Understanding
Church
Growth
and
Decline:
1950-1978

Understanding Church Growth and Decline: 1950-1978

Edited by
Dean R. Hoge
and
David A. Roozen

The Pilgrim Press
New York/Philadelphia

Biblical quotations, unless otherwise indicated, are from the Revised Standard Version of the Bible, copyright 1946, 1952 and © 1971 by the Division of Christian Education, National Council of Churches, and are used by permission. Scriptural excerpts marked NEB are from *The New English Bible* © The Delegates of the Oxford University Press and the Syndics of the Cambridge University Press, 1961, 1970. Reprinted by permission.

Library of Congress Cataloging in Publication Data
Main entry under title:

Understanding church growth and decline, 1950-1978.

    Bibliography: p. 374
    Includes index.
    1. Church membership—Addresses, essays, lectures, 2. Church growth—Addresses, essays, lectures. I. Hoge, Dean R., 1937-   II. Roozen, David A.
BV820.U5   301.5'8   79-4166
ISBN 0-8298-0358-0 pbk.

The Pilgrim Press, 287 Park Avenue South, New York, New York 10010

Contributors

JACKSON W. CARROLL is a sociologist who serves as coordinator of research at The Hartford Seminary Foundation. He is the editor of *Small Churches Are Beautiful* (Harper & Row, 1977) and coauthor of *Religion in America, 1950 to the Present* (Harper & Row, 1978).

RUTH T. DOYLE is research associate, Office of Pastoral Research, Catholic Archdiocese of New York. She is a Ph.D. candidate at Fordham and is a research consultant. Formerly, she was on the research staff of the Executive Council of The Episcopal Church.

JOHN E. DYBLE is an independent religious researcher. He is a research consultant to the national boards and agencies of several mainline denominations and to the Princeton Religion Research Center and the Gallup Organization, Inc.

ROBERT A. EVANS serves as theologian for The Hartford Seminary Foundation. Previously, he was professor of theology at McCormick Seminary, in Chicago. His books include *Christian Theology* (Harper & Row, 1976) and *Casebook for Christian Living* (Knox, 1977).

C. KIRK HADAWAY has authored a number of articles on religious commitment and on denominational trends. He recently completed his Ph.D. in sociology and is now a research analyst with the Southern Baptist Home Mission Board, in Atlanta.

DEAN R. HOGE is a sociologist at Catholic University. Formerly, he taught at Princeton Theological Seminary. He is the author of *Commitment on Campus* (Westminster, 1974) and *Division in the Protestant House* (Westminster, 1976).

PHILLIP BARRON JONES is a research consultant in the Planning Section of the Home Mission Board, Southern Baptist Convention. He is a graduate of Southern Baptist Theological Seminary, Louisville, and Georgia Institute of Technology, Atlanta.

DEAN M. KELLEY is executive for religious and civil liberty of the National Council of Churches. He is the author of *Why Conservative Churches Are Growing* (Harper & Row, 1972, 1977) and *Why Churches Should Not Pay Taxes* (Harper & Row, 1976).

SHEILA M. KELLY is research analyst with the United Church Board for Homeland Ministries. She was formerly on the research staff of the Episcopal Church Center and was research associate to the National Council of Churches' Clergy Support Study, 1974.

MARTIN E. MARTY is the Fairfax M. Cone Distinguished Service Professor at the University of Chicago, the associate editor of *The Christian Century*, and the author of, among other books, *A Nation of Behavers* (University of Chicago, 1976).

WILLIAM J. McKINNEY JR. is secretary for research and evaluation with the United Church Board for Homeland Ministries and is a doctoral candidate at Pennsylvania State University.

WADE CLARK ROOF is a sociologist at the University of Massachusetts, Amherst. He is the author of *Community and Commitment* (Elsevier, 1978) plus numerous articles on religion. He is currently researching Protestant, Catholic, and Jewish subcultures in the United States.

DAVID A. ROOZEN is assistant coordinator of research at The Hartford Seminary Foundation. He is a United Church of Christ layperson, with a Ph.D. in the sociology of religion. Among his recent publications is *The Churched and the Unchurched in America* (Glenmary, 1978).

LYLE E. SCHALLER is parish consultant on the staff of the Yokefellow Institute, Richmond, Indiana. He is the author of sixteen books, including *Assimilating New Members* (Abingdon, 1978) and is general editor of the *Creative Leadership Series* for Abingdon Press.

JAMES H. SMYLIE is professor of American religious history at Union Theological Seminary in Virginia. He was formerly secretary of the American Society of Church History and is currently editor of the *Journal of Presbyterian History*.

C. PETER WAGNER is associate professor of church growth at the Fuller Theological Seminary School of World Mission. He is the author of fourteen books on missiology and church growth, including *Our Kind of People* (Knox, 1979) and *Spiritual Gifts and Church Growth* (Regal, 1979).

DOUGLAS A. WALRATH is a social researcher and church planner. His major concern is the effect of social change upon churches. He is the author of many articles and of an upcoming book (Abingdon, 1979) on church leadership effectiveness.

Contents

Foreword

by Martin E. Marty

To: Participants in, Observers of, or Participant/Observers in and of Mainline American Protestantism

Re: Generalizations about the causes of church growth and decline

A Warning: Do not open your mouth about trends and patterns in church membership and participation unless you have read this book. The reason for that is simple: it is possible that the person or people to whom you are talking will have read it. If they found its data and arguments convincing, they will be skeptical of anyone henceforth who says something that begins as follows:

"The single big reason why mainline churches have been declining and conservative churches have been growing is . . ."

Or: "The factors in growth and decline are all in the context of churches. Study their environments and you can foresee the trends . . ."

Or: "The factors in growth and decline are all in the inner life of churches. Study what they believe and how they believe it and you can interpret trends . . ."

Or: "The simple explanation is . . ."

All such openings will betray a lack of information about the web of explanations that concern a drastic change in American cultural and religious life. Through half a year, as first drafts of chapters for this book came in over my transom, it happened again and again that I had to revise a lecture or an article. The chapters were all marked "not for quotation or attribution in this form." While I could therefore give no credit, my privileged reading, at least on the negative side, prevented my making false or rash statements about what everyone, or at least what the people I had been reading and observing, thought was "true." Until now there had been too few scientific studies of mainline fates and fortunes to give us confidence about generalizations. But we had to make them, often on the basis of hunches, and these hunches are proving to be debatable.

Not that the chapters in this book will clear up everything. They could not, because most of their authors confess to being confused by much of what they know and bemused over what they cannot yet and may never know. If each individual reading the book were to set forth a careful analysis of all the reasons why he or she makes certain religious commitments or refuses to make them, there would be a maze of issues. They have to do with the womb from which each sprang, their child-rearing, adolescent traumas, philosophical commitments, psychological needs, fate, fortune, habit, and behavior—all unsorted and left vague in their lives. Multiply that by a few tens of millions and you have a beginning picture of the complex of motivations. To complicate matters further, let your scholarly guides through the maze bring competitive outlooks. Let some of them be objective inquirers who merely want to understand the processes that affect national life, as church trends do. Let others of them be impassioned advocates of church growth or doleful rescuers of meaning in the face of church decline. Let some be historians, some sociologists, some statisticians, some theologians. Out of all this it is not likely that you would find complete agreement.

The diverse disciplines and outlooks, as well as the disagreements in this book, are aids to understanding, then; they are not barriers. We need to be tentative at this stage of inquiry. But being tentative and modest does not mean being paralyzed into silence. The guides assembled here have brought talents and energies to this task as have few others, and the few others are cited in the references that course through the volume. They are able not only to do some demolition work on cherished generalizations, some demythologizing of most favored myths, but also to offer some positive clues. A profile begins to emerge.

A seismic shift has been occurring and continues in American religion. While church growth and decline are far from being the only ways of measuring religious health, they give at least some indication of how citizens are voting with their bodies. From the birth of the republic until around 1965, as is well known, the churches now called mainline Protestant tended to grow with every census or survey. While the public gives evidence of thinking that the founders of America were religious in the churchgoing sense and that there has been decline ever since, later Americans confuted the prophets from Europe by supporting their churches during all the "-ations" that were supposed to lead to their decline: modernization, secularization, urbanization, pluralization, industrialization. Let come a new assault of the sort that led to European decline, and Americans answered by building more churches, bringing more offspring to their nurturing care, supporting them better, filling their pews. Until 1965.

The rates of growth were never consistent, despite the overall trends. One could write the history of American religion in terms of the "overtakers" in successive waves. The colonial "big three"— the mainline Congregationalists, Presbyterians, and Episcopalians—without ever losing out, were quickly overtaken by the nineteenth-century revivalist rivals—the Baptists, the Methodists, and the cluster of Disciples of Christ and Christian churches. By midcentury they were overtaken by the "immigrant" arrivals from Ireland and then, more from the Continent, the Roman Catholics. All but two of the old mainline were outpaced by the Lutherans. Psychically, Jews and Eastern Orthodox churches also jostled them by adding to pluralism, although without actually numbering more people than the standard brand churches.

In the 1950s the overtaken churches, still at ease in the culture and able to prosper with its prosperity, experienced a boom that to the prophets of that decade looked superficial and in retrospect had an artificial character. For reasons too complex to review here, postwar Americans found reasons, in the very decade when they were telling poll-takers that religion meant less and less in their lives, to join and support churches. The momentum of their joining carried them into the midsixties.

Then came cultural crisis. As everyone knows—or knew, until they read books like this—the mainline then suffered, because it acquired the image of being controversial and social activist in matters of race, peace, and justice. And the slide has continued. Be careful! The reasons for the relative decline are far more complex than that flip explanation suggests, and some data suggests that activism had very little at all to do with the changes. Well, then, for whatever reason—keep on reading these chapters to find whatever reasons—the mainline started slipping.

Change in the mainline is painful to its leaders and harmful to the morale of its followers. As some of the historians and theologians in this book like to remind them and us, it is arguable whether or not calculated and contrived growth was ever designed to be part of the original package of Christianity. They go on to say that decline can be a measure of faithfulness. They are unwilling, for good reason, to go a step further and claim that the mainline churches have been especially faithful, particularly inconvenienced, and for that reason have known losses.

Change in the mainline has an effect on the larger culture. Several authors here speak of "the collapse of the middle," of the churches (and other agencies) that mediated particular value systems to the general culture. The survivors were polarized into right-wing churches—I do not use the term invidiously—who made up an important subculture but had little to say to the larger world, and secular humanist culture, which could not have cared less what was going on in the subculture of conservative religion. The "middle" began disappearing. In it were theologians and artists, pastors and literary figures, doers and thinkers, who construed reality in the light of faith in Christ but who were critically open to the idea of using that faith to transform (not merely to judge) the culture; they began disappearing. The gap between one kind of believer and others in the environment grew. While it is possible to read the New Testament in such sectarian terms and say that this is what God had in mind all along, it is hard to read the rest of the New Testament or the whole Bible and picture such distance and disengagement. The collapse of the middle, therefore, has and will have fateful consequences for religious communication in a pluralistic culture. That is one more reason it must be understood, one more occasion for the inquiries in this book.

If there were the overtaken, there were also overtakers. The American landscape and peoplescape are too diverse, too full of spiritual nooks and crannies, to permit a void. The search for meaning and belonging go on, and people will look elsewhere when something declines or collapses. Many found what they looked for in nondescript secular culture or its descript movements. Others went searching in cult and occult, in Africa and in Asia, for new centers of meaning and focus for belonging. But at their side was the growth of a large subculture made up of pentecostalists, conservative Catholics after Vatican II, fundamentalists, and neo-evangelicals, later evangelical Protestants.

This book concerns itself with the mainline yin and, consistently if implicitly, with the evangelical yang that complements it in Protestantism. The yang was not, of course, a new force. The complementary halves shared common roots and never completely untangled them. I think one could make the case that every enduring mainline (moderate to liberal although probably never modernist) Protestant is, at heart, an evangelical. The basic regard for biblical authority, Christic faith, devotional centrality, and often even the impulse to be converted and to convert, were nurtured at the evangelical font. And a similar case can be made that every fulfilled evangelical, when he or she reaches out to give expression to the wholeness of Christian life, learns something from the modes perfected by the mainliners through the decades. But the outlines of division also grew sharper through these decades.

Before 1965 a few revivalists foresaw a new outpouring of the spirit; revivalists do such foreseeing because it is their nature and business to do so. But you will find precious little evidence that secular or religious prophets and analysts at that mid-decade foresaw the new prosperity of this large faction. In public stereotype, the fundamentalists, having been disgraced in 1925 at the Scopes trial and defeated in their efforts to win denominational control, went off to the hills and the Bible Belt. There they wore hobnail boots, let spittle drip down their chins, started Bible schools for illiterates and radio programs for the prejudiced, and, in general, were settling in to become fossils. Now and then a Billy Graham might become visible in the culture, but for the rest they made up a sub-subculture.

Not at all. Through the religious depression during the Great Depression they began to regather. During the war they formed associations. In the 1950s they rode Graham's coattails and sought and found the beginnings of new academic respectability, whether as old evangelicals renewed or as old fundamentalists reshaped into moderates. After about 1968 their inning came. People looked for authority, security, the end of the world then, and rationales for affluence now. Most of all they looked for inner experiences, as people did whenever religion was being renewed. And the evangelical-pentecostal cluster was well poised to meet their needs. The leaders acted as if they were working against the zeitgeist, the spirit of the times. Instead, they were the spirit of the times, although they had to compete for the monopoly with some new therapies, secular apocalyptic movements, and Eastern styles of inwardness. The full meaning of their recovery is no more easily available than are the full explanations of mainline decline. Their future is not simply assured either. As Dean Hoge reminds us in this book, students of the context of American religious change have learned or ought to learn not to project much about that context into the future.

Whatever happens to the context, a seismic shift has occurred, power relations are different, and even after fads and fashions disappear, evangelicalism should remain as big and strong as a monadnock on the horizon.

What of the mainline, the concern of this book? I see no one here foreseeing a sudden spurt of growth and prosperity. It was not the business of the present writers to project the future of the evangelicals, but it would be a fairly safe reading of all present trends to see them converging on a new kind of mainline, dropping their distance from much of the culture and, as *The Worldly Evangelicals* by Richard Quebedeaux suggests, turning most worldly. Then a new generation of social scientists can muse as the present one does in this volume.

I have mentioned that two sets of writers are in the present panel, and I expect there will be two sets of readers. Some are sociologists who take on the mainline "because it is there," because they are social scientists and the churches are social institutions. They write dispassionately, question their own assumptions, and qualify all that they write. At the other end of the spectrum are theologians, like Robert Evans, who look for divine purpose in the chastening and hope for responsible recovery of the collapsed middle; or historian James Smylie, who knows "the limits to growth" but wishes there were a more visible compensatory faithfulness among those who do not grow; and there is Peter Wagner, a passionate advocate of church growth who uses scientific instruments to support his commitment.

So with readers. Some will welcome this book as they would a work on the prosperity or decline of political parties, labor movements, fraternal orders, or cooperatives—anything that helps explain America and modern life. To others it will be, if not a manual of arms, at least a description of tactics and terrain. They will canvass it for clues about what went wrong (if they are in the mainline) or what went right (if from the Protestant right they saw the devil's doings in the compromises of moderate Protestantism).

As comprehensive as this book is, it does not pretend to be everything that is needed on this subject. Only a couple of chapters debate the issue of measurement and statistics or speculate as to the theological meaning of church decline and growth. Sometimes when I watch how often the exploitative, the ominous, the banal, the trivial entrepreneurs on the Christian right—and not everyone on the Christian right is of those sorts—prosper and draw crowds, I wish I knew whether Jesus really *wanted* his church or that kind of church to grow. It so often seems that a God who cares about the humanizing of the world would bless churches that care for wholeness and civility and not merely for aggressive pouncing on prospects as possible converts. But those are my musings based on prejudices and precommitments. This book checks or feeds those biases and inspires other heartfelt inquiries. At such a point do sciences and arts, the reason's reasons and the heart's reasons, meet. It takes a special kind of book to minister to both levels or types of curiosity.

Maybe readers will look back in a few decades on this dusty book in the library and wonder what the fuss was about. It may be that the mainline churches were the accurate harbingers, that institutional church life in America went the way of Europe, that the evangelical boom was a mutation, a last gasp. There are signs that the born-again movement is not leading so much to the prosperity of congregations as to the formation of clienteles for entrepreneurs on television or authors of best-sellers. The conservative denominations grow impressively, yet they seem to be losing out to the "invisibly religious" who are born again but who need no organized religion, no institutional church to sustain them. If the latter win out, in a future generation I would hope that the efforts here begun would help illumine such a fascinating or portentous turn in the ageless religious search. For now, the book should take a more than modest place in the religious research of our decade.

Introduction

An unprecedented period in the life of the North American church began in the mid-1960s. For the first time since records allow us to recall, many major denominations actually stopped growing in membership and began to decline, and the growth rate of most others slowed considerably. National church attendance also fell off significantly, the declines being felt most sharply among Catholics.

The downturn of the 1960s continued into the 1970s. While the latest Gallup polls hint that the declines may be coming to an end, we still look back over more than a decade of continual abatement. This period of decline, which came after nearly two centuries of growth, appears especially stark in comparison with the surge of membership and attendance during the so-called religious revival of the 1950s.

The reversal caught many denominational leaders by surprise. Why did the declines occur, and why were they most acute in the more theologically "liberal" denominations? By 1973 this question had attracted much attention. Denominational leaders began asking earnest questions. At least three denominations—the United Church of Christ, the United Methodist Church, and the United Presbyterian Church—commissioned major studies of their membership declines (their reports are incorporated in chapters 6, 9, and 10). These investigations were undertaken largely in isolation from one another.

In 1975 a group of academic and church researchers became convinced that the seriousness of the question deserved intensive and interdenominational study by a working group which could pool data, analyses, and insights. With initial support from The Hartford Seminary Foundation, we worked with Jackson W. Carroll to pull such a group together and to find financial support for it. In 1976 the Lilly Endowment, Incorporated, made a grant to The Hartford Seminary Foundation for the study.

The project was designed to bring together a group of academic sociologists, denominational researchers, theologians, and historians who had been working on the issue to pool their knowledge and expertise in a systematic review, reevaluation, and extension of existing research on church trends over the past quarter century. The purpose was to provide information and interpretation to denominations and local congregations, enabling them to make better-informed decisions.

Working group meetings were held in June 1976, June 1977, and February 1978. Smaller meetings of researchers were held at four additional times. In February 1978 the group sponsored a national symposium, held in Hartford, entitled "Church Growth and Decline: Implications for Evangelism." It drew over 250 persons from across the country, representing twenty-one denominations. The purpose of the symposium was to provide an initial forum for the findings of the working group.

This book represents a second forum for sharing the findings. The first fourteen chapters are papers prepared by members of the working group. Most of the material was prepared prior to the symposium and was revised in light of the symposium and critiques by group members. The final two chapters are commentaries on the fourteen papers; they are written by noted interpreters of modern church life.

As a third vehicle for the presentation of the findings of the working group, a shorter, less technical volume, *Where Have All Our People Gone? New Choices for Old Churches* has been written by Carl S. Dudley (The Pilgrim Press, 1979) as a companion piece to this book. It deals more specifically with the implications for pastors, laity, and church leaders.

The focus of the working group was on understanding mainline Protestant church membership and participation since about 1950, through collation, reevaluation, and interpretation of existing information. This consisted mainly of yearbook data, past denominational studies, and national public opinion surveys. No new surveys were commissioned.

The writers of the various papers have brought together the available data in new and highly informative ways. Prior to our study, we found that religious trends in general, and church trends in particular, were not well understood by historians, sociologists, and church leaders. One heard widely varying predictions about the future of the church, ranging from total demise to unparalleled growth; most of them were uninformed by careful analysis of past trends. We came to believe that much could be gained through careful scrutiny of data on hand. This book is the result.

We would like to thank all members of the working group, both those who have contributed chapters to this book and those who have not, for their contributions to the project as a whole. Especially we thank Jackson W. Carroll and the administration of The Hartford Seminary Foundation for guidance and support. We also thank the Lilly Endowment, Incorporated, for financial support. And we thank Marion M. Meyer of The Pilgrim Press for her impressive editorial help.

The original drafts of many of the papers comprising the present volume were longer and more technically detailed than their present form. They were rewritten so that the main arguments and conclusions appear in this volume, with additional details put into an appendix that has been printed separately. This 100-page technical appendix is available for $3 from The Bookstore, The Hartford Seminary Foundation, 111 Sherman Street, Hartford, CT 06105. Copies have also been deposited in the libraries of The Hartford Seminary Foundation, Candler School of Theology, Fuller Theological Seminary, McCormick Theological Seminary, and Princeton Theological Seminary.

Dean R. Hoge

David A. Roozen

Participants in all or some of the working group meetings:

Jackson W. Carroll, The Hartford Seminary Foundation
Ruth T. Doyle, Roman Catholic Archdiocese of New York
Carl S. Dudley, McCormick Theological Seminary
John E. Dyble, Research Consultant
Robert A. Evans, The Hartford Seminary Foundation
George Gallup Jr., American Institute of Public Opinion
C. Kirk Hadaway, Southern Baptist Convention
Peter Halvorson, University of Connecticut
Warren J. Hartman, United Methodist Church
Dean R. Hoge, Catholic University of America
Phillip B. Jones, Southern Baptist Convention
Dean M. Kelley, National Council of Churches
Sheila M. Kelly, United Church of Christ
Donald W. Kimmick, The Episcopal Church
G. Douglass Lewis, The Hartford Seminary Foundation
William J. McKinney Jr., United Church of Christ
William G. McLoughlin, Brown University
Robert L. Montgomery, United Presbyterian Church

Orrin D. Morris, Southern Baptist Convention
Philip J. Murnion, Roman Catholic Archdiocese of New York
William M. Newman, University of Connecticut
Everett L. Perry, United Presbyterian Church
Donald L. Ploch, University of Tennessee
W. Clark Roof, University of Massachusetts
David A. Roozen, The Hartford Seminary Foundation
A. Wayne Schwab, The Episcopal Church
James H. Smylie, Union Theological Seminary, Richmond
Margaret J. Thomas, United Presbyterian Church
C. Peter Wagner, Fuller Theological Seminary
Douglas A. Walrath, Reformed Church in America

CHAPTER 1

Recent Trends in Church Membership and Participation:
An Introduction

David A. Roozen
and
Jackson W. Carroll

The concern with statistical religious trends is by no means an invention of the twentieth-century bureaucrat. After poring over a mass of church statistics, nineteenth-century churchman Daniel Dorchester (1888:742) wrote:

All persons familiar with the history of Christianity will agree that the above exhibit of religious progress cannot be paralleled in the history of God's Kingdom in any land or any age. It is all the more remarkable because only about ninety years ago it was a common boast of infidels that "Christianity would not survive two generations" in this country. Instead of that, Christianity, since then, has achieved her grandest triumph. How often has the progress of Christianity in the apostolic age been cited as a marvel of growth which the church of our time should emulate. Such persons forget that the growth of the churches in the United States in this century has far transcended that of the first centuries. (Between 1800 and 1886, the number of adherents of Evangelical Christianity in our country has seen an increase of 41,287,226, or more than in the whole world at the close of the first nine centuries of the Christian era.) "Not unto us, O Lord, not unto us, but

22

unto thy name give glory, for thy mercy, and for thy truth's sake."

Such celebrations of growth and progress in American Protestantism continued at least through the 1960s, as the trend lines of denominational membership continued to move upward; however, the situation since the midsixties has been considerably different.[1] Since 1966 total Protestant and Catholic membership has remained relatively unchanged, but, in light of population growth during this period, it has actually declined as a percentage of the adult U.S. population (see Figure 1.1). More significantly, at least ten of the largest (and theologically more liberal) denomina-

FIGURE 1.1
PROTESTANT AND ROMAN CATHOLIC MEMBERSHIP,
1952-1974, AS A PERCENTAGE OF THE U.S. POPULATION
18 YEARS OLD AND OLDER

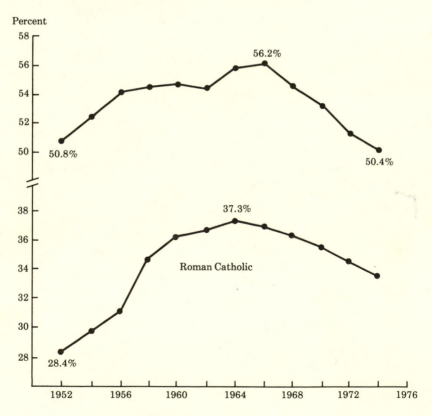

Source: *Historical Statistics of the U.S.* (U.S. Census, 1975)
Statistical Abstract of the U.S. (1976)

tions have had membership losses in every year after 1966. Since most of these denominations had grown without interruption from colonial times, their declines reverse a trend of two centuries.

Most, but not all, major denominations experienced declines after the midsixties. Figures 1.2 and 1.3 present the actual

FIGURE 1.2

MEMBERSHIP TRENDS IN THREE DENOMINATIONS

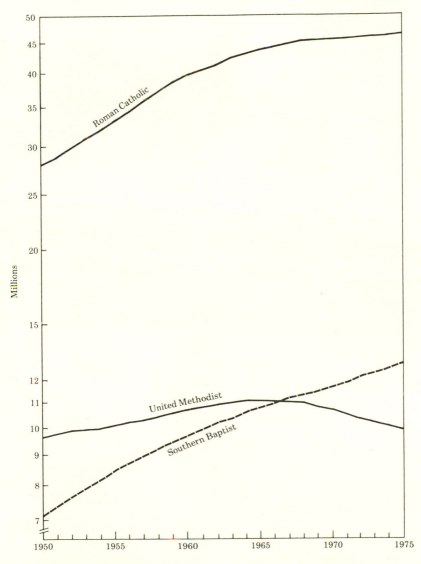

Source: Yearbook data; see Chapter 6.

FIGURE 1.3
MEMBERSHIP TRENDS IN SEVEN DENOMINATIONS

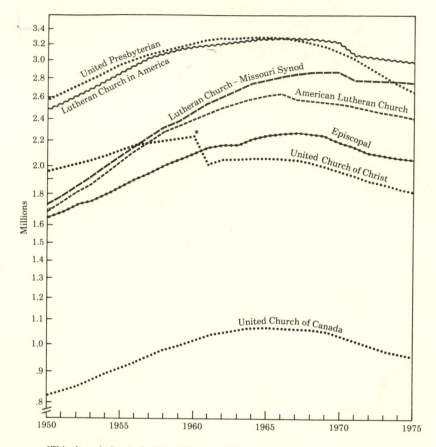

*This sharp decline in the United Church of Christ is due to withdrawal of
congregations after the merger.

Source: Yearbook data.

membership trends for nine of the ten largest American denominations (for others see Kelley, 1977). Figure 1.4 presents the same
trends, but this time as a percentage of 1950 membership. Of the
nine denominations, only the Catholics and the Southern Baptists
have not experienced recent membership losses, although their
growth rates have slowed. Of the other seven denominations, all
but the Missouri Synod Lutherans peaked in membership between
1964 and 1967.

Since the publication of Dean Kelley's *Why Conservative
Churches Are Growing* (1972), it has been common to distinguish
growing denominations from declining denominations in terms of

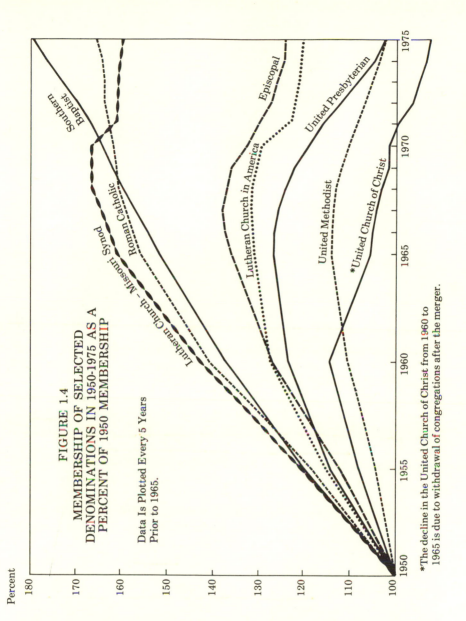

FIGURE 1.4
MEMBERSHIP OF SELECTED
DENOMINATIONS IN 1950-1975 AS A
PERCENT OF 1950 MEMBERSHIP

Data Is Plotted Every 5 Years
Prior to 1965.

Percent

*The decline in the United Church of Christ from 1960 to
1965 is due to withdrawal of congregations after the merger.

their theological orientation. Whether or not theology has a causal impact on growth is subject to debate (see chapters 8 and 15), but it does appear to be descriptively accurate—at least in regard to denominational growth.

The rise and decline pattern in many denominations is not limited to church membership. It has also occurred in church attendance and in religious giving. National survey data from both the Gallup poll and the Survey Research Center of the University of

25

FIGURE 1.5

COMPARISON OF CHURCH ATTENDANCE TRENDS AS MEASURED
BY THE GALLUP POLL AND THE SURVEY RESEARCH CENTER,
UNIVERSITY OF MICHIGAN

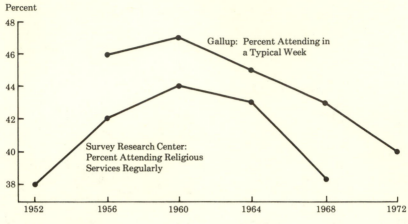

Source: Roozen (1977).

Michigan show that church attendance increased throughout the 1950s, peaked about 1960, and then descended steadily through the mid-1970s (see Figure 1.5).[2] Attendance data by denomination from 1966 to 1975 (Gallup Opinion Index, 1978a:32) shows that the recent declines are not characteristic of all denominations. Baptist attendance over this period shows no change, but decreases are found among Methodists, Lutherans, Presbyterians, and Episcopalians.

Concerning religious giving, a recent analysis of financial contributions to religious institutions over the past quarter century (Carroll, 1978a:22-24) shows an upswing in giving during the 1950s, followed by a general downtrend through the 1960s (see Table 1.1). The analysis, using figures adjusted to control for the effects of inflation, again shows that the declines of the late sixties and early seventies are not characteristic of all denominations; rather, as before, they are limited to the more liberal groups.

Available indicators all reveal a similar pattern: the 1960s were a time of reversal in a previously long-term trend of growth in American religious participation. Declines were greatest in the so-called liberal, mainline denominations. But knowing what the trends look like is not the same as knowing why they occurred. And it is the *why* question that is the focal concern of this book. The emphasis is moved from charting the trends to understanding them.

For whatever reasons, the long history of growth in American religious participation prompted little serious research concerned

TABLE 1.1: PER CAPITA GIVING TO SELECTED PROTESTANT CHURCHES, 1950-1974
(Adjusted to 1967 Constant Dollars)

Denomination	1950	1955	1960	1965	1970	1974
Church of God (Anderson, Ind.)	--	$135.92	$148.76	$177.72	$182.35	$203.72
Percent Change		--	+9.4	+19.4	+2.6	+11.7
Church of the Nazarene	145.14	156.61	160.41	178.09	190.94	190.05
Percent Change		+7.9	+2.4	+11.0	+7.2	-0.5
Episcopal Church	58.87	60.52	72.70	112.99	96.83	100.11
Percent Change		+2.8	+20.1	+55.4	-14.3	+3.4
Lutheran Church in America*	49.26	68.08	82.23	83.90	83.33	85.31
Percent Change		+38.2	+20.8	+2.0	-0.6	+2.4
Lutheran Church-Missouri Synod	68.75	95.18	108.39	112.84	107.88	102.60
Percent Change		+38.4	+13.9	+4.1	-4.4	-4.9
Southern Baptist	39.58	55.54	62.75	62.65	65.97	72.74
Percent Change		+40.3	+13.0	-0.1	+0.5	+10.3
United Church of Christ*	51.52	71.48	83.88	83.91	79.91	78.99
Percent Change		+38.7	+17.3	+0.03	-4.8	-1.1
United Methodist Church*	37.25	53.45	62.93	60.58	67.10	63.04
Percent Change		+43.5	+17.7	-3.7	+10.8	-6.0
United Presbyterian, USA*	55.30	84.63	95.03	101.30	99.44	106.63
Percent Change		+53.0	+12.3	+6.6	-1.8	+7.2
U.S. Per Capita Disposable Income (in 1967 dollars)	1982	2077	2183	2577	2903	3136
Percent Change	--	+4.8	+5.1	+18.0	+12.6	+8.0

*Corrected for merger by including members of merged denominations for each time period.
Source: After Table 4 of Jackson W. Carroll, Douglas W. Johnson, and Martin E. Marty, Religion in America: 1950 to the Present (Harper and Row, Publishers), by permission. Copyright 1979 by Jackson W. Carroll, Douglas W. Johnson, and Martin E. Marty.

with isolating the causes of that growth. The declines of the 1960s, however, launched several rather large-scale efforts to uncover the dynamics that lie beneath the figures on the charts. The works that are drawn together in this book represent the core of this material.[3]

These works concentrate primarily on Protestant trends, and within the Protestant tradition, primarily on the mainline denominations.[4] This limited focus is partly a matter of choice and partly a matter of necessity. Catholics, for example, are not included beyond brief mention (see chapters 2, 4, and 6), because their trends have been analyzed in other works (Greeley, McCready, and McCourt, 1976, for instance) which suggest that recent changes in Catholic participation are considerably influenced by factors specific to the Catholic situation.

Black, other minority, ethnic, and most smaller and evangelical denominations are not included, because reliable trend data for them is not currently available. Unfortunately, therefore, one is unable to treat these groups with the same type of careful scrutiny afforded mainline denominations.

Neither is membership or participation in various "new" religious movements (for example, Hare Krishna, Transcendental Meditation, Children of God) treated here, despite their fascination to students of American religion. This is an important area of commentary and research, but it is beyond the scope of the present inquiry.

This book focuses its inquiry primarily through statistical lenses. This is done in full appreciation of the fact that it is only one of several important ways of viewing American religious life. This is also done in awareness of the limits it places on the scope of our inquiry. In particular, we are tied to existing sources of reliable data. Not only does this prohibit attention to several segments of America's religious community as noted above; it also means that important theoretical and/or theological distinctions that do not easily lend themselves to quantification cannot be adequately treated. We have tried to be sensitive to a number of these issues. Chapter 3, for example, provides a historian's perceptions of the history of the church growth movement in America. Chapter 15 calls attention to what might be learned from studying denominations and movements out of the mainstream. And chapters 10, 12, and particularly chapter 13 keep before us the theological issues at stake in what we are about. Nevertheless, the bulk of what appears in the following pages is statistical and social scientific in its orientation and is an attempt to identify as carefully and rigorously as possible those factors affecting the trends in religious participation we are concerned to understand.

DATA SOURCES

Because our inquiry is primarily statistical in orientation, a note regarding the quality of data used is in order. The data comes from four principal sources: denominational self reports such as those contained in denominational yearbooks and the *Yearbook of American and Canadian Churches;* national public opinion surveys such as the Gallup poll; denominational surveys of churches and church members; and case studies of especially noteworthy growing or declining congregations. Specifics regarding the data used in any particular chapter are included in that chapter, but a few general observations can be made.

Denominationally reported membership statistics have always had their detractors, with written critiques of this process appearing as early as 1893 (Carroll, 1893). More thorough and recent critiques can be found in Landis (1959), Demerath (1968), and Newman et al. (1977). The problems discussed by these critics are multiple, but three deserve comment here. The first is the vexing problem of differing definitions of membership from one denomination to another. For example, most Baptist denominations practice adult baptism and only those who have been baptized are counted as members. The Roman Catholic Church and most Lutheran denominations also count all baptized persons as members, but these groups practice infant baptism and count persons from infancy onward as members. Most other major denominations count only confirmed persons as members, with confirmation typically taking place around 13 years of age. Such differences in definition of membership should not have much effect on the trends of the various denominations relative to one another if the definitions have remained the same across time. Fortunately, this has generally been the case over the time span with which we are concerned.[5]

A second criticism of denominational membership figures is that local churches sometimes carry members' names on their rolls long after these members have left the church. A recent United Methodist study found that, nationally, 10 percent more persons were reported each year as new members of local churches received by transfer from other United Methodist churches than were reported as losses by transfer to other local United Methodist churches (Hartman, 1976:16). This means that some persons have their names on at least two United Methodist church rolls simultaneously. Such laxness in roll-cleaning is not peculiar to the United Methodist Church. It should not, however, have a major effect on the long-term membership trend of any denomination, so long as the practice does not change appreciably from year to year. But that such change has occurred is claimed by many. They argue that at least a portion of the recent declines in membership have been due to more rigorous and accurate roll-keeping, as local congregations seek to reduce denominational financial assessments based on the number of local members. Two denominations that have seriously studied this possibility, however, both conclude that a more judicious cleaning of the rolls has had a minimal impact on their membership declines (Hartman, 1976:2; Presbyterian Committee, 1976:226).

A third problem in trend studies using denominational membership figures is how to handle mergers, particularly when not all local churches in the merging bodies opt to join the newly formed denomination. This can be seen, for example, in charting United Church of Christ trends. The denomination was formed out of the 1957 merger of the Evangelical and Reformed Church and the Congregational Christian Churches. A sizable number of local congregations, especially in the latter body, did not initially join the merger. Although many of these have continued as the National Association of Congregational Christian Churches, others have remained unaffiliated with any national group or have affiliated with the merged body some time after 1957. A similar problem is encountered in denominations (for example, American Baptists and Disciples of Christ) where local congregations have the option of not reporting their yearly statistics if they choose not to. A congregation may report one year, choose not to report for a year or two, then resume reporting. Such a practice, if widespread, could obviously cause considerable yearly fluctuation that has nothing to do with real membership gain or loss.[6]

In sum, anyone dealing with denominationally reported statistics must proceed with caution and with a good bit of foreknowledge concerning the varying reporting practices used. Still there is risk of error. To minimize this risk, the denominational statistics reported in this book have undergone careful scrutiny. For example, denominational data reported in this chapter and further discussed in chapter 6 has been limited to those major denominations that are generally considered to have the most reliable reporting procedures. In addition, denominational offices were asked to recheck the figures where possible and make necessary adjustments for errors or inconsistencies. The authors then rechecked the data once more. As a result, some of the figures depart slightly from those reported elsewhere; however, we believe that they provide the most accurate statistics available.

The second major data source used in this book is various national public opinion surveys. The careful methods of probability sampling and data collection used in these surveys (the same type of survey that has allowed the Gallup poll and others to predict national elections within one or two percentage points over the past twenty or more years) make them a considerably more reliable source of information than denominational self reports. However, a number of cautions must be kept in mind when interpreting them. Perhaps the most troublesome is whether or not persons interviewed in such surveys are answering truthfully or, rather, are giving what they perceive to be socially accepted answers. For example, if persons think they *should* be attending church regularly, they might be hesitant to tell an interviewer that they are not. While this distorts the findings of individual surveys, it should not affect trend studies that compare the results of several surveys. It becomes a problem only if the tendency to give socially desirable answers changes from survey to survey. Although we assume that this has not been a major factor in the data cited in this book, there is no way of knowing for sure.

A second caution concerns the type of questions asked. Interview questions for such national surveys need to be relatively brief and to allow for a fixed range of responses. Thus, the richness, complexity, and subtlety of the issues being addressed in the question are often sacrificed, and many areas of considerable interest in the study of religious beliefs or practice are treated rather superficially, if at all.

3. A third major data source, denominational surveys, must also be viewed with the above cautions firmly in mind. In addition, the reader must pay more attention to the specific sampling procedures used in denominational surveys, because they tend to vary more in both quality and design than those used in national public opinion surveys. The major advantage of the denominational surveys, in comparison with national surveys, is that they deal more specifically and intensely with the question under consideration, covering a much broader range of factors potentially related to church growth and decline.

4. Case studies provide a fourth source of data. Their major liability is the difficulty of generalizing their findings. Case studies of a limited number of churches allow a more in-depth analysis than is possible through other research methods. However, the cost in time and money of such intense study typically limits the number of congregations that can be included. Because of the limited focus of case studies, it is often difficult to tell if what is found in the church or churches being studied is peculiar to that type of church or is really a general characteristic of many different church types. For example, case studies of rapidly growing churches may indicate that these churches have exceptionally skillful pastors. Before one could conclude that a skillful pastor is a major factor in church growth, one must also know that most declining churches do not have skillful pastors. Despite this restriction, these analyses

provide an invaluable glimpse into the dynamics of a congregation's life, and generalizability increases as more cases are studied over a widening spectrum of church types.

In summary, anyone working with quantitative data on religion must acknowledge its limitations. However, when these limitations are acknowledged and efforts are made to counter their negative effects, the data is quite helpful. While it does not tell us everything we need to know, it provides important insights into the dynamics of church life, both of growth and decline.

CHURCH PARTICIPATION AND RELIGIOUS LIFE

Although this book concentrates on church growth and decline as measured by membership and participation, such a focus should not imply that the various authors necessarily accept membership and participation as theologically appropriate indicators of congregational or denominational performance, or even of individual religious commitment. In chapter 13, Robert Evans addresses this issue directly. The authors of other chapters adopt a more neutral, empirical orientation, asking at most what relationship exists between membership growth and other possible performance or commitment criteria.

Sociologists of religion have found that there are various ways in which an individual may express commitment to a particular religious tradition. Charles Glock and Rodney Stark (1965:18-38) identify five dimensions of commitment: the belief or ideological dimension; the practice or ritualistic dimension; the feeling or experiential dimension; the knowledge or intellectual dimension; and the effects or consequential dimension. Not only is commitment recognized to be multidimensional, but empirical studies show that the various dimensions are not as strongly related as one might think. A recent national survey of the churched and the unchurched in America (Gallup Opinion Index, 1978b) clearly illustrates this with reference to the relationship between religious membership and participation and other aspects of religious commitment. For purposes of that study, a person was considered to be unchurched if he or she had not attended religious services (apart from weddings, funerals, or special holidays) in the six months prior to the survey or was not a member of a local congregation. Figure 1.6 shows a comparison of findings for the churched and the unchurched regarding other aspects of religious commitment. Attention is directed to the sizable portion of the unchurched who subscribe to traditional religious practices or beliefs, not to differences between the churched and the

FIGURE 1.6
COMPARISON OF THE CHURCHED AND UNCHURCHED

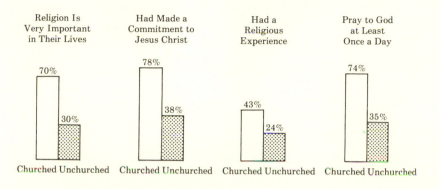

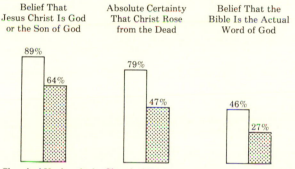

Source: Gallup Opinion Index, 1978b.

unchurched. Also note that quite a few of the churched do not follow traditional religious practices or do not hold basic Christian beliefs. For example, 64% of the unchurched believe Jesus Christ to be God or the Son of God, 38% indicate having made a commitment to Christ, and 35% pray at least daily. Twenty-six percent of the churched do not pray daily, 22% have not made a commitment to Christ, and 54% do not believe the Bible to be the actual word of God.[7]

As the data shows, church membership and participation are not perfect reflections of other dimensions of religious commitment. This suggests that the forces which influence religious participation are at least somewhat different from the forces that influence other dimensions of religious commitment. This same supposition is supported by the limited trend data we do have on aspects of

TABLE 1.2

TRENDS IN RELIGIOUS PREFERENCE OF U.S. ADULTS, 1947-1976

Year	Protestant	Catholic	Jewish	All Others	None
1947	69	20	5	1	6
1952	67	25	4	1	2
1957	66	26	3	1	3
1962	70	23	3	2	2
1967	67	25	3	3	2
1972	63	26	2	4	5
1975	61	27	2	4	6
1976	60	28	2	4	6

Source: Percentages for all years except 1957 are based on a combination of at least four Gallup Surveys in that year. 1957 percentages are from Current Population Reports (U.S. Bureau of the Census, P-20, No. 79, 1958). 1976 and 1977 percentages are from Religion in America 1976 and Religion in America 1977-78 (published by the Gallup Organization).

religion other than membership and participation, such as belief and private devotions. Generally, the trends show little resemblance to those for church membership and participation. A brief look at these trends helps to set the broader religious context within which the membership and participation shifts studied in this book are located.

National public opinion polls regularly ask about one's religious preference, and responses are usually categorized as either Protestant, Catholic, Jewish, other, or none. The trend in these religious preferences since 1947 is presented in Table 1.2 Two aspects of the table are of interest. First, a considerably larger percentage of the population states a preference for a particular religious tradition than actually holds membership within a church of that tradition. Second, while the Protestant majority is clearly intact, its size has eroded over the past twenty-eight years. Part of the change is due to the increased percentage of Catholics in the population and to increases among the "other" and "none" categories. How much of this latter growth ("other" and "none") is due to Jewish and Catholic defections cannot be seen from the data.

Trend data on the importance of religion in one's life is relatively scarce, but three national surveys spanning the period 1952 to 1978 show evidence of a long-term decline that is especially sharp since 1965 (see Figure 1.7). While it is common to expect that declines have been greatest among young adults, their falloffs are only a fraction greater than those of the population as a whole. One must also note that the importance of religion in individuals' lives was decreasing during the 1950s and early 1960s, a period of almost

FIGURE 1.7
INDICATORS OF RELIGIOUS SALIENCE: 1952-1978

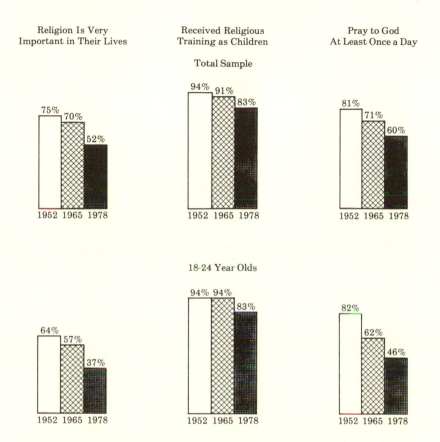

Source: Marty, Rosenberg, and Greeley (1968) and 1978 Gallup data.

universal membership growth for American denominations. A second, less direct indicator of a general decline in the importance of religion in the lives of Americans is also contained in these three surveys: the percentage of persons who received religious training as a child. Like the more direct measure of the importance of religion noted above, the percentage of persons receiving religious training fell slightly from 1952 to 1965, then dropped more sharply from 1965 to 1978 (see Figure 1.7). There is virtually no difference between the trends for young adults and the total population.

A third indicator of the importance of religion is the frequency of prayer. As shown in Figure 1.7, the percentage of persons who prayed at least daily went down ten points in each thirteen-year period. But unlike the above two measures of saliency, the decline in daily prayer was almost twice as great for young adults as it was for the total population. Additionally, if one disregards frequency and only looks at the percentage of persons who say they pray, there is almost no change from 1952 to 1978 (92 percent in 1952 versus 89 percent in 1978). Whether or not people pray has not changed significantly over the past twenty-five years, but the frequency of praying has lessened considerably.

Before one concludes too quickly that the importance of religion in America has been in constant decline since the early 1950s, it is important to look at trends in religious beliefs. If asked to name the most important dimension of religious commitment, most persons say religious belief. Regrettably, trend data on the religious beliefs of the American public is sparse.

Available national trend data on religious beliefs shows little change over time in the percentage of Americans affirming traditional Christian beliefs—such as belief in God and in life after death—when the belief questions are stated in simple "Yes" or "No" terms. For example, in both 1947 and 1975, 94% of the population responded yes to a question concerning whether or not they believed in God. Similarly, in 1958, 68% of the population said they believed in life after death; in 1975, 69% gave the same response. It has been argued, however, that such stability might be an artifact of the simplistic, all-or-nothing way in which the

TABLE 1.3

BELIEFS ABOUT GOD: 1952–1965

	1952	1965
Percent Absolutely Certain There Is a God		
All Adults	87	81
18–24 Years Old	87	71
Percent Thinking of God As a Loving Father		
All Adults	79	73
18–24 Years Old	80	67
Percent Believing in the Trinity		
All Adults	89	83
18–24 Years Old	90	80
Percent Believing Jesus Christ Was God		
All Adults	74	72
18–24 Years Old	76	68

Source: Marty, Rosenberg, and Greeley (1968).

questions were asked. Carroll (1978a:29), citing data from two questions dealing with beliefs about God from the 1952 and 1965 *Catholic Digest* national surveys of religion in America, shows that when the certitude of one's belief and the specific content of one's belief in God are addressed, significant declines are evident over time, especially among young adults. Table 1.3 contains the relevant information and shows that from 1952 to 1965 there was a marked decline in the certainty of belief in God and in the percentage of persons holding traditional Christian conceptions of God.

Comparable national survey data from 1963, 1976, and 1978 concerning beliefs about the Bible also depict a gradual shift from fundamentalist or literal interpretations of traditional Christian doctrines to more liberal or symbolic explanations. As shown in Table 1.4, the percentage of persons who believe the Bible is the actual word of God decreased from 65% in 1962 to 37% in 1978, while the percentage of persons who believe the Bible to be the inspired word of God increased from 18% in 1963 to 46% in 1968.[8]

Although admittedly sketchy, these trends in aspects of religious commitment other than church membership and participation all point to the same general conclusion. Over the past twenty-five years there has been a steady, gradual decline in the importance of religion in the lives of the American population, and a shift from literalistic to more symbolic interpretations of traditional Christian doctrines has taken place. These changes appear to have been

TABLE 1.4

BELIEFS ABOUT THE BIBLE: 1963-1978

	1963	1976	1978
Percent Indicating:			
Bible is the actual word of God and is to be taken literally, word for word	65	38	37
Bible is the inspired word of God but not everything in it should be taken literally, word for word	18	45	46
Bible is an ancient book of fables, legends, history, and moral precepts recorded by men	11	13	11
None of the above, or can't say	6	4	6

Source: Gallup Opinion Index (1967; 1978a; 1978b).

somewhat greater among young adults than among the total population and somewhat greater since the mid-1960s than from 1950 to the 1960s.

Juxtaposing these trends with those previously outlined for church membership and participation presents a number of interesting contrasts. Most obvious is that the two sets of trends move in opposite directions during the 1950s and early 1960s. Traditional Christian beliefs and the saliency of religion eroded, while church membership and participation grew. One possible explanation for this divergence is provided by Andrew Greeley's (1972) distinction between the meaning and belonging functions of religion. Meaning, as Greeley uses the term, refers to the cognitive framework that religious systems provide to help persons order the otherwise chaotic and frustrating world in which they live. Belonging refers to the care, support, and fellowship that are found as one is incorporated into a community. It is plausible to argue that the 1950s marked a decided transition period in the motivations for religious participation, one that saw an increasing number of people enter into the life of a religious institution primarily for reasons of fellowship and belonging, despite the fact that some traditional religious beliefs and practices (the meaning function) were declining in importance in their lives.

The second contrast in the two sets of trends is that, although the national polls show a marked shift from literal to symbolic interpretations of traditional Christian doctrines since the mid-1960s, it is the theologically conservative denominations that have continued to grow in membership during this time and the more liberal denominations that have experienced membership decline. At least two explanations for this contrast may be offered. One is that conservative denominations are gaining an increasing percentage of a decreasing market, while liberal denominations are gaining a decreasing percentage of a growing market. A second interpretation is that the membership of conservative denominations is becoming less fundamentalistic in orientation, while the mainline denominations, long without much sway over members' beliefs, are losing persons to competing, more secular, sources of fellowship or belonging.[9]

AN INTERPRETIVE FRAMEWORK FOR UNDERSTANDING PATTERNS OF CHURCH GROWTH AND DECLINE

In *Your Church Can Grow*, C. Peter Wagner (1976:29) states: "Simply put, *church growth is complex*. There is no way it can be reduced to a simple formula or canned program." The summary

report of the Special Committee to Study Church Membership
Trends, of the United Presbyterian Church (Presbyterian Commit-
tee, 1976:48), begins: "Our study . . . clearly demonstrates that
there is no single cause or simple pattern of causes for growth."
Jackson W. Carroll (1978a:37) concludes in his "Continuity and
Change: The Shape of American Religion":

> Single cause explanations of the [religious] trends . . . attract
> attention. But to explain them by any one factor alone
> oversimplifies an exceedingly complex set of relationships.
> Thus, we look not to single factor explanations, but to the
> impact of multiple factors whose interrelationships we
> cannot trace out or understand.

Study after study reaches the same conclusion: There is no single
cause or simple pattern of causes related to church growth or
decline. Rather, growth or decline involves a complex pattern of
multiple and often interacting factors.

The contributors to this book have found that a useful framework
for organizing and interpreting the wide variety of factors that
contribute to church growth or decline can be developed by
crosscutting two distinctions. The first distinction is between
contextual factors and institutional factors. Contextual factors are
external to the church. They are in the community, the society, and
the culture in which a church exists. A church has little control
over them. Institutional factors are internal to the church and are
aspects of its life and functioning over which it has some control.
The second distinction is between national and local factors.
National factors are those affecting all churches regardless of the
local setting, while local factors are those specific to a given locale.
Four different categories result from this crosscutting.

1. *National contextual factors*, representing forces operating at
   the national level external to the church—Here fall the broad
   sociostructural, economic, political, and value commitment
   changes that have occurred in the United States over the past
   quarter century.

2. *National institutional factors*, representing factors internal to
   the church but whose control is located at the national
   level—Most generally, this would include the activities of the
   national denominational and interdenominational bureaucracies; for example, their approach to and emphasis of
   evangelism and new church starts.

3. *Local contextual factors*, representing characteristics of the
   local community of a particular congregation and over which
   the congregation has little or no control—These may include
   population shifts, neighborhood changes, local economic
   trends, and so on.

4. *Local institutional factors,* representing factors internal to the local parish, those characteristics and structures of a local church that attract or dissuade membership and participation—Here may be included the quality and scope of program and leadership.

These four types of influences on church membership and participation act conjointly to determine the overall growth patterns of American Protestantism as a whole, of any given denomination, and of any given local congregation. This is to say that the growth or decline of a local congregation is dependent upon the impact of broad social and cultural forces, the impact of denominational resources and polity, and the impact of local contextual and local institutional factors. Similarly, the growth of a particular denomination is dependent upon the impact of broad social and cultural forces, the impact of its own characteristics and policies, and the impact of local contextual and institutional factors on its constituent congregations. Given the limits of presently available data sources, we cannot study the simultaneous or cumulative impact of all four types of factors taken together on either national, denominational, or local congregational trends. We are forced to deal with each type of factor and each type of trend somewhat independently. Specifically, we are limited to the study of national and denominational trends to discern the effect of national factors. And we are limited to the study of local parish trends to discern local contextual and local institutional factors. These areas of inquiry constitute the major organizing principle for the chapters in this book.

This chapter and the two that follow form an extended introduction to the subject of church growth and decline. Chapter 2 provides an extensive review of past research dealing with the dynamics of church commitment, and chapter 3 gives a historical overview of the growth movement in American Protestantism.

Chapters 4 through 12 contain empirical studies of the causal determinants of church growth and decline, organized according to the fourfold conceptual framework. Chapters 4 and 5 deal with the impact of national contextual factors on overall national trends. Chapter 4 focuses on the relationship of value changes to religious change, while chapter 5 deals with the explanatory usefulness of a variety of popular demographic theories of religious change.

Chapters 6, 7, and 8 shift the focus to denominational trends. Chapter 6 is primarily descriptive, providing a variety of trend data on Catholics and on nine of the largest Protestant denominations.

Chapter 7, also primarily descriptive in orientation, offers a comprehensive and systematic review of statistical trends for the Southern Baptist Convention, the largest Protestant denomination in the United States and one of the few major denominations that has not experienced overall membership declines since the mid-1960s. Chapter 8 presents an empirical test of the theories concerning denominational growth and decline set forth in Dean Kelley's influential *Why Conservative Churches Are Growing.*

Chapters 9 through 12 are concerned with an explanation of membership growth and decline in local congregations. Chapter 9 is a re-analysis of data originally gathered by the Special Committee to Study Church Membership Trends of the United Presbyterian Church. It addresses the question of the multiple factors related to growth and their relative impact, as well as the question of whether growth can be attained only at the cost of other possibly desirable areas of congregational performance.

Chapter 10 asks similar questions, using data from a study of United Church of Christ congregations. Chapter 11 focuses specifically on the relationship of the social context to the growth or decline of local congregations, and chapter 12 presents a summary of learnings derived from the case study research paradigm developed by the Church Growth Institute.

Chapters 13 through 16 provide a concluding section of reflection and reaction to the empirical studies contained in the book. Chapter 13 contains a theologian's response that raises questions about church growth and decline based on the distinction between faithfulness and effectiveness. Chapter 14 summarizes what we currently know and have yet to learn about the sociological analysis of church growth and decline. The final two chapters contain commentaries written by noted interpreters of modern church life. They offer not only their reactions to the material presented in the book, but also begin to draw out the implications of this material for the life of the church.

One final note by way of introduction: In gathering together the chapters that follow, the editors have sought to give voice to those researchers who have been most intimately involved in the study of church growth and decline over the past five or more years. The criteria of inclusion have been experience and the quality of the work produced rather than agreement on the issues. Consequently, there is not total agreement among the authors. At the very least, the disagreements remind us of the complexity of the subject matter.

CHAPTER 2

Research on Factors Influencing Church Commitment

Dean R. Hoge
and
David A. Roozen

Fundamental to any investigation of church growth or decline is a clear understanding of why individuals become involved in religious organizations, maintain or increase their involvement, or drop out. These questions have been dealt with in many previous studies. The result has been a diverse collection of hints and partial explanations but not any definitive theory clearly supported by empirical evidence. This chapter aims to provide a thorough review of the past research on factors influencing individuals' church commitment and states several conclusions for orienting future research of church trends.[1]

The scope of this chapter is limited in two ways. First, it is restricted to the study of church membership and participation. We are not concerned with other aspects of religious commitment such as devotionalism, theological beliefs, or religious experience except as they influence church membership and participation. We make no assumption that motivations for church participation are intrinsically religious in a way making them different, for example, from motivations for country club participation; this is an empirical question. But we do assume that motivations for church participation are varied and multiple, and that they are partly unconscious.

Second, this chapter deals specifically (as does the entire book) with the more established and traditional denominations in America. Mainline Protestant denominations and the Catholic Church are typically culture-affirming and supportive of the social status quo. Research on new religious movements, sects, and cults is not reviewed here. Characteristically, such groups remove themselves self-consciously from the general American culture, and the motivations for participation in them are different.

Although past research on this topic is quite diverse, it can be grouped into three types. One is atheoretical research on single social factors related to church participation and commitment, such as sex, age, or rural-urban differences. Another is more theoretical research, setting forth and testing theories purporting to explain levels of church participation. The third is research looking at motivation arising from church life itself. The organization of our review follows this grouping: Part I deals with research on single factors, Part II with research testing six theories, and Part III with studies of church life and its effects. Finally, Part IV attempts to summarize and integrate the findings.

I: RESEARCH ON SINGLE FACTORS

Sex

All research on Protestants and Catholics shows higher church attendance and religious commitment for women than for men (for an extensive review see Argyle and Beit-Hallahmi, 1975:71-79). Females attend church more, hold more orthodox beliefs, and are more devotional—regardless of age, race, education, or subjective social class (see Carroll and Roozen, 1975:98ff).

For Jews the sex ratios are different, and the data is not consistent. Lazerwitz (1970) found greater male than female pietism, synagogue attendance, and traditional beliefs, especially among more orthodox Jews and especially in the first generation or two after immigration. Mueller and Johnson (1975:790), however, reported higher religious participation for Jewish females than males in 1970 data. Probably, as Lazerwitz suggests, American culture influences the Jewish community so that, in time, the traditional level of male participation decreases and the sex ratio reverses.

Cross-cultural studies of religion find a wide variety of sex ratios (see Yinger, 1970:134), indicating that they are cultural products, not anything universally human.

What is the explanation for the Protestant and Catholic sex ratios in America today? Several have been proposed. Lazerwitz (1961), Lenski (1963:51), and Luckmann (1967) hypothesize that participation in the labor force might be important, with nonparticipation being associated with more church attendance. If this is so, then sex differences in church attendance should decrease when labor force participation is controlled. Lazerwitz (1961), Carroll and Roozen (1975), and Hoge and Carroll (1978) tested this with various kinds of data. In every test the sex differences did not decrease, indicating that participation in the labor force has little effect on church attendance.

Yinger (1970:133) suggests that sex differences in religious commitment may occur because females have narrower social contacts and thus experience somewhat less secularization. Carroll and Roozen (1975) found that females do indeed belong to fewer voluntary organizations than males, but when church attendance is studied, while controlling for nonchurch organizational involvement, the sex differences remain. Yinger also intimates that females play a more central role in the socialization of children than do males. Since religious training of children is an important function of churches, one would expect church attendance of mothers with school-age children to be higher. Carroll and Roozen checked and found this to be true not only for mothers, but also for fathers. Hence, the socialization of school-age children does not explain sex differences.

None of these proposed explanations of sex differences has found empirical support. We are left, then, with indisputable data about sex differences in America today but with no clear explanations for them. Since the sex differences occur across a wide range of subgroups, it appears that they result from general normative expectations about sex roles. Indeed, sex-role research has found a broad structure of male-female differences in America today, a structure in which religious behavior fits well. Women, in general, are found in all research to be more conforming to social norms, more anxious, more nurturant, and more affiliative (see, for example, Argyle and Beit-Hallahmi, 1975:77-78), and these traits are congruent with traditional church behavior. Sex differences in church behavior are apparently components of broader sex-role differences. They are mostly learned behavior and are acquired early in life.

Age

The relationship between age (during adulthood) and church behavior has been studied many times. Good reviews are found in Bahr (1970), Argyle and Beit-Hallahmi (1975), and Finney and Lee (1977). Several studies done in 1947-55 showed a sharp decline in religious activity between ages 18 and 30, followed by a continuous increase from 30 onward; this pattern came to be known as the traditional pattern. However, more recent studies have shown different and inconsistent patterns, suggesting that the traditional pattern was a product of a particular time in history. Several recent studies have been able to distinguish aging, cohort, and period effects. The aging effect refers to the effect of becoming older in the typical American life cycle, apart from all else. The cohort effect relates to the impact of having been socialized at a certain time in history; the crucial age in regard to religion and values is usually understood to be high school or early college, although research is not conclusive (see Freedman, 1956; Hastings and Hoge, 1976). The period effect refers to the influence of social factors in any particular historical period.

Which of these three effects is strongest in middle-class America? Two studies have been able to distinguish the three effects on church attendance (Wingrove and Alston, 1974; Carroll and Roozen, 1975), and both find the aging effect to be the weakest and the period effect to be the strongest.[2] This finding makes us cautious about drawing conclusions from cross-sectional studies at any one time.

A few outlines of each effect can be summarized from existing research. Carroll and Roozen found the cohort effect in recent decades to cause each cohort of young persons to enter adulthood at a lower church attendance level. This finding matches research on youth and college students showing declining religious commitments over the past twenty years (Hoge, 1974). Wingrove and Alston found no single discernible cohort effect in their data. However, they did identify a definite period effect—that all cohorts had their highest church attendance rates between 1950 and 1960, and that all cohorts declined in church attendance after 1965. Wingrove and Alston found no clear aging effects, but Carroll and Roozen found one pattern—that religious activity increased from the 21- to 30-year-old group to the 31- to 40-year-old group. Argyle and Beit-Hallahmi reviewed all past research and concluded that one aging effect is visible throughout—a decrease in religious activity between ages 18 and 30 (1975:66). Bahr similarly reviewed all research but concluded that no constant overall aging effect was visible (see Bahr's summary table, 1970:61).

Recent cross-sectional research has usually found a modest positive relationship between age and church attendance (Carroll and Roozen, 1975; Hoge and Polk, 1976; Hoge and Carroll, 1978; Wuthnow, 1976b; Finney and Lee, 1977) but not always (Johnson et al., 1974). The relationship is probably the product of cohort effects, since trend research on youth shows a decided decline in church commitment.

We are left with a conservative conclusion. Aging, in itself, has a small effect on church behavior, although many studies indicate a decline between 18 and 30 that may be well-nigh universal over recent decades. Beyond that no general statements about age differences can be made. This conclusion calls into question any demographic theories purporting to explain church participation trends by pointing to variations in the size of each age stratum in America from decade to decade (for example, Schroeder, 1975).

Denomination

All research agrees that denominational differences exist in church participation. In all studies Catholics have the highest level of church attendance, followed by Protestants, and then by Jews, who have the lowest level (Lazerwitz, 1961; Marty, Rosenberg, and Greeley, 1968; Stark and Glock, 1968; Alston, 1972). These differences have been quite stable over time, with the exception of a sharp decline in Catholic church attendance after about 1964, causing some convergence between Catholic and Protestant attendance rates.

Analysts have found that denominational differences cannot be explained by demographic factors (see Lazerwitz, 1961; Alston, 1972). Rather, they result from group norms maintained in the denominations and transmitted via socialization and sanctions. Like sex roles, they are social facts not explainable by characteristics of individuals.

An illuminating research finding is that church attendance is considerably lower for members of interfaith families (Leiffer, 1949; Lenski, 1953; Anders, 1955; Prince, 1962; Babchuk, Crockett, and Ballweg, 1967; Carroll and Roozen, 1975). The differences are large. For example, Carroll and Roozen (1975:132) found that of married Protestant adults whose spouses had the same religious preference, 62% reported at least monthly church attendance; of those whose spouses had a different preference the figure was 33%.

Among Catholics the corresponding figures were 73% and 43%. The size of the differences was little affected by social class, age, or the presence vs. absence of school-age children in the home. The reason for the lower church attendance of mixed-marriage families is unclear. A convincing explanation, if found in future research, would probably have far-reaching implications for understanding motivations for church participation today. Apparently, a mixed marriage reduces the identity or belonging functions that church-going serves for the family or for its individual members.

Community Size

Much research has related community size to church participation and church attendance (for reviews see Fischer, 1975; Newman, 1975; Roozen, 1978a). The findings have varied considerably but in one respect have been in agreement—all research has found *weak* relationships, if any at all. The bulk of recent research has found no relationships at all (Bouvier and Weller, 1974; Gaede, 1975; Carroll and Roozen, 1975; Roof, 1976; Hoge and Polk, 1976).

These largely negative findings exist alongside some widely believed theories purporting to explain rural-urban differences in religion. For example, Herberg (1955) argues that urbanization and suburbanization create identity loss and encourage church participation to help people regain a sense of identity and social location. Wirth (1938) and Cox (1965) argue, on the contrary, that urban life leads to secularization, relativism, and loss of tradition. Tests of these theories (Fischer, 1975, for example) have found little support for them.

In summary, community size alone appears to have little impact on church behavior, and current theories of urbanism are very weak at best. Perhaps community size in combination with other factors—such as age of population, rate of transiency, level of localism, and amount of familism—might be predictive of church behavior.

Region

All research agrees that regional differences in church attendance exist. First, it has been consistently found that southern Protestants attend church more often than Protestants in other regions. The difference has been quite constant over time. It is not attributable to regional differences in race, education, occupation, or rural versus urban residence (Reed, 1972:78; Gallup Opinion

Index, 1975:3). Among Catholics, however, higher church attendance levels in the South have usually not been found (Alston, 1971; Carroll and Roozen, 1975:131; Gallup Opinion Index, 1975:3).

Second, the West has been found in all research to have lower church attendance rates than the rest of the nation. This is true for both Protestants and Catholics (Gallup, 1972; Gallup Opinion Index, 1975:3; Carroll and Roozen, 1975:131).

The regional differences are rather large. Carroll and Roozen found that 54 percent of persons with Protestant preference attended church monthly or oftener in the entire nation, but the figure was 73 percent in the East South Central region and 38 percent in the Pacific region. These differences are not new; they were quite clear, for example, in the 1926 Census of Religious Bodies. Douglass and Brunner (1935:240) tried to explain them as resulting from differences in population mobility and density of population per square mile. Most observers have suggested a cultural rather than a demographic explanation, speculating that lower church attendance in the West is due to the greater rootlessness of the population and the emergent Western culture of individualism (for example, Metz, 1965). No researchers, however, have found empirical support or disconfirmation, to our knowledge, for any of these theories.

II: RESEARCH ON SIX THEORIES[3]

Deprivation Theory

The deprivation theory is the most common theory of religiosity found in the literature. Dittes (1971:394) has called it the most "standard" theory of religion in the history of social science. It is actually a group of related theories, all stating that persons suffering deprivation or dispossession look to religion as a means of compensation and thus become committed to the church. The theory has roots in the Marxist view that "religion is the sigh of the oppressed creature" and finds support in the work of Troeltsch (1931) and Niebuhr (1929).[4]

In 1965 Glock and Stark published an article outlining and defending the deprivation theory. They defined deprivation as "any and all of the ways that an individual or group may be, or feel, disadvantaged in comparison to other individuals or groups or to an internalized set of standards [1965:246]." They distinguished five kinds of deprivation: economic, social, organismic, ethical, and psychic. Although their definition of deprivation allows for an objective deprivation not subjectively felt, the thrust of the argument is on subjectively felt deprivation. This is a crucial point for testing the theory, as we will see.

Glock and Stark argue that the five kinds of felt deprivation lead to different kinds of social movements. Economic deprivation tends to lead to revolutionary movements or to sectarian religious movements. Social deprivation (defined as a feeling that one's social status is less than that of others) leads to reform movements or to churchlike religious movements. Organismic deprivation leads to healing movements. Ethical deprivation (defined as a feeling of value conflict between oneself and the wider society) tends to lead to reform movements. Psychic deprivation (defined as a feeling of being without a meaningful system of values) tends to lead to religious cults. Glock and Stark (1965:256) say that to understand church life today, one must look at social deprivation.

> The ability of churches to survive in basically unchanged form is, in substantial part, a consequence of the persistence of social deprivation. Participation in a church, we would suggest, functions to provide individuals with a source of gratification which they cannot find in the society-at-large.

This theory must be tested using measures of subjectively felt deprivation, but in practice it has usually been tested using objective measures of socioeconomic status or status-related variables such as sex and age.

Many researchers have studied socioeconomic status in relation to church behavior. Although it is difficult to summarize the research because of its diversity in method, measures used, and results, some statements can be made. Table 2.1 sums up the principal studies of the relationship between church attendance and socioeconomic status. Every study except one has found either no relationship between socioeconomic status and church attendance or a positive relationship. This research does not support the deprivation theory. The one study supporting the theory was done by Glock and his associates using a 1952 nationwide sample of Episcopalians (Glock et al., 1967). Perhaps its unusual sample or the method of data analysis (using no significance tests or measures of association) accounts for the uncommon conclusions.[5]

The introduction of control variables uncovers no changes from the pattern summarized in Table 2.1. When Catholics and Protestants are studied separately or when sexes and age groups are studied separately, the same patterns remain in each group

TABLE 2.1

SUMMARY OF CHURCH ATTENDANCE-SOCIOECONOMIC STATUS RELATIONSHIPS FOUND IN PAST RESEARCH

	Sample	Findings			
Year	Characteristics	Education	Occupation	Income	Source
1952	National sample of adult Episcopalian church members	Composite Index: Negative*			Glock, Ringer, and Babbie (1967)
1952	National sample: adults	None	None	Slight +	Marty, Rosenberg, and Greeley (1968)
1956	National sample of adult Congregationalists	Positive	Positive		Goode (1966)
1957	Three national samples: adults	Positive	Positive	None	Lazerwitz (1961)
1957	Adult church members from nine denominations	None	None		Estus and Overlington (1970)
1958	Adult Detroit area sample		Positive		Lenski (1963)
1959	Appalachian sample: church members and non-members	None	Positive		Goode (1966)
1960	National sample: adults	Positive	Positive		Glock and Stark (1965)
1965	National sample: adults	Positive	None	Positive	Marty, Rosenberg, and Greeley (1968)
1965	National sample: adults	Positive	Positive	None	Alston (1971)
1967	National samples: adults†	Positive	Positive	Positive	Gallup Opinion Index (1968)
1968	North Carolina adult Episcopalian church members	Positive			Roof (1976)
1969	National sample: adults	None	Slight +	None	Alston (1971)
1970	Adult suburban church members, two denominations	None	None	None	Hoge and Carroll (1978)
1970	National non-farm sample: adults	Slight +	Slight +	Slight +	Mueller and Johnson (1976)
1971	National sample of Protestant church members	None	None	None	Hoge and Polk (1976)
1973	National sample pooled with 1974 national sample: adults	None	None	None	Carroll and Roozen (1975)#
1974	National samples: adults†	(	Slight +	(	Gallup Opinion Index (1975)

*Composite index including education and income.
†Pool of all AIPO national samples which included a question on church attendance.
#Carroll and Roozen found a positive relationship between church attendance and subjective social class.

(Lazerwitz, 1961; Lenski, 1963; Alston, 1971; Gallup Opinion Index, 1975; Mueller and Johnson, 1975; Carroll and Roozen, 1975).

Two important studies have concluded that different types of religiosity relate differently to socioeconomic status. Both Demerath (1965), in his study of members of five mainline Protestant denominations, and Campbell and Fukuyama (1970), in their study of members of the United Church of Christ, found that church attendance and organizational involvement correlated positively with socioeconomic status, while traditional beliefs and personal devotionalism correlated negatively. Campbell and Fukuyama suggested that "religion is largely an expression of social captivity for people of privilege while it is largely an expression of compensation for social deprivation for underprivileged people [1970:104]." Such a reformulation, limiting the deprivation theory to beliefs and personal devotional life, fits the research data, but it does not help to explain patterns of church commitment and participation. It does imply, however, that motivations for church participation might be different in upper and lower classes, with the former being more social and the latter more theological.

What about the status-related variables of sex and age? Glock and other theorists have assumed that females and elderly people are accorded less prestige in American society than males and young people. It has already been shown that females participate more in the church than males. Whether deprivation is the explanation for this is doubtful, since sex ratios in religious participation vary greatly from culture to culture, and we find it incredible that the relative levels of felt deprivation by men and by women would vary so greatly. But this is merely speculation. The topic deserves study.

As regards age, we indicated earlier that age patterns in church participation vary from decade to decade. We doubt that deprivation feelings of older persons vary so much from decade to decade, and hence we are skeptical about a deprivation explanation for age differences.

In summary, the social deprivation theory as expounded by Glock and Stark has received only a modicum of support, while most of the research has directly contradicted it. To many analysts this suggests abandoning the deprivation theory as an explanation of participation in mainline churches. But not all persons have abandoned the deprivation theory; some defend it (see examples in Argyle and Beit-Hallahmi, 1975:194ff). Two main arguments are used. The first is that church attendance and church organizational participation are not "really" religiosity but are merely another instance of voluntary social activity. This argument leads to a reduced formulation of the deprivation theory as suggested by Campbell and Fukuyama (noted above), leaving it to explain personal religiosity but not church behavior. The argument may be correct, but it is not relevant for our concern, which is *church participation*.

The second argument is that the research has used only objective measures of deprivation, not subjective measures. Hence, it cannot show true levels of feelings of deprivation held by individuals. This argument has been tested in about a dozen studies that have utilized subjective measures of deprivation. The studies, which usually use measures of anomie, vary widely in quality (for reviews of earlier studies see Lee and Clyde, 1974; Carr and Hauser, 1976). They generally showed that anomie is unrelated to religiousness. When a relationship was found, it was usually that religious persons were slightly *lower* in anomie, contrary to the deprivation theory. Four recent studies have found the same—in every case, churchgoing persons were lower in anomie than others (Carroll and Roozen, 1975; Hoge and Polk, 1976; Alston and McIntosh, 1977; Hoge and Carroll, 1978). Generally, tests using subjective measures also fail to support the deprivation theory of church participation.

It could be objected that feelings of deprivation were high among these persons prior to church membership or prior to high levels of involvement, but the feelings subsided thereafter. Both the Hoge-Polk and the Hoge-Carroll studies checked variations in anomie or dissatisfaction with life as related to length of time in the congregation. No patterns were found, making the objection unconvincing. Also Hoge and Polk argue that if the objection is true and feelings of deprivation subside after joining a church, then if deprivation is the main motivation for involvement, the involvement should also subside. The likelihood remains that motivations for initial joining of a church differ greatly from motivations for sustained or increased involvement at a later time. Since most research has been cross-sectional and not longitudinal, perhaps the research has not uncovered deprivation factors present at the time of initial church joining but largely absent later. This is a possibility that may identify a limited role for the deprivation theory for certain persons at the time of initial joining.

Deprivation Theory Continued: The Family Surrogate Theory

The study by Glock and his associates [1967] based on Episcopalian data spawned a family surrogate theory. The study found that persons without spouses or married persons without children participated more in churches than did married persons with children. The relationship held true regardless of sex or age. Glock and his associates extended the deprivation idea to include family status, saying that persons either unmarried or married but without children were accorded lower social status than those married and with children. Hence, such persons participated more in the church, which functioned for them as a family surrogate.

A number of studies have investigated church involvement of married or unmarried adults and of married couples with children compared with those without children (Lenski, 1953; Lazerwitz, 1961; Hobart, 1974; Carroll and Roozen, 1975; Mueller and Johnson, 1975; Hoge and Polk, 1976; Alston and McIntosh, 1977; Hoge and Carroll, 1978). No studies have found the pattern predicted by the family surrogate theory. The Glock et al. (1967) study is unusual in its findings, different from all others; the reason is unclear.

Returning to the scrutiny of the deprivation theory in general, we may ask where all the research leaves the theory. For explaining church participation patterns in mainline churches, the deprivation theory seems unimportant and should be abandoned (for a similar conclusion see Alston and McIntosh, 1977). The family surrogate theory should also be given up. The deprivation theory, however, does seem apt for understanding commitment to some sectarian movements and new social movements. Possibly it is also useful in explaining initial participation in mainline churches; on this question we lack information. But it is not a major explanation for participation in mainline churches. A different theory is needed.

Child-rearing Theory

The child-rearing theory was most clearly formulated by Nash and Berger (1962). They interviewed new members of suburban churches and concluded that the presence of school-age children was a foremost factor leading to membership. They pointed out that churches usually include programs of religious education for children, and that many Americans believe in these programs. Hence, when young adults begin to have children of school age, they increase their church participation for the sake of child-rearing (also see Fairchild and Wynn, 1961; DeJong and Faulkner, 1972). This theory is strengthened by a series of surveys on church priority preferences of Protestant laity, all of which show Christian education for children as the highest or nearly highest priority (Hoge, 1976b).

The theory has been tested in a number of studies. Anders (1955) found, in a study of one church, that families with children participated more than those without children, and if the children were of minor age, the participation was higher than if they were very small children. In a survey of Indianapolis Protestants, Lenski (1953) found that the more children were living in the family, the higher was the interest in religion. Lazerwitz (1961) and Metz (1965) found that if couples had children 5 years old or older, their church attendance was significantly higher; Davis (1962) found the same if the couples had young children. Mueller and Johnson (1975:795) and Hoge and Carroll (1978) found the same. The clearest pattern occurred in the Carroll and Roozen study (1975) based on nationwide survey data. In that study parents with children 5 years or younger attended less than average, while parents with school-age children attended more than average.

Two studies failed to find support for the child-rearing theory. Alston (1971) and Hoge and Polk (1976), both using nationwide survey data, failed to find the predicted pattern. However, both studies lacked information on age of children, which is a crucial variable to control when testing the theory.

We can summarize that studies which have controlled for age of children and have tested the effect of *presence* of children in the home (not the total *number* of children) have always found the predicted relationship, while those not controlling for age and those looking only at the total number of children have found no relationships or weak relationships. We conclude that the child-rearing theory has some explanatory power which is visible in research using appropriate controls. The patterns found are sometimes moderately strong and sometimes quite weak.

Status Group Theory

Earlier we found that many studies indicate that upper and middle status groups participate more in the church than do lower status groups, even though the latter are more orthodox and more devotional. Is middle- and upper-class participation based on another motivation?

Lenski (1963:44) argued that the greater middle- and upper-class church activity occurs because these persons have a higher level of associational activity in general. They participate more in organizations of all kinds, and the church is one kind. Lazerwitz (1964), Goode (1966), Estus and Overington (1970), Blaikie (1972), and Mueller and Johnson (1975) tested the theory. The outcomes were similar—when the association of social class and church participation was measured while controlling for overall associational activity, the original relationship weakened but by less than half. Therefore, the relationship between class and church participation is not wholly a product of the more general relationship between class and organizational activity.

The problem of explaining upper- and middle-class church participation levels remains mostly unsolved. Another approach to it begins with Weber's description of status groups (Gerth and Mills, 1958:186). Status groups are associations in which participation by members bestows status, identity, and honor. Persons who take an active part have their social status confirmed. Weber discussed businessmen's clubs and lodges, and we would add country clubs, college alumni associations, and organizations such as Rotary and Junior League (see Stub, 1972). It is also true that some persons who take part in these activities derive additional benefits; for insurance agents and stockbrokers, for instance, business success depends partly on social connections.

Several authors have suggested that middle- and upper-class churches approximate being status groups. Campbell and Fukuyama (1970:101) argue that mainline Protestant churches elicit more participation from the middle and upper classes than from working-class persons because these churches affirm middle- and upper-class values. "If the church is simply expressing the views of the dominant social classes, it would be expected that the privileged social groups would find satisfaction in associating with the church in its programs and organizations." They speak of a "country club at prayer" theory, and Winter (1962) describes the "social captivity of the church." Winter points out that most mainline congregations are composed of single social class groups and single ethnic groups.

The status group theory states that for some persons church participation is motivated by the status, honor, and recognition it bestows. The theory is difficult to test convincingly. One element of the theory, the point that most congregations are single class and single ethnicity in composition, finds abundant research support (see Warner and Lunt, 1941; Pope, 1942; Hollingshead, 1949;

Laumann, 1969). But demonstration of the motivations for participation in status groups is elusive. Hoge and Polk (1976) found that the statement "Church membership has helped me to meet the right kind of people" correlated at .21 with church attendance in a cross-denominational Protestant sample. But Hoge and Carroll (1978) did not find the same result in a study of Methodist and of Presbyterian church members; the statements "The church is most important as a place to formulate good social relationships" and "One reason for my being a church member is that such membership helps to establish a person in the community" had no correlations with church attendance. However, in the same study the number of a respondent's five closest friends who are also members of her or his congregation correlated .28 with church attendance (for a similar finding see Roof, 1976).

What can be concluded? Perhaps being embedded in gratifying social relationships is important in motivating church attendance, but church members do not report status-group-related motivations as being important. This is a tentative conclusion, but since the research is so sparse, nothing definite can be said. The status group theory needs articulation and careful testing in future research.

Doctrinal Belief Theory

It has long been believed that commitment to orthodox doctrinal beliefs produces church participation. Thus, if individuals hold orthodox Christian beliefs, their participation in the church will be relatively high. If, in addition, they believe that the church is necessary for salvation, their participation will be higher. If they also believe that their church and no other has God's truth, their participation will be even higher.

All research shows a strong association between orthodox theological belief and church involvement (Faulkner and DeJong, 1966; Stark and Glock, 1968; King and Hunt, 1975). For instance, in a nationwide sample of Presbyterians, King and Hunt (1975:18) found a correlation of .34 between an index of orthodox beliefs and a measure of church attendance.

How strong is the explanatory power of doctrinal beliefs after controlling for background variables? Hoge and Polk (1976) assessed the variance in church attendance explained by doctrinal factors after socioeconomic, personal, and familial factors were controlled. They found that doctrinal factors explained about 4 percent of the variance in theologically conservative denominations and about 15 percent in theologically liberal denominations. In conservative denominations, doctrinal beliefs varied much less than in liberal denominations, thus allowing them less explanatory power. Hoge and Carroll (1978) made a similar analysis using both Methodist and Presbyterian church member data. The amount of variance explained by doctrinal beliefs after other factors were controlled was only 2.3 percent. It seems that the causal power of doctrinal beliefs is only moderately strong when other background and group factors are taken into consideration.

What is the direction of causation between beliefs and church participation? This question has been much discussed (see Gaede, 1977). Some researchers (for example, Lofland and Stark, 1965) have shown that religious beliefs evolve in the midst of church life and that church life is initially based on personal relationships. Other researchers emphasize the causal power of beliefs. Hoge and Polk (1976) and Hoge and Carroll (1978) constructed and tested simple path models positing causation in first one direction, then the other, and they concluded in both studies that the models positing causation from beliefs to church participation were stronger than those positing the opposite direction. This evidence is not very conclusive, but we have warrant for speaking of some causation from doctrinal beliefs to church attendance.

Value Structure Theory

Theories based on the structure of values held by an individual are prominent in the discussions of church participation. Some research has found much explanatory power in them. A vexing problem is establishing direction of causation, for even though church participation is shown to be correlated with certain value structures, the values cannot be considered to be causal without strong theoretical reasons.

In this section we discuss the work of three researchers—Hoge, Wuthnow, and Roozen. All three have investigated the relation of church participation to value clusters. Our review will give much attention to the problem of direction of causation.

Hoge studied trends in the religion of college students and emerged with some theoretical conclusions important for understanding relationships between religious commitments and values. He used a concept "meaning-commitment system."

> The term "meaning-commitment system" will refer to the total system of values, attitudes, commitments, and behavior of any individual person. It is somewhat similar to Tillich's

concept of ultimate concern in that it refers to the central elements of one's personal religion [1974:30].

It is composed of attitudes and values. Its structure is vaguely hierarchical, but it is not tightly unified. It is more like a network than a rigid structure. It is subject to change due to imputs from one value area or another.

Adequate interpretation and explanation of religious change must work from the total meaning-commitment system of the individual. The reason is that investment in traditional religious doctrines or institutions may be affected indirectly by changes in other portions of the meaning-commitment system. For example, changing commitment to particular expressive styles, particular political programs, or particular community organizations, though apparently distinct from traditional religious doctrines and institutions, will affect the latter indirectly [1974:180].

Hoge showed how trends in several value areas were similar over four decades and interpreted the total pattern of trends in terms of shifts in the modal meaning-commitment system of students.[6] The sources of the trends were impacts from the overall political and social climate. The Cold War era, the McCarthy period, and political conservatism of the early 1950s influenced political and national values, which, in turn, affected religion (1974:ch. 6).

It follows that the relative closeness to one another of various value components is a measure of the relative influenceability of one from the other. Of all the value areas studied by Hoge, sex and family values were found to be closest to traditional religious values. Other values, such as political or economic, were much less close. We may conclude, therefore, that social changes in the area of sex and family will have greater impact on religion (and vice versa) than changes in the areas of politics or economics.

What is the direction of causation between religious participation and other values? Hoge says that no general statement can be made; sometimes causation is in one direction, sometimes in another, depending on the relative impacts on the total system from one direction or another. A religious conversion would, for example, constitute an important change in religious commitments, and it would, in turn, influence other value areas. A personal event in the realm of politics, such as resisting the draft, would cause an impact, in turn, on religious commitments. In methodological terms, values alone are not seen as causal on religious commitments or vice versa, but demonstrated changes in certain value areas, especially when traced to important events, can be considered causal for changes in closely related commitments.

Wuthnow (1976b) made an important analysis of recent religious change. He focused on the counterculture that arose among many young people in the 1960s and outlined a number of respects in which it opposed organized churches: civil rights militancy, antiwar activism, homosexuality, drug use, alternative life-styles, and sexual freedom. Then he addressed the problem of causality.

> To the extent that a relation between religious trends and the emergence of the counterculture can be posited, it also appears reasonable to suggest that the dominant direction of influence was from the counterculture to religion rather than from religion to the counterculture, especially during the late 1960's and the early 1970's [1976b:854].

Wuthnow argues that the counterculture was little concerned with organized religion, and no visible link between organized religion and the rise of the counterculture can be found. He also argues that recent panel study data at Berkeley indicates causation from counterculture trends to religious trends (see Wuthnow, 1978:ch. 7). His explanation of overall trends in American church participation is centered on changes in the young generation of liberally educated bearers of new cultural values. The changes in this generation were due largely to the alienating political and social events of the 1960s. Hence, the logic of analysis is similar to that used by Hoge—from events to broad values to religious commitments. Wuthnow found that the value areas most in conflict with established churches were use of drugs and marijuana, unmarried persons living together, freedom for homosexuality, and participation in political demonstrations (1976b:859).

Wuthnow's analysis has other dimensions, but for us his demonstration of relationships between church participation and other values, his handling of the problem of causation, and his explanation of trends in generational terms are most pertinent. His causal model, based on California data, is a strong one, with a beta of − .47 for the crucial relationship between counterculture values and church participation.

Roozen (1977) analyzed nationwide survey data in an attempt to explain levels of church attendance. He adopted a social-psychological approach to the study of religion, taken partly from Estus and Overington (1970) and Roof (1976; 1978).

> This perspective maintains that religious expressions are essentially symbolic representations of broader sets of values, commitments and meanings; and that traditional religious institutions generally are expressive of meanings found plausible only within a particular context of broader value commitments [1977:1].

Thus, the logic of explaining levels of church participation is to discern the values espoused by churches and then compare them with the values held by groups and categories of persons in the population. The better the match, the higher will be the church participation of the group. This approach leads directly to an explanation for change, since any discernible value changes in segments of the population, in which values associated with church life shift, will predict changes in levels of church participation.

Roozen reviewed past research depicting the values, commitments, and meanings symbolized by mainline churches. The research agrees rather well on what they are. They include a world view focused on the private sector of life and with such immediate social orientations as the family, ethnic group, or local community. They are associated with conformity and conservatism in all attitude realms and with personal and privatistic commitments not oriented to social change. They value conformity and tradition more than individual freedom and tolerance of diversity, social conservatism more than social change, and definite moral codes more than individualized moral orientations.

Roozen tested this theory with nationwide survey data. He identified values and attitudes associated with traditional religion and used them as an explanation of church attendance. The principal causation he saw as from value orientation to religion, not vice versa. He created a value index from items asking about abortion, extramarital sexual relations, homosexuality, whether a book written by someone who was against all churches should be removed from the public library, whether a person should be allowed to make a speech against private enterprise, and whether an admitted Communist should be allowed to teach in a college. This index, called the New Morality Index, alone accounted for 9.8 percent of the variance in church attendance.

To summarize the work of these researchers, the value structure theory is clearly important in understanding church participation and commitment, since the association between certain value areas and church participation is quite strong. The problem of direction of causation is crucial, but already we can conclude that there is some warrant for speaking of causation from general value orientation to church participation.

Localism Theory

The localism theory has recently been proposed by Roof (1972; 1976). It holds that an understanding of church participation patterns requires a thorough analysis of subgroups in society having divergent values and orientations. The theory argues that modern industrial society is highly differentiated, including many areas where traditional religious norms are segregated from institutional sectors (see Luckmann, 1967), thus producing a variety of religious and secular value configurations. In the process, traditional local values are confronted by new cosmopolitan values.

> As the scale of societal integration has increased, primarily through large bureaucratic organizations and mass communication facilities, choices of reference perspectives and affiliational patterns of a local-versus-extralocal type have become more and more available. Societal-wide configurations of rational values and norms have come to be differentiated from localistic, traditional cultural patterns [1972:4].

In an increasingly pluralistic society, maintenance of any value orientation requires a community of persons committed to the values and supporting others in that commitment.

> A sociology of knowledge perspective suggests that the primary prerequisite for any belief system is the presence of an adequate socio-communal support structure. That is, definitions of social reality are "real" insofar as they are confirmed through day-to-day interactions among those who share a similar perspective. Such a social base—what Peter Berger refers to as "plausibility structure"—is indispensable for maintaining any kind of world view, religious or otherwise [1976:197].

In modern society the plausibility structures for church religion have diminished in size and now consist of local social enclaves. They are usually made up of family networks, ethnic groups, and local communities. An individual's relation to these structures is crucial to know for understanding his or her degree of church involvement. To measure it, Roof developed an index of local (versus cosmopolitan) orientation. He predicted that locally oriented people would be more involved in churches than cosmopolitan people.

Roof tested his predictions with two sets of data. One was from North Carolina Baptists. He found that localism was strongly associated with doctrinal orthodoxy and communalism (measured by the number of one's closest friends who are members of the congregation) but only moderately associated with church involvement (attendance and organizational involvement). In regression analysis the beta for localism as a determinant of church involvement was .33. The second set of data was from North Carolina Episcopalians. The results were the same: localism was the single strongest predictor of church attendance and organizational involvement. Also localism was associated with length of residence in the community $(r = .38)$, with community size $(r = .31)$, and with education $(r = .31)$.[7]

Roof recognizes the difficulty in establishing direction of causation between local orientation and religious participation. He argues that local orientation is an indicator of social differentiation and thus has structural meaning as well as value meaning; as such it would have some claim to be causally prior. But the claim is weak, in our opinion, since we do not know the closeness of association between social differentiation and local orientation. Possibly localism and church participation should be seen as joint products of prior variables such as mobility, strength of community friendship networks, or social makeup of the community. In any event, Roof made an important contribution by calling attention to the importance of local plausibility structures.

III: RESEARCH ON CHURCH LIFE FACTORS

Most research attempting to explain church commitment has looked at preexisting factors such as age, socioeconomic status, or beliefs. But without doubt continued levels of church participation are explained partly by factors *in church life itself*. Killian (1964:445) states a crucial point.

> To attempt to account for the dynamics of a social movement in terms of common, pre-existing psychological states of individual members is to obscure the nature of the movement as a collectivity with emergent properties. What happens to the members as a consequence of their interaction within the

movement is vastly more important than the reasons why they first came into the movement.

We agree. Causes of initial entry into a church are certainly different from the causes of continued participation over months and years, since the experience of church participation itself has an effect. Research on religious participation should more clearly distinguish initial joining from ongoing involvement.

Research on the consequences of church participation for continued involvement is rather sparse and scattered, but many factors have been identified. They include having a positive feeling toward one's pastor (Bell, 1971), a number of friendships with church members (Bender, 1968), positive feelings from belonging in the church community (Gaede, 1975), the level of church programming (Moberg, 1962:395ff), the ease of transportation to the church building (Moberg, 1962), and the congruence between the individual's goals and the church's goals (Scalf et al., 1973). The extant research is of two general kinds: (1) typologies of church members according to their motivation and (2) studies of persons who dropped out of church membership. We review each in turn.

Typologies of Church Members

Several researchers have tried to discern motivations for church involvement and have found that the identifiable motivations are multiple. Hartman (1976) studied a large number of Methodist church members and identified five types, which he calls "audiences." Four of the five are distinct; the fifth is defined as a mixture of the other four.

1. *Fellowship audience* (about 17%)—These persons heavily stress the friendliness of other church members. They are looking for a supportive Christian community in which they will be accepted and loved. Often they are moved about frequently by business, industry, or military employers.

2. *Evangelistic concerns audience* (about 11%)—These persons are committed to the evangelistic function of the church, and they value personal witness to the faith and efforts at winning others to Christ. They attend church frequently and tend to be older, less educated, less affluent, and more rural than the other audiences.

3. *Study audience* (about 8%)—These members are eager to acquire a better knowledge of the faith through study. They are younger and more educated than persons in the other groups. Many are junior executives and professional persons.

They attend church and church school regularly and provide much progressive leadership.

4. *Social concerns audience* (about 6%)—These persons tend to be moderately old, and many are women. Their theology is inclined to be liberal and their church attendance rather low. Their involvement in church life is largely in activities representing their church in its ministries in the community and the world.

5. *Mixed concerns audience* (about 58%)—Sometimes these persons stress two or three of the concerns, but not the others. Yet, they cannot be clearly placed in any of the other audiences.

Hartman believes that analysis of audiences can help explain changes of involvement in particular congregations. Either a change in the sizes of the audiences or a change in the congregational program related to audience interests would have an impact on both attendance and participation levels.

Two other attempts to typologize church members by motivation should be noted. Monoghan (1967) interviewed members of a fundamentalist church and factor-analyzed the data. He found three types—the authority-seeker, the comfort-seeker, and the social participator. Gorlow and Schroeder (1968) studied college students' motivations for church participation and found seven distinct factors in the responses.

We are convinced that mainline Protestant congregations have diverse audiences and motivations among their members, and we believe the Hartman approach is promising for understanding levels of participation by diverse members in any congregation. Possibly future research could look into complementarity or conflict between audiences and between audience and church program.

Research on Church Dropouts

Several researchers have interviewed church dropouts in an attempt to find out why they left (Metz, 1965; Hartman, 1976; Presbyterian Committee, 1976; Savage, 1976). Hartman surveyed Methodist ex-members and asked their reasons for dropping out.

The most frequently mentioned reason on their list was their failure to feel that they were accepted, loved, or wanted. They felt that they did not belong and that others in the church and church school did not demonstrate any real love and concern for them. . . . The second most frequently mentioned factor related to a number of personal reasons. These included such things as illness in the family, changes in work schedules, transportation problems, lack of support or opposition from other family members, too busy with other responsibilities, and leisure pursuits. . . . The third most frequently mentioned group of reasons clustered around the feeling that what the church or church school was offering was not relevant. Specifically, they mentioned such things as poor sermons or teaching, too much boredom and busy work, irrelevant curriculum resources, and apathy among the church workers [1976:40-41].

Hartman (1976:42) summarizes:

A deep yearning to be accepted and loved by others in the church and church school is a dominant and recurrent theme among all persons. Church growth may be more closely related to a sense of acceptance by a warm, supportive Christian community than by any other factor.

A United Presbyterian Committee (1976) used the telephone to interview 225 persons who had recently been removed from church rolls. As a control group they studied a sample of active members. Compared with the active members, the dropouts (1) less often said that the church to which they had belonged was friendly, warm, and personally satisfying; (2) less often said that the pastor was effective and inspiring; (3) knew Presbyterian doctrines well but disagreed with them; and (4) agreed much more that "an individual should arrive at his own religious beliefs quite independent of the church." Also, the dropouts were younger than the active church members. The dropping out, in short, had occurred for both social and theological reasons, with the social reasons appearing more important.

Savage (1976) interviewed 101 Methodist church members, some active and some inactive, in an attempt to discern why some seemed to lose interest and become uninvolved. He found definite sequences in the processes of becoming apathetic or bored, leading to dropping out of the church. The beginning was usually some incident that produced a sense of uneasiness, most commonly conflict with the pastor, conflict with a family member, or conflict with another church member. If the conflict was unresolved over a period of time, the sense of anxiety spread to other areas of life, so that worship attendance, interest in the church, and even thinking in religious terms receded (1976:68). After several weeks, if no one from the church reached out to the person, he or she got a feeling that no one cared or that nothing could be done about the situation. Typically, the person would then reinvest his or her energies elsewhere.

Savage describes the strong personal attachments which grow in church life:

> Each of the 23 persons interviewed in the non-active group indicated that no one from the church had ever come to find out why they were losing interest or had dropped out. It reinforced their belief that no one cared, and that they were not missed. One third of this group cried during the interview, indicating the intensity of unresolved feelings.
>
> When the individual begins to move away from the church, there is expressed a considerable amount of grief mixed with the anger. The church, for most of these non-actives, was a very important object in their lives. They still talk about it as being "their" church and "that minister (or other persons or situation) is there and they cannot return until he/it goes away" [1976:58].

In summary, Savage depicts the motivations stemming from church participation itself. If the experience is gratifying, members invest more and more of themselves into the church. And if, after a time, they experience rejection or lack of appreciation, they react in anger or disillusionment, as with the loss of any love object.

Metz (1965) interviewed attending and non-attending members in two Methodist churches. Among the inactive persons, past activity levels had fluctuated over time. One of the most common reasons given for inactivity was a difficulty within the family.

> Almost one-fourth of the inactives in this study reported some form of family difficulty with regard to religion as the main reason for their lack of participation. These family situations are usually one of two kinds: either there is a lack of religious interest on the part of the spouse, or there is some change with regard to the children. The differences between husband and wife are the most common (with the husband typically being less interested in the church) [1965:44].

Another common explanation for inactivity was a higher priority given to some leisure time pursuit such as camping, boating, or involvement in another organization.

Metz asked about criticisms of the church. There were four main criticisms: the lack of personal contacts in the church, the financial concerns of the church leaders, modern versus traditional orientation, and the church's involvement in social action. Many inactives had found the church too impersonal; they had wished that church members would reach out to them but had not found it.[8]

In summary, the studies of dropouts point to an undeniable factor influencing levels of church participation and commitment—personal investments and gratifications in church life. Involvement in church life often produces recognition and esteem, which, in turn, strengthen motivation for further involvement. When recognition, esteem, and a feeling of belonging are denied a person, that person will probably become frustrated and drop out. Research on these motivations arising from church life itself is quite unintegrated with other sociological studies of church participation. Future research should include both and relate them.

IV: SUMMARY AND INTEGRATION

The research reviewed above produces thirteen summary statements that appear to have solid support.

1. Women participate more in churches than men, and this is true in all Christian denominations in America.
2. Denominational differences in rates of church participation are rather great, and they have persisted for decades.
3. The West is lower in church attendance than the rest of the nation for all denominations; the South is higher than the rest of the nation for Protestants.
4. Age alone, apart from cohort and period effects, has little impact on church participation except that in all research, participation has been shown to decline from the teenage years to about age 30.
5. Church participation correlates positively with socioeconomic status, but in most studies the correlation is very weak.
6. Interfaith marriages result in greatly reduced church participation by the spouses.
7. Married persons increase church participation if and when they have children of school age; often they join churches at that time.
8. For some people, church participation is motivated by the status and honor it bestows or by the occupational or life-style benefits it provides.
9. The holding of certain doctrinal beliefs has a moderately strong influence, on the average, on church participation.
10. Persons favoring alternative life-styles, sexual experimenta-

tion, and related cultural innovations tend to participate less in churches than others; in general, persons influenced by the recent counterculture tend to participate less in churches than others.

11. Persons with cosmopolitan values and outlooks, in contrast to local values and outlooks, participate less in churches; in general, the less they are embedded in family, ethnic group, and local community structures, the less they participate in churches.

12. The more that members are satisfied with their church and pastor, the higher will be their level of participation.

13. The more that persons feel accepted, loved, and supported in the church, the greater will be their participation in it; if they experience unresolved conflicts, they will tend to withdraw from participation.

Future analysts should distinguish explanations for initial church joining from explanations for continued levels of church involvement. Also they should work on the assessment of theories of church participation rather than on more tests of single variables such as socioeconomic status.

Some of the thirteen statements can be integrated into broader theoretical statements. For example, statements 9, 10, and 11 are specifications of a broader theory saying that the more an individual is immersed in traditional social structures such as family, ethnic group, or local community structures, the more he or she will participate in a church. This is a social structural theory, akin to Durkheimian theory, in which the church is seen as a kind of totemic religion for a single social group. Also statements 12 and 13 can be combined in a broader theory of interpersonal gratification.

Past research indicates that at least five separate theories are required to explain all the variance in church participation. First, a social learning theory must be maintained, as indicated by our discussion of sex and denominational differences. Second, a theory of immersion in traditional social structures is needed. Third, the impact of theological beliefs is important and should be maintained as a separate theory. Fourth, the child-rearing theory has some explanatory power among young and middle-aged adults. Fifth, a theory of satisfaction with church life is essential for explaining ongoing participation.

CHAPTER 3

Church Growth and Decline in Historical Perspective:
Protestant Quest for Identity, Leadership, and Meaning

James H. Smylie

"No Christian Marshall Plan," Karl Barth warned Americans in *The Christian Century* of December 8, 1948. Barth was commenting on the papers prepared for the first Assembly of the World Council of Churches in Amsterdam of that year. At one point he raised a question that he would certainly put to those who are currently discussing the growth and decline of the churches.

> What objection could we really make if it should please God to carry his work onward and reach his goal, not through a further numerical increase but through a drastic numerical decrease of so-called Christendom? It seems to me the only question in this matter is: How can we free ourselves from all quantitative thinking, all statistics, all calculation of observable consequences, all efforts to achieve a Christian world order, and then shape our witness into a witness to the sovereignty of God's mercy, by which alone we can live—a witness to which the Holy Ghost will surely not refuse his confirmation [1948:1332]?

Some observers, unable to relieve themselves of "all quantitative thinking," might observe that Barthians in Europe have succeeded in lowering membership and participation without necessarily lifting the quality of life of the body of Christ.

After World War II and into the 1950s there was an upsurge of church membership and interest in religion. George Sweazey, a Presbyterian pastor and evangelist, told of the upsurge in a pamphlet, *Evangelism in the United States,* in 1958. He suggested reasons for the phenomenon: (1) the "higher regard for religion," symbolized by the simple faith of President Dwight D. Eisenhower and piety along the Potomac; (2) the "national situation," in which religion was considered essential for the country's survival and triumph in the struggle against Communism; (3) the "personal situation," in a turn from materialism as a rival religion because it had ceased to satisfy; (4) the "cultural factors," since membership in a church was, to a degree, still a sign of upward movement on the social scale; and (5) because of simpler personal factors, more conscious than the zeitgeist of the period. Sweazey was not uncritical of this growth of interest and affiliation. He warned of an American Shinto and the "cult of the comfortable" as well as shallowness, recalling Marilyn Monroe's testimony to a reporter about her religious views: "I just believe in everything—a little bit." Sweazey (1958:7-14) also maintained that the interest was a great opportunity for the denominations to increase the quality of Christian faith and life.

Since the 1960s, however, several mainline denominations have suffered serious drops in participation and losses in membership. Denominational governing bodies and agencies have not been able to free themselves of all thought of statistics. Dean M. Kelley, Methodist minister and executive of the National Council of Churches—a mainline insider—heightened anxiety in a provocative volume, *Why Conservative Churches Are Growing* (1972). To simplify a complex case, Kelley suggested that liberal churches had declined in membership because of a loss of ability to respond to the basic human search for meaning. Conservative churches have been better able to do so. Moreover, controversy has broken out over the work of the department of church growth of the nondenominational Fuller Theological Seminary, which makes church growth the very essence of faithfulness to the gospel of the Great Commandment. In response to positive thinking volumes from the Fuller writers—*How Churches Grow* (McGavran, 1959), *Ten Steps for Church Growth* (McGavran and Arn, 1977), and *Your Church Can Grow* (Wagner, 1976)—Robert K. Hudnut (1975) wrote a challenge, *Church Growth Is Not the Point!* He called for a smaller "grace-filled, spirit-charged" membership and participation in the body of Christ (1975:xi). The controversy over church growth has reached beyond particular denominations and beyond the National Council of Churches. McGavran carried the debate to the World Council in a discussion of the meaning of mission for Christians today. He presented his church-growth approaches, if not over against, then in such a way as to question the value of international Christian missions not primarily concerned for numerical growth (McGavran, 1972).

In the meantime, denominations losing membership have mounted studies of why churches grow and decline, with the help of staff sociologists and statisticians. Among these studies *Membership Trends: A Study of Decline and Growth in the United Methodist Church, 1949-1975* (Hartman, 1976) and *Membership Trends in the United Presbyterian Church in the U.S.A.* (Presbyterian Committee, 1976) are the most massive and impressive. Jackson W. Carroll has summarized the findings in "Understanding Church Growth and Decline," *Theology Today* of April 1978. These studies and Carroll's summary tell us much about church growth and decline. Relying upon these findings, denominations—statistically self-conscious—have not only begun to plan strategy for growth, but they have the confidence that with proper leadership and in the planting of new churches, the denominations will once again grow. Martin E. Marty (1977) supports this judgment. In his view, denominations will survive. But while there is currently an expanding religious interest throughout the country, it does not appear that denominations which have experienced the greatest decline will be the chief benefactors of the widespread concern about spiritual matters. People are not translating this concern into denominational affiliation. Thus, churches continue to face problems having to do with growth and decline.

The following remarks attempt to place the problem of church growth and decline in historical perspective. They are intended to ascertain how some of the larger currents flowing in our history have affected those denominations that have lost membership in recent years, and they form a supplement to the thorough studies that have already been made of this subject. After dealing with what has been called the "decline of the Wasp," we move on to discuss how the basic problems of mainline Protestant denominations, associated with the National Council of Churches, have been related to factors that seem to affect church growth and decline.

These are the quest for identity and the social action factor, the quest for leadership and the success factor, and the quest for meaning and the ecumenical factor.

THE DECLINE OF THE WASP

In 1972 Sydney E. Ahlstrom published *A Religious History of the American People*, in which he described judiciously and at length America's spiritual heritage. Ahlstrom placed what was happening to American Protestantism in a larger historical perspective. In writing about the decade of the sixties (1972:1079), he stated that

It may even have ended a distinct quadricentennium—a unified four-hundred-year period—in the Anglo-American experience. A Great Puritan Epoch can be seen as beginning in 1558 with the death of Mary Tudor, the last monarch to rule over an officially Roman Catholic England, and ending in 1960 with the election of John Fitzgerald Kennedy, the first Roman Catholic president of the United States. . . . Histories of the rise of organized Puritanism begin their accounts with the decisive first decade in the reign of Queen Elizabeth; and the terms "post-Puritan" and "post-Protestant" are first popularly applied to America in the 1960s.

The age of the Wasp—the white Anglo-Saxon Protestant—was drawing to a close. Ahlstrom's suggestion is certainly open to question. There are, of course, still a good many Wasps around, if Protestant is defined in the broadest terms. But we should look closer at Ahlstrom's overarching generalization in discussing the condition of mainline Protestantism today.

Seen from a longer historical perspective, the bodies that have lost membership in recent years have become, over the centuries, a smaller portion of the population that claims to have some formal religious affiliation. The Reformation churches that gave to colonists the great controlling metaphor about God's design and American destiny, especially with the help of such formative documents as *The Book of Common Prayer* and the *Westminster Confession of Faith*, actually lost numerical dominance in the early years of the nineteenth century. William Warren Sweet, of the University of Chicago, traced this growth and decline in American religious bodies. In an overview of "The Protestant Churches" in 1948, Sweet pointed out that the Anglicans, Congregationalists, Presbyterians, Dutch and German Reformed, and Lutherans—the right-wing, established churches of the Reformation—constituted the largest and most powerful religious bodies in America during the seventeenth and the eighteenth centuries. They soon lost out numerically to Baptists, Methodists, and other left-wing sectarian bodies in the latter part of the eighteenth and the early nineteenth centuries. These denominations adapted to American conditions, Sweet wrote, as Americans swarmed westward, and they adopted more vigorous strategies of enlisting members than did the older ecclesiastical bodies. Later, he points out, Roman Catholicism, Judaism, and Orthodoxy began to catch up numerically with particular Protestant denominations. This was due largely to immigration of Catholics, Jews, and Orthodox from Europe (Sweet, 1948:43-52). In 1960 Benson Y. Landis summarized "Trends in Church Membership in the United States" for the preceding decade. In this period of growth, expansion in some mainline bodies—the United Church of Christ, the United Presbyterian Church, and the United Methodist Church—had taken place, in part, because of ecumenical efforts and mergers. Edwin Scott Gaustad dramatically illustrated the position of American mainline bodies in his *Historical Atlas of Religion in America* (1962). What Sweet wrote about in 1948 shows up clearly on Gaustad's map of religion in 1950. Only Southern Baptists, Lutherans, Methodists, Mormons, and Roman Catholics show up as representing 50 percent of the reported membership in various areas of the United States. In a later edition of the *Atlas* (1976), Gaustad indicated the membership decline of the mainline Wasp of recent years. The demographic portrait illustrates vividly how these bodies have lost space and place in American life.

With the growth of a non-Protestant religious pluralism, the power and prestige of mainline Protestant bodies have been challenged. There has been a considerable amount of Wasp-swatting in recent years, along with some disconcerting self-criticism and self-examination by Wasps themselves about the role of Protestantism in the modern world. In the same year in which Sweet took the Protestant pulse, Liston Pope (1948), religious sociologist of Yale University, observed that churches illustrated the social stratification of American life. Social, economic, and political mobility led some people to move from Roman Catholicism into Protestantism. Within Protestantism the drive for status led from Pentecostalism through the Baptist and the Methodist churches, and then into the upper-class churches of the Episcopalians, the Presbyterians, and the Congregationalists (Pope 1948:84-91). As late as 1958, Vance Packard (1958:194) suggested that it was still a long road from Pentecostalism to Episcopalianism. In status-seeking in the United States it has been up from Anabaptism, up from Methodism, up from Pentecostalism, up from Catholicism.

Perhaps there still is a Wasp Establishment in some areas of American life, for example, in economic power, but now status-seeking by religious affiliation may be limited to those wanting one kind of status in a religiously pluralistic society. E. Digby Baltzell (1964:x), writing from within Waspdom, issued a warning in *The Protestant Establishment, Aristocracy and Caste in America.*

> A crisis in moral authority has developed in modern America largely because of the White-Anglo-Saxon-Protestant establishment's unwillingness, or inability, to share and improve its upper-class traditions by continuously absorbing talented and distinguished members of minority groups into its privileged ranks.

In this same time frame, a rise in self-esteem and in the status of lower-class and non-Wasp groups indicates that an American did not have to be part of mainline Protestantism to be "in" in America. For example, the formation of the Full Gospel Business Men's Fellowship International helped to change the image of the once-deprived Holy Rollers. Indeed, the FGBMFI encouraged the charismatic movement even among established Protestants. The emphasis on the value of different racial, ethnic, and religious characteristics and backgrounds has been a serious challenge.

Will Herberg celebrated the existence of a non-Wasp pluralism in the United States in *Protestant, Catholic, Jew* (1955). Since then, Moynihan and Glazer in *Beyond the Melting Pot* (1963), Michael Novak in *The Rise of the Unmeltable Ethnics* (1972), and Andrew Greeley in his various studies have shown that non-Wasps have survived and prosper. They are gaining on and sometimes surpassing Wasps in both prestige and power in some areas of American society. At the same time we have been celebrating racial, ethnic, and religious differences, there has been a serious depreciation and debunking of the Wasp and of Wasp contributions to America. Peter Schrag's *The Decline of the Wasp* (1973) is a sample of this view. Schrag maintained that the once-great Wasp defaulted on a birthright and brought into existence all our present wasteland. The Wasp is thus deservedly in decline. In this open season on Wasps someone has suggested that the appropriate term should be Asp. The use of white and Anglo-Saxon in the designation represents a redundancy. Such social, racial, ethnic, and religious-upping may have made it unnecessary for social status to be associated with the Episcopalians, the Presbyterians, the United Church of Christ, the Dutch Reformed, and the Lutherans.

Something else should be noted about this period. Protestants themselves have been engaged in a process of self-criticism and self-evaluation in order to determine the nature and the role of the Christian in contemporary life. Paul Tillich called for a reformation within Protestantism in *The Protestant Era* as early as 1948. The most important contribution of Protestantism to the world in the past, present, and future is, Tillich maintained, "the principle of prophetic protest against every power which claims divine character for itself—whether it be church or state, party or leader." In Tillich's eyes, this included any tendency within Protestantism itself to absolutize any particular manifestation of Christian faith and life. Tillich (1948: 230) called upon Protestants to shape new communities on the basis of what he called "an active expression of a Gestalt of grace." Following Tillich's lead, Protestant writers— Hugh T. Kerr, *Positive Protestantism* (1950); George W. Forell, *The Protestant Faith* (1960); Robert McAfee Brown, *The Spirit of Protestantism* (1961); Charles W. Kegley, *Protestantism in Transition* (1965), to mention a few—defined Protestantism as a life of faith, a process, and continual pilgrimage and pioneering. The church reformed must ever be reformed—*ecclesia reformata semper reformanda.* Kerr (1950:107-108) ended his volume with this comment in calling Protestantism to be the "evangelical conscience of Christendom":

> If Protestantism will commit itself in an act of self-dedication to the consummation of this divine commission, the tomorrow of Protestantism will involve not only self-renunciation but also self-realization. To this end Protestantism must apply to itself the repeated warning of the Lord to his disciples: "Whoever would save his life will lose it; and whoever loses his life for my sake and the gospel's will save it."

Looked at from the perspective of Tillich's Protestant principle, this self-criticism and self-evaluation may be read as a sign of the rejuvenating spirit within Protestantism. Obituaries may be premature.

Yet, looked at from the perspective of the discussion about church growth and decline, the diminished position of Protestantism, the direct attack upon Wasps, and the discussion within

Protestantism of the dangers of Waspishness to Wasps themselves may not have been conducive to quantitative growth. Many mainline American Protestants have believed that God not only brought ancestors to this continent, but that the United States has been the Promised Land of milk and honey for vast multitudes of people. Moreover, in this most recent period God has transformed the country into a place of peace and prosperity, which, despite our problems, has exceeded the wildest visions of earliest pioneers. Many Protestants have felt a proprietary role in this achievement, and to have this called into question has been unsettling, to say the least. To do so at a time when other social, racial, ethnic, and religious groups have been celebrating themselves—their own traditions and their own achievements—at the expense of the Wasp may have been too much to bear, even with some honest recognition that the Wasp has not always been easy to live with in this environment. Other members of mainline denominations have been impressed with the Ahlstrom warning and have been on a quest for fresh identity, leadership, and meaning in a pluralistic society come of age.

IDENTITY AND THE SOCIAL ACTION FACTOR

During the period of growth in the 1950s there was considerable awareness of the displacement of Protestants, of a non-Protestant pluralism, and a discussion of a "second chance" for Protestants in a new religious situation. In 1951 H. Richard Niebuhr published *Christ and Culture,* widely read and influential in mainline religious circles. He analyzed different ways in which Christians might relate to culture. With the imaginative use of prepositions, Niebuhr wrote about the "Christ of Culture," "Christ Above Culture," and "Christ Against Culture." He also argued that Christ may be confessed as the transformer of culture. The Christian may believe that human nature is fallen and perverted and that this perversion appears in culture and is transmitted by it. Hence, Christ may be seen in opposition to all human institutions and customs. Yet, Niebuhr (1951:43) continued,

> the antithesis does not lead either to Christian separation from the world . . . or to mere endurance in the expectation of a transhistorical salvation. . . . Christ is seen as the converter of man in his culture and society, not apart from these, for there is no nature without culture and no turning of men from self and idols to God save in society.

With this typology in mind, mainline Protestant bodies have been seeking to free themselves from "quantitative thinking." They have been trying to shape a witness to God's mercy in a fresh way. In the discussion of church growth and decline, important aspects of identity are often reduced to the social action factor. Church growth movement experts suggest that it is axiomatic that those denominations which engage in social action will not grow, although Carroll (1978b) points out that there is no clear correlation in the studies done by denominations. This matter should be discussed in terms of a Protestant quest for identity, not simply as social activism.

First, it should be noted that the mainline Protestant bodies which are our chief concern here have taken up an identity as transformers of culture. They have done this in a natural evolutionary process from earlier traditions and in light of new conditions. All these bodies—the Episcopalians, the Congregationalists, the Presbyterians, the Dutch and the German Reformed, the Lutherans, and even the Methodists with the Anglican connection—belong to what Ernst Troeltsch called the churchly rather than the sectarian tradition. They were part of the magisterial Reformation. Each, except for the Methodists, enjoyed an established position in the nation-states in which they were dominant at the time of the Reformation. They held a monopoly of ecclesiastical prestige and power, and they felt responsibility for the total life of the culture. Sectarian bodies, or groups in the left-wing of the Reformation, were not established and were more concerned about the individual and interior life of the Christian. As Niebuhr pointed out in his study of *Christ and Culture*, the relationship between the churches and culture was based upon theological convictions about God's concern for the public affairs of human beings and their institutions and not merely for their private lives. In the American colonies and in the nineteenth century, these churches evolved into denominations. While churches gave up a monopoly of prestige and power, they did not give up concern for corporate problems. Indeed, in the recent attacks upon Waspdom we have seen how Protestants are perceived as enjoying, despite the celebration of religious liberty, a Protestant Establishment. While not governmentally supported, we created a cultural Protestantism to which all peoples had to more or less conform. It is this cultural Protestantism and Waspishness that has been under attack in recent years, even by Protestants.

In connection with this development, Martin E. Marty called

attention in *The Righteous Empire* (1970) to the emergence of a two-party system in American Protestantism. The first is the party of public Protestantism, members of which are interested in social order and in social destiny; the second, a private party, is concerned about personal salvation out of the world, a personal fulfillment of rewards and punishments in another world, and a personal moral life congruent with these ideas of the saved (1970: 179). Marty sees these parties emerging at the beginning of this century. These tensions began to show much earlier in American Protestantism, as denominations wrestled with such societal problems as slavery, economic injustices, and war throughout the nineteenth century. These parties cut across denominational lines and expose division not only within Protestantism generally, but within each denominational body. It may be, of course, that public Protestantism is more concerned about the personal life of men and women than Marty's definition suggests, and that private Protestantism is more concerned about culture. Indeed, it has been argued that the party of private Protestantism, because of its uncritical acceptance of the culture as it is, is now more acculturated and supportive of the American Way than is the party of public Protestantism.

Public Protestantism was organized ecumenically in the Federal Council of Churches (1908) and later the National Council of Churches (1950). Henry J. Pratt has described in *The Liberalization of American Protestantism* (1972) how the churches associated with the NCC have been more aggressive in urging a transformation of the society than denominations have been in the past, thus sowing seeds of modern Protestant discontent. Church growth advocates suggest that public Protestantism has forgotten the nature of a denomination as the American form of the church, responsible for preaching God's mercy, administering the sacraments, and exercising discipline within Christ's body. Denominations have evolved into voluntary societies, according to this argument, run by social activists who speak and do for the denominations when they have no such mandate. This suggestion ignores the fact that denominations have always been voluntary societies since the founding of the Republic, and throughout history most of them have been deeply involved in debates over public policy and practice. To be sure, the media have given much attention to activists. But the basic method denominations have adopted to deal with public affairs has been educational—the discussion of "cases of conscience," to use a time-honored Protestant phrase, and the development of policy statements for issue clarification. Denominations have an obligation, according to these voices, to help Christians deal with public matters—local, national, and global—from the perspective of Christian faith and to show to the non-Christian the concern of the Christian community for human welfare.

Engagement in the transformation of culture has been, second, stimulated by mainline Protestant concern over the nature and the character of the church, the body of Christ, as well as its role in modern society. For those in the party of private Protestantism, the church does not seem to be a primary concern. Deep involvement in the civil rights, antiwar, and antipoverty movements of the fifties, sixties, and early seventies has been cited as illustrative of how social activists have taken over the churches. To be sure, each of these movements has involved social activism. However, each one illustrates the struggle of the mainline denominations to gain a new identity and a new expression of faithfulness, to transcend the culture as well as to transform it. This cannot be reduced to a mere matter of social action. Prior to the period we have just mentioned, mainline Protestants had been engaged in serious discussion of the faces of modern idolatry. People seek salvation through identification with a particular race, nation, or economic system, either of the capitalist or communist type. The church has often fed these idols covertly and overtly—racism, nationalism, and economic absolutism. Awareness of these idols grew in the national and international turmoils of the 1930s and 1940s. Reinhold Niebuhr made a brilliant analysis of the false messiahs of the modern world in *The Nature and Destiny of Man* (1941, 1943), while bombs fell on Britain at the beginning of World War II. During these years discussion of the different nature and character of the Christian community, in the light of these idols, was carried on in the FCC, the NCC, and the World Council of Churches. In 1954 the World Council of Churches met in Evanston, Illinois, to discuss the theme "Christ, the Hope of the World." Christians directed attention toward "rival hopes" and sent out a warning [*The Evanston Report*, 1954:152] in one of the reports against finding safety in "the power of their race or class or nation." This warning followed the McCarthy hysteria in America, and enormous growth in American economic and military power.

The church of Jesus Christ, mainline Protestants decided, is a fellowship that transcends racial, national, and economic barriers. Insofar as it is shaped primarily by these factors and not by Christian imperatives, the church ceases to be the church. The way in which this fresh perception of the nature and character of the

Christian community touched public affairs may best be seen in the mainline denominational reaction to the challenge of racism. Denominations associated with the FCC had already called for a desegregated church in a desegregated society in the 1940s. In the 1950s Martin Luther King Jr. incarnated that vision dramatically in his word and work and as he called upon the churches to help transform American society. George D. Kelsey discussed the matter in Christian perspective in *Racism and the Christian Understanding of Man* (1965). He wrote of the problem not as a matter for social action, but in terms of Christian heresy. Christian faith, he confessed for himself and for others, "knows only one race: the human race," and it declares that racism is a manifestation of the sin of pride which must be overcome by faith. "The racist self is transformed," Kelsey suggested (1965:176-77), "from the state of hostility, fear and anxiety for itself, because it lives in the security of the love of God, knowing for the first time the fulness of God's covenant community and hoping for the first time for the redemption of all creation." This was not the peculiar insight of public Protestantism alone, and many leaders in the private Protestant party came to this conclusion. Many public Protestants saw this matter as one of personal faith and the "desegregated heart" and then went on in a more decisive manner to help transform the church and culture in the light of a new identity.

Closely related to attempts to deal with racism have been attempts to deal with American nationalism and materialism, focused in the antiwar and the antipoverty movements. Our consciousness of these matters expanded as we began to shift our attention from the East-West world conflict to the North-South struggle, between the industrial and developing nations, with dangers of the population explosion and massive starvation. Members of mainline denominations have differed over our approaches to these interrelated and complicated problems. What happened in the 1960s was that many began to realize more clearly than ever how we as Christians in the United States have tended to accept the American Way in getting and spending and in conducting foreign affairs as the Christian Way, quite unconscious and quite uncritical of ourselves and the way in which we were dealing with these matters. At the beginning of this period of time, Reinhold Niebuhr noted the "irony of American history," that in our pursuit of happiness and of security in material success and military superiority, we were gaining neither. At the conclusion of the period, William Stringfellow (1973), Episcopal layman and lawyer, wrote of becoming an alien in his own land. America had turned out to be, not the Promised Land, but modern Babylon. These problems—racism, nationalism, materialism—may not be reduced to social action matters, regardless of how much social activism they have involved in recent years. They must be seen in terms of a deepened appreciation of the Christian church as a community that transcends race, nation, and class and of a commitment to transform the church and the society into more inclusive and just communities.

Another facet of this quest for a new identity has to do with the problem of discipline within mainline denominations. Dean Kelley has argued that mainline denominations have not grown because they do not impose a discipline upon their members, and they suffer from "the dynamics of diminishing demands." Other bodies have grown because of stricter discipline—adherence to special beliefs, attendance at meetings, attachment to a code of behavior, a missionary commitment. Kelley seems to be right in that some religious bodies which expect more of their adherents seem to be growing, although not all these denominations that do so grow. Mainline Protestant bodies have had problems with discipline ever since disestablishment and the development of a genuine freedom of choice in religious affiliation. Kelley is right in suggesting that Protestants have grown lax in discipline over the past hundred years. Franklin H. Littell called our attention to this problem in *From State Church to Pluralism* (1962), especially in his description of American Methodism. It grew by leaps and bounds in the early years of the nineteenth century, but it has suffered from lack of discipline in the twentieth. Peter Berger summarized the ineffectiveness of Christians and of their institutions in *The Noise of Solemn Assemblies* (1961), a book widely influential among students and a perception that summarized the contempt in which many held the churches.

But Christian discipline must be seen in terms of the quest of mainline denominations for a new identity as institutions that transcend race, nation, and class and in terms of the Christian imperative to transform the society. Littell (1962:118,133) pointed this out in his study. He suggested that the Christian community must deal with racial discrimination by reinvigorating discipline, by insisting that members exercise greater faithfulness in dealing with racial prejudices within the heart, the Christian community, and American society. In one way this perception of discipline is closely related to the problem of growth for mainline denominations. Church growth movement experts observe that churches and congregations grow if they follow a homogeneous strategy—like attracts like, and we should make the most of it. Mainline denominations did not need church growth people to point this out. Gibson Winter noted it in *The Suburban Captivity of the Churches* (1962). Growth in the 1950s was white growth among people leaving the cities and the blacks for the greener crabgrass of the suburbs and leaving behind many of their urban responsibilities. While the homogeneous model for growth seems sociologically obvious, it is not new. The strategy is troublesome biblically, theologically, and ethically, despite disclaimers by church growth movement writers, because it fails to deal seriously with the identity of the Christian community as a community that is inclusive and that transcends the prejudices of race. Debates over American patriotism and materialism are not so dramatically related to church growth. But the problem of discipline must be discussed in the light of the attempt of mainline denominations to get their members, many of whom preside over American enterprise, to think more responsibly about the way in which our power and possessions are gotten and employed in relation to other people in the nation and throughout the world. This may be seen as an unwarranted meddling in political and economic affairs, a meddling unhealthy for the growth of the church, quantitatively thinking. Yet, mainline denominations have been calling members to pay the "cost of discipleship," commensurate with the influence we still may have, to transcend and transform the world.

LEADERSHIP AND THE SUCCESS FACTOR

Leadership seems to be an important aspect in the cultivation of participation and membership in denominational bodies. In connection with this matter, there has been much discussion about the nature and character of Protestant leadership and considerable concern about measuring the ministry by quantitative thinking and American success models. Sociologist Paul M. Harrison (1969:977) put the matter poignantly:

> The dilemma of the clerical professional may be rooted in the nature of the Judeo-Christian tradition itself. Exemplified in the ministry and passion of Jesus as recorded in the synoptics, the pastoral and prophetic archetype is presented for every subsequent clergyman to attempt to emulate, however finite his efforts may be. Judged by any standards of the professional clerics, Jesus was in the end less successful than most ministers, but the "paradox of the crucifixion" presents all

subsequently successful clergy with an insolvable problem; it is impossible, historically and sociologically, to actualize both living by and dying on the cross. This is the root ambiguity of the Christian ministry.

Harrison has put the dilemma of leadership in bold terms and has raised the question about what kind of leadership, given the current challenges, fills the need today.

In past decades mainline Protestants have lost their most prominent national figures. The great shapers of mainline public Protestantism have died, while those of private Protestantism have flourished and have gone from success to success. In 1955 *Life* printed a special issue on Christianity, celebrating the vitality of faith and life of the times. Toward the conclusion of the issue the editors featured dramatic portraits of H. Richard Niebuhr, Reinhold Niebuhr, and Paul Tillich, aging leaders who were helping Christians face contemporary challenges. These three were shakers and shapers of mainline Protestantism and of the national ethos—not parochial, but international figures. These men are now dead. Although they influence us through their numerous writings, we no longer live with the same confidence since their strong voices have been stilled. Some years after that edition of *Life*, Martin E. Marty (1968:178) called attention to our need of models as well as theologians. Marty mentioned several recent saints who were part of American Protestant ecumenical hagiography: Dietrich Bonhoeffer, Albert Schweitzer, Martin Luther King Jr., Pope John XXIII, and Adlai Stevenson, John F. Kennedy, and Dag Hammarskjöld from the secular realm. These persons were admired primarily in mainline Protestant circles—not by all, to be sure, but by many. They had charisma and provided inspiration. They were followed as transformers of the church and the world. They are now all gone.

Quite different has been the lot of other national religious leaders. In the *Life* issue of 1955 Norman Vincent Peale is pictured preaching to his large congregation in New York City. He is described in this way:

> An outstanding phenomenon of the revival has been the success of mass communication media in reaching massive and interested audiences. Dr. Peale, through his cheery doctrine of positive thinking, has become a one-man religious industry. He has a popular television show and a busy lecture schedule and still finds time to operate a publishing house which distributes some one million items monthly [*Life*, 1955:52-53].

Not as cheery, but every bit as effective, youthful Billy Graham is pictured preaching repentance and calling for commitment to Christ at a crusade. The *Life* article on Graham shows him "Resting Up to Save Souls" at his mountaintop retreat in North Carolina, praying as well as playing golf, to find strength at home for his evangelistic meetings. These men are older, but they are alive and well in America, still shaping our religious consciousness. They have been joined by other superstars. Robert Schuller, with his "Hour of Power," carries on the Peale tradition of positive thinking, while Oral Roberts, Herbert W. and Garner Ted Armstrong, Pat Robertson, Jim Bakker, Rex Humbard, and Jerry Falwell seem more like Graham, with differing formats for their programs of salvation. Some, like Falwell, herald millenarian doom, made all the more eminent because of the ways and means of liberals. Paradoxically, Falwell, as well as other such leaders, seems to be overwhelmed with prosperity, much profit and not much loss, and is overflowing with patriotic nationalism. In the American ethos, these are the leaders by whom many members of Protestant congregations measure ministerial effectiveness; at the same time others suspect them of being manipulative and panderers of "cheap grace."

Over this same period of time, in the second place, there has been some confusion over just what clergy should be doing in the church and in the world. This confusion has been reflected in what has been going on in theological education. Since the 1950s, theological institutions in which mainline Protestant leadership is trained have passed into the hands of presidents and professors, many of whom found Peale "appalling" and were wary of supporting Graham-type evangelistic efforts. Moreover, they were influenced by the famous studies of H. Richard Niebuhr, Daniel Day Williams, and James Gustafson, who wrote and edited *The Ministry in Historical Perspective* (1956), *The Purpose of the Church and Its Ministry* (1956), and *The Advancement of Theological Education* (1957). The chief pattern for the Christian leader projected in these studies was that of the pastor-director. While clergy would continue to fulfill the ministry of the word and sacrament, they would actually focus on administering the affairs of the congregation and on enabling others to fulfill the witness of the body of Christ, in the love to God and to neighbor. While this model, descriptive of what many ministers were already doing, may be, theoretically, a good one for encouraging participation and membership in the church, it may also have the effect of reducing the minister to an "organization man"—in gray flannel clerical garb. As Robert Lee (1962:208) has pointed out, training for the role of pastor-director may lead to the "depersonalization of charisma" and to the education of functionaries at the expense of personal inspiration, which leaders also need.

The Niebuhr studies called attention to two fields of importance in theological education that should be mentioned in connection with church growth and decline—religious education and pastoral counseling. Both these fields have grown at a time of uncertainty about the role of the ministry and out of some desire for the legitimation of the ministry as a profession. The Sunday school movement in the nineteenth and early twentieth centuries was a major instrument for the recruitment of membership, and churches took advantage of this means of growth. But with the development of progressive education theory, graded lessons, and a variety of course offerings, the church school became less a means of conversion and more a means of nurture within the Christian community, already gathered. Pastoral counseling arose in the midtwentieth century. It has not been a major instrument for increasing the membership of the church. It has been, rather, a means of practicing the "cure of souls" within the body of Christ. It should be noted that professionals in these two fields are often suspicious of manipulation in religious affairs, especially among the champions of revivalism portrayed as Elmer Gantrys and as Marjoes.

In addition to this concern for the nature and character of ministry, Protestants have been troubled about the lack of what has been called spiritual formation in theological education. There has been a growing realization that people will have no reason to respond to a pastor-director or, in terms of the broader perspective of this essay, to respond to the challenge to transcend and transform the culture if Protestant leaders are not perceived as spiritual leaders. Mainline Protestants have sung, in recent years, a "requiem for a lost piety." This loss has been a grave one in theological education. The American Association of Theological Schools mounted a study about spiritual formation, and the report (1972:171) expressed this desire:

> We would wish that seminaries today accept as their task the spiritual formation of people who will be more than able scholars, or vital human beings, or dedicated social change agents; of people also, whom—with considerable risk—we may speak of as sacramental or holy people; that is people whose life strikes upon other people as lived from God and unto God, people whose presence somehow both communi-

cates and evokes the divine. Indeed, perhaps the term sanctity best conveys our meaning.

Some of this loss of spiritual vitality may be the result of the increasing intellectualization and professionalism of the ministry. Mainline Protestants are also having trouble shaping a new holistic piety, which, on the one hand, will embrace the personal yearning for God-centeredness, and yet one that will also embrace the social order and destiny of human beings in their corporate existence.

In the third place, discussion of the nature and the character of Protestant leadership has been touched by a profound communications revolution. Walter J. Ong, S.J., has analyzed a seismic change in a seminal volume, *The Presence of the Word* (1970). Human history, according to Ong, may be periodized in three stages: the first that of oral-aural communication; the second, the invention of the alphabet and of movable type; the third, the development of electronic devices, revolutionized by mass market television beginning in the 1950s. Mainline Protestantism was born and spread during the end of the second period, with the invention of movable type. Now mainline denominations have been outmaneuvered by enterprising religious entrepreneurs, who have effectively exploited the mass market with printed materials and with radio and television. In the 1940s and 1950s Charles Fuller pioneered with the masterfully planned "Old Fashioned Revival Hour." Now Jerry Falwell exploits TV with "The Old Time Gospel Hour," and Robert Schuller, with the "Hour of Power." Electronic churches, as they have been called, reach millions. Programs are conducted by leaders who have a certain charisma, and they mix nostalgia, informality, and intimacy with spiritual uplift. Religious personalities on radio and television no longer feel it necessary or beneficial to refer people to local congregations, as revivalists did in the past. The new radio and TV denominations appear to be on good terms with the divine and offer religious education and counseling in a variety of ways. Mass audiences join for prayer and praise, and they pay by mail for the support of these new churches, which now exceed in number some of the older Reformation bodies. Furthermore, they allow members to tune in or drop out at will.

Mainline Protestant leaders have recognized radio and television as important media for bearing witness to Christian faith and life. But the new means of communication have raised serious questions about how they may be used responsibly without manipulation contrary to Christian standards. Radio and television superstars present programs that are definitely lowbrow and offer oversimplistic approaches to spiritual problems and to social concerns and social destiny. Furthermore, their lavish success vividly raises the problem of the "paradox of crucifixion" in the new electronic age. Mainline Protestants have often used the electronic media in creative and in imaginative ways, but not in such a manner as to attract huge audiences, nor to stimulate dramatic denominational growth. Moreover, television especially may have complicated mainline Protestant life during the turbulent sixties and early seventies by identifying Protestant leadership with the social activism of the civil rights, antiwar, and antipoverty demonstrations, without, at the same time, clarifying the basic biblical, theological, ecclesiological, and ethical rationale for such activity. Protestant leaders, in confrontation with public officials, appeared as social agitators, not as spiritual leaders.

The career of Eugene Carson Blake exemplifies both the mainline Protestant approach to the new electronic age and also the problems of leadership arising in the late 1950s. Blake was a successful pastor-director of a large Presbyterian congregation in California. He rose in ecclesiastical circles to be one of America's foremost church leaders—president of the National Council of Churches and, later, secretary of the World Council of Churches. He became a church executive, one who may have dressed in gray flannel, but one who carried a prophetic portfolio. Blake used the media and, in turn, was used by it. He was host to an NBC religious talk show for five years. The show was called "Frontiers of Faith," and Blake moderated highbrow discussions of such topics as "Ethics in a Business Society," "The Church and Labor," "National Security and Individual Liberty," "The Negro in Higher Education" among many others, which demonstrated the attempt of mainline Protestants to transcend and transform the culture. In 1963 he was arrested while trying to integrate an amusement park in Baltimore, Maryland. Through this arrest, widely broadcast throughout the nation and the world, Blake identified mainline Protestantism with the civil rights movement and with the struggle for racial justice. As a media event, Blake also associated mainline Protestantism with antiwar and antipoverty causes in later years. Blake was, in his way, endeavoring to live by, if not die on, the cross and to give a model of ministry for others. Blake's media image stands in stark contrast with that of successful media entrepreneurs. When Eugene Carson Blake speaks, people hear a clerical meddler. Yet, Billy Graham is seen by many to represent what Christian faith and life is all about. Despite his sermons on judgment, Graham still manages to pronounce a benediction upon our big, buzzing, booming, affluent culture, which mainline leaders have been trying to transcend and transform (see Brackenridge, 1978).

MEANING AND THE ECUMENICAL FACTOR

"The business of religion," Kelley wrote, "is meaning [1972: 38]." Mainline ecumenical denominations associated with the NCC and the WCC have been losing members, Kelley suggests, because they have not been addressing themselves to essentially religious questions. They have given themselves over to the tasks of administering churches after the pastor-director model and to the transformation of culture, but they have not been helping people to explain the "meaning of life in ultimate terms." This is an important aspect of the church growth and decline discussion.

The problem of meaning has been made urgent because of the cloud of nuclear terror under which we live on this spaceship Earth. At the same time Ahlstrom was reflecting on the end of the Protestant era, his Yale colleague, Robert Jay Lifton, was pondering the impact upon us of the use of atomic bombs on Hiroshima and Nagasaki in 1945. Lifton (1969:5-9) believes that we have entered into a new age in human history. We live with the anxiety that we have the power to end the existence of the human species as we know it. Mainline Protestant denominations have been aware of the crisis of meaning in our time. What is it, however, that Christians have to say and do in this foreboding present and for the future? It should be noted that the decline of the Wasp has taken place over a 400-year period in which there has also been a decline in a belief in hell and heaven, a belief that has to do with meaning—the ultimate resolution of life's problems. While confessing hope in the resurrection and in the presence and coming of God's kingdom, many Protestants have not been willing to exploit anxiety of the nuclear age with anxiety about a future age of rewards and punishments, as do some religious bodies and leaders. While mainline Protestant bodies may not have been able to address the problem of ultimate meaning to satisfy the multitudes, they have been struggling with this matter in several ways.

Ecumenism has been a deterrent to growth, so Kelley's argument runs, because the denominations involved in the ecumenical movement have not been addressing themselves to the problem of ultimate meaning. The ecumenical denominations may not have been able to market ecumenism for the masses, but these denominations have truly been addressing themselves to the problem of meaning. The modern ecumenical movement came into being as Protestants began to discuss with one another common problems of "life and work" and "faith and order" in order to arrive at some common witness about God's love for the world in which we live. Among Protestants there has been an increasing awareness that problems which have divided generations past should not be allowed to keep Christians apart as we are called upon to meet new challenges. Ecumenism may be described as a new kind of discipline within the church and as an attempt to overcome those things that have divided us in the household of God in order to better serve the world with a common faith and love and hope.

In this connection, ecumenical dialogue should be mentioned. The Consultation on Church Union, currently known as the Church of Christ Uniting, is especially significant for these years. In 1960 Eugene Carson Blake suggested that Protestants seize the opportunity to form a new Christian community that would be truly catholic, truly evangelical, truly prophetic. It was a call to resolve problems left over from the Reformation. This effort was not meaningless, nor simply an attempt to develop a superchurch, an image conjured by the opponents of the proposal. It represented a vision of Christian reunion in a religious community too long and too much divided. In recent years mainline Protestants have also engaged in dialogue with Roman Catholics, the Orthodox, and with non-Christian faiths, including Marxism, in order to reach great understandings. Thus, with attempts to de-escalate racial, national, and economic conflict, there has also been an attempt to curb religious conflict around the globe. This ecumenical spirit may appear to some to be void of ultimate meaning. Indeed, it has been interpreted as watering down and a sellout of Christian meaning. Yet, it has been motivated by a belief that God's ultimate purpose for the Christian family and for the human family is not division, hostility, and even mutual destruction, but a supportive global community.

In addition to the ecumenical quest, mainline denominations have been exploring fresh ways of celebrating and confessing the faith, while at the same time preserving the treasured traditions of the Christian and the Reformation past. In seeking new directions, churches have been touched by discussions about the nature of God, which to an unreflective public may appear frivolous, faddist, not to say confusing. God is dead! God is black! God is red! God is a woman! While these discussions may not appear to some people to have anything to do with ultimate meaning, they have been serious efforts by participants to deal with questions about meaning from a captivity in which God appears to many as a Wasp, maybe a Blake, a Graham, or one or another of the present religious superstars. Mainline denominations have, in fact, been very responsible in dealing with the problem of religious meaning not only in their ecumenical endeavors, but in educational and in counseling programs that have helped widen horizons and provide the "cure of souls." While these strategies have not netted large numbers, quantitatively thinking, they have helped thoughtful and anxious people with the question of meaning, while using the least amount of manipulation.

Some other things already alluded to in terms of the passing of the Protestant era should be mentioned here. The *Book of Common Prayer* of the Episcopalians and the *Westminster Standards* of the Presbyterians were among the great formative documents of Protestant faith and life. These denominations have been exploring ways of continuing to use these treasures, while at the same time adapting celebration and confession to the twentieth century. Episcopalians have revised the *Book of Common Prayer*, a process that has been aggravated by the debate over the ordination of women to the priesthood, but a process that has addressed the question of the ultimate meaning of Christian worship. Over the past two decades Presbyterians have been engaged in serious theological discussions. The United Presbyterian Church in the United States of America adopted *A Book of Confessions* in 1967, which contained creeds shared in common with all Christians, confessions of the Reformed tradition of the sixteenth and the seventeenth centuries, including the majestic Westminster Confession, the Barmen Declaration of the Confessing Church of Germany (an attack upon the neopaganism of Nazism), and a new statement entitled "The Confession of 1967." The new confession was based upon the biblical testimony that God was in Christ reconciling the world to God. It carried a call to Christians that what is confessed about reconciliation with the lips must also be demonstrated in disciplined lives. The confession challenged Christians to deal with modern problems of race, nationalism, poverty, and human sexuality. Members of the Presbyterian Church in the United States, in the South, also engaged in serious theological discussion in the 1970s, but efforts to alter the church's sole dependence on the seventeenth-century *Westminster Standards* were not successful. If the problem of our time is anomic terror under a balance of nuclear terror, then Presbyterians and others were attempting to witness to that problem.

Despite mainline Protestant efforts to give expression to a new Christian community, to give new expression to ultimate meaning in the nuclear age, we have not found the vision in which to both challenge and comfort the multitudes. Mainline Protestants have not gotten their act together in this new age. It was Hal Lindsey, in *The Late Great Planet Earth* (1970)—an apocalyptic scenario dramatized on television by Orson Welles—who spoke a word of ultimate meaning for numerous people, not the World Council of Churches at Evanston in 1954, or the Presbyterians in the sober but quietly confident "Confession of 1967." The Church of Jesus Christ of Latter-Day Saints presents a message, cosmic in nature, that seems to appeal to others. In the Mormon visitors' center in Salt Lake City well-groomed guides conduct guests on a tour that begins with God's creation of the earth, depicted on murals, and climaxes under a rotunda in which stands a statue of Christ with outstretched arms under a starry universe. Without apologies, a guide reminds the listener that Christ visited America and called into being the community of the Latter-Day Saints. The visitor is invited to become part of this great cosmic drama. An observer, imbued with the Protestant principle and endeavoring to transcend the situation, might see in this an American Shinto, as George Sweazey put it—a new manifestation of cultural religion. The place of the declining Wasp has been taken by one of mainline American Protestantism's embarrassing offspring. But this attempt to set the person in the middle of a clear and meaningful divine drama may suggest why Mormonism is one of America's fastest growing bodies. It was not until 1978, however, that blacks were allowed into the Mormon priesthood.

Protestantism gave American Christians a sense of being part of an elect people and an elect nation. Jonathan Edwards, during the Great Awakening of the 1740s, preached highly effective sermons on the awesome sovereignty of God and on the justification by faith alone—the principal hinge of the Reformation. At the same time, he preached sermons on what was to be for him his magnum opus, which were finally published as *The History of the Work of Redemption*. In these sermons he gave members of his congregation the sense of being part of the grand creative and redemptive purpose of God, the conclusion of which was about to occur in America, in New England, and perhaps even in Northampton. Since Edwards' day mainline Protestants have become less confident in speaking in such terms about God's purpose, especially in a complex nuclear age. In *The Search for America* (1959:146) Reinhold Niebuhr focused attention on our ambiguous situation. His essay was entitled "From Progress to Perplexity." Challenging our illusions of bygone ages, he called us to Christian responsibility with caution about ultimate meaning.

> Nothing worth doing is completed in our lifetime; therefore, we must be saved by hope. Nothing true or beautiful or good makes complete sense in any immediate context of history; therefore, we must be saved by faith. Nothing we do, however virtuous, can be accomplished alone; therefore, we are saved by love. No virtuous act is quite as virtuous from the standpoint of our friend or foe as from our standpoint. Therefore, we must be saved by the final form of love which is forgiveness.

Niebuhr called people to an uncertain life of faith and love and hope as a witness to God, who alone knows the ultimate meaning of life. The problem of mainline Protestantism is that it has not developed what has been called a "controlling metaphor," which points to the one God and one world toward which we are moving.

CONCLUSION

These remarks about the decline of the Wasp and about the quest by Protestants for identity, leadership, and meaning in a new age in history have been made to put the current discussion of church growth and decline in a larger historical framework and to help evaluate data on growth and decline. Karl Barth (1948:1332-33) ended his warning about freeing ourselves from all "quantitative thinking" with these further words about what is required of Christians:

> What is required of us is that we should be watchful, willing and ready to make Christian decisions in the midst of an evil world. We are not the ones to change this evil world into a good world. God has not resigned his lordship over it into our hands. The salvation of the world, which has already been accomplished, was not our work. And so also that which still remains to be done—the revealing of the world's salvation in a new heaven and a new earth—will not be our work but his. All that is required of us is that in the midst of the political and social disorder of the world we should be his witnesses, disciples and servants of Jesus. We shall have plenty for all our hands to do, just being that!

Mainline Protestants need not return to Barthianism to join his confession of confidence in God's power to realize a new heaven and a new earth and then answer the call to be faithful witnesses, disciples, and servants of Jesus. Apparently, God is intending to carry out divine will, as Barth suggested God might, by reducing Christians to a minority status in the world and indeed, at the present time, by decreasing the number of mainline Protestants in America. The church is not a no-growth institution, although true discipleship and servanthood may not be very popular, and may be very lonely at times. What Protestants need to do continually is to try to live responsibly under Christ's lordship, to bear witness to the sovereignty of God's mercy, and to invite others to take part in this ministry. Perhaps, as Hugh T. Kerr wrote in 1950 in *Positive Protestantism*, by losing its life for Christ's sake and the gospel's, Protestantism may find new life.

CHAPTER 4

National Contextual Factors Influencing Church Trends

Dean R. Hoge

Nationwide social and intellectual influences—what we have called national contextual factors—undoubtedly are important for explaining church trends. On that everyone agrees. But identifying and weighing the specific factors having an effect has been difficult. As a result, no precise model is available that shows exactly what national factors are important or where and when they have an impact. What exists in its place is a collection of efforts by many observers to discern social and cultural changes that help explain church trends. Church historians have done this most earnestly; the works of Ahlstrom (1970; 1972; 1978) and Marty (1976) are widely read examples. In addition, many persons have made arguments pointing to one social trend or another as the main explanation for recent religious trends. I have attended dozens of meetings in which speakers have explained church trends by one or more changing contextual factors, ranging widely from "the disillusionment of youth with science" to the increase in women in the work force, to the impact of space exploration, to the increase in vacation houses. Which factors actually have an impact and how? Even more interesting is the fact that the most discussed book on church trends today, Dean Kelley's *Why Conservative Churches Are Growing*, virtually ignores national contextual factors.

A sociological set of guidelines for evaluating contextual factors as possible explanations of church trends is adopted in this chapter. We will ask of each factor under study that (1) changes in it resemble the changes in congregations or denominations it purports to explain, in terms of social "location," time span, and direction; (2) it demonstrably correlate with church participation or commitment; and (3) some evidence of a causal relationship (as opposed to mere correlation or even accidental similarity) between it and church participation or commitment be available. These guidelines should aid us in sorting out the issues in this difficult area.

This chapter has three parts. First is a review of past sociological research on contextual factors. Second is an investigation of the relationship between a series of attitudes and church commitment. Third is an inspection of trends in some attitudes that may be important for understanding church trends.

PAST RESEARCH

This section discusses four writers who have tried to describe national contextual factors influencing church trends.

Donald McGavran

McGavran is a mission theorist whose thought derives from Christian mission growth or decline in many cultures. He distinguishes contextual and institutional factors in church growth, calling them "receptivity" and "mission strategy." Several of his conclusions are important. He finds that receptivity changes greatly from time to time.

> The receptivity or responsiveness of individuals waxes and wanes. No person is equally ready at all times to follow the Way. The young person reared in a Christian home is usually more ready to accept Jesus Christ at twelve than at twenty. The skeptic is often more willing to become a disciple after serious illness or loss than he was before [1970:216].

> Sudden ripenings, far from being unusual, are common. No one knows or has counted the ripenings of the last decade, but it is safe to say that they total hundreds. . . . One thing is clear, receptivity wanes as often as it waxes. Like the tide, it comes in and goes out. Unlike the tide, no one can guarantee when it goes out that it will soon come back again [1970:218].[1]

Also, McGavran concludes that social psychological factors are more influential than theological ones. He outlines certain social situations that produce higher receptivity, including movements of peoples from older settings to new lands or to the cities, changing government policies that free populations from strong social controls, and nationalistic feelings that are associated with religion (1970:219-21).

Dean Hoge

Several years ago I did some replication studies to measure trends in religious commitment among American college students, and I tried to explain the patterns that were found. The studies agreed fairly well that traditional religious commitments of students had been relatively strong in the mid-1920s, weakened until a low point in the middle 1930s, then rose again about 1940 and hit a high point in 1952-55. After the middle 1950s they weakened constantly throughout the 1960s (Hoge, 1974:54). In searching for convincing explanations, I found several other social indicators that had the same fall-rise-fall pattern since the 1920s. One was fear of Communism or subversion (the same fall-rise-fall pattern), a second was conformity to college social norms and other-direction (the same pattern), a third was age-specific birthrate of women 20 to 24 years old (the same pattern), and a fourth (in reverse direction) was college student political activism (absent in the 1920s, high in the 1930s, absent in the early 1950s, high in the late 1960s). Two others were also found. See Table 4.1, which depicts how these indicators varied in similar directions over the decades. I intercorrelated the measures wherever possible and found consistent correlations in the predicted direction. These commitments of college students formed an overall system, and they all shifted together.

Explanations for religious change must work from the total system of commitments, which I called the meaning-commitment system. Religious commitments are linked to others, and they may change indirectly when the other commitments change. An impact on the total system at any point will affect all the components to a greater or lesser extent, depending on the closeness of the ties in the structure. Historical events having a strong impact on any of the components closely related to religious commitments will indirectly influence those commitments. The direction of causation within the system varies, depending on the direction of external impact and its reverberations on various commitments. In the case of the strengthening religious commitments of college students in the 1940s and early 1950s, Cold War anxieties and conservative political pressures had a major influence, which, in turn, strengthened the churches and traditional religious life.

This research on religious change among college students is not only important to us due to the theoretical model that emerged. It is also important since the population group and the time period under study is the same (middle-class Americans, last three decades) and since all research shows that religious trends are more extreme among youth than among the total adult population (see Hoge, 1974:169).

Robert Wuthnow

The work of Robert Wuthnow is probably the most powerful recent attempt to explain religious trends in America. In an article entitled "Recent Patterns of Secularization: A Problem of Generations?" (1976b), which is directly pertinent to us (also see Wuthnow, 1976a), he reviews indicators of religious change in the United States from 1950 to 1972 and finds a rise-and-fall pattern in all of them. Because the changes are too discontinuous and short run in nature, they cannot be explained by overall modernization processes, including upgrading of education, diffusion of science, urbanization, or energy consumption (1976b:853).

The explanatory factor, in Wuthnow's view, is the emergence of a distinct youth generation in the 1960s. He takes from Mannheim

TABLE 4.1

CHANGES IN INDICATORS OF PERSONAL COMMITMENTS OF COLLEGE STUDENTS

	Middle 1920s	Middle 1930s	Early 1950s	Late 1960s
Traditional religious commitment and orthodoxy	high	low	high	low
Fear of Communism or subversion	high	low	high	low
Conformity to college social norms; other-direction	high	low	high	low
Commitment to family life (measured by the age-specific birthrate)	high	low	high	low
Commitment to military duty and patriotic war	--	low	high	low
Political activism toward change	low	high	low	high
Criticism of college education	--	high	low	high

Source: Hoge (1974:181).

the concept "generation unit," meaning a biological age group in a society having a common location, a common experience, and a common response. Any event that disrupts the normal socialization of youth in a society may increase the chances of distinct generation units forming. Wars and migrations have done so in the past, and the events in America in the 1960s did so again. The emergence of self-conscious generational units typically causes some religious change, and in the 1960s it caused an important disaffection of youth from established churches.

Wuthnow shows in survey data that the disaffection of youth from established churches in the late 1960s and 1970s is much greater than any disaffection among older adults. He also shows that age differences in religious commitment in the 1970s are greater than they were in the 1950s and 1960s. Then, using 1972 survey data from the bay area in California, he shows that a strong factor in disaffection of specific youth from the church is a prior contact with the counterculture. Hence, he argues that the counterculture was the creation of a large generation unit in America, a group to which only a minority of youth belonged but which affected large portions of the youth population.

All of Wuthnow's data is cross-sectional, and thus the direction of causation must be established by external evidence. Wuthnow argues that the dominant causation is from the counterculture experience to religious commitment. He says that the counterculture was never as concerned with organized religion as organized religion came to be with the counterculture. The church took somewhat of a follower role in the cultural changes among youth in the 1960s (1976b:860). And, most important, panel data on Berkeley students demonstrates that defection from parental religion is strongly predicted by certain value commitments held by the students a year or two earlier in the areas of drug use, living together before marriage, and alternative life-styles (1978:ch. 7).

Wuthnow's analysis of recent religious change as a generational phenomenon is supported by considerable data, and it seems important in helping explain the short-range variations in church trends. His demonstration that counterculture exposure is a predictor of defection from church life is also theoretically important.[2]

Ronald Inglehart

Inglehart (1977) carried out value surveys in nine European nations and in the United States in 1970-73. He accepted the conception of a value hierarchy by Abraham Maslow, a view which held that for any person survival and subsistence needs are foremost until they are routinely and securely met, after which other needs such as esteem, belonging, and self-actualization begin to intensify and become central in one's life. Inglehart devised a value measure that divided respondents into "Materialists" and "Post-Materialists." The latter are persons who are accustomed to material well-being and who therefore have greater stress on quality of life, personal freedom, and participation in decision-making in government and occupation (see Inglehart, 1977:ch. 2).

In all ten nations studied, the younger, more affluent persons tended disproportionately to be Post-Materialists. Men were more so than women. Jews were more so than other religious groups, and in some European nations Protestants were more so than Catholics. The greatest concentration of Post-Materialist values was found among college-educated young adults. "The Post-Materialist type is much more prevalent among the younger university-educated cohorts than elsewhere. Indeed, this seems to be the only sector of society where the Post-Materialists outnumber the Materialists—a fact that may have great significance [1977:82]." In trend data, young people were found to change more rapidly than older people; Inglehart (1977:103) says they are more "malleable." Today, in most of these nations, age cleavages are as important in politics as social class cleavages, and the age cleavages are greatest in those nations that experienced the most rapid social change.

Post-Materialists tend not to be affiliated with a church or to attend church. Of the respondents affiliated with a church, 10 percent scored as Post-Materialists; of those not affiliated, 26 percent did so (1977:89). Inglehart posits no causation here, for he interprets all the values as being the result of structural changes in society. Events in the affluent Western nations since World War II have produced vast, pervasive value changes. These events have included (1) a sharp increase in higher education; (2) an increase in mass media and foreign travel; (3) technological innovation and an increased standard of living; (4) changes in the occupational structure, with large increases in the tertiary sector; and (5) increased employment of women. These changes have introduced new values for youth, and among them are new attitudes about religion. They are in the direction of greater egalitarianism, personal freedoms, and rejection of institutional authority.

Inglehart sees generational differences as gradual products of social changes over the decades. He differs with Wuthnow, who stresses the short-run variations in religious trends and argues that only generational differences can explain them. Inglehart puts little stress on such sharp reversals or changes in values and looks instead at longer-range trends over several decades. He makes no attempt to measure or explain short-range fluctuations.

Summary

Three summary statements can be made: (1) National contextual factors favoring or disfavoring religious commitment change quickly, often rising or falling within a few years. Thus, projections into the future are very risky. (2) Religious changes are usually part of broader changes in values, attitudes, and sentiments. The precise theoretical model needed to explain interrelations of changes is still unclear. (3) Religious changes in modern America are disproportionately great among young adults, disproportionately small among older adults.

RELATIONSHIP OF RELIGIOUS COMMITMENTS TO OTHER VALUES

If religious changes are components of broader changes, what is the exact shape of the broader package? How are religious commitments related to other commitments? One method of answering these questions is to look at intercorrelations of religious commitments and other values.

Evidence from College Student Surveys

My research on college student values (Hoge, 1969; 1974) yielded two studies of intercorrelations among religious attitudes and other attitudes. A 1969 survey at the University of Michigan (see Appendix) found that church commitment correlated .24 with a Fear of Communism Index but only weakly with a Social Constraint of Deviants Index, Free Business Enterprise Index, Small Government Index, and Intellectualism Index. A Religious Orthodoxy Index correlated .34 with the Fear of Communism Index, .24 with the Free Business Enterprise Index, and .22 with the Social Constraint of Deviants Index, but weaker with the others. In a 1974 study at the University of Michigan the correlations were similar (see Hoge, 1976a).

At the University of Wisconsin in 1968 a measure of traditional religious commitment was correlated with a Sex and Family Index, a Political Attitude Index, and an Economic Attitude Index. The strongest correlation was with the Sex and Family Index; traditional religious views were associated with traditional views about sex and family. The correlation with the Economic Attitude Index was very weak (see Appendix).

Evidence from Adult Surveys

In an informative study of Lutheran church members, Kersten (1970) surveyed a sample of Lutheran laity in metropolitan Detroit in 1967. He asked many attitude questions and related the responses to a measure of orthodox theological beliefs and a measure of church involvement. Of the twenty-eight attitude areas tapped, only ten had any noteworthy relationships with religious beliefs and church involvement. In every case traditional and conservative attitudes were associated with greater church involvement. Six are in the area of sexual behavior, abortion, and divorce. Two are in the area of women's roles in the church. One is in the area of civil liberties ("A person who says there is no God is likely to hold dangerous political ideas"), and one is in the area of racial prejudice. By contrast, none of the items in the other attitude areas had any associations with the religion indexes—political party preference, social welfare, the Vietnam War, foreign aid, treatment of criminals, sex and violence in movies and TV, anti-Semitism, anti-Catholicism, dancing, smoking, women's family role, and women's careers (see Appendix).

The best data for our purposes are the General Social Surveys, gathered annually by the National Opinion Research Center since 1972. They include data from a random sample of Americans 18 and older. Table 4.2 depicts correlations between three religious commitment measures and a large number of attitudes, as found in the 1975 survey. The three religious measures are (1) an item asking about belief in life after death, (2) an item on frequency of church attendance, and (3) an item asking "Would you call yourself a strong ———— (whatever the religious preference)?" Correlations weaker than plus or minus .15 are not shown.

Twenty-seven items were deleted from the table, since none of the correlations with the religious commitment measures was as strong as .15. Five items were on race relations, four were on the roles of women in modern society, twelve were on how much confidence the respondent had in business leaders, leaders of banks, education leaders, the federal government, labor leaders, the press, medicine, television, the Supreme Court, the scientific community, Congress, and military leaders, two items were on our

TABLE 4.2

CORRELATIONS OF ATTITUDE ITEMS WITH THREE MEASURES OF RELIGIOUS
BELIEFS AND COMMITMENT, 1975 N.O.R.C. GENERAL SOCIAL SURVEY*

	Belief in Life After Death	Church Attendance	Strongly Religious Person
Political Attitudes			
Self-identification with political party (1=yes, 2=independent)	--	--	--
Strength of party identification (1=none or weak, 2=strong)	--	--	--
Political views (semantic differential: 1=extremely conservative, 7=extremely liberal)	--	-.17	--
Should marijuana be made legal? (1=no, 2=don't know, 3=yes)	--	-.24	-.17
Do you approve of the Supreme Court ruling against required Bible reading or prayer in public schools? (1=no, 2=don't know, 3=yes)	--	--	--
Attitudes on Sex, Pornography, and Birth Control			
Ideal number of children for a family	--	.18	.17
Should birth control information be available to anyone wanting it? (1=no, 2=no opinion, 3=yes)	--	--	--
Would you be for sex education in the public schools? (1=no, 2=don't know, 3=yes)	--	-.17	--
Should birth control information be available to teenagers who want it? (1=no, 2=no opinion, 3=yes)	--	-.20	-.19
Should divorce be easier or more difficult to obtain? (1=more difficult, 2=stay as is, 3=easier)	-.17	-.23	-.16
Should abortion be legally available if the woman is married and does not want more children? (1=no, 2=don't know, 3=yes)	-.15	-.28	-.20
...if the family is poor and cannot afford more children?	-.15	-.24	-.19

	Belief in Life After Death	Church Attendance	Strongly Religious Person
...if the woman is single and does not want to marry the man?	--	-.25	-.20
Have you seen an X-rated movie in the past year?	--	-.16	--
Sexual materials lead to breakdown of morals. (1=no, 2=don't know, 3=yes)	--	.25	--
There should be laws against the distribution of pornography whatever the age. (1=agree, 2=favor lesser restriction or no law)	--	-.25	-.15
Is premarital sex always wrong, almost always wrong, wrong only sometimes, or not at all? (1=always wrong, 4=not at all)	-.16	-.36	-.26
Items on Personal Satisfaction			
For each area of life, tell me how much satisfaction you get from it: (semantic differential: 1=low, 7=high)			
The city or place you live in	--	.16	.15
Your non-working activities such as hobbies	--	--	--
Your family life	--	--	--
Your friendships	--	--	--
Your health and physical condition	--	--	--
Would you say that your marriage is very happy, pretty happy, or not too happy? (1=not happy, 2=pretty happy, 3=very happy)	--	--	--
Taken all together, how would you say things are these days--would you say that you are very happy, pretty happy, or not too happy? (1=not too happy, 2=pretty happy, 3=very happy)	--	.19	.15

*N=1490. Correlations weaker than .15 are not shown; those shown are significant at the .001 level. Actual questions are abbreviated here.

country's role in world affairs, and four items were on crime (on harsh treatment of criminals, the death penalty, wiretapping, and gun control). We were a bit surprised that all these correlations were so weak.

Table 4.2 shows that the area with strongest correlations with religious commitment is clearly that of sex, pornography, divorce, and abortion. Nothing in the area of politics correlates with the religious commitment measures except for the issue of legalization of marijuana and an item asking about strength of party identification. The items on personal satisfaction correlate only very weakly with religious commitment.

The 1974 General Social Survey included a series of attitude items not asked in 1975, and they are correlated with two religious commitment measures in Table 4.3. Eight items were deleted from the table because their correlations with religious commitment were all weaker than .15. They are five items on what characteristics are most important in a job, an item on whether life is generally exciting or dull, an item on whether hard work or lucky breaks are more important in getting ahead, and an item asking whether the respondent would continue working if he had enough money to live comfortably. The correlations in Table 4.3 are weak. The strongest ones are in the area of sexuality. Again church-oriented persons are more conservative than other persons.

We checked the correlations in Tables 4.2 and 4.3 within two age groups (39 and younger; 40 and older). On attitudes regarding sex, pornography, Communists, and civil liberties, the correlations were stronger in the younger group. We also checked the correlations for Protestant-preference persons only and for Catholic-preference persons only. In the area of sex, abortion, and pornography the correlations are somewhat stronger for the Catholics than for the Protestants. Also, the Catholics had noteworthy correlations between church involvement and political party involvement (as opposed to being an independent in politics) and between church involvement and strength of party identity; the Protestants did not.

Roozen (1978b) made a similar analysis using the General Social Survey data, but in addition to the relationships in the tables here, he compared persons having a religious preference with those having no preference. This provides additional information. Roozen found that persons with no religious preference (7 percent of all adults) differ from all other adults in that (1) they more often are political independents and less often declare a political party identification; (2) they see themselves as less happy with life in

TABLE 4.3

CORRELATIONS OF ATTITUDE ITEMS WITH TWO MEASURES OF CHURCH ATTENDANCE
AND COMMITMENT, 1974 N.O.R.C. GENERAL SOCIAL SURVEY*

	Church Attendance	Strongly Religious Person
Political Attitudes		
What do you think of Communism as a form of government? (1=worst kind of all, 2=bad, 3= all right for some countries, 4=good)	-.16	-.15
Most public officials are not really interested in the problems of the average man. (1=agree, 2=don't know, 3=disagree)	--	--
Attitudes on Civil Liberties		
If a person who is against all churches and religion wanted to make a speech in your city against churches and religion, should he be allowed to speak? (1=no, 2=don't know, 3=yes)	--	-.16
...Should he be allowed to teach in a college or university, or not? (1=no, 2=don't know, 3=yes)	--	--
...Should a book he wrote be taken out of your public library? (1=yes, 2=don't know, 3=no)	--	--
If a person who favored government ownership of all the railroads and all big industries wanted to make a speech in your community, should he be allowed to speak? (1=no, 2=don't know, 3=yes)	--	--
...Should he be allowed to teach in a college or university, or not? (1=no, 2=don't know, 3=yes)	--	--
...Should a book he wrote be taken out of your public library? (1=yes, 2=don't know, 3=no)	--	--

	Church Attendance	Strongly Religious Person
If a person who admits he is a Communist wanted to make a speech in your community, should he be allowed to speak? (1=no, 2=don't know, 3=yes)	--	--
...Should he be allowed to teach in a college or university, or not? (1=no, 2=don't know, 3=yes)	--	--
...Should a book he wrote be taken out of your public library? (1=yes, 2=don't know, 3=no)	-.15	-.15
If a man who admits that he is a homosexual wanted to make a speech in your community, should he be allowed to speak? (1=no, 2=don't know, 3=yes)	--	-.15
...Should he be allowed to teach in a college or university, or not? (1=no, 2=don't know, 3=yes)	--	--
...Should a book he wrote be taken out of your public library? (1=yes, 2=don't know, 3=no)	--	--
Attitudes on Sex		
What is your opinion about a married person having sexual relations with someone other than the marriage partner? (1=always wrong, 2=almost always wrong, 3=wrong sometimes, 4=not wrong)	-.20	-.16
What about sexual relations between adults of the same sex? (1=always wrong, 2=almost always wrong, 3=wrong sometimes, 4=not wrong)	-.18	-.16

*N=1484. Correlations weaker than .15 are not shown; those shown are significant at the .001 level. Actual questions are abbreviated here.

general; (3) they more often favor easier divorce and accept broader roles for women in society; (4) they are more liberal about premarital and extramarital sex relations and homosexuality; (5) they more often favor legalization of marijuana use and pornography; and (6) they are more liberal about birth control information, abortion, and civil liberties for such persons as Communists, atheists, and homosexuals.

Summary

Religious commitments are associated with some attitude areas but not with others. The strongest associations are with attitudes in the area of sex and family (especially regarding premarital sex, extramarital sex, homosexuality, abortion, divorce, and pornography). They are moderately associated with attitudes toward Communism. And weak associations exist with attitudes about civil liberties of Communists and atheists and with attitudes about marijuana. Among Catholics there is an association with having a political party commitment.

The attitudes are interrelated enough that we can speak of a total attitude cluster. Any important changes in particular attitudes in the cluster will have some impact on others in the cluster. The most hopeful form of inquiry regarding national contextual factors influencing the church would appear to be the assessment of changes in other attitudes in the cluster and the explanation for any such changes.

TRENDS IN ATTITUDE AREAS RELATED TO CHURCH COMMITMENT

This section reviews evidence on trends in each of the attitude areas in the cluster outlined above. The review is in six parts, looking at data on (1) religious beliefs and church commitment; (2) attitudes toward sex behavior, marriage, and divorce; (3) attitudes toward abortion and birth control; (4) attitudes toward civil liberties; (5) political party identification; and (6) other attitude areas.[3]

Trends in Religious Beliefs and Church Commitment

Most of the trend data in this area is reviewed in chapter 1. The long-term trends in basic Christian beliefs in the American population show little change. Belief in God, the Bible, or life after death has changed little in overall pervasiveness over three or four decades. However, the self-estimated importance of religion in people's lives decreased from 1952 to 1978, and where survey data includes a measure of certitude or literalism of beliefs, it has also decreased from the 1950s to 1978. The changes in certitude and literalism have been greater among the young adults than among the total population and greater after the mid-1960s than in the period of 1950 to the mid-1960s.

Religious participation trends are reviewed by Roozen in chapter 5. He found that different age groups had different trends since the late 1950s. The most changeable group in the adult population are those under age 30. Also college-educated persons are more changeable than other persons. Roozen found that after 1960 the age strata diverged sharply in their patterns of church attendance; those under 30 dropped sharply, those 31 to 55 remained quite constant, and those over 55 increased attendance. We doubt if aging itself is a causal factor, since chapter 2 concluded that aging by itself has little effect on church commitment.

Figure 4.1 depicts trends in church attendance within age groups, as found by the Gallup poll. In about 1960 the church attendance rates of the age groups diverged, with those under 30 attending less and less during the 1960s. Beginning about 1970 the divergence stopped, but the under-30 group remains much lower than the others. This figure is the counterpart to Figure 5.3 found by Roozen in quadrennial election surveys. Both sets of data agree that the main declines in church attendance have been among persons under 30 years old and that the divergence of age groups began about 1960. Apparently, whatever is causing the overall drop in church attendance had its greatest impact on the under-30 group, and the impact came after about 1960. Figure 4.1 also shows that in times of both increase and decrease in church attendance, the under-30 group changed most rapidly, suggesting that it is most subject to sharp short-run change in *either* direction; this agrees with the conclusions in college student research.

Several other studies substantiate the differences in age groups. The *Catholic Digest* studies in 1952 and 1965 included many replications. While the overall changes in religious belief over thirteen years were small, among young adults they were much larger. For example, while the overall decline in belief in God as a loving parent was 6 percent, it was 13 percent in the 18 to 24 group and 12 percent in the 25 to 34 group (see Hoge, 1974:168).

Greeley and his associates (1976) checked apostasy rates for American Catholics from 1955 to 1974 by looking at three

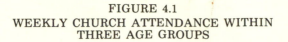

FIGURE 4.1
WEEKLY CHURCH ATTENDANCE WITHIN
THREE AGE GROUPS

—— 21-29
--- 30-49
••••• 50+

Source: AIPO polls.

nationwide polls. At all three times the apostasy rate (calculated by the number not giving Catholicism as their present preference divided by the number reared as Catholics) was greater in the under-30 group than in the 31 to 49 and over-50 groups. For example, in 1974 the figures were 22 percent, 13 percent, and 11 percent in the under-30, 31 to 49, and over-50 groups respectively. Also, the figures for the young increased faster from 1955 to 1974 than figures for the other age groups.

Trends in Attitudes About Sex Behavior, Marriage, and Divorce

Table 4.4 depicts trend data. Although the data is rather sparse, the consistent trend is toward greater tolerance and freedoms, with greatest changes since the 1950s. Item 2 in the table includes a replication of a 1943 item, and it shows that virtually all the attitude change came after 1965. Item 4, on the importance of having children, shows that child-rearing was seen as less important in marriage in 1971 than in 1955.

For item 1 we were able to secure age and regional breakdowns of the 1960, 1968, and 1975 surveys. See Figure 4.2, which depicts the trends within each age group. The overall pattern is the same as in

TABLE 4.4

TRENDS IN ATTITUDES IN THREE AREAS (IN PERCENTAGES)

Sex Behavior, Marriage, and Divorce

Question	1945	1950	1955	1960	1965	1970	1975
(1) Should divorce in this country be easier or more difficult to obtain than it is now? Easier.				9		18	32 29
(2) Would you be for or against sex education in the public schools? For.	68				69		79 76
(3) From the moral standpoint, how do you feel about divorce? Always wrong or usually wrong. (Detroit only)				43		18	
(4) Which one of these five things would you say is the most valuable part of marriage? The chance to have children. (Detroit only)			26			13	
(5) Approve of sexual relations between an engaged couple. (Catholics only)					12		43
(6) Approve of remarriage after divorce. (Catholics only)					52		73
(7) Approve of premarital coitus. (Midwestern college students only) Males				47	55		
Females				17	38		

Abortion and Birth Control

(8) Should a pregnant woman be able to obtain a legal abortion if the woman's own health is seriously endangered? Yes.

(9) Should a pregnant woman be able to obtain a legal abortion if the family cannot afford any more children? Yes.

(10) Do you think birth control information should be available to anyone who wants it, or not? Yes.

Civil Liberties and Freedoms

(11) There are always some people whose ideas are considered bad or dangerous by other people. For instance, somebody who is against all churches and religion. If such a person wanted to make a speech in your city, should he be allowed to speak, or not? Yes.

(12) ...Should such a person be allowed to teach in a college or university, or not? Yes.

(13) ...Should a book he wrote against churches and religion be taken out of your public library? No.

(14) Consider a person who favored government ownership of all the railroads and all big industries. Should he be allowed to make a speech in your community? Yes.

(8)				83 91 90 88 89
(9)			18	46 52 52 51 51
(10)	72	72 74 81	77	91 89
(11)			37	65 65 62 64
(12)			12	40 41 42 41
(13)			35	60 61 60 60
(14)			58	77 77 76

(15) ...Should such a person be allowed to teach in a college or university, or not? Yes.	33			56	57	57
(16) ...Should a book he wrote favoring government owner-ship be taken out of your public library? No.	52			67	71	69
(17) How about a man who admits he is a Communist. Should he be allowed to make a speech in your community? Yes.	27		52	60	58	55
(18) ...Should such a person be allowed to teach in a college or university, or not? Yes.	6		32	39	42	41
(19) ...Should a book he wrote be taken out of your local public library? No.	27		53	58	58	56
(20) College officials have the right to ban persons with extreme views from speaking on campus. Agree. (College freshmen only)		40	32	26	23	
(21) College officials have the right to regulate student behavior off campus. Agree. (College freshmen only)		23		13	14	

Sources: (1) Roper Research Center; N.O.R.C. (1974;1975). The 1960 item is a slight variant.
(2) Erskine (1966:501); N.O.R.C. (1974;1975).
(3,4) Duncan et al. (1973:72,8).
(5,6) Saldahna et al. (1975:17-18).
(7) Christensen and Gregg (1970).
(8,9) Gallup (1972:1985); N.O.R.C. (1972-76).
(10) Gallup (1972:1785,1823,1915,1654); N.O.R.C. (1974;1975).
(11 thru 19) Stouffer (1955); N.O.R.C. (1972-1976).
(20,21) Bayer and Dutton (1976:167).

Figure 4.1—the age groups were similar in 1960 but diverged in the following years, with the young adults changing the most in the direction of personal freedom. The regional breakdowns did not have a distinct pattern.

We searched for replications of nationwide poll items on extramarital sex relations and pornography but found none spanning more than a few years. Yet, all indications are that tolerance has increased in these areas during the past decade.

The Yankelovich surveys of college students found increases in approval of sexual freedom from 1969 to 1973. For example, the percentage saying that extramarital sexual relations are wrong declined from 77 in 1969 to 60 in 1973; the percentage saying that relations between consenting homosexuals are wrong declined

FIGURE 4.2

PERCENT IN THREE AGE GROUPS SAYING DIVORCE SHOULD BE MADE EASIER TO GET

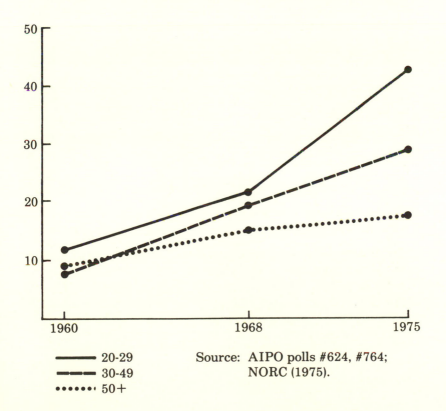

from 42 in 1969 to 25 in 1973; the percentage saying that casual premarital sexual relations are wrong declined from 34 to 22 (Yankelovich, 1974:13, 67; also see Perlman, 1974).

The practice of premarital sex relations increased in recent decades. Finger (1975) carried out replication studies of college students and found large increases in premarital sexual experiences of college men from 1944 to 1973. Bell and Chaskes (1970) found an increase in reported premarital sex among comparable samples of women college students from 1958 to 1968; for instance, the percentage while going steady was 15 in 1958 and 28 in 1968. Udry, Bauman, and Morris (1975) found similar patterns of increased premarital coitus in a large study spanning four decades. Alston and Tucker (1973) analyzed breakdowns of surveys on sexual freedom and found urban areas to be more permissive than rural areas; also, the West is the most permissive region in the United States, while the South is the least.

Divorce rates in the United States have the same pattern of accelerated change since about 1960. The divorce rate was stable during the 1950s and until 1962 at about 9 or 10 per 1,000 married women age 15 and over. Then it zoomed upward, hitting 15 per 1,000 by 1970 and 19 per 1,000 by 1975 (U.S. Bureau of the Census, 1977).

Trends in Attitudes About Abortion and Birth Control

Table 4.4 includes three replications of items on abortion and birth control. All show sharp increases in acceptance after 1965 (also see Blake, 1971).

Among college students Yankelovich (1974:93) found an increasing acceptance of abortion from 1969 to 1973. The percentage saying that having an abortion was wrong dropped from 36 to 32 in those four years.

Trends in Attitudes About Civil Liberties and Freedoms

The bottom of Table 4.4 includes eleven items on civil liberties accorded to various kinds of persons. Items 11 through 19 are on atheists, socialists, and Communists. There was a considerable gain in tolerance for all three from 1954 to the early 1970s. Items 20 and 21 are from college student surveys and show much change over seven years toward a demand for more student freedoms.

Two groups of researchers have done further analysis of the replication data on civil liberties. Nunn, Crockett, and Williams (1978) looked for the determinants of the change in attitude.

Education turned out to be the most important determinant. By use of controls they distinguished the cognitive and personality effects of higher education from the socioeconomic effects. The former were the only important effects influencing attitudes of tolerance of nonconformists (1978:63). Nunn and his associates found that college education had an effect or not at any time depending on the larger political climate; in the 1950s, for example, it had no liberalizing effect on attitudes toward civil liberties, since the entire political climate at that time was one of fear of deviants. Hence, the analysis of the changing political climate was found to be necessary for understanding the sources of attitude change.

Nunn and his associates interpreted the data in generational terms, following Mannheim. They adopted Mannheim's idea that young people make "fresh contact" with the world and with tradition in a way that produces changes. The events of the 1960s, preeminently the Vietnam War and the decreasing perception of threat from Communism, were the new social elements that caused formation of different attitudes among the youth. Young persons changed most from 1954 to 1973. Figure 4.3 indicates the pattern, showing attitudes on whether or not Communism is a serious threat. Whereas the age groups had similar attitudes in 1954, in 1973 they did not.

Davis (1975a) also analyzed the trend data on attitudes about civil liberties. He was able to distinguish several sources of attitude change over the nineteen years. Most important was the change in political climate, independent of demographic or educational changes in the population. Figure 4.4 plots the average tolerance level in each age group in 1954 and in 1972-73. As the Nunn study found, young adults changed more than older adults. Davis (1975a:510) speculates that these attitude changes are one part of a broad attitude shift.

> I would say that there is solid empirical ground for suspecting that the changes observed here were not isolated changes in these particular attitudes, but part of a general movement including all sorts of issues of the liberalism-dogmatism variety (not economic liberalism), including civil liberty, racial prejudice, women's rights, tolerance of nudity, and sexual experimentation.

This speculation is similar to the argument being set forth in the present chapter. However, according to our evidence, the attitude cluster that co-varies over time is not as broad as Davis guesses.

114

FIGURE 4.3

PERCENT IN THREE AGE GROUPS SEEING
COMMUNISM AS A SERIOUS THREAT, 1954 AND 1973

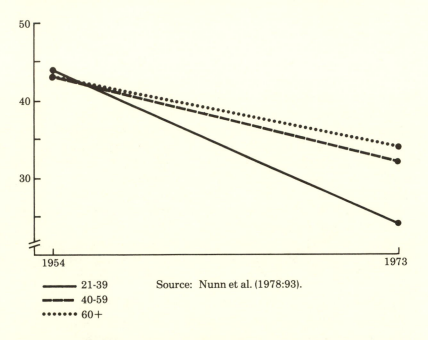

Source: Nunn et al. (1978:93).

——— 21-39
– – – 40-59
••••••• 60+

Trends in Political Party Affiliation

Recently, a major study of political party affiliation by Nie and
his colleagues (1976) has given us new information on trends. The
Nie study analyzed the Michigan Election Studies data from 1952
to 1974 and found sharp increases in the percentage having no
party affiliation during that time. The percentage calling themselves "independents" was roughly constant from 1952 to 1964 (23
or 24 percent), then rose sharply to 40 percent in 1974.

The possible analogy between political independents and
religious independents has stimulated discussion. It is reasonable
to believe that persons shying away from political party identification might, for similar reasons, shy away from religious
identification too. However, the correlation is very weak except
among Catholics. And the analogy is a loose one, since the social
functions of political parties and churches are quite different; a
party lacks most of the local community-building and child-rearing
functions of churches. However, for young persons without
children the analogy would appear to be somewhat closer. Values
of cosmopolitanism, individualism, or noninvolvement in organi-

FIGURE 4.4
PERCENT GIVING TOLERANT RESPONSES ON
CIVIL LIBERTIES ATTITUDE INDEX,
1954 AND 1972-73

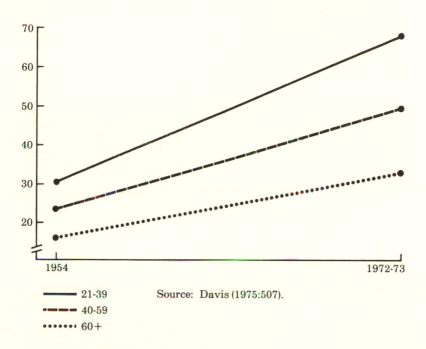

Source: Davis (1975:507).

——— 21-39
−−−− 40-59
•••••• 60+

zations may lie behind the tendencies toward "independence" in both areas.

Figure 4.5 shows the cohort analysis done by Nie and his associates. It is constructed differently from the other figures in this chapter; the lines connect *the same cohort* of people over time, not persons of equivalent age. The figure shows that the increased numbers of independents derive from the young adults who enter the electorate, not from a tendency of persons formerly politically affiliated to drop out and become independents. A partial exception occurs with the "new voters, 1964," who did tend to drop out and become independents between 1964 and 1968. Glenn and Hefner (1972) made a separate analysis of Democratic and Republican party identification and aging and came to the same conclusion.

Figure 4.5 is relevant to us, since it is the political party equivalent to the Carroll and Roozen (1975:119) analysis of age cohorts and church attendance. Church attendance rose and fell more dramatically due to short-run period effects, but otherwise

FIGURE 4.5
PERCENTAGE OF POLITICAL INDEPENDENTS BY
AGE COHORTS, 1952 TO 1972

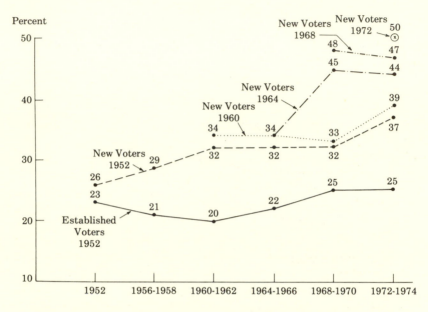

Source: Norman H. Nie, et al., *The Changing American Voter.* Harvard
University Press, 1976, page 63. Reprinted by permission. Copyright ©
1976 by the Twentieth Century Fund.

the figures are similar in showing that overall trends in recent years have been due largely to the behavior of the new cohorts entering adulthood—not due to changes in behavior among older adults.

When I began this analysis I expected that political alienation would be part of the attitude cluster. This was because alienation from government seemed somehow associated with alienation from the church, and also because Wuthnow and the Berkeley researchers concluded that among California youth, rejection of the church was one element of a broad rejection of established American institutions. However, several tests of the relationship, done with the 1974 and 1975 General Social Survey data, failed to find a noteworthy correlation. This raises the question of how broad the total attitude cluster is that explains alienation from churches among young adults in the nation. Apparently, the broad cluster, including political alienation, described by Wuthnow and the Berkeley researchers is overdrawn. Either the California setting is different from the total national setting, or the time period (1972 for the California data, 1974-75 for the nationwide data) is different.[4]

Trends in Other Attitude Areas

Table 4.2 included two correlations that we have not discussed due to paucity of data: correlations with attitudes toward marijuana legalization and toward ideal family size.

Survey questions on marijuana date back to only the late 1960s. In nationwide polls the percentage agreeing marijuana should be legalized was 12 in 1969, 15 in 1972, 20 in 1975, and 28 in 1976 (Gallup, 1972:2219; National Opinion Research Center, 1972-76). In nationwide polls of college freshmen, those agreeing that marijuana should be legalized were 19 percent in 1968, 26 in 1969, 38 in 1970, 39 in 1971, 47 in 1972, 48 in 1973, and 47 in 1974 (Bayer and Dutton, 1976:164). Youth were more tolerant than adults, and changes among youth were faster than changes among adults. This is the pattern found several times above.

Table 4.2 also found that persons with stronger church commitment tended to desire larger families. We saw in Table 4.4, item 4, that the perceived importance of children decreased from 1958 to 1971 (at least in Detroit). Also, research has shown that the ideal family size as seen by the total population has been falling (Blake, 1974; Current Opinion, 1973). Indeed, the birthrate in the United States has been falling since about 1960; it fell sharply all during the 1960s and then fell gradually in the early 1970s. The age-specific birthrate of young women under age 24 varied more dramatically over these years, but the overall timing was similar (U.S. Bureau of the Census, 1975).

It is noteworthy that the birthrate in the United States has matched trends in traditional religious commitment for at least a half century. Both fell during the early 1930s and then rose in the 1940s, and both were very high during the 1950s (see Hoge, 1974:176). The two trend lines are remarkably similar, but the theoretical meaning of the parallelism is not clear. Several sociologists have commented on the relationship. For example, Herberg (1955:61) suggested that during the 1950s young people turned to the security to be found in the elemental ways and institutions of humankind—the family and religion. "Indeed, the two have been closely linked from the very earliest times." In Herberg's view, a turn to the private life, reflecting the attempt to find meaning and security in basic, unchanging ways of life, led both to the upswing in church participation and the upswing in the birthrate.

There are three possible linkages between church participation rates and birthrates. First is simply that higher birthrates produce more babies who find their way into Sunday schools and then churches. If this linkage is the primary one, birthrate variations should anticipate church membership variations by ten or fifteen years. Second is the child-rearing theory of church participation, which has been proven in a series of studies. It holds that married persons with children of school age participate more in church because of the perceived assistance of church life for child-rearing. If more children exist in the population, their parents will participate more in churches for child-rearing reasons. Third is an association between traditional religious commitments and larger desired families, so that rising religious participation (for example, in the early 1950s) is associated with a desire among parents for more children.

Of these three, the second and third seem most convincing to us, although decisive data to test them is only partly available. Probably the third linkage is the most powerful one. An association between traditional religious commitments and larger families (either larger desired families or actual number of births) has been found in all research. Whelpton and his colleagues (1966) found that when Protestant women were divided into those in liberal, intermediate, and fundamentalistic denominations, those in the fundamentalistic groups were the most fertile; this could not be explained by differences in education, income, occupation, or community size (1966:74). Also, wives who said that religious activities were "very important" in their present families were more fertile than those reporting no religious activities in their family life. This was true for both Protestants and Catholics. The Westoff study (1961) found church attendance and two measures of traditional religious attitudes to be associated with preferred family size (Lenski [1963:254] found the same for both Protestants and Catholics).

Whelpton and his associates (1966) also asked the women in their nationwide survey if they worked, and if so, why. Women who worked had had fewer births and expected fewer more in the future than those not working. Also, women who worked because they liked to work had fewer births and fewer expected future births than those who worked because their families needed the income or because of other reasons. Peterson (1975:537) reviewed fertility differentials in recent research and concluded that couples striving for upward mobility have fewer children for that reason. These research findings begin to depict the nature of the association between birthrates and changes in other life commitments.

Trends in the birthrate resemble trends in church participation in several other ways. The baby boom in the 1950s and the subsequent sharp decline in the birthrate were phenomena largely of younger women, not older women. The young changed much more than the old. Also, educated women changed more, in one direction or the other, than uneducated women (for the research see Freedman et al., 1959; Rindfuss and Sweet, 1977). Attempts by demographers to explain the baby boom and the drop in fertility through demographic analysis looking at different categories and aggregates of people have proven unfruitful (see Rindfuss and Sweet, 1977). This is exactly the conclusion in Roozen's study of church participation trends using demographic analysis (chapter 5 in this book).

We believe that birthrates can be seen as indicators of commitment of young adults to traditional family life and other privatistic values. The explanation for birthrate trends is probably in part the trends in such values.[5] This was Herberg's (1960) view, and it seems substantiated by all research. Trends in family and privatistic values are very likely explanatory, to some degree, for church participation trends as well (on this question see Hoge, 1974:176ff).

Finally, two trends widely discussed as possible explanations for church trends deserve mention: the increase in leisure-time pursuits and the increase in economic well-being. The first is often noted by church leaders who see empty churches on Sundays and hear about vacation homes, recreational vehicles, and camping trips that occupy their parishioners on weekends. This theory is most obviously an explanation for season-specific rates of church attendance, not membership, yet its proponents suggest it has wide application. But the theory is weakened by available trend data. The average length of workweek in the United States declined for decades but leveled off in the late 1960s. It was 43.4 hours in 1948, 41.0 hours in 1958, 38.7 in 1968, and 39.2 in 1972 (Kando, 1975:80). If leisure produces depressed church attendance, then church attendance should have decreased steadily during the 1950s. Trends in recreational participation (attendance at sports events, participant sports, expenditures on sports equipment as percentage of family income, for instance) all have smooth ascending curves during the 1950s, the 1960s, and the 1970s, often with a leveling-off in the 1970s (Kando, 1975:216, 219, 224). It is difficult to see how religious trends, which have short-run changes during these years, can be explained by smooth trends over the whole period.

Purported explanations of church trends by economic trends have the same problem. Economic indicators since the 1940s (for example, family income in constant dollars, real disposable income in constant dollars, GNP per capita) show quite constant growth, and religious trends cannot easily be explained by such smooth, steady curves (see Carroll and Roozen, 1975; Moss, 1968). In my study of trends in religion of college students, I found economic indicators to be useless (Hoge, 1974:ch. 6).

CONCLUSIONS

This chapter has tried to bring a measure of specificity into discussions of nationwide social factors influencing church trends. It has produced, I believe, several conclusions.

1. National trends in church participation change rather quickly, often fluctuating in five- or ten-year segments. The trend lines are not straight for very long, and projections of church trends from one decade cannot be reliably made into the next decade.

2. National changes in church participation in the past two decades cannot be explained by demographic changes such as migration, educational trends, or urbanization. Nor are they explainable by increases in standard of living or leisure, or by birthrates in the mechanical sense that more or fewer births produce more or fewer church members. The analyst of national change in the churches must turn to the scrutiny of religious climate, just as the political scientist must scrutinize political climate. This is a rather elusive entity not closely associated with social structural conditions.

3. Changes in church commitment are part of a broader pattern of value changes. All data supports this view. Other areas in the overall cluster undergoing change are attitudes about sex and family, birth control, ideal family size, civil liberties, legalization of marijuana, and (among Catholics) political party identification. In all these areas, change since the 1950s has taken the same pattern. It has been in the direction of individualism, personal freedom, and tolerance of diversity. The change has been much greater among young adults, especially the college-educated young adults, than among any other persons. It took place mostly after 1960.

4. The reasons for the overall attitude changes are not easily known. Wuthnow and Nunn and his associates argue for a generational explanation, saying that the social and political events of the late 1950s and the 1960s caused a large segment of youth in those years to form a separate culture; the rapidity of the changes seems to support this view. Inglehart prefers to look at the confluence of longer-range trends in educational level, affluence, and mass media exposure that produced rapid social changes. It is possible that the rapid changes in attitudes in the 1960s came after the waning of the Cold War climate, a climate that impeded the individualizing and liberalizing pressures attending gradual social changes all during the 1950s. Thus, the rapid changes were a kind of "catching up" with underlying social change. An explanation having this logic is possible and is the most convincing kind for understanding the rapid changes in American Catholicism following the events of Vatican Council II.

Many questions remain, of which I will mention two. Is it possible to understand differences in denominational membership trends from the point of view of this chapter? Is there something about the overall value shifts which, by itself, has produced declines in some denominations but not in others? We have been unable to make much progress toward answering this question. The approach to it would entail distinguishing social class differences and regional differences in the value shifts, since denominations vary by social class and region. Because value shifts were greater among more educated persons, they would appear to affect upper socioeconomic denominations most adversely. This matches the trend data and appears to be a partial explanation of denominational trends. Regional patterns should have additional explanatory power, but our initial attempts (see chapter 8) to understand them in these terms were not successful.

The other question is one raised by church leadership. If the values of more educated young adults are moving in the direction of individualism, personal freedom, and tolerance of diversity, would churches benefit from adjusting their value emphases (insofar as doctrines allow) in these directions? In short, if youth are becoming more liberal, would they become involved in more liberal churches? We lack reliable data on this question, but all observers agree that the answer is no. The value shift seems to conduce people to no church participation at all, not to participation in liberal churches. The majority of young adults undergoing the value shift cease church participation, but a minority become committed to churches. This minority appears more often to find church commitment in some kind of reaction or defense against the value shift than to find it as an inherent part of the shift. The strongest church commitment recently among educated young adults is more often in conservative churches, who oppose the individualism and freedom of the value shift, than in liberal churches, who affirm it. This question is discussed further in chapter 14.

CHAPTER 5

The Efficacy of Demographic Theories of Religious Change:
Protestant Church Attendance, 1952–68[1]

David A. Roozen

National contextual theories of religious change typically assert one of three general types of causal process: (1) demographic change, (2) massification or differentiation, or (3) pervasive normative change. Demographic change refers to changes in the relative size of various subgroups of the population.[2] The increasing percentage of young adults and decreasing percentage of middle-age adults in the United States since the mid-1960s provides an excellent example. Assuming that young adults are less inclined toward religious participation than are older adults, the shift in the relative sizes of these two subgroups provides a plausible explanation for the overall national decline in religious participation over this period.

Massification and differentiation refer to the increasing similarity or dissimilarity, respectively, between various subgroups in the population.[3] Wuthnow (1976b), for example, argues that the difference in religious participation between young adults and older adults increased significantly during the 1960s, and that this differentiation in religious participation between the age groups is critical for understanding the overall national decline in religious participation for this period. The decline was almost totally limited to the young adult segment of the population; the level of participation for older adults remained generally constant.

Pervasive normative change refers to change in attitudes or behaviors that has become widely diffused throughout the population, touching all major subgroups. Most secularization theories of religious change are couched in such terms. Another example is Kelley's (1977:91) suggestion that one contributing factor to recent declines in church membership and participation has been the disappearance of the general social expectation that people should attend church.

Demographic change, massification/differentiation, and normative change are conceptually distinct. But, in reality, all three tend to be found operating at the same time and in varying degrees, sometimes in tandem and sometimes in opposition. The problem for the analyst of religious change, therefore, is that of disentangling the three effects and specifying how much and in what direction each is contributing to the change.

The primary purpose of this chapter is to test empirically the efficacy of some widely discussed demographic theories of the change in American religious participation over the past quarter century. In addition, I will note those instances identifiable in the data where nondemographic processes seem especially important for understanding the religious change.

DATA

The data for this study is from five national surveys conducted by the Survey Research Center (SRC) of the University of Michigan as part of their American Election Study Series, one conducted in each Presidential election year beginning in 1952. Each is designed to be representative of the total population of persons of voting age living in private households in the continental United States at the time of the survey.[4]

For present purposes three modifications have been made to the original samples. Persons under the age of 21 have been excluded to control for changes in the voting age. Nonwhites have been eliminated to control for the confounding effects of race. Persons expressing a religious preference other than Protestant have been excluded to control their confounding effect.[5]

Each sample, therefore, represents a cross section of the white, Protestant preference population of the continental United States 21 years of age and over. Sample sizes range from 827 in 1968 to

1,202 in 1960. Combining all five samples produces a total of 5,112 white adult Protestants.

DEMOGRAPHIC THEORIES OF RELIGIOUS CHANGE

Before turning to a review of demographic theories of religious change, I should clarify what is meant by a demographic theory and how it differs from the two mentioned alternatives. A simple path diagram (Figure 5.1) is instructive. Figure 5.1 posits four possible relationships: (1) religious participation may change over time; (2) the relative size of population subgroups may change over time; (3) religious participation may vary between population subgroups; and (4) time may affect the subgroup religious participation relationship. The first relationship (time → Y) can be understood to represent period change—that change in religious participation unaccounted for by other variables in the theory and often accounted for by theorists in terms of normative change. The second relationship (time → X) represents demographic change. Massification/differentiation effects are represented by the fourth relationship (T → XY). A pure demographic theory of social change assets a TX relationship, an XY relationship, a TY relationship that approaches O when X is controlled, and a negligible T → XY relationship (that is, the subgroup/religious participation relationship is constant over time). The key is finding an explanatory variable that defines the right set of population subgroups. That

FIGURE 5.1
PATH DIAGRAM OF
RELIGIOUS CHANGE

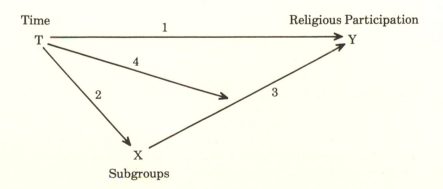

variable must be related to religious participation, and its distribution must change over time.

Chapter 2's review of previous research on church commitment reveals that several variables are consistently found to be related to religious participation. For present purposes I shall focus on sex, age, religious preference, religious belief, region, education, child-rearing, and value commitments.[6] To the extent that the distribution of any of these variables changes over time, they become logical possibilities as the key explanatory variable (X in Figure 5.1) in a demographic theory of religious change.

The distribution of two of these variables, however, has not changed, and I drop them from further consideration. The sex distribution of both the national adult population and the national adult population of white Protestants has remained virtually constant since 1950 (see Appendix). Similarly, the proportions of adult Protestants, Catholics, Jews, and non-Judeo-Christians (defined by religious preference) in the population have remained virtually unchanged since the early 1950s (see Appendix). For the remainder of the variables, however, change has occurred.

From chapter 1 it is known that American religious participation increased through the 1950s, peaked in the early 1960s, and then declined through the late 1960s and 1970s. The curvilinear nature of this twenty-five-year trend has a critical implication for the search for appropriate demographic explanations. If one is seeking single variable explanations, then the twenty-five-year trend in the distribution of the explanatory variable must match that of religious participation, that is, must be curvilinear, reversing itself in the early 1960s. Of the variables related to religious participation noted above, there is solid evidence indicating such a trend for the age structure of the population and the proportion of parents of school-age children (see Appendix). Considerably softer data indicates such a trend in value commitments (see chapter 4).

Each of these trends has been noted by previous analysts of religious change and has been proposed as a major contributing factor to the rise and fall of religious participation since 1950. The related changes in the age structure of the population and the proportion of parents with school-age children are the explanatory core of the child-rearing theory (Nash and Berger, 1962; Lazerwitz, 1961; Mueller and Johnson, 1975; Carroll and Roozen, 1975). Religious participation, the theory holds, is relatively low among young adults because their major commitments are focused on the establishment of career and families; relatively high during the middling or parenting years, motivated largely out of a desire to see one's children receive religious instruction; then dropping off somewhat as one's children mature and leave the household. Accordingly, as the relative proportion of young adults in the population increases, the overall national rate of religious participation should decrease. Concomitantly, as the proportion of young adults decreases, religious participation should increase.

The child-rearing theory of religious change has typically been analyzed using either age or the presence or absence or number of children in the household as the key operational variable. This study shall use both a measure of age and of the presence of school-age children. In addition, a composite family life cycle variable constructed by combining the age and presence of school-age children measures with a measure of marital status shall be used.

Value changes—changes in the proportion of the population expressing different value orientations—have been theoretically linked to religious change by Hoge (1974; 1976b), Wuthnow, (1976b), and Roozen (1977). In the most radical formulation of the position, religious change is asserted to be directly dependent upon value change. Specifically, it is held that traditional religious involvement is positively related to privatistic, familial, and conformist values, a value set dominant in the 1950s, but coming under severe critique in the mid to late 1960s. Accordingly, religious participation should have a curvilinear trend over this period, peaking in the mid to late 1960s—as of course it did. Unfortunately, no direct empirical test of the impact of value changes on religious participation over this period is possible. No series of surveys covering the appropriate time spans (the five surveys of this study included) contains measures of both religious participation and value commitments.[7]

The best national survey data regarding the value theory of religious change comes from a recent publication by Nunn, Crockett, and Williams (1978). The data is from two national cross-sectional surveys, one conducted in 1954 and the other in 1973, each containing a measure of religious participation and tolerance of nonconformity. Although the two surveys are inadequate to map the curvilinear nature of the religious participation trend over this period, a quick look at their findings in regard to the relationship of tolerance to changes in religious participation is suggestive.

Table 5.1 presents the relevant information. Section A of the table shows that in both 1954 and 1973 the percentage of active participants in religion was significantly greater among the "less

TABLE 5.1

TOLERANCE OF NONCONFORMITY AND RELIGIOUS PARTICIPATION, 1954-1973:
ADULT NATIONAL SAMPLES*

	1954	1973	Change
Section A: Percent Religiously Active by Tolerance Level by Year			
In the More Tolerant Group	57	47	-10
In the Less Tolerant Group	66	62	-4
Section B: Percent More Tolerant and Percent Religiously Active by Year			
Percent of the Population Who Are More Tolerant	31	55	14
Percent of the Population Who Are Religiously Active	63	54	-9
Section C: Demographic Effect (Percent Religiously Active by Year Removing Polarization and Period Effects)			
Percent Religiously Active	63	61	-2
Section D: Polarization and Period Effects (Percent Religiously Active by Year Removing Demographic Effect)			
Percent Religiously Active	63	59	-4

*Reported in Nunn, Crockett, and Williams (1978). Tolerance of noncon-
formity is measured by an index of Stouffer items, divided into three
categories: more tolerant, in-between, and less tolerant. We have combined the in-between and less tolerant categories here. Religious participation is measured by church attendance; those who attended in the
past month were classified as religiously active. The percentages in
Section A, which formed the basis for the standardizations in Sections
C and D, were reconstructed from Nunn, Crockett, and Williams (1978:
51, 127, 130).

tolerant" than among the "more tolerant." This would be expected,
based on previous findings regarding the relationship of values to
religious participation. Section A also indicates that the percentage
of religiously actives declined from 1954 to 1973 for both the "more
tolerant" and "less tolerant" (a period effect), but that the decrease
was more than double among the "more tolerant" (evidence of
differentiation). Section B of the table shows that the "more
tolerant" proportion of the population increased significantly over
the nineteen years, suggesting that demographic change might also
have contributed to the overall decline in religious participation
measured in these two surveys.

If one assumes tolerance of nonconformity to be a valid value indicator, the Nunn, Crockett, and Williams data suggests that both differentiation and demographic effects are involved in the relationship of value change to religious change since the mid-1950s. Can one estimate the relative contribution of each? Using a standardization procedure, the relative effects are estimated in Sections C and D of Table 5.1. They show that (1) other things remaining equal, the increase in tolerance from 1954 to 1973 (the demographic effect associated with value change) would have resulted in the percentage of religiously actives declining by two percentage points; and (2) that if there would have been no change in the relative sizes of the "more tolerant" and "less tolerant" segments of the population (if only differentiation and period effects were operating), religious participation would have declined by four percentage points.

It has already been noted that the five SRC surveys focused on in this chapter contain no value measure appropriate to a more rigorous test of the value theory than that provided by the Nunn, Crockett, and Williams surveys. The SRC surveys do, however, contain a measure of political party affiliation that allows one to test a theory of religious change suggested by some to be related to the value theory. This theory is touched on in Hoge's discussion of religious participation and national contextual factors (chapter 4) but more formally proposed by Currie, Gilbert, and Horsley (1977:108-10). Using their terminology, it shall be referred to as the political mobilization theory. The theory asserts that whatever mobilizes one to political party affiliation will concomitantly lead one to affiliation with religious institutions. Given that the trend in American political party affiliation over the past twenty-five years shows a curvilinear pattern somewhat similar to that of religious participation (Nie et al., 1976; Converse, 1976), the theory appears worthy of serious consideration.

There has been demographic change associated with a number of other variables shown in past research to be related to religious participation. However, rather than this change matching the curvilinear trend in religious participation, it has been linear. The educational attainment of both the population as a whole and white Protestants, for example, has steadily increased since the 1950s (see Appendix). Similarly, there has been a steady increase in the proportion of the population living in the West, although this increase is reflected in our data for white Protestants only from 1956 to 1960 (see Appendix).

Because of the linear nature of these demographic changes, they cannot be expected to account for both the rise and the fall pattern in religious participation over the past quarter century. This does not necessarily mean that they contributed nothing to this change. The increasing educational attainment of the population, for example, might have exerted an inflationary force on rates of religious participation over the entire period, an inflationary force hidden by more powerful deflating effects since the mid-1960s.

MEASURES AND METHODS

Trend analyses of national public opinion surveys are commonly plagued by inconsistencies in the way data pertaining to the same variable is gathered over the spectrum of surveys in the time series. Slight differences in question wordings or response codings are especially common. This study is no exception. In fact, some adjustment of items to achieve compatibility is required for every variable in our study except sex and religious participation. The latter is measured by: Would you say you go to church regularly, often, seldom, or never?[8] For purposes of our analysis, I have dichotomized this range of responses as "regular" and "less than regular."

In regard to education, age, religious preference, marital status, region, and political party affiliation, the adjustments required to achieve compatibility across survey measures involve little more than collapsing response categories until a desirable set of least common denominators is found. For purposes of analysis the following categories are used. Educational attainment is coded "less than high school graduate," "high school graduate," and "more than high school." Age is coded "21 to 30 years old," "31 to 55," and "over 55." Marital status is coded "married, currently living with spouse" and "other." Political party affiliation is coded "party member" and "not a party member."

The greatest leap of faith in this study concerning the compatibility of indicators over time involves the indicator of the presence or absence of school-age children in the household. The 1952, 1964, and 1968 surveys contain a question of direct relevance: Do you have any children in school? The 1956 and 1960 surveys, unfortunately, do not ask such a question. Here a more approximate measure has been constructed from information concerning the number and ages of one's children under 18.[9]

The composite family life cycle variable consists of the following seven categories: (1) 21 to 30 years old and not married; (2) 21 to 30, married, but with no school-age children present in the household;

(3) 21 to 30 and married with school-age children present in the household; (4) 31 to 55 and not married; (5) 31 to 55 and married with children of school age present in the household; (6) 31 to 55 and married but with no children of school age present in the household; and (7) over 55 years old.[10]

The purpose of my analysis is (1) to disentangle the demographic, massification/differentiation, and period effects on religious participation associated with each explanatory variable; and (2) to specify their relative magnitude. Unfortunately, when two or more of these effects are present at the same time (which, as we shall see, is most of the time), such a decomposition becomes complex. To simplify matters I shall not initially differentiate between massification/differentiation and period effects, thereby having only to be concerned with the measurement of (1) the effect of demographic change, (2) the joint effect of massification/polarization and period change (hereafter referred to as the "joint period effect"), and (3) the interaction of (1) and (2).

To estimate these three effects a statistical method called test factor standardization is used (for a full description of this procedure see Rosenberg, 1961). The method allows one to remove either the demographic effect (statistically simulating no demographic change) or the joint period effect (statistically eliminating all effects except the demographic effect) on religious participation associated with any given explanatory variable between two points in time.[11] The removal of either of these two effects allows the measurement of the impact of the other. Frequently, the sum of these two effects will not total the actual measured change. The difference is due to the interaction of the two effects and is an indicator of the presence of massification/differentiation.

FINDINGS

Figure 5.2 plots the trend in regular church attendance for white Protestants as measured in the five SRC surveys. It shows the expected pattern of gradually increasing attendance from the early 50s through the early 60s, followed by a rather distinct decline in the late 60s. Even though the change in the trend is not particularly great, just over five percentage points in each direction, it is statistically and substantively significant (5 percent of adult white Protestants equals approximately 3.5 million persons).

How much of this change can we attribute to the various effects associated with age, the presence of school-age children, stage in

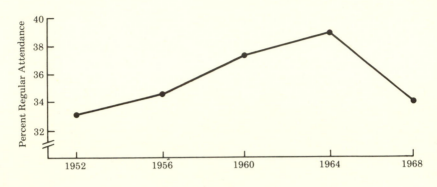

FIGURE 5.2
WHITE PROTESTANT CHURCH ATTENDANCE,
1952-1968

TABLE 5.2

DECOMPOSITION OF RELIGIOUS PARTICIPATION CHANGE
INTO EFFECTS ASSOCIATED WITH AGE

	Percentage Point Change in Regular Church Attendance			
	1952–1956	1956–1960	1960–1964	1964–1968
Actual Change	1.6	2.9	2.1	−5.5
Demographic Effect	0.0	0.0	−0.1	−0.4
Joint-Period Effect	1.6	2.8	2.0	−5.0
Interaction Effect	0.0	0.1	0.2	−0.1

the family life cycle, political party membership, region of residence, and education? The first three of these variables all relate to the family life cycle theory of religious change.

As that theory has been proposed, the demographic changes associated with each should contribute significantly to both the increase in religious participation experienced in the early 1950s through the early 60s and to the declines that followed. Tables 5.2, 5.3, and 5.4 show that the predicted demographic effect is weak, if present at all, and sometimes is opposite of what the theory predicts.

Table 5.2 deals specifically with age effects. It shows no demographic effect for the periods 1952-56 and 1956-60; an extremely weak negative effect (equal to a change in the religious participation of one tenth of one percentage point) from 1960-64; and an only slightly greater effect from 1964 to 1968. Almost all the actual change is due to the joint period effect, with a slight interaction effect present from 1960 to 1964.

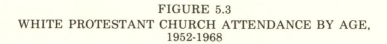

FIGURE 5.3
WHITE PROTESTANT CHURCH ATTENDANCE BY AGE,
1952-1968

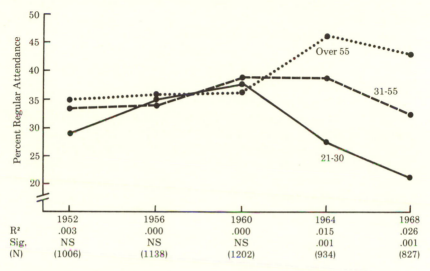

	1952	1956	1960	1964	1968
R²	.003	.000	.000	.015	.026
Sig.	NS	NS	NS	.001	.001
(N)	(1006)	(1138)	(1202)	(934)	(827)

Why have changes in the age structure had such a slight impact on changes in religious participation? Figure 5.3 suggests the reason. From 1952 to 1960 the relationship between age and religious participation is negligible. In 1964 and 1968 the relationship is statistically significant but is hardly of substantive significance (explaining less than 3 percent of the variance in white Protestant attendance). The differences in religious participation between various age groups are, generally speaking, not large enough to cause significant changes in religious participation given the level of demographic changes in the age structure of the population.

Figure 5.3 provides grist for another comment concerning the child-rearing theory of religious participation as specified in terms of age. The theory assumes a certain constant relationship between age and religious participation, namely, that religious participation is relatively low in young adulthood, increases in the middling or parenting years, then declines slightly in the postparenting years. The SRC data seriously challenges this assumption. Figure 5.3 shows that the relationship varies across time in both magnitude and direction, with religious participation usually, but not always, highest in the postparenting years. Figure 5.3 also indicates (1) that, overall, changes in religious participation have been greatest among young adults; (2) that differences in religious participation between age groups clearly polarized from 1960 to 1964, with the level of participation increasing over this period for postparenting-age adults but decreasing for young adults; and (3) that the decline in religious participation from 1964 to 1968 was similar across all age groups.

The impact on religious participation associated with the presence of school-age children is presented in Table 5.3. A slight demographic effect (equal to three tenths of one percentage point) in the expected direction is found for 1952-56 and 1956-60. A considerably larger effect (in fact, the largest pure demographic effect present in this analysis, equaling a change in religious participation of 1.1 percentage points) is found for 1960-64. It is, however, a negative effect, meaning that although religious participation increased from 1960 to 1964, the demographic change in the percentage of parenting adults was actually acting to reduce it. The percentage of parenting adults declined during this period of increasing religious participation. To put it another way,

TABLE 5.3

DECOMPOSITION OF RELIGIOUS PARTICIPATION CHANGE INTO EFFECTS
ASSOCIATED WITH THE PRESENCE OF SCHOOL-AGE CHILDREN

	Percentage Point Change in Regular Church Attendance			
	1952–1956	1956–1960	1960–1964	1964–1968
Actual Change	1.2	3.1	1.2	-4.7
Demographic Effect	0.3	0.3	-1.1	0.0
Joint-Period Effect	1.0	2.4	1.3	-4.7
Interaction Effect	-0.1	0.4	1.0	0.0

FIGURE 5.4
WHITE PROTESTANT CHURCH ATTENDANCE BY PRESENCE
OF SCHOOL-AGE CHILDREN, 1952-1968

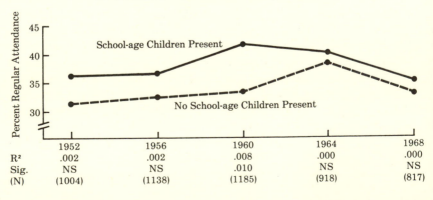

	1952	1956	1960	1964	1968
R^2	.002	.002	.008	.000	.000
Sig.	NS	NS	.010	NS	NS
(N)	(1004)	(1138)	(1185)	(918)	(817)

if the percentage of parenting adults had stayed the same over this period, the increases in religious participation would have been higher than they in fact were.

Table 5.3 also indicates a relatively large interaction effect for the 1960-64 period. This, in turn, indicates the presence of a massification or differentiation effect. The nature of this latter effect is clearly visible in Figure 5.4. From 1960 to 1964 religious participation decreased among parents of school-age children but increased sharply among those not having school-age children. This massification of religious participation rates in the 1960-64 period is preceded by a differentiation effect from 1956 to 1960. The data certainly suggests that the relationship between religious participation and the presence of school-age children is not constant over time.

Figure 5.4 also suggests why the demographic effects associated with the presence of school-age children are generally small over the entire period of our study. The relationship between presence of school-age children and religious participation, although consistently in the expected direction, reaches statistical significance only in 1960, and even then is hardly of substantive significance (R^2 = .01). In addition, Figure 5.4 indicates that the declines in religious participation characteristic of the 1964-68 period are similar for both parents and nonparents.

Table 5.4 summarizes the effects on religious participation associated with our composite family life cycle variable. Although the specific magnitude and direction of the effects vary somewhat from those found for either age or presence of school-age children, the general conclusions are similar: (1) the relationship between family life cycle and religious participation is hardly of substantive significance and varies over time; (2) the pure demographic effects associated with family life cycle are small because the family life

TABLE 5.4

DECOMPOSITION OF RELIGIOUS PARTICIPATION CHANGE INTO EFFECTS
ASSOCIATED WITH STAGES IN THE FAMILY LIFE CYCLE

	Percentage Point Change in Regular Church Attendance			
	1952– 1956	1956– 1960	1960– 1964	1964– 1968
Actual Change	1.6	3.1	1.4	−5.0
Demographic Effect	−0.2	0.7	−0.3	−0.6
Joint-Period Effect	1.4	2.8	0.9	−4.2
Interaction Effect	0.4	−0.4	0.8	−0.2

136

cycle/religious participation relationship at any given point in time is small; and (3) the decrease in religious participation characteristic of the 1964-68 period is generally similar across all stages in the family life cycle.

The political party mobilization theory of changes in religious participation over the past quarter century asserts that the causes of party membership and religious affiliation are similar. This implies that party membership and religious participation should be related, and that changes in party membership should parallel changes in religious participation. Table 5.5 and Figure 5.5 present relevant data. Figure 5.5 speaks directly to the question of the relationship between party membership and religious participation. It shows that from 1952 to 1964 the relationship is in the expected direction but is extremely weak, becoming progressively weaker over time. By 1964 the relationship is no longer of statistical significance, and by 1968 there is a hint that the relationship might even have reversed itself.

Given such a weak party membership/religious participation relationship, it is not surprising, as shown in Table 5.5, that demographic changes in party membership have little effect on religious participation.

As already noted, the five SRC surveys show a change in the West/non-West distribution of white Protestants only from 1956 to 1960. Accordingly, one would expect to find a regionally associated demographic effect on religious participation only for this period. Table 5.6 confirms this expectation. Between 1956 and

FIGURE 5.5

WHITE PROTESTANT CHURCH ATTENDANCE BY PARTY MEMBERSHIP OR NONPARTY MEMBERSHIP, 1952-1968

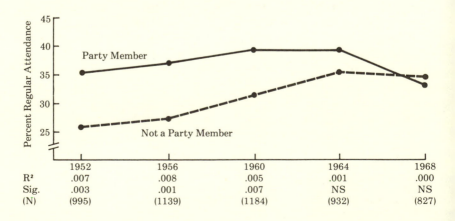

	1952	1956	1960	1964	1968
R²	.007	.008	.005	.001	.000
Sig.	.003	.001	.007	NS	NS
(N)	(995)	(1139)	(1184)	(932)	(827)

TABLE 5.5

DECOMPOSITION OF RELIGIOUS PARTICIPATION CHANGE INTO EFFECTS
ASSOCIATED WITH POLITICAL PARTY MEMBERSHIP

	Percentage Point Change in Regular Church Attendance			
	1952–1956	1956–1960	1960–1964	1964–1968
Actual Change	1.4	3.1	1.0	-4.6
Demographic Effect	-0.2	0.2	0.1	-0.3
Joint-Period Effect	1.6	2.9	1.0	-4.7
Interaction Effect	0.0	0.0	-0.2	0.4

TABLE 5.6

DECOMPOSITION OF RELIGIOUS PARTICIPATION CHANGE INTO EFFECTS
ASSOCIATED WITH REGION OF RESIDENCE

	Percentage Point Change in Regular Church Attendance			
	1952–1956	1956–1960	1960–1964	1964–1968
Actual Change	1.2	2.9	1.5	-4.9
Demographic Effect	0.0	-0.6	0.0	0.1
Joint-Period Effect	1.3	3.3	1.5	-5.0
Interaction Effect	-0.1	0.2	0.0	0.0

1960 the increased proportion of white Protestants living in the West resulted in about a half percentage point decrease in the overall percentage of regular church attendance among white Protestants. In all other periods the demographic effects associated with regional distribution are negligible.

Not only are these negligible demographic effects found, but, as shown in Figure 5.6, the relationship between region and religious participation itself varies in magnitude and is generally weak.

Past research has shown education to be positively related to religious participation. In a situation characterized by rising educational attainment, therefore, one would expect an associated positive demographic effect on religious participation. The entire period of our study is characterized by rising educational attainment, and, as indicated in Table 5.7, this rising educational attainment has exerted an almost constant inflationary force on the overall rate of religious participation. This upward pressure is equal to a change in the overall proportion of white Protestant regular church attenders of one half of one percent every four years. Such a change is certainly not much to speak of, but it is generally

138

FIGURE 5.6

WHITE PROTESTANT CHURCH ATTENDANCE BY REGION,
1952-1968

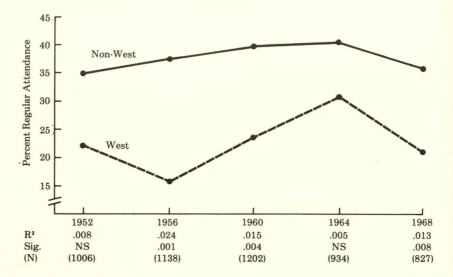

	1952	1956	1960	1964	1968
R²	.008	.024	.015	.005	.013
Sig.	NS	.001	.004	NS	.008
(N)	(1006)	(1138)	(1202)	(934)	(827)

constant over the sixteen-year period and therefore is the only demographic effect in the study that could possibly be trusted for future predictions.

The reason for the weakness of the demographic effect associated with educational attainment is evident in Figure 5.7. As is the case for all the relationships considered thus far, the relationship between education and religious participation is not great, reaching a maximum R^2 = .04 in 1960.

Also evident in Figure 5.7—as well as indicated by the presence of interaction effects in Table 5.7—is the fact that the education/religious participation relationship varies somewhat over time. This means that the constant demographic effect detected in Table 5.7 is really an oversimplification of counteracting massification and differentiation effects. In particular we find that (1) both the most extreme increases and the most extreme decreases in religious participation are located among those with more than a high school education; (2) from 1956 to 1960 those who were less than high school graduates declined in religious participation while everyone else increased, but from 1960-64 just the reverse occurred—those who were less than high school graduates increased in religious participation while everyone else decreased; and (3) although all three educational groups showed declines in participation from 1964-68, the change was considerably less among those who were less than high school graduates.

DISCUSSION

The primary concern of this chapter has been to test several demographic theories of religious change. The conclusions are generally negative. Of those demographic changes followed across the five SRC surveys—age, presence of school-age children, stage in the family life cycle, region, education, and political party membership—all have, at best, weak and/or unpredictable effects

TABLE 5.7

DECOMPOSITION OF RELIGIOUS PARTICIPATION CHANGE INTO EFFECTS
ASSOCIATED WITH EDUCATION

| | Percentage Point Change in Regular Church Attendance | | | |
	1952–1956	1956–1960	1960–1964	1964–1968
Actual Change	1.1	2.9	1.4	-4.7
Demographic Effect	0.6	0.4	0.4	0.6
Joint-Period Effect	0.2	2.2	1.3	-5.0
Interaction Effect	0.3	0.3	-0.3	0.3

FIGURE 5.7
WHITE PROTESTANT CHURCH ATTENDANCE
BY EDUCATION, 1952-1968

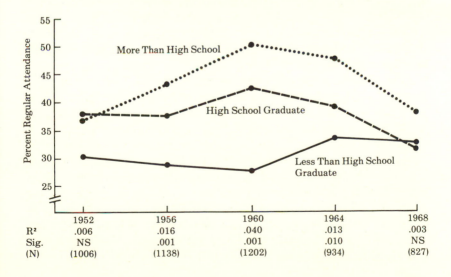

	1952	1956	1960	1964	1968
R²	.006	.016	.040	.013	.003
Sig.	NS	.001	.001	.010	NS
(N)	(1006)	(1138)	(1202)	(934)	(827)

on changes in religious participation. And although the more limited Nunn, Crockett, and Williams data on value change precludes a definitive response, the data does suggest that the effects of value change on changes in religious participation will not be much greater nor more predictable than those we have been able to study in more depth.

Of particular importance is the finding that in all cases the relationship between the explanatory variable and religious participation varies over time, often in direction as well as magnitude. Not being able to assume that this relationship is constant robs a demographic theory of its predictive potential. For example, the U.S. Bureau of the Census can provide very reliable projections of the age structure of the population through at least the year 2000 (see, for example, Current Population Reports, Series P-25, No. 704, July 1977). If there were clear evidence that the age/religious participation relationship had remained constant over time in the past, then one could use this relationship in conjunction with future age structure projections to predict with some confidence future changes in the overall rate of religious participation. In the absence of a constant age/religious participation relationship, such predictions are meaningless.

In addition to being unpredictable because of massification/differentiation effects, the demographic effects found in the five SRC surveys, with one exception, account for relatively little of the actual observed change in religious participation. They can hardly be seen as major causes of religious change. The exception is the 1952-56 increase in educational attainment. The associated pure demographic effect accounts for just over 50 percent of the actual change in religious participation over this four-year period, and the demographic effect coupled with the massification effect accounts for just over 80 percent of the actual change.

There are two reasons for the generally limited explanatory power of the demographic changes we have investigated. First, although the relationships of the explanatory variables to religious participation varied over time, in no instance were they of substantive significance (using the criterion of R^2 greater than .05 as our indicator of substantive significance). Second, in most instances the actual demographic change was not large enough to effect significant changes in religious participation. The West/non-West distribution of regional residence is a good case in point.

The general ineffectiveness of demographic change to account for the observed change in religious participation raises for us the poignant question posed by Davis (1975b:98) in regard to the inability of demographic change to explain changes in either racial attitudes or attitudes toward civil liberties.

> How can we account for social change in attitudes and opinions (and behavior) when they are changing faster than the variables we introduced to explain them? The invocation of "secular trends," "zeitgeists," and similar specters will not fill the gap for long.

That heretofore unknown and/or unmeasured factors have been the dominant cause of religious change over the period of this study is reflected in the size of joint-period effects obtained in the analysis. The joint-period effect, it will be remembered, is that portion of the change in religious participation contributed by massification/differentiation effects and otherwise unspecified period change. Unfortunately, both of the latter are really descriptions of change rather than specifications of the factors responsible for the change. For example, the presence of a massification or differentiation effect says only that whatever is causing change in religious participation is affecting the various subgroups defined by the explanatory variable in different ways. It does not identify the "whatever." Similarly, the presence of what we have called period effects says only that whatever is causing change in religious participation is affecting the various subgroups defined by the explanatory variable in the same ways. It does not say what the "whatever" is.

The identification of massification/differentiation and period effects, however, can provide some clues as to what the "whatever" might be and where to look for it.

The trends in religious participation for each subgroup considered in the SRC surveys, except for family life cycle, are presented in Figures 5.3 to 5.7. The one pattern of change common to all these trends is their downward slope from 1964 to 1968. It appears that whatever was responsible for the overall declines in religious participation during this period was rather pervasive in its effect, touching all segments of the population.

Nevertheless, not all segments were affected to the same extent. The declines experienced by those who were less than high school graduates and by nonparty members are almost negligible. On the other extreme, the percentage of regular church attenders among those with more than a high school education and those living in the West dropped ten points, and among those 21 to 30 years old and those who were high school graduates dropped 8 points. What is more, of these four subgroups all but those living in the West also experienced significant declines in religious participation from 1960 to 1964.

The data also indicates that the increases in religious participation from 1952 to 1960 were greatest among those 21 to 30 years old and those with more than a high school education. The distinctive pattern of these two trends supports previous research that has occasioned Hoge (1974:165) to conclude that either (1) the causes of religious change should be sought in factors especially affecting the young and the college educated or (2) the factors producing religious change touch all groups equally but that the young and college educated are in some way freer to respond, or quicker to respond, than others.

One further point in this regard should be noted. Although religious participation declined among the college educated, among high school graduates, and among young adults from 1960 to 1964, the overall change for this period was positive. This net increase was due to sharp increases among those over 55 and among those who had not graduated from high school. If, therefore, one seeks to understand the trend in religious participation during the early 1960s in terms of specific historical events or broad-based cultural change, one would do well to look to those things that could simultaneously cause the elderly and less educated to increase their participation, and the young and highly educated to decrease their participation.[12]

CONCLUSIONS

In summary, the demographic changes associated with age, presence of school-age children, stage in the family life cycle, education, region, and political party membership over the last quarter century have had little effect on the overall level of Protestant religious participation. They have had little effect for any or all of three reasons: (1) the demographic change is minimal; (2) the relationship between religious participation and the explanatory variable is minimal to negligible; and/or (3) the relationship between religious participation and the explanatory variable changes unpredictably over time. This is not to say that demographic effects associated with these variables are altogether absent in the SRC data. It is only to say that they are extremely weak and generally unpredictable. That the same might be true for demographic changes associated with value change is suggested by the Nunn, Crockett, and Williams data, but more study of this area is needed.

The only consistent demographic effect on religious participation that I have found is the increasing educational attainment of the population. But even this effect is small (equal to an increase of about one half of one percentage point in regular church attendance every four years) and is complicated by a number of significant massification and differentiation effects. It appears that all future projections of religious change based on the theories I have investigated, including value theories, are highly tenuous.

An investigation of the nondemographic effects present in the SRC data suggests two things in particular: (1) that the change in religious participation of the late 1960s was pervasive, touching all segments of the population; and (2) because young adults and the college educated show the most extreme changes in religious participation, it appears that new efforts to identify the causes of religious change should begin with an investigation of those forces most affecting these groups.

It must be noted, however, that the focus of this study is the overall national trend for Protestants. Whether demographic theories of change have more efficacy for understanding participation changes in specific denominations or local congregations is beyond the scope of the data used in this chapter. These questions are addressed more directly in the following chapters.

CHAPTER 6

Comparison of Trends in Ten Denominations 1950-75[1]

Ruth T. Doyle
and
Sheila M. Kelly

Future church leaders may look back to the third quarter of this century as a dramatic turning point in U.S. church history. The 1950s saw substantial growth in membership and church school enrollment within the major denominations, and throughout the period many church members became involved in social issues as an expression of their religious values. And yet, during the 1960s, some unfavorable, perplexing trends set in. Sunday-morning congregations began to shrink, and church school enrollments dropped sharply. Some denominations experienced a loss of membership for the first time in decades.

Concern about such developments and the factors associated with them has led several denominations to compile and analyze information on church school membership and other relevant trends. This chapter brings together results of a number of these denominational studies, as well as statistics newly compiled for cross-denominational comparisons. In all, comparable data for nine major U.S. and one Canadian denomination has been assembled through the use of denominational yearbooks and research reports.[2]

This chapter examines trends in church membership, baptisms, and church school enrollment for the ten denominations for the period 1950 through 1975. Interrelationships among these three indicators of denominational change are analyzed, and changes in denominational trends are compared with population trends. This is the first time that data on the Roman Catholic Church and the Southern Baptist Convention has been available for comparison with other denominations. Moreover, since most of the data is based on special reports prepared by denominational research offices, figures have been subject to scrutiny and adjustments have been made to correct inaccuracies. Figures are therefore more accurate than those based solely on yearbooks.

The ten denominations discussed in this chapter include nine of the ten largest church bodies in the United States (based on membership figures in the *1977 Yearbook of American and Canadian Churches*).[3] For comparative purposes the United Church of Canada, the largest Protestant denomination in Canada, has been added as the tenth denomination. The ten, in order of size, are as follows: the Roman Catholic Church (RC), the Southern Baptist Convention (SBC), the United Methodist Church (UMC), the United Presbyterian Church in the United States of America (UPC), the Episcopal Church (EC), the Lutheran Church in America (LCA), the Lutheran Church-Missouri Synod (LCMS), the American Lutheran Church (ALC), the United Church of Christ (UCC), and the United Church of Canada (UCN).

TRENDS IN CHURCH MEMBERSHIP

In studying trends in membership, one must look carefully for changes in definition of membership during the time period at issue. In checking this it was found that while the definition of membership differs from one denomination to another, *within* each denomination it has remained fairly constant over time. The reported trends are therefore not simply an artifact of changing definitions.

Some churches record both baptized and communicant membership. The former is generally a broader category of membership, while the latter denotes a more active participation. Six of the denominations considered report only one membership category: Roman Catholics and Southern Baptists report only baptized membership; United Methodists, United Presbyterians, United Church of Christ, and United Church of Canada report only communicant membership. The Episcopal Church and the three Lutheran denominations report both baptized and communicant membership (communicants generally represent two thirds of the baptized body). For this chapter we have used the membership statistic emphasized in each denomination's reports and the one most commonly utilized (for Episcopalians, communicants; for the Lutherans, baptized). It should be noted that in any case, the categories correlate highly with each other over time.

In chapter 1 (Figures 1.2, 1.3, 1.4) the basic membership trends are presented. Table 6.1 summarizes the trends. From 1950 to 1975 the number of persons affiliated with nine of the ten denominations increased substantially. The growth of four bodies—the Roman Catholic Church, the Southern Baptist Convention, the Lutheran Church-Missouri Synod, and the American Lutheran Church—exceeded the rate of growth of the U.S. population. The only denomination that declined is the United Church of Christ, due largely to the union of the Congregational Christian Churches and the Evangelical and Reformed Church in 1957, which created the United Church of Christ. Eighteen percent of the Congregational Christian Churches did not join the new denomination.[4]

All ten denominations experienced net membership increases from 1950 to 1965, but patterns are rather different in the 1965-75

TABLE 6.1

MEMBERSHIP CHANGE 1950 TO 1975

Denomination*	Percent Change					
	1950-55	1955-60	1960-65	1965-70	1970-75	1950-75
RC	18.2	19.3	10.5	4.0	2.1	65.5
SBC	19.7	14.8	10.7	8.0	9.5	79.9
UMC	4.3	5.8	3.3	-3.2	-7.1	2.6
UPC	14.3	20.5	3.2	-6.4	-13.9	14.5
EC	12.1	13.5	7.2	-2.7	-6.1	24.5
LCA	15.0	10.8	2.9	-1.1	-7.5	19.9
LCMS	20.1	18.9	12.9	3.2	-4.0	59.9
ALC	20.6	17.6	9.5	-3.0	-5.0	43.2
UCC	8.1	5.8	-7.8	-5.4	-7.2	-7.4
8 U.S. PROT	12.5	11.9	5.9	0.3	-2.2	30.7
UCN	11.2	11.4	4.6	-2.9	-7.9	15.9
U.S. POPULATION[†]	8.9	8.9	7.5	5.5	4.3	40.3

*All tables in this chapter arrange denominations by size of membership from the largest to the smallest. To correct membership data for mergers, the figures for groups which merged are added together for prior years. This correction was not done for the 1958 United Presbyterian merger due to its small effect on trends.
†U.S. population data in all tables in this chapter is from Statistical Abstracts of the United States, 1977 and earlier.

decade. Seven of the ten denominations had substantial membership losses averaging 10 percent, with the United Presbyterian
Church showing the largest decrease, over 19 percent. The Roman
Catholic Church and the Southern Baptist Convention continued
to grow in this decade, but the growth pattern changes. The rates of
increase for the Roman Catholic Church and the Southern Baptist
Convention for 1965-70 and 1970-75 are substantially lower than
those of earlier periods. Within the Lutheran Church-Missouri
Synod there was some increase from 1965-70, but a decline in the
first half of the 1970s and an overall small decline of less than one
percent between 1965 and 1975.

Analysis of year-by-year membership trends indicates that all
ten denominations have experienced decelerated growth or
declines in the last few years. Even the Southern Baptist
Convention's growth has been decelerating, with annual gains of
less than 2 percent each year since 1973.

Regional Membership

To examine variation in church membership trends for the nine
U.S. denominations, membership figures were assembled for the
nine U.S. census regions by five-year intervals, from 1950 to 1975
(Southern Baptist data commences with 1962).[5] Two tables on
regional membership are presented here.

The membership per thousand population for every five years is
shown in Table 6.2. It indicates the largest Roman Catholic
representation is in both the New England and Middle Atlantic
census regions, while the smallest is in the South Atlantic and the
East South Central regions. Southern Baptist concentration is in the
East and West South Central and the South Atlantic states, as is the
United Methodist. United Church of Christ concentration and the
largest Episcopal representation are in New England. The
American Lutheran Church and the Lutheran Church-Missouri
Synod are strongest in West North Central. The United Presbyterians and the Lutheran Church in America both have their greatest
strength in the Mid-Atlantic and the West North Central regions.
Note that a denomination may have its greatest concentration in a
region but may not be the most predominant church there; for
example, the Episcopal Church in New England.

Over the twenty-five-year period the relative regional strength of
each denomination has not shifted. A denomination's greatest
regional concentration in 1975 is the same as it was in 1950. This
pattern holds even for the Episcopal and the United Methodist

TABLE 6.2

MEMBERSHIP PER 1,000 POPULATION 1950-1975 BY U.S. CENSUS REGION

Year	RC	SBC*	UMC	UPC	EC	LCA	LCMS	ALC	UCC	U.S. Pop. (in 000's)
New England										
1950	400	NA	19	3	24	7	3	0	39	9,314
1955	458	NA	18	3	23	7	2	0	40	9,619
1960	465	0	16	3	24	7	3	0	40	10,532
1965	465	0	15	3	23	7	3	0	37	11,329
1970	468	0	13	2	21	6	3	0	33	11,883
1975	465	1	11	2	18	6	3	0	28	12,187
Mid-Atlantic										
1950	285	NA	47	27	17	36	5	2	12	30,164
1955	307	NA	46	28	16	37	5	2	12	32,244
1960	345	0	45	31	16	36	5	2	11	34,270
1965	358	0	43	29	15	33	6	2	11	36,122
1970	356	1	39	26	14	30	5	2	10	37,274
1975	347	1	37	22	12	28	5	2	10	37,269
East North Central										
1950	228	NA	66	19	7	17	24	18	18	30,399
1955	225	NA	61	21	7	18	25	19	17	33,604
1960	245	7	58	23	7	19	27	20	17	36,291
1965	256	8	58	22	7	19	28	21	16	38,406
1970	256	9	51	20	7	17	28	20	15	40,313
1975	255	11	45	17	6	16	27	19	14	40,945
West North Central										
1950	157	NA	85	24	7	25	36	55	16	14,061
1955	166	NA	82	25	7	29	39	62	17	14,843
1960	186	33	82	28	8	31	42	65	17	15,424
1965	198	34	77	28	8	32	45	68	16	15,819
1970	198	35	72	25	7	31	45	65	15	16,360
1975	194	38	64	21	7	31	44	62	14	16,690
South Atlantic										
1950	40	NA	96	6	12	12	2	1	5	21,182
1955	49	NA	91	6	12	12	2	2	5	23,447
1960	68	135	89	6	13	12	3	2	5	26,091
1965	72	128	83	6	14	12	4	2	4	28,743
1970	77	127	78	6	14	12	4	2	4	30,805
1975	81	126	70	5	13	11	4	2	4	33,658
East South Central										
1950	35	NA	102	3	5	1	1	0	2	11,477
1955	41	NA	102	3	5	2	1	0	2	11,668
1960	45	219	100	4	6	2	1	0	2	12,073
1965	50	218	97	4	6	2	2	0	2	12,627
1970	47	229	93	4	6	2	2	0	1	12,839
1975	47	235	84	3	6	2	2	0	1	13,515
West South Central										
1950	151	NA	80	6	7	1	5	2	1	14,538
1955	173	NA	79	6	8	2	6	2	2	15,694
1960	185	171	78	6	10	2	7	2	2	17,010
1965	189	167	77	6	11	2	8	2	2	18,209
1970	177	168	70	5	11	2	8	2	1	19,388
1975	174	172	63	5	10	2	8	2	1	20,867
Mountain										
1950	172	NA	36	17	9	4	8	8	7	5,075
1955	174	NA	36	19	9	6	10	10	7	5,931
1960	192	24	36	22	10	7	11	12	7	6,916
1965	193	25	34	20	10	8	12	13	7	7,740
1970	173	26	29	16	9	8	13	13	6	8,348
1975	162	28	22	13	7	7	12	11	5	9,625
Pacific										
1950	175	NA	26	15	9	5	7	6	7	15,115
1955	177	NA	25	18	9	6	8	9	7	17,253
1960	197	10	26	20	10	7	9	10	7	21,368
1965	197	11	24	18	11	7	10	12	6	24,464
1970	194	12	20	16	10	6	10	11	5	26,600
1975	196	13	18	12	8	6	9	9	4	28,274

*1950, 1955, and 1960 figures for the Southern Baptist Convention are not available. For 1960 in this table, 1962 figures, the earliest available, are used.

churches, which are somewhat less geographically concentrated than other denominations.

Table 6.2 also shows that the proportion of the population belonging to these denominations varies considerably from one region to another. Church membership in these nine denominations constitutes more than half the population of New England, while it comprises less than one third the population of both the Mountain and Pacific states.

The regions of the United States experienced varying rates of growth over the twenty-five-year period. Percent changes in church membership are compared with regional population changes in Table 6.3 to show the relationship between population growth and membership change. The table suggests that to some extent regional population growth parallels membership growth, with some exceptions. In general, the churches grew most where the population increased most. Church growth, however, is not directly proportionate to population change and the relationship between the two is not sufficient in itself to explain membership trends for the various denominations.

Of the two denominations that have shown continued increases, the Southern Baptists report increases in every census region for every time period. Moreover, the reported increases are greater than population increases in all but the South Atlantic. For the Roman Catholics there were only slight membership losses in 1965-70 in the Mountain and the South Central regions and in 1970-75 in the Mid-Atlantic. Other denominations show more regional declines in recent years. The United Methodists, the American Lutherans, and the United Church of Christ show declines in every region in 1970-75, while the Episcopal Church shows declines in all but the South Atlantic and the United Presbyterian in all but the East South Central. The Lutheran Church in America and the Lutheran Church-Missouri Synod show recent increases in the South Atlantic, the South Central, and the Mountain states. (See Appendix for detailed five-year figures.)

TRENDS IN BAPTISMS

New church members come through baptisms, professions of faith, and transfers from other churches. The major source of new members is through baptism. Baptismal records are available for all the denominations except the United Church of Christ.

Figure 6.1 and Table 6.4 depict the trends (year-by-year data is in the Appendix). With the exception of the Southern Baptists,

TABLE 6.3

PERCENT MEMBERSHIP CHANGE 1950–1975 BY U.S. CENSUS REGION

Region	Denomination Membership									Total U.S. Population
	RC	SBC*	UMC	UPC	EC	LCA	LCMS	ALC	UCC	
NE	52.2	†	-19.8	-10.2	-3.0	15.3	60.3	#	-5.6	30.9
M-At	50.4	†	-3.9	0.9	-11.7	-2.4	36.1	23.1	-2.6	23.6
ENC	50.6	68.9	-7.5	17.7	-18.3	30.9	49.1	47.8	2.2	34.7
WNC	46.9	27.5	-10.0	5.0	12.1	43.7	44.4	33.9	0.3	18.7
S-At	221.1	22.0	15.0	29.7	68.6	53.0	258.3	135.2	25.2	58.9
ESC	57.2	21.6	-2.8	36.1	34.0	63.8	202.6	#	-15.5	17.8
WSC	66.0	25.2	14.0	15.7	87.1	151.4	121.3	62.5	4.5	43.5
MTN	79.0	63.4	16.6	47.1	45.1	214.8	181.3	162.1	49.7	89.7
PAC	109.3	75.4	24.4	50.0	64.1	113.0	137.7	224.9	1.0	87.1

*Southern Baptist figures are from 1962.
†The 1962 figure is less than 10,000.
#The 1950 figure is less than 10,000.

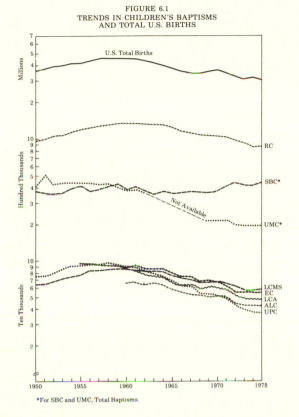

FIGURE 6.1
TRENDS IN CHILDREN'S BAPTISMS
AND TOTAL U.S. BIRTHS

*For SBC and UMC, Total Baptisms.

baptisms have declined for all the denominations in the twenty-five-year period. The declines have been especially dramatic since 1960 and, in general, are proportionately larger than the declines in church membership. The drop in baptisms commenced earlier than the drop in church membership, suggesting a relationship between the changing rate of baptisms and changes in church membership in these denominations.

Why have the baptisms declined so much? An initial clue can be seen by distinguishing between baptisms of children and adult baptisms. Half the denominations make this distinction. For the Catholics and the Episcopalians the drop in adult baptisms is proportionately much greater than the drop in child baptisms. For the Catholics, one out of eight baptisms in 1950 was an adult baptism; in 1975 one out of twelve persons baptized was an adult. For the Episcopalians the proportion was one out of four in 1950, but one out of ten in 1975. These trends point to either a decrease in evangelism efforts or lack of success of such efforts.

TABLE 6.4

CHANGE IN TOTAL BAPTISMS 1950–1975

Denomination	Percent Change					
	1950–55	1955–60	1960–65	1965–70	1970–75	1950–75
RC	22.7	7.5	−3.3	−16.1	−16.9	−11.0
SBC	10.8	−7.3	−6.4	2.0	14.4	12.2
UMC	5.9	−13.1	NA	NA	−9.3	−53.0
UPC	30.8	−14.0	−24.1	−28.4	−23.3	−53.0
EC	15.2	5.5	−13.8	−19.2	−16.5	−36.6
LCA	NA	NA	−16.8*	−13.8	−19.2	−42.1
LCMS✝	24.6	23.7	−12.3	−9.5	−14.0	−5.6
ALC	NA	NA	−9.9	−15.1	−16.2	−35.7
UCN	22.5	6.6	−25.6	−27.5	−11.3	−37.4
U.S. BIRTHS	13.0	3.8	−11.7	−0.8	−15.3	−13.0

*1961–65
✝Children only; adult figures are not available.

Child baptisms have also declined, and they have done so faster than the decline in the total number of births in the United States. Figure 6.1 depicts the changes in baptism and changes in the birthrate of the population. Quite clearly, the decline in child baptisms is not entirely due to the decline in births; indeed, it seems that the major explanation must lie elsewhere. A purely demographic analysis that merely counts births is not sufficient. While we have no hard evidence as yet, factors explaining the drop in baptisms in addition to the declining birthrate may include a high dropout rate in membership among the youth of the sixties; increasing numbers of disaffected young parents who no longer participate in church activities or present children for baptism; a movement away from infant baptism among some parents in favor of baptism as a mature decision to be made at a later age. For the Roman Catholics, differing baptismal practices of the newer ethnic groups may be contributory.

Some of the declines in baptisms are drastic. Compared with their peak years of baptisms, 1975 baptisms for the Presbyterians and the Methodists are less than one half, and for the Catholics and the three Lutheran churches they are about two thirds. This suggests that for these denominations, baptism rates are a major explanation for membership change and that trends in acquisition of new members, both children and adults, may be much more explanatory in recent years than trends in dropping out by existing members.

The Southern Baptists are the only group for whom baptisms have generally increased from 1950 to 1975. Why have the

Southern Baptists experienced this continued baptismal growth while none of the other denominations has done so? Interestingly, baptism in this denomination is seen as a normal rite of early adolescence or early adulthood. In 1975, 49 percent of the Southern Baptist baptisms were of persons between the ages of 12 and 29; less than one percent of those baptized were preschool age (see chapter 7 for a discussion).

TRENDS IN CHURCH SCHOOL ENROLLMENT

Church school enrollment from 1950 to 1975 is depicted in Figure 6.2 and is summarized in Table 6.5. (For year-by-year figures see Appendix.) As in the case of membership figures, categories included in church school statistics vary from one denomination to another, although the definitions within each denomination have

FIGURE 6.2
TRENDS IN CHURCH SCHOOL ENROLLMENT*

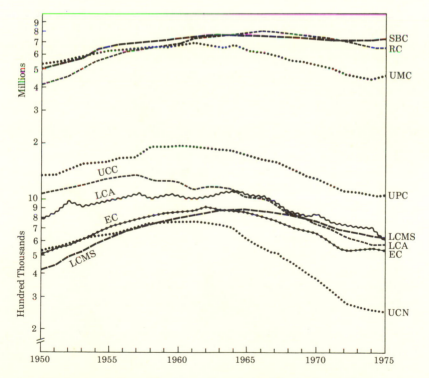

*The American Lutheran Church is not shown; its trend line closely resembles that of the Episcopal Church.

TABLE 6.5

CHURCH SCHOOL ENROLLMENT 1950-1975

Denomination	Percent Change					
	1950-55	1955-60	1960-65	1965-70	1970-75	1950-75
RC	42.1	19.5	14.3	-4.8	-14.8	57.4
SBC	32.2	11.2	3.8	-4.8	-0.1	44.9
UMC	18.4	8.0	-6.7	-16.1	-12.0	-11.8
UPC	22.9	17.7	-9.9	-24.5	-18.9	-20.3
EC	42.2	17.9	-0.3	-22.2	-18.4	6.2
LCA	24.7	1.7	6.4	-22.0	-31.9	-28.4
LCMS	48.4	27.4	12.0	-12.5	-20.8	46.7
ALC	20.0	16.3	7.9	-19.4	-22.5	-5.9
UCC	19.7	2.7	-14.5	-29.5	-24.5	-47.0
8 U.S. PROT	25.6	10.2	-1.6	-13.8	-10.1	5.5
UCN	22.6	14.9	-19.5	-39.3	-31.8	-53.1
U.S. POPULATION UNDER 18	17.9	16.3	8.1	-0.1	-4.9	40.9

remained fairly consistent over time.[6] Because of differences in reporting categories and other problems in the accuracy of yearbook information, this section concentrates on general trends indicated by the data.

Table 6.5 shows that 1950 to 1960 saw overall gains in church school enrollment. All the denominations increased during this period, and the average annual increase ranged from a high of 6.7 percent (Roman Catholics) to a low of 1.6 percent (United Church of Christ).

Detailed figures for the 1960s indicate that between 1960 and 1966 nine denominations reported their highest church school enrollment for the entire 1950-75 period. (The tenth, the United Church of Christ, reached its highest enrollment in the 1950s.) The highest total church school enrollment in the eight U.S. Protestant denominations taken together occurred in 1962. The Roman Catholic Church peaked in 1966, and the United Church of Canada in 1961.

For the period 1970-75 all ten denominations averaged annual declines. Six denominations show declines every year. The United Methodist and the United Presbyterian churches have increases in 1975. The Episcopal Church has an increase of one percent in 1974, followed by a decrease of about one percent in 1975. The Southern Baptists, after declines in 1970 and 1971, show yearly increases averaging 0.5 percent a year beginning in 1972.

Table 6.5 also shows the percentage in the U.S. population under 18 years of age for the twenty-five-year period. In the 1950s church school enrollment grew at a faster rate than the increase in the under-18 population. This pattern is reversed in later years, with church school enrollments declining at a faster rate than the under-18 population. Even the Southern Baptists report a net church school decrease from 1965 to 1975.

Table 6.6 shows figures for every five years on church school enrollment as a percentage of membership. Because the definitions of church school enrollment vary by denomination, the figures cannot be compared across denominations. Within each denomination, however, church school enrollment as a percentage of membership is lower in 1975 than in any other year. The decline in the under-18 population may be one factor, especially for the Roman Catholics, whose figures are for elementary school children only. Since the declining ratios of church school to membership are greater than population figures alone can explain, it is possible that some churches may be adopting other forms of instruction that are not reported in church school statistics, while others may simply be dropping formal education programs altogether. The declining ratios may also be caused by a rising dropout rate among young persons.

INTERRELATIONSHIPS BETWEEN MEMBERSHIP, BAPTISMS, AND CHURCH SCHOOL ENROLLMENT

Analysis of the relationship between membership and the number of baptisms revealed some significant changes over the twenty-five-year period. In general, the rate of baptisms per 100 members in 1975 is half that of 1950. The decline was slightly less

TABLE 6.6

CHURCH SCHOOL AS A PERCENTAGE OF MEMBERSHIP 1950–1975

Denomination	1950	1955	1960	1965	1970	1975
RC	14.7	17.6	17.7	18.3	16.7	14.0
SBC	71.0	78.4	75.9	71.1	62.7	57.2
UMC	54.6	62.0	63.3	57.1	49.5	46.9
UPC	57.3	61.6	60.2	52.5	42.4	39.9
EC	31.1	39.5	41.0	38.1	30.5	26.5
LCA	32.1	34.8	32.0	33.1	26.1	19.2
LCMS	24.6	30.4	32.5	32.2	27.3	22.6
ALC	32.8	32.7	32.3	31.8	26.4	21.6
UCC	55.2	61.1	56.2	52.1	38.9	31.6
8 U.S. PROT	52.5	58.6	57.7	53.7	46.1	42.4
UCN	65.4	72.1	74.4	57.3	35.8	26.5

dramatic for the Southern Baptist Convention and the Lutheran Church in America, and it was more drastic for the Presbyterians. This would indicate that the greatest potential source of new members is much smaller proportionately to the total membership in 1975, even in those denominations that are still growing. Unless these denominations reverse this trend, or begin to increase membership through other means, they may well show continued declines in membership.

The rate of baptisms per 100 church school members also shows declines between 1950 and 1975, although these declines are not so great as the baptism/membership drop. Only the United Methodists show a drop of one half; all the other U.S. denominations show smaller declines, and the United Church of Canada shows an increase.

In a study of United Methodist Church membership changes, Hartman (1976) found that church school and membership changes were strongly correlated over time and indicated that changes in church school enrollment were leading predictors of subsequent trends in membership for the United Methodist Church. Does this relationship between church school enrollment changes and membership growth or decline exist in other denominations? Table 6.7 shows Pearson's correlations between church school enrollment and membership for all ten denominations across the twenty-five years. Since Hartman had found a five-year lag between church school and membership trends, church school enrollments were correlated with the membership figures five years later. The results are in the second row of Table 6.7. All correlations in the table are positive, and most are strong. The relationship between church school enrollment and membership is present for all the denominations whether membership is increasing or decreasing. The unlagged correlations (at the top of Table 6.7) are quite strong for all the denominations except the Lutheran Church in America. The lagged correlations are very strong, even for the Lutheran Church in America. These figures suggest that church school participation supports continued involvement in the churches and that church school enrollment change is an extremely strong predictor of membership change five years later. Indeed, church school enrollment is more highly correlated with membership change than are baptisms.

We also correlated baptisms with church membership. Some correlations were positive and others were negative. The reason is not clear. The relationships between trends in baptisms, church school enrollments, and membership can be seen more clearly

TABLE 6.7

CHURCH SCHOOL AND MEMBERSHIP CORRELATIONS

	RC	SBC	UMC	UPC	EC	LCA	LCMS	ALC	UCC	UCN
Correlation of Church School Enrollment with Membership in Same Year	.87	.76	.59	.53	.50	.29	.77	.61	.88	.67
Correlation of Church School Enrollment with Membership 5 Years Later	.99	.87	.73	.90	.99	.82	.99	.89	.74	.85

when the peak years of each are compared across denominations. This is shown in Figure 6.3. In the figure, membership peaks for the Roman Catholics and the Southern Baptists are shown as 1975, although their memberships did not, in fact, peak during the years 1950-75 but rather continued to grow.

Figure 6.3 has a kind of chronological sequence in most of the denominations. Declines in baptisms began mostly in the late fifties, with declines in adult baptisms preceding declines in child baptisms. Declines in church school enrollment began in the early and middle sixties (except for the UCC, where it began in 1957). The two denominations that had not peaked in membership as of 1975 (Roman Catholic and Southern Baptist) are not much different from the others in the peaks of church school. Roman Catholic baptism peaks are also not much different from other denominations. Only the Southern Baptist Convention shows a different baptism pattern. As noted earlier, baptism has a different function in the Southern Baptist Convention than in most mainline denominations, hence its trends could be different.

Figure 6.3 suggests that the underlying causes for the membership decline in the mainline denominations were present for some time before those declines actually set in. The declines are one part of a more general sequence of changes, a sequence that was visible (in retrospect) already in the late fifties. As noted above, one cause of the sequence is the decline in births, but this is not the sole cause.

SUMMARY

Membership, baptisms, and church school enrollment in ten major U.S. and Canadian denominations grew in the fifties and early sixties but declined thereafter. Only the Southern Baptist

158

FIGURE 6.3
PEAK YEARS FOR MEMBERSHIP, CHURCH SCHOOL
ENROLLMENT, AND BAPTISMS

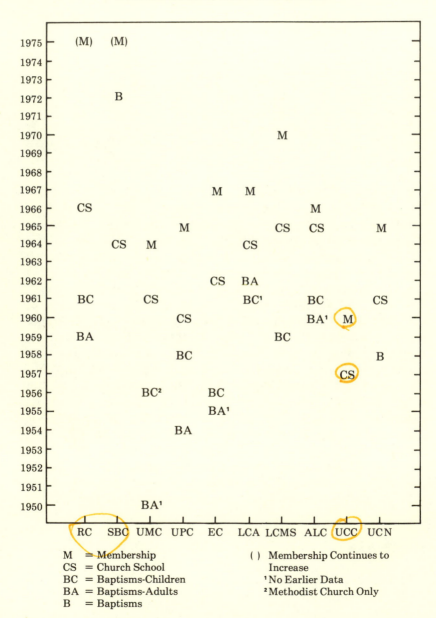

	M = Membership	( ) Membership Continues to
	CS = Church School	Increase
	BC = Baptisms-Children	¹ No Earlier Data
	BA = Baptisms-Adults	² Methodist Church Only
	B = Baptisms	

Convention and the Roman Catholic Church have continued to experience increases in membership in the 1970s.

Membership figures by U.S. census region indicate that the regional concentration of denominations has remained stable over time. In 1975 each denomination is strong in those regions where it was strong in 1950 and weak in those where it was underrepresented in the fifties. Within each denomination, however, the rate of change differs widely from region to region, and these changes are similar for a number of denominations. This finding indicates some impact of population change and regional variation in birthrates on church membership change.

Baptisms declined beginning in the late fifties and early sixties, and their dropoff has been the most extreme of any statistic. Since baptisms are a major source of new members for most denominations, this precipitous decline in baptisms is an area that warrants further investigation.

Church school enrollment declined more than membership over the twenty-five-year period, with all ten denominations experiencing losses by the late sixties. Church school enrollment is a strong predictor of church membership five years later.

Since 1950 there has been a regular sequential pattern of declines, in which baptismal changes were followed by church school enrollment changes and then by membership changes.

While there are differences between denominational patterns over the last twenty-five years (especially among Roman Catholics and Southern Baptists), the considerable similarity of trends across most of the large denominations strongly suggests that the causes of the trends are to be found in conditions external to each and common to all. Internal denominational developments, such as policy changes or theological changes, cannot explain trends in any one denomination if other denominations with different internal developments had the same overall trends. The most that internal developments can explain would appear to be the variations from denomination to denomination—such as the earlier church school enrollment peak in the United Church of Christ or the later membership peak in the Lutheran Church-Missouri Synod. But even here we cannot be sure that internal rather than contextual causes predominate.

CHAPTER 7

An Examination of the Statistical Growth of the Southern Baptist Convention

Phillip Barron Jones

The Southern Baptist Convention is unique in American Protestantism. It is the largest denomination, and it is the only large body among the older Protestant denominations to have experienced sustained growth in recent decades. Southern Baptist growth data is important for understanding the Protestant church in America, yet it is not widely known. A summary and interpretation of this data is presented in this chapter.

The visible vital signs of the Southern Baptist Convention are analyzed. Other vital signs, such as personal spiritual growth, are equally important but are not measurable. Most of the data is from the yearly handbook issues of the *Quarterly Review: A Survey of Southern Baptist Progress*, published by the Sunday School Board. This publication is based on the Uniform Church Letter, a questionnaire sent out yearly to every church in the convention. Most letters are returned and form the basis for the data reported in this chapter.

MEMBERSHIP TRENDS

Figure 7.1 charts the long-term growth of the total membership of the Southern Baptist Convention from 1900 through 1977. It also charts other Southern Baptist organizational statistics. The figure shows the relatively stable increase in membership from 1900 through 1977. There was no decline in membership during the 1960s as reported by some of the major denominations. Table 7.1 lists population and membership growth in five-year increments from 1900 to 1975. It shows that the largest percentage increases for the United States population and for the Southern Baptist Convention were in the periods 1905-10 and 1945-50. The U.S. resident population has shown a gradual decrease in its rate of growth for the past twenty years. The Southern Baptist Convention total membership has shown a corresponding slowdown for the

FIGURE 7.1
SOUTHERN BAPTIST CONVENTION STATISTICS,
1900-1976

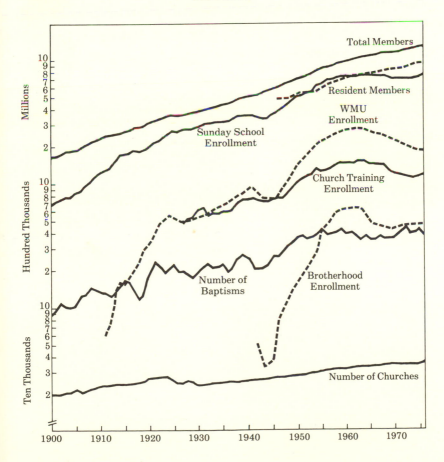

first fifteen of these twenty years and then has increased in the 1970-75 period.

REGIONAL GROWTH PATTERNS

The membership of the Southern Baptist Convention is predominantly in the South and is primarily white. When Southern Baptist membership and the white southern U.S. population are compared for each decade beginning in 1900, it is evident that Southern Baptists have grown faster than that population from which they have traditionally drawn the bulk of their membership (see Appendix).

Table 7.2 shows Southern Baptist church membership change by geographic region from 1962 through 1977. The largest numerical increase is in the South followed by the North Central, West, and Northeast regions respectively. The largest percentage increase is in the Northeast. The bulk of the Southern Baptist Convention growth is still in the South, while the rate of fastest growth is outside the South.

TABLE 7.1

GROWTH OF THE UNITED STATES POPULATION AND SOUTHERN BAPTIST MEMBERSHIP AND BAPTISMS IN FIVE-YEAR INTERVALS FROM 1900 TO 1975

Year	U.S. Resident Population*	Percent Change in Population	SBC Total Membership	Percent Change in Membership	No. of Baptisms (average of 5 preceding years)	Annual Baptism Rate (av. of 5 preceding years)
1900	76,094	9.36	1,657,996	12.86		
1905	83,822	10.15	1,899,427	14.56	103,259	5.92
1910	92,407	10.24	2,332,464	22.79	135,240	6.62
1915	100,546	8.80	2,685,552	15.13	142,588	5.77
1920	106,461	5.88	3,149,346	17.26	143,939	5.10
1925	115,829	8.79	3,649,330	15.87	217,629	6.49
1930	123,077	6.25	3,850,278	5.50	189,533	5.14
1935	127,250	3.39	4,389,417	14.00	215,782	5.31
1940	131,954	3.69	5,104,327	16.28	233,606	5.02
1945	132,481	.39	5,865,554	14.91	219,189	4.07
1950	151,235	14.15	7,079,889	20.70	311,943	4.93
1955	164,308	8.64	8,474,741	19.70	361,094	4.99
1960	179,979	9.53	9,731,591	14.83	399,553	4.45
1965	193,526	7.52	10,772,712	10.69	375,240	3.69
1970	203,810	5.31	11,629,880	7.95	370,002	3.32
1975	213,032	4.52	12,735,663	9.50	420,333	3.48

*Population in thousands.

Sources: The Quarterly Review: A Survey of Southern Baptist Progress. Historical Statistics of the United States: Colonial Times to 1970, Part I (Bureau of the Census).

TABLE 7.2

MEMBERSHIP AND PERCENT CHANGE BY REGION
OF THE COUNTRY, 1962-1977

Region	Total Members			
	1962	1967	1972	1977
United States	10,193,050	11,142,720	12,067,280	13,074,020
Northeast	6,391	15,753	28,028	42,292
South	9,060,568	9,760,912	10,474,999	11,254,064
North Central	765,594	879,147	989,940	1,103,849
West	384,319	484,400	567,967	673,823

	Percent Change in Total Members		
	1962-67	1967-72	1972-77
United States	9.32	8.30	8.34
Northeast	146.49	77.92	50.89
South	7.73	7.32	7.44
North Central	14.83	12.60	11.51
West	26.04	17.25	18.64

Source: Data from Uniform Church Letter compiled by
           Sunday School Board, Southern Baptist Convention.

RURAL AND URBAN DISTRIBUTION PATTERNS

Limited data is available that provides a classification of the Southern Baptist membership by community size (see the Appendix). In 1950, communities of over 2,500 population contained only 45 percent of the membership. In 1977 they contained about two thirds. This corresponds with the shift of the total population from rural to urban areas.

CLASSIFICATION OF MEMBERSHIP

The total Southern Baptist membership can be broken down into resident and nonresident membership. Resident members include those persons who live close enough to their church to attend; nonresident members, those persons who no longer live close enough to attend their church yet maintain their membership in it. Obviously, the resident membership would more closely approximate the active membership of the denomination. Data for resident membership is available beginning in the late 1940s and is graphed in Figure 7.1. After fluctuations in the early years, resident membership growth has paralleled that of total membership. Since 1950 nonresident membership has averaged between 27 and 28 percent of total membership.

SOURCES OF CHURCH MEMBERSHIP GAIN AND LOSS

New members are incorporated into Southern Baptist churches by two means. The first is through baptism by immersion. In order to join a Southern Baptist church new converts to Christianity must make a statement of their personal faith in Jesus Christ and then submit to the ordinance of baptism. Children are not automatically baptized when they reach a certain age. They must go through the same process as adults. Normally, very few children under 6 years of age are baptized into a church, since it is generally believed that they are not yet accountable before God for their actions. Children between the ages of 6 and 11 make up 30 percent or more of the baptisms reported each year by the churches. Youth from 12 to 17 normally account for more than 27 percent of the baptisms.

A second way in which new members are incorporated into a church is through transfer of membership. Persons who have already been baptized in a Southern Baptist church can transfer membership into another Southern Baptist church. This is called an addition by letter or by transfer of letter. Additions by letter also include those few persons from non-Southern Baptist churches whose baptisms by immersion are recognized as valid by the receiving churches. (Most persons received from non-Southern Baptist churches are baptized or "re-baptized" by immersion.) For the whole convention, additions by letter should not affect the total membership, since they should merely represent the migration of members between churches.

There is no uniform policy for maintaining church membership rolls. Members are removed due to death or transfer to another church inside or outside the denomination. Many times members move and do not join churches elsewhere. These persons may or may not be removed from church rolls. Maintenance of membership rolls is left to the discretion of the individual churches. Some churches carefully maintain their rolls while others are lax. Thus, it is difficult to make generalizations about the reliability of membership data.

Figure 7.2 graphs the number of persons received into Southern Baptist churches from non-Baptist churches and those lost to non-Baptist churches. In 1975 there was a surplus of persons

FIGURE 7.2
MEMBERS RECEIVED FROM NON-BAPTIST DENOMINATIONS AND
LOST TO NON-BAPTIST DENOMINATIONS, 1966-1977

transferring into the Southern Baptist Convention over those leaving. However, for other years there has been a net outflow. Price (1977:5-6) indicates that the majority of these gains and losses represent transfer to and from the mainline Protestant denominations (also see Hayes, 1969:19). Roughly a third of the gains and losses involve transfer between the Southern Baptist Convention and Methodist denominations.

BAPTISM TRENDS

Figure 7.1 shows the number of baptisms recorded for all Southern Baptist churches from 1900 through 1977. The numbers range from a low of 80,365 in 1900 to a high of 445,725 in 1972 (see Appendix for yearly data). Table 7.1 includes five-year averages of baptisms and baptism rates. The baptism rate per 100 members was generally between 5 and 6.5 until the 1930s, when it began dropping gradually. At the end of World War II it was about 4, and then it rose during the late 1940s and early 1950s. Since the middle 1950s it has been gradually declining. In 1977 the baptism rate dropped below 3 per 100 resident members. In recent years the membership of the convention has become less evangelistic, or society is less receptive to its evangelistic efforts.

Figure 7.1 shows that there has been no major increase in the number of baptisms since 1950. Although there has been some yearly variation, in the years 1950-77 baptisms have remained on a plateau. This stagnation in the number of yearly baptisms has resulted in the slowdown of the membership growth of the convention.

Reporting of baptisms by age groups began in 1966, but a slight change in categories in 1971 makes it difficult to compare the earlier and later data. Prior to 1971, children and youth were grouped into categories of ages 6 to 16; adults were 17 and above. In 1971 children were redefined as 6 to 17 and adults as 18 and above. Still, it is clear that over the twelve-year period since 1966 the adult category has had an overall increase in the number of baptisms. In seven of the twelve years the under-18 category shows losses. If the classifications had not been changed in 1971, the overall losses for the twelve-year period for the under-18 category and the gain for the adult category would have been more pronounced. Although the under-18 category has decreased as a percentage of total baptisms, it still comprises about 57 percent of total baptisms. Baptisms of preschool children comprise about one half percent of the yearly total. (For detailed breakdowns of baptisms by age see Appendix.)

In Figure 7.3 the number of baptisms for each year since 1900 is graphed along with the net change in total membership. Notice how closely the peaks and valleys of the membership change follow those for baptisms. The difference between these two lines is the number of persons who have been removed from church rolls during a given year through death, the negative net change in the number of persons transferring into and out of the denomination, and the number of persons who have been removed because of inactivity. The net change in persons who have transferred in and out represents a small percentage of the change. Note that since 1950 there is a decreasing net membership change. By 1977 it appears that only one of every two baptisms results in a positive net membership change. The other replaces someone who has died or has otherwise been removed from church rolls.

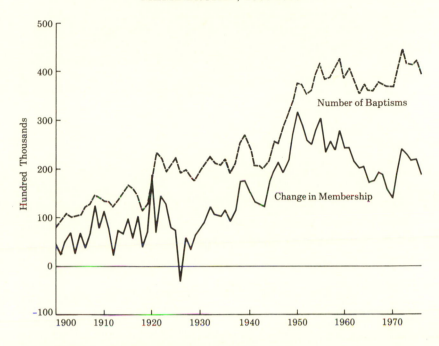

TRENDS IN NUMBER OF CHURCHES

The number of Southern Baptist churches is another indicator of the overall church growth (see Figure 7.1 and Appendix). The early 1900s was one of the periods of fastest growth in the number of churches in the convention. The years from 1919 through 1930 were volatile years, with much short-term variation. They reflect the impact of a series of controversies that raged throughout the decade. Slower rates of growth marked the years of the 1930s and the early 1940s. The late 1940s and 1950s were years of fairly substantial percentage increases in the number of churches. Slower rates of growth characterize the 1960s and 1970s, with the years between 1969 and 1974 having especially low rates of increase. This data represents only the yearly net change in churches. Data is readily available only since 1969 on the number of churches that are organized and the number that disband or disaffiliate themselves from the convention each year. See Table 7.3, which indicates that the convention must have 200 to 300 new churches each year just to replace those that are lost.

Figure 7.4 shows the number of Southern Baptist churches

TABLE 7.3

THE NUMBER OF SOUTHERN BAPTIST CHURCHES ORGANIZED; DISBANDED,
MERGED, OR WITHDRAWN; AND THE NET CHANGE: 1969-1977

Year	New Churches Organized	Number of Churches Disbanded, Merged, or Withdrawn from the Convention	Net Change in Total SBC Churches
1969	323	283	40
1970	297	272	25
1971	314	233	81
1972	316	223	93
1973	323	192	131
1974	338	269	69
1975	395	227	168
1976	372	201	171
1977	373	191	182

Source: James Lowery, Research Department, Baptist
          Sunday School Board.

FIGURE 7.4
SOUTHERN BAPTIST CHURCHES EXISTING IN 1976, PLOTTED BY YEAR ORGANIZED (1900-1975)

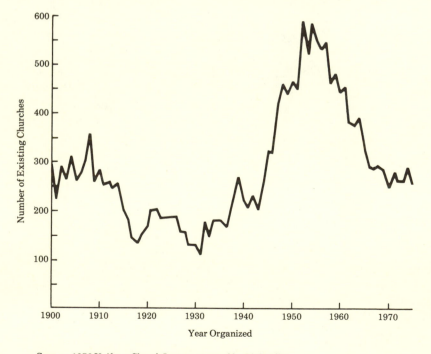

Source: 1976 Uniform Church Letter; prepared by Phil Miller.

TABLE 7.4

NUMBER OF CHURCHES AND PERCENT CHANGE BY REGION
OF THE COUNTRY, 1962-1977

	Total Members			
	1962	1967	1972	1977
United States	32,892	34,147	34,534	35,212
Northeast	42	93	175	248
South	28,014	28,594	28,667	29,014
North Central	3,315	3,637	3,766	3,922
West	1,581	1,788	1,903	2,028

	Percent Change in Total Members		
	1962-67	1967-72	1972-77
United States	3.82	1.13	1.96
Northeast	121.43	88.17	41.71
South	2.07	.26	1.21
North Central	9.71	3.55	4.14
West	13.09	6.43	6.57

Source: Data from Uniform Church Letter.

existing today, plotted by the year they were organized.[1] Although many of those churches organized in a given year have not survived, we can still see that the years from 1948 to 1961 were the peak years of successful new church development. Interestingly, comparison of the data in Table 7.3 and Figure 7.3 shows that 20 percent of the churches organized from 1970 to 1975 were not part of the convention by 1976.

Table 7.4 gives the number of churches by regions of the United States. The trends for churches are the same as for membership. The greatest increase in number of churches was in the South, and the largest percentage increase was in the Northeast.

The locations of Southern Baptist churches have been changing from rural to urban but not as fast as the membership (see Appendix). In 1950 over 83 percent of the Southern Baptist churches were located in open country, in villages, and in towns; in 1977 it was 63 percent. (While about one third of the churches are in areas defined as urban, they account for two thirds of the membership.)

In 1950, 79 percent of the churches in the Southern Baptist Convention had less than 300 members. By 1977, 62 percent of the churches had a membership of less than 300. Actually, in 1976 the median church in the convention had 158 resident members. It is interesting that in 1976, 60 percent of those churches under 100 members were more than forty years old.

NEW CHURCH DEVELOPMENT

It is frequently argued that new church development is the primary reason for the growth of the Southern Baptist Convention. This assertion can be tested with our data. Since baptisms are the primary source of membership growth for the convention, we broke down the 1976 baptisms by categories of church age. In Table 7.5 the breakdown represents 94 percent of all Southern Baptist churches and 90 percent of the total baptisms reported in 1976.[2] Table 7.5 indicates that the bulk of the growth in the convention comes from older, more established churches; 77.3 percent of the baptisms in 1976 were in churches twenty-one years old or older. The Southern Baptist Convention still would have increased by more than 100,000 members in 1976 even if it had not started any churches or missions in the past ten years. It would have increased by 50,000 even if it had not started any new work in the last twenty years.

If baptism rates per 100 resident members (1976 baptisms divided by 1976 resident members × 100) are used as a measure of efficiency for a church, then young churches are more efficient than old churches (see Table 7.6). The older a church gets, the less efficient it is in baptizing new converts.

TABLE 7.5

NUMBER OF BAPTISMS IN 1976 BY AGE OF CHURCH

Years of Age	Number of Baptisms	Percent of Baptisms	Number of Churches	Percent of Churches
Less than 11	26,142	7.6	2,356	7.1
11–20	51,822	15.1	3,796	11.5
21–30	61,200	17.8	4,646	14.1
31–40	27,671	8.0	2,305	7.0
41+	177,322	51.5	19,867	60.3
Total	344,157	100.0	32,970	100.0

TABLE 7.6

AVERAGE NUMBER OF BAPTISMS PER 100 RESIDENT MEMBERS
PER CHURCH BY AGE OF CHURCH*

Years Old	Average Number of Baptisms Per 100 Resident Members	Number of Churches
Less than 11	9.5	2,314
11-20	6.3	3,732
21-30	5.7	4,577
31-40	4.6	2,274
41+	3.7	19,651

*Calculated from 32,548 churches.

Source: Data from Uniform Church Letter.

This same phenomenon is found for the size of a church—the larger the church, the less efficient it tends to be. Since the large majority of young churches (less than ten years of age) are small churches (less than 200 members), it might be inferred that baptism rate is a function of size rather than age. However, when church size is controlled, the same relationship between baptism rate and age of church holds (see Table 7.7).

Most new churches are missions before they are constituted as churches. There are two broad categories of missions—church-type missions and other-type missions. Church-type missions are those that intend to constitute as churches. Other-type missions include places of ministry such as jails, juvenile homes, YMCAs, community centers, or other established witnessing points. New churches usually begin as church-type missions, because it takes time to establish membership, leadership, and financial support. In addition, to constitute as a Southern Baptist church requires a mission's acceptance into a local Baptist association. This normally requires being sponsored by a mother church. It may or may not involve leadership and financial aid from the mother church. In either case the mother church empowers a church-type mission to receive new members by baptism or by transfer of letter on the mother church's behalf and to conduct or administer the ordinances. Thus, the members of the church-type mission are technically members of the mother church. As a result, only very limited data is available for church-type missions as well as

TABLE 7.7

1976 BAPTISM RATE BY 1976 RESIDENT MEMBERSHIP
BY AGE OF CHURCH*

Number of Resident Members	Age of Church				
	Less Than 11	11–20	21–30	31–40	41+
1–49	11.4	7.1	7.8	5.5	3.3
50–99	10.2	7.6	5.7	5.4	4.1
100–149	8.9	6.3	5.5	4.8	4.1
150–199	8.0	6.4	5.3	4.5	3.8
200–299	7.9	5.9	4.9	4.2	3.7
300–399	7.3	5.4	4.7	4.4	3.5
400–499	6.6	5.0	4.4	3.9	3.2
500–749	6.1	4.7	4.1	3.7	3.0
750–999	5.7	5.1	4.2	3.2	2.9
1000–1499	7.1	5.6	3.8	3.4	2.9
1500–1999	7.8	4.8	4.8	3.4	2.9
2000–2999	–	5.3	4.7	2.2	3.6
3000+	–	2.6	3.6	6.4	3.5

*Calculated from 32,548 churches.

other-type missions; their statistics are included with those of the mother church. The only available data is included in Table 7.8, which shows the number of missions started each year and the number currently operating. This table also shows overall decreases in the number of both types of missions.

The initiative for starting new missions generally comes at the local level through associations, churches, and sometimes individuals. State and national agencies provide help through the publication of planning guides and sometimes offer financial assistance; however, either the association, the sponsoring church, or the mission itself is responsible for its pastoral support, its facilities, and its development. Local initiative and support are crucial.

FINANCIAL TRENDS

Financial contributions in the Southern Baptist Convention have increased yearly since 1950. Per capita contributions were $27.86 in 1950 and $129.27 in 1977. When corrected for inflation using the consumer price index, the per capita contributions increased 84 percent over twenty-six years. Generally, the trends have been steady and continuous (see the Appendix for data).

TABLE 7.8

NUMBER OF CHURCH-TYPE AND OTHER-TYPE MISSIONS STARTED
AND OPERATING FROM 1964 THROUGH 1977*

Year	Church-Type Missions		Other-Type Missions	
	Started	Operating	Started	Operating
1964	–	4,027	–	–
1965	–	3,759	–	–
1966	–	3,512	–	–
1967	–	3,733	–	–
1968	–	3,541	–	–
1969	–	3,211	–	–
1970	–	2,516	–	–
1971	535	2,460	1,281	2,760
1972	–	–	–	–
1973	431	2,071	891	2,171
1974	487	1,811	720	2,005
1975	557	1,823	649	1,984
1976	602	1,800	639	1,697
1977	756	1,856	612	1,827

*Only the 1976 data represents actual counts; the others are
estimates based on a sample of 5,000 churches.

Source: The Quarterly Review: A Survey of Southern Baptist
Progress, published by the Sunday School Board,
Southern Baptist Convention.

TRENDS IN MAJOR CHURCH PROGRAMS

Another way of examining the growth of the Southern Baptist
Convention is by examining its major organizations. The major
organizations are the Sunday School program, the Church Training
program, the Woman's Missionary Union (WMU), and the
Brotherhood. Almost all churches have a Sunday school program
on Sunday mornings that is devoted primarily to Bible study. The
Church Training program is similar to the Sunday school program
except that it is normally scheduled for Sunday evenings and often
includes a broader range of studies than just biblical subjects. The
primary function of the Woman's Missionary Union, an organization of Baptist women, is the support of mission activities. This is
accomplished by promoting and conducting mission projects, by
promoting special mission offerings, and by sponsoring mission
groups for youth and children. The Brotherhood is the corresponding missions organization for men. Membership in any of

these programs or organizations is not necessarily dependent upon church membership.

Figure 7.1 shows rapid growth in these organizations until the early 1960s. Enrollments for Church Training, the WMU, and the Brotherhood all peaked in 1963. Sunday school enrollment peaked in 1964. These four organizations showed a decrease each successive year for at least seven years after enrollment had peaked. Sunday school enrollment bottomed out in 1971 and has shown mostly increases since that time. Statistics for the Brotherhood show that it bottomed out in 1970 and started to increase in 1971. Part of the increase for Brotherhood and part of the decrease in WMU in 1971 represents a shift in sponsorship of the 6-to-8-year-old boys' mission group from the WMU to the Brotherhood. Because of this shift, data for 1971 and for succeeding years for these two organizations is not directly comparable to previous years, but the statistics reported on the graphs still show long-term trends. WMU bottomed out in 1973 and has continued to increase in enrollment since that time. Only Church Training continues to decline in its organizational enrollment. The decrease in enrollment for these organizations from the early sixties to the early seventies is similar to the decrease in membership and organizational enrollment as recorded by other major denominations. While church membership for the Southern Baptist Convention continued to grow for this period, the decreases of enrollment in its major church organizations show there was a decrease in active church involvement. Unfortunately, no records are collected for worship service attendance.

Some age group data is available for Sunday school enrollment back to 1950. The three age groups are preschool (0 to 5 years), children and youth (6 to 16 or 17), and adults (17 or 18 years plus). The main problem in establishing comparable data for these years is the redefinition of age group categories in 1971 (discussed earlier). However, by charting the data in Figure 7.5, the overall trend for these age groupings can be established. While the 1950s were a period of rapid growth for Sunday school enrollment in all three age groups, the rate of increase slowed in the latter part of the decade. Actually, fairly consistent losses for the 0 to 5 age category began in 1958 and continued through 1972. Losses began for the 6 to 16 (6 to 17) age group in 1963 and, with a few exceptions, continued through 1977. The first losses for the 17-plus group (18-plus) occurred in 1965 but were reported in only three other years up through 1977. Even then the losses were not as dramatic as those for the younger age groups. Both the 0 to 5 and the 18-plus age

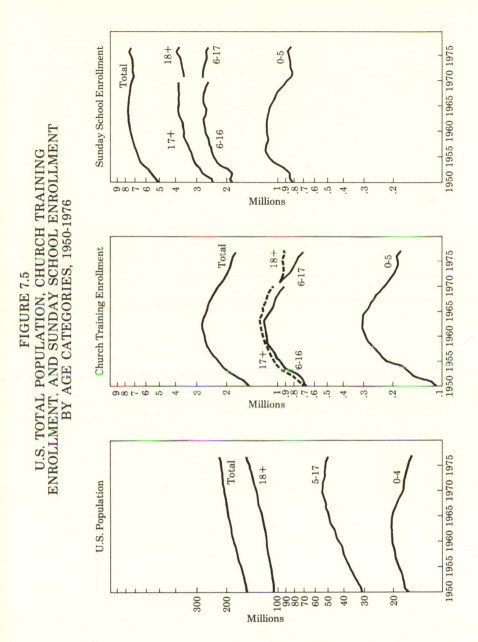

FIGURE 7.5

U.S. TOTAL, POPULATION, CHURCH TRAINING ENROLLMENT, AND SUNDAY SCHOOL ENROLLMENT BY AGE CATEGORIES, 1950-1976

groups have been growing rapidly since 1971. It appears that the overall losses in total Sunday school enrollment between 1964 and 1971 are largely due to the losses in the enrollment in the under-17 (or 18) age categories.

Data is available back to 1950 for breakdown of the total Church Training enrollment into the three age categories used for Sunday school (see Figure 7.5). Like Sunday school, there was rapid increase for each of the age groups in the 1950s. Figure 7.5 shows that all age categories for Church Training slowed their rates of growth in the early 1960s and have shown fairly consistent losses since 1962 or 1963. The most serious percentage losses have occurred in the under-18 categories. Since the under-18 categories comprise over half the total enrollment, they account for large numerical losses.

Consistent age group data for WMU and Brotherhood back to 1967 and 1968 can be compiled for only the under-18 and 18-plus age categories (see Appendix). Almost half those enrolled in these two organizations are under 18. The largest losses for WMU over this period of time, as in Sunday school and Church Training, have been in the under-18 age category. By contrast, Brotherhood had an overall increase in its under-18 enrollment in this period.

CHURCH TRENDS AND POPULATION TRENDS

In an effort to analyze why Sunday school, Church Training, WMU, and baptisms are decreasing in the under-18 age groups, data for the age breakdown of the U.S. population was collected (see Appendix). The age categories in the census data approximate the age categories used for the church data but do not parallel them exactly. (The categories for the census data are 0 to 4 years, 5 to 17 years, and 18 years and older.) The periods of slowest growth for the total population were in the 1930s and the latter 1960s, continuing into the 1970s. These periods of slower growth were preceded several years by losses in the 0 to 4 age category. This category slowed its rate of growth in 1960 and began declining in 1962. The decline has accelerated and continued through 1976. The 5 to 17 age category had a slowdown beginning in 1965, followed by losses after 1971. The 18-plus population has grown consistently since 1960. For our purposes, the longitudinal age structure of the southern white population would have been better information, but it was not available.

When the population age-group trends are compared with the Southern Baptist enrollment trends, we see many similarities. In Sunday school enrollment the slowdown in the under-18 age group closely coincides with the decrease in the under-18 population. However, the 0 to 5 Sunday school enrollment has been increasing recently, while the number in this population age group has not increased.

The Church Training program, unlike the total population, has had decreases in enrollment for all age categories since 1964. Probably the decreases since the early 1960s resulted from decreasing interest of all age groups in the Sunday evening program.

The trends for the Woman's Missionary Union are similar to those of the Sunday school and Church Training. However, the trends in the under-18 Brotherhood enrollment are inconsistent with the shrinkage of the under-18 U.S. population. Obviously, other factors are at work here.

The data for baptisms since 1966 seems fairly consistent with population data. The under-18 age category shows frequent yearly losses. The 18-plus category shows a considerable gain over the twelve-year period. Otherwise, baptisms, as well as Sunday school enrollment, Church Training enrollment, and WMU enrollment, appear to be, in part, dependent upon population change.

How about the total membership? If the decrease in the under-18 age group in the total population was responsible for the declines in organizational enrollments during the 1960s, why was not total membership affected? The answer lies in the age composition of the total membership. It is mainly adult, and therefore it is not as susceptible to shrinkages in the under-18 population as its organizations would be, whose membership is about half under 18 years of age. However, shrinkage in the under-18 population has had some effect on total membership. Since about 60 percent of the yearly baptisms are persons under 18 years of age, and since baptisms are the main source of membership growth, shrinkage in the under-18 population has caused some of the slowdown in Southern Baptist total membership growth.

SUMMARY

The membership of the Southern Baptist Convention continues to grow. The denomination has consistently grown faster than the population. Membership has shifted from rural to urban areas, with the large majority now in large cities. However, the majority of the churches are still small and are in rural areas. The Southern Baptist Convention is still a regional denomination, with almost 86 percent of its membership residing in the South. The largest numerical increases are occurring in the South, while the largest percentage increases in churches and membership are taking place outside the South. Young and small churches are growing the fastest, yet the bulk of Southern Baptist growth is in older and larger churches. Baptisms, the main source of growth for the Southern Baptist Convention, appear to have maintained a plateau since the 1950s. The stagnation of baptisms in recent years is due to a decrease of baptisms for the 6 to 17 age group. The rate of growth for the denomination has slowed down since the early 1960s due to a lack of growth in baptisms.

All the major church organizations grew rapidly in enrollment during the 1950s. Their rate of growth slowed in the early 1960s and declined beginning in 1963 or 1964. Most organizations recovered in the 1970s. Only Church Training shows continued substantial losses. Many of the fluctuations in enrollment for these organizations are due to the shifts in the under-18 age group of the U.S. population, because a large percentage of enrollment in each organization is under 18. The total church membership in the Southern Baptist Convention did not show corresponding losses in the 1960s partly because the membership is predominantly adult.

CHAPTER 8

A Test of Theories of Denominational Growth and Decline

Dean R. Hoge

As is generally known, recent church trends vary from denomination to denomination. Some denominations are growing; others are declining. Seldom have the reasons for this been analyzed, partly because studies comparing denominations have been hindered by lack of data.

This chapter reports on a new study, comparing sixteen Protestant denominations, made possible by the availability of new survey data. Some key variables were still not available in any existing data, so expert ratings had to be used.[1] The study was designed largely as a test of Dean Kelley's theories in *Why Conservative Churches Are Growing* (1972; second edition, 1977).

Kelley's Theories of Church Growth

Kelley's book has been central in recent discussions of denominational trends. His main argument is that churches can be "strong" or "weak." Strong churches (denominations or congregations) grow, while weak ones decline. Strong churches are characterized by (1) a demand for high commitment from their members, including total loyalty and social solidarity. They (2) exact discipline over both beliefs and life-style. They (3) have missionary zeal, with an eagerness to tell the good news to all persons. They (4) are absolutistic about beliefs. Their beliefs are a total, closed system, sufficient for all purposes, needing no revision and permitting none. They (5) require conformity in life-style, often involving certain avoidances of nonmembers or use of distinctive visible marks or uniforms. Weak churches, by contrast, are characterized by relativism and individualism in beliefs, tolerance of internal diversity and pluralism, lack of any enforcement of canons or doctrine, an attitude of dialogue with outsiders rather than proselytism, limited commitment to the church, and little effective sharing of convictions or spiritual insights within the group (1972:84, 95).

Kelley's theorizing is concerned almost entirely with institutional characteristics, not social or historical context or anything external.[2] He says that, "other things being equal," strong churches will grow and weak churches will diminish in numbers (1972:90). He does not deny the existence of contextual factors but pays little systematic attention to them.

Three more institutional factors are noted by Kelley. First is emphasis on social action. He holds that social action is good or bad depending on the relation of that action to the ultimate meanings of the religion as understood by members. It is strengthening when its implications for the ultimate religious meaning of the members are clearly understood and accepted by them. But if the action lacks this religious meaning, it threatens church life. In such cases, the members' evaluations of church social action are derived as much from their other loyalties and interests as from their religion. Second is a "growing secularism" of the life of mainline denominations and a "consequent neglect of spiritual concerns." Third is the "increasing dominance of the clergy in these churches, subordinating the laity to passive roles [1972:98]."

The only social contextual factor interesting to Kelley is social class. He quotes Wesley's law, that "wherever riches have increased, the essence of religion has decreased in the same proportion" and seems to agree that strong church commitment is most common in lower social classes (1972:54-55).

Kelley ponders the historical shifts in church trends, especially the declines in the mainline denominations in the mid-1960s, after fifteen years of strong growth. Characteristically, he looks to institutional factors as the explanation for such historical changes; he points to the attention given to social action in these denominations beginning in the mid-1960s, their worry about minority agendas and their overconcern about ecumenism and dialogue. In effect, he says that they shifted from being strong to being weak churches. At one point Kelley notes the possibility that changes in the total social context may have caused some denominational trends (1972:91), but he comes to no firm conclusion about what they are, partly because he lacks information on contextual factors.

Other Theories

Other theorists have proposed other explanations for the trends. Two institutional factors, other than those discussed by Kelley, have been proposed as important. One is change in energy given to new church development. Since the American population is constantly moving and new suburbs and towns are always being developed, any denomination failing to keep up with population shifts in new church development will fall behind. If it does not establish congregations in the new suburbs, other denominations will do so and will benefit in growth. There is evidence that denominations have varied in the attention and energy given to new church development over the past two decades.[3]

The other is organizational skill and management of potential divisiveness (see Perry, 1973:199). In the difficult 1960s some denominations were not able to maintain internal unity and commitment, hence they experienced membership losses.

Four kinds of contextual factors have been suggested as explanations for the denominational trends. First is the impact of region, both demographically and culturally. Demographically, the impact occurs due to differential birthrates and interregional migration. Culturally, it occurs from region-specific value changes. Most observers discuss the South and the West as being most important in regional variation. Possibly, denominations located in these regions will have different experiences than others.

Second is change in the birthrate. Data on denomination-specific birthrates has never, to our knowledge, been gathered. We would expect such rates to be associated with regional or social class variations.

Third is the vertical social mobility of members of any denomination. Troeltsch (1931) and H. Richard Niebuhr (1929) described how lower-class groups could sustain strong church commitment, but with upward social mobility the commitment weakened. Upward social mobility in any denomination may affect membership and commitment.

Fourth is value change in some specific population group. Most important is youth, the population group most susceptible to rapid value shifts. Affluent youth are especially susceptible. Such shifts would be expected to affect some denominations more than others (see the discussion of youth in chapter 4).

Here we are listing single factors, but probably interactions occur among the factors. Kelley (1977:viii) mentions one: "Though environmental influences may sway the more attenuated forms of religious life, they have much less effect upon the 'purer' or more vigorous forms." Such interactions deserve investigation.

Past Research

Four studies have tested aspects of Kelley's theories. Bibby and Brinkerhoff (1974) investigated the sources of new members in twenty conservative congregations in one city to see if the factors stressed by Kelley were important to the growth of these congregations. They found that most of the new members came through transfer or reaffiliation of persons formerly members of other evangelical churches. Thus, the patterns of switching from one congregation to another were important in understanding overall trends. The factors stressed by Kelley were not very important.

Bibby (1978) scrutinized Canadian survey data to find the reasons for the greater growth in conservative denominations. He found that the conservatives had a higher birthrate, a higher rate of religious education for their children, and higher rates of participation during adult life. He concluded that the Kelley thesis is correct with respect to retention of children in the church but not with respect to proselytizing outsiders.

A Presbyterian study of 681 congregations looked at five of the factors stressed by Kelley (Presbyterian Committee, 1976; chapter 9 in this book). The key outcome variable was growth or decline in each congregation over a six-year period. All the tests of the Kelley hypotheses about determinants of growth came out very weak. The researchers concluded that other factors are more crucial for Presbyterian congregations.

Biersdorf (1975) studied thirty-six religious communities (congregations, alternative communities, and voluntary task forces) nominated by others as having outstanding religious vitality. He tested the Kelley theories using these groups and found that Kelley was right in stressing the importance of meaning-laden experiences in religious life, but that Kelley was wrong in saying that such experiences occurred mainly in conservative groups. In Biersdorf's opinion, such experiences occur in many kinds of religious groups.

The present study tests several elements of the Kelley theories and also looks at contextual factors that might explain some denominational trends.

METHOD

A search turned up no available reliable data for Protestant denominations on some theoretically important variables. We were forced to rely on expert judgments. We designed a questionnaire for experts, asking for some ratings for the 1966-75 decade. We asked several researchers and ecumenical leaders for nominations, then phoned or wrote to the nominees to ask their help. We asked twenty-five experts, of whom twenty-one completed the ratings.[4]

In choosing the denominations to study, we began with the twenty-seven largest Protestant denominations in the United States and the two largest in Canada. Then we deleted those having no current membership statistics in the *Yearbook of American and Canadian Churches* in 1976 or 1977 and those that our pretest experts said were too unknown.[5] This left only sixteen eligible for analysis.

Statistics on membership and contributions were taken from the *Yearbook of American and Canadian Churches*. Information on demographic backgrounds of members was taken from the pooled 1972-77 General Social Surveys done by the National Opinion Research Center (a rich set of data, with 9,120 cases). Information on geographic distribution of denominations was taken from *Churches and Church Membership in the United States* (Johnson, Picard, and Quinn, 1974), based on 1971 reports.

Measures

The rating form for experts included eight dimensions related to the Kelley theories, to be rated on 1-to-7 scales whose poles were defined.[6] The ratings were for the years 1966-75:

1. *Strength of Ethnic Identity*, with "strong ethnic or nationality identity" = 7 and "no ethnic or nationality identity" = 1.

2. *Theological Conservatism or Liberalism*, with "most conservative" = 1 and "most liberal" = 7. The rating form explained that "conservative" included literal accuracy of scriptures, literal heaven and hell, and suspicion of science or rationality as a source of truth or authority. Liberalism was defined in opposite terms.

3. *Attitudes Toward Ecumenism*, with "most positive to ecumenism" = 1 and "most negative to ecumenism" = 7.

4. *Centralized or Congregational Polity*, with "centralized polity" = 1 and "congregational polity" = 7. The rating form defined "centralized" as indicating central or regional authority over appointments, finances, and programs.

5. *Emphasis on Local and Community Evangelism*, with "low priority on community evangelism" = 1 and "high priority on community evangelism" = 7. The rating form described evangelism as "such as canvassing, visitation, promoting Sunday school or Bible study groups in the community, or sponsoring revival services."

6. *Involvement in Social Action*, with "not involved in social action" = 1 and "heavily involved in social action" = 7. Social action was defined as efforts directed to social, political, or economic change, such as programs in the areas of race relations, poverty, and community self-help; it does not refer to individual charity or relief.

7. *Emphasis on Distinctive Life-style and Morality*, with "maximal affirmation of American life-style" = 1 and "maximal distinctiveness from American life-style" = 7. The rating form explained that the dimension was on whether the denomination emphasized a distinctive life-style or morality involving such matters as dress, diet, drinking, entertainment, use of time, marriage, sex, child-rearing, and the like.

8. *Attitude Toward Pluralism of Beliefs Among Members*, with "demands strict standards of beliefs" = 1 and "affirms individuality and pluralism in belief" = 7. This dimension referred more to leadership than average lay viewpoint.

We did not know how much the experts would agree in their ratings, but actually they agreed quite well.[7] The ratings are shown in Table 8.1.

From the *Yearbook of American and Canadian Churches* we took inclusive membership and per capita contributions for the sixteen denominations in 1940, 1955, 1965, and 1975. The membership data was adjusted to eliminate the effects of mergers and schisms (see Appendix for procedures). The inclusive membership figures are inferior to the adult confirmed membership figures for our purposes, but since many denominations did not report the latter, we had no choice.

From the NORC data we got six variables on persons giving each denomination as their preference—mean occupational prestige, mean years of education, mean family income, mean number of children (for adults 40 or over), the percent attending church "nearly every week" or oftener, and the percentage living in Standard Metropolitan Statistical Areas. Since the NORC data did not distinguish among Baptist, Presbyterian, and Lutheran denominations, we had to refer to other data to do so. For the Baptists and the Presbyterians we used geographical breakdowns;

TABLE 8.1

MEAN RATINGS BY 21 EXPERTS ON EIGHT DIMENSIONS*

	Ethnic Ident.	Conserv. Liberal	Ecumen- ism	Polity	Evan- gelism	Social Action	Distinc. Style	Plural- ism
American Baptist Churches	1.71	4.24	3.05	5.71	3.86	4.91	2.95	5.14
American Lutheran Church	4.65	3.45	3.88	3.63	3.38	4.28	3.16	3.50
Assemblies of God	1.76	1.15	6.17	5.63	6.48	2.00	6.00	1.48
Christian Church (Disciples)	1.90	4.67	2.33	5.00	3.26	5.00	2.95	5.50
C.J.C. of Latter-Day Saints	2.67	1.56	6.87	1.87	6.32	2.57	6.28	1.40
Church of the Nazarene	2.00	1.80	5.89	4.26	5.67	2.60	5.30	2.24
Churches of Christ†	1.84	2.05	6.47	6.12	5.78	2.12	5.00	2.17
Episcopal Church	2.67	5.57	2.63	2.24	1.52	5.33	1.55	5.52
Lutheran Church in America	4.25	4.40	3.28	3.21	3.00	4.84	2.84	4.20
Lutheran C.-Missouri Synod	5.29	1.62	6.32	2.86	4.11	2.85	3.85	1.38
Presbyterian Church, U.S.	2.43	3.76	3.68	3.29	3.71	4.24	2.75	4.00
Reformed Church in America	4.81	3.29	3.83	3.30	3.50	4.00	2.95	3.57
Seventh-Day Adventist Church	2.05	1.48	6.37	2.92	6.05	2.71	6.26	1.15
Southern Baptist Convention	1.95	2.00	6.21	5.38	6.57	2.76	4.45	2.71
United Church of Christ	2.05	6.62	1.32	4.57	1.76	6.43	1.60	6.52
United Methodist Church	2.00	5.57	2.16	2.05	3.14	5.76	2.25	5.91
United Presbyterian, U.S.A.	1.95	5.05	1.95	2.95	3.00	5.76	2.05	5.19

*The eight dimensions are: Ethnic Ident. = Strength of Ethnic Identity (7=strong, 1=none). Conserv.-Liberal = Theological Conservatism or Liberalism (7=liberal, 1=conservative). Ecumenism = Attitudes Toward Ecumenism (7=negative, 1=positive). Polity = Centralized or Congregational Polity (7=congregational, 1=centralized). Evangelism = Emphasis on Local and Community Evangelism (7=high priority, 1=low priority). Social Action = Involvement in Social Action (7=heavily involved, 1=not involved). Distinc. Style = Emphasis on Distinctive Life-style and Morality (7=maximal distinctiveness, 1=affirmation of American life-style). Pluralism = Attitudes Toward Pluralism of Beliefs Among Members (7=affirm individuality and pluralism, 1=demand strict standards).

†Ratings of the Churches of Christ are shown here even though the denomination had to be excluded from the analysis.

for the Lutherans we used data from three other sources (see the Appendix).

From Johnson et al. (1974) we took the percent of members within each denomination who reside in the South, the percent in the Far West (including Alaska and Hawaii), and the percent in the Far West and the Mountain states. In the case of the Assemblies of God, who were not in the data, we procured information from the denominational research office.

To test the impact of regional factors, William McKinney computed a Regional Growth Index for 1955-65 and a Regional Growth Index for 1965-75. They are based on the regional distribution of each denomination (broken into the nine census regions) multiplied by the population change in each region for each decade. Most of the population change is due to migration, but some is due to natural growth differences. Thus, for example, if the Church of Jesus Christ of Latter-Day Saints is located largely in the West, and if the regional growth rate of the West was high in one decade, then for this reason the denomination would have a high score on the Regional Growth Index for that decade. Similarly, denominations mostly located in out-migration areas will have low index scores. The index shows denominational changes predictable from population shifts on the assumption that persons migrating to any region will join the denominations already strong in that region and will not continue earlier denominational membership. (Whether or not this assumption is true is unknown; the purpose of the index is solely to distinguish demographic from cultural factors related to specific regions.) The index scores and computation methods are shown in the Appendix.

FINDINGS

Contextual Factors: Historical and Social

Table 8.2 shows growth rates for the sixteen denominations in 1955-65 and 1965-75. The two decades were very different in overall growth rates, yet rankings show that the relative rates of growth in the various denominations were similar in the two decades. That is, the fastest growing denominations in 1955-65 tended to be also the fastest growing in 1965-75. The correlation between the 1955-65 and 1965-75 growth rates for the sixteen denominations is .69. *Relative to each other*, the denominations grew or declined at somewhat constant rates. To check this question further, we correlated 1940-55 growth rates with the

TABLE 8.2

GROWTH RATES, 1955-1965 AND 1965-1975, BY DENOMINATION

	Growth Rate* 1955-65	Growth Rate 1965-75	Growth Rate 1955-65 Rank	Growth Rate 1965-75 Rank
C.J.C. of Latter-Day Saints	1.45	1.31	1	3
Assemblies of God	1.43	1.37	2	1
Lutheran C.-Missouri Synod	1.34	1.03	3	7
American Lutheran Church	1.33	.95	4	9.5
Seventh-Day Adventist Church	1.32	1.36	5	2
Southern Baptist Convention	1.27	1.18	6	5
Church of the Nazarene	1.27	1.29	7	4
Reformed Church in America	1.21	.92	8	11
Episcopal Church	1.20	.83	9	15
Presbyterian Church, U.S.	1.17	.97	10	8
United Presbyterian, U.S.A.	1.14	.80	11	16
Lutheran Church in America	1.14	.95	12	9.5
United Methodist Church	1.10	.90	13	13
United Church of Christ	1.09	.88	14	14
American Baptist Churches	1.02	1.04	15	6
Christian Church (Disciples)	1.01	.91	16	12

*Growth rate figures are ratios of the endpoint figure divided by the beginning figure, thus in the first column, 1965 membership divided by 1955 membership. The unweighted overall mean for 1955-65 is 1.298 and for 1965-75 is 1.043. Rankings were done before rounding off growth rates.

1955-65 and 1965-75 growth rates for the sixteen denominations (we used 1940 data since 1945 data is lacking). The 1940-55 growth rates were divided by 1.5 to make them comparable with the others, which are based on one decade. The 1940-55 growth rate correlated .90 with the 1955-65 growth rate and .67 with the 1965-75 growth rate. These strong correlations strengthen our conclusion that relative growth rates are somewhat constant over the decades. It suggests (but does not prove) that changes in denominational growth rates from one decade to another are caused more by external changes, which are common to many denominations, than by institutional changes, which are not.

The variation in growth rates across the sixteen denominations changed from decade to decade. The standard deviation for the sixteen growth rates was .17 in 1940-55, .13 in 1955-65, and .19 in 1965-75. An interaction factor occurred in the last period; whatever factors caused the declines in 1965-75 hit those denominations hardest that had generally been the slowest growers in earlier decades.

Table 8.3 shows correlations of growth rates with nine contextual factors. We have shown correlations with regional factors for both decades since regional distributions are quite stable (see chapter 6 in this book). The zero-order correlations are quite strong for family income, number of children, regional growth, and percent in the West. They are weak for percent living in SMSAs and percent living in the South. The weak correlation with living in metropolitan areas corresponds with findings in past research; the weak correlation with living in the South, however, surprised us. The strong correlation with living in the West also surprised us; to check on it we also computed correlations with the percent living in the West plus the Mountain states. The correlations were so similar to those with percent in the Far West that we did not show them in the table.

Is the relationship between percentage in the West and denominational growth a product of demographic patterns or of a separate religious subculture in the West? The two regional growth indexes provide some information. The zero-order correlations between them and growth rates resemble the zero-order correlations between percentage in the West and growth rates. When the regional growth indexes are controlled, the partial correlation between percentage in the West and growth in 1955-65 is .19; in 1965-75 it is .39. We conclude that in 1955-65 migration was the largest single source of regional differences in denominational growth, but in 1965-75 it was somewhat less important. Evidently, in 1965-75 other regional factors unknown to us, such as subcultural variations, had a notable effect.

The intercorrelations among the nine contextual factors are sometimes high (see Appendix). The correlation between years of education and family income is .88; between education and occupational prestige it is also .88. Therefore, we shall look solely at family income as our indicator of socioeconomic status in further

TABLE 8.3

CORRELATIONS OF CONTEXTUAL FACTORS WITH DENOMINATIONAL GROWTH:
ZERO-ORDER AND PARTIAL CORRELATIONS

	Zero-Order Correlation		Control: Income		Control: Percent in West		Control: Children	
	1955-65	1965-75	1955-65	1965-75	1955-65	1965-75	1955-65	1965-75
Years of Education, 1970s*		-.50						
Family Income, 1970s		-.64				-.55		-.56
Occupational Prestige, 1970s		-.40						
No. of Children (adults 40 or older), 1970s		.66		.58		.60		
Percent in SMSAs, 1970s		.23						
Regional Factors:								
Regional Growth Index, 1955-65	.55		.54				.37	
Regional Growth Index, 1965-75		.59		.71				.35
Percent in South, 1971	-.06	.13						
Percent in West, 1971	.50	.67	.46	.59			.39	.62

*The factors labeled "1970s" are from the pooled 1972-77 NORC data.

analysis. For our best indicator of regional factors we will use percentage in the West; it encompasses demographic and cultural factors in regional patterns.

We have said that three contextual factors are strong predictors of denominational growth—family income, percent living in the West, and number of children. To check on overlap among the three we computed partial correlations as shown in Table 8.3. It would have been desirable to control more than one variable at a time, but our low N of 16 prevents more elaborate multivariate analysis. The partial correlations indicate that the overlap is not large, and the three variables are not simply equivalent to one another. In particular, number of children is not simply a restatement of family income.

Some conclusions may be drawn at this point. First, contextual factors indeed have an impact on denominational growth or decline. Second, contextual factors that impinged on the denominations after 1965 had most impact on the upper socioeconomic denominations. In general, after 1965 the higher the social class of the denomination, the less it grew (or more it declined). Possibly the socioeconomic differences could be due to differences in family size, so that lower socioeconomic denominations grow solely because of the large numbers of children being reared in them. This factor is undoubtedly present, but it is not the main explanation for the socioeconomic differences. Even when family size is controlled (see Table 8.3, line 2), the correlation between family income and denominational growth in 1965-75 is still − .56.

Third, the percent living in the West is a strong predictor of a denomination's growth or decline. This was largely due to migration patterns in the 1955-65 decade but much less so in 1965-75.

Do contextual factors explain most of the variance in denominational growth rates? Our N of 16 prevents us from calculating the variance explained by all the contextual factors combined. We did, however, calculate multiple correlations of two contextual variables at a time by growth rates. Highest was .80 for the multiple correlation of number of children and percentage in the West by growth in 1965-75. Equivalent multiple correlations for the 1955-65 period are impossible, but preliminary analysis indicates that they would be a bit weaker. We conclude that contextual factors alone can explain over half the total variance in denominational growth rates in 1965-75 and a bit less in 1955-65.

Institutional Factors

Table 8.4 shows zero-order and partial correlations with eight institutional factors and three indicators of members' church commitment. For five of the institutional factors we have used the 1966-75 ratings for both decades, since we judge them to be quite stable from decade to decade. For the others (marked with an

TABLE 8.4

CORRELATIONS OF INSTITUTIONAL FACTORS WITH DENOMINATIONAL GROWTH:
ZERO-ORDER AND PARTIAL CORRELATIONS

	Zero-Order Correlation		Control: Income		Control: Percent in West	
	1955-65	1965-75	1955-65	1965-75	1955-65	1965-75
Strength of Ethnic Identity, 1966-75	.26	-.25	.29	-.24	.42	-.17
Theological Liberalism, 1966-75	-.80	-.86	-.85	-.78	-.73	-.81
Congregational Polity, 1966-75	-.22	.22	-.35	-.06	-.19	.41
Emphasis on Local and Community Evangelism, 1966-75	*	.93	*	.88	*	.92
Emphasis on Social Action, 1966-75	*	-.88	≠	≠	≠	≠
Ecumenism, 1966-75	*	-.87	≠	≠	≠	≠
Emphasis on Distinctive Lifestyle & Morality, 1966-75	.75	.97	.82	.95	.65	.95
Affirms Individualism and Pluralism in Belief, 1966-75	-.87	-.84	-.90	-.77	-.82	-.75
Indicators of Personal Commitment:						
Church Attendance Rate, 1970s	*	.90	*	.82	*	.84
Per Capita Contributions, 1955	.55	*	.51	*	.29	*
Per Capita Contributions, 1965	*	.70	*	.61	*	.34

*Correlations are not shown here if the institutional factor ratings for 1966-75 cannot plausibly be applied to 1956-65 or if the data is for different time periods than the decade of growth in question. This is to avoid misleading conclusions.
≠Partial correlations are not shown for institutional factors considered theoretically to be correlates, not determinants, of denominational growth.

asterisk) there is evidence of institutional change over the years, hence we do not use the ratings for both decades.

The zero-order correlations in the first two columns of Table 8.4 are extremely strong. Only two of the eight characteristics measured by the expert ratings correlate weakly with denominational growth—strength of ethnic identity and congregational versus centralized polity. The rest have very strong correlations. We conclude that the denominational characteristics attributed by Kelley to growing denominations are strongly upheld by independent ratings of experts. The factors Kelley stressed most—emphasis on evangelism, emphasis on distinctive life-style and morality, and disallowing individualism in belief—came out the strongest. Furthermore, the correlations with growth in 1955-65 were almost as strong as those in 1965-75, indicating the relevance of these factors in different historical settings.

The three variables at the bottom of the table are indicators of church members' commitment, and all three demonstrate the crucial character of such commitment for denominational growth. Church attendance is a stronger predictor of growth than per capita contributions. In addition, we looked into correlations of growth rates with size of denomination in each decade. The correlations were quite weak—they were $-.23$ for the correlation of 1955 membership with growth in 1955-65 and $-.21$ for the correlation of 1965 membership with growth in 1965-75. Overall denomination size does not appear important.

Two of the variables in Table 8.4 were seen by Kelley as correlates of, but not causally important for, denominational growth. They are emphasis on social action and on ecumenism. Accordingly, we have not shown partial correlations involving them. Given the other strong correlations in the table, we believe that they are not very crucial for explaining denominational growth or decline.[8]

Intercorrelations among the institutional factors in Table 8.4 are not shown here, but most of them are very strong. Of the eight dimensions measured by expert ratings, only two do not strongly intercorrelate with the others; they are strength of ethnic identity and congregational versus centralized polity. All the correlations among the other six are stronger than .80. These six represent slight variations on a single axis, which might be called "liberal-pluralistic-culture-affirming" on one end, "conservative-disciplined-distinctive from culture" on the other end. Denominations near the latter end grow more than others and tend to have higher levels of church attendance than others (see Appendix for the correlations).

They also have higher rates of per capita contributions. We conclude that denominational growth is indeed closely associated with certain denominational traits during the 1965-75 period and to a slightly lesser extent during 1955-65.The associations argued by Kelley have been strongly borne out in our analysis. But the question of causation remains. Which of these characteristics, if any, are causal for denominational growth, and which are merely correlates, maybe even accidental correlates? Are some other factors not measured in our study the crucial causal ones?

The question of causality demands serious scrutiny, and we can only begin the process in this study. We have made initial tests for spuriousness of institutional factors by calculating some partial correlations in the last four columns of Table 8.4. Due to the low N, we had to control the variables one at a time. In addition to the controls shown in the table, we controlled for percentage in the Mountain and the Western states and also for number of children; since the outcomes were similar but slightly weaker than those in the table, we did not show them.

When income and region (the two strongest predictors of denominational growth among our contextual variables) are controlled, the principal correlations with institutional factors do not weaken greatly. For example, the zero-order correlation between distinctive life-style and growth in 1965-75 was .97 and weakened only slightly to .95 when income or region was controlled. The zero-order correlation with individualism in belief was −.84 and weakened to −.75 when region was controlled. Relationships are depicted graphically in Figures 8.1 and 8.2, where the strongest contextual variable and the strongest institutional variable are plotted with denominational growth.

The partial correlations tell us that the institutional characteristics so strongly associated with denominational growth are not just extensions or artifacts of socioeconomic status, family size, or region; they are determinants in their own right.

Relative Importance of Factors

Most of the debate about denominational growth or decline has been over the relative importance of factors causing them. This issue involves two separate questions. First, what determinants seem most important for denominational growth or decline at *any* point in time? We have tried to assess various determinants in the pages above. We believe that contextual factors should be seen as causally prior, since they form the backdrop for institutional

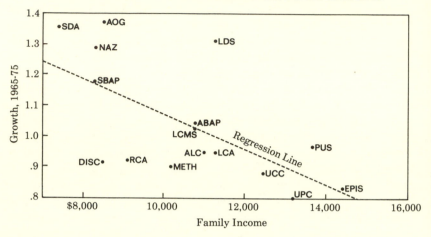

FIGURE 8.1
PLOT OF FAMILY INCOME BY GROWTH 1965-1975

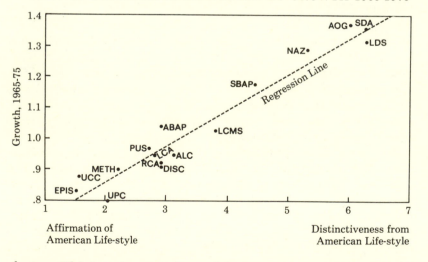

FIGURE 8.2
PLOT OF DISTINCTIVE LIFE-STYLE BY GROWTH 1965-1975

factors. This is a theoretical simplification of a set of relationships that are complex in reality; without question, institutional factors influence contextual factors as well as vice versa. But the main causation should be seen as being from contextual factors first, then from institutional factors, not the opposite. The contextual factors taken alone can explain over half the variance in denominational growth in 1965-75 and a bit less in 1955-65.

This conclusion is somewhat different from Kelley's view, which puts most emphasis on institutional factors. Perhaps Kelley underemphasized contextual factors due to the hortatory purpose of his book. Contextual factors are, after all, serious limits to options for action by church leaders and pastors, usually immovable and frustrating. Our purpose is explanation, not advocacy, and we estimate that contextual factors comprise over half the explanation for denominational growth or decline rates.

The most important contextual factors found in our data are socioeconomic status and region. Both have been prominent in past analyses of social factors in denominationalism. H. Richard Niebuhr (1957), following Max Weber, emphasizes social contexts in which religious movements flourish, and social class is very important. Niebuhr (1929:70) quotes Wesley's law about the inevitable loss of religious commitment among people whose riches have increased. Donald McGavran (1970:ch.14) discusses this same sociological dynamic, calling it "halting (in growth) due to redemption and lift," that is, lift in social status among church members. This sort of analysis of social class should be integrated with Kelley's discussion of institutional factors to produce a clear explanation of denominational growth trends. Kelley's own depictions of exemplary "strong" churches should be carefully analyzed to discern the social contexts in which they flourished. Our impression is that they grew in distinctive social settings, usually involving some separateness from the mainline culture and main power structures. The committed members felt alienation from "the world"—from the social and political powers. They were not wealthy or cosmopolitan people, and they often had a sort of pariah status in the society.

To reiterate, Protestant denominations live in particular social contexts and are both influenced and limited by them. No analyst should say that denominations have broad freedom of movement in remaking themselves or in changing future directions, for the objective conditions of social life do not, in fact, allow for great overall changes. These external conditions account as much for denominational growth or decline as do institutional decisions and actions.

The institutional characteristics of denominations are quite strongly associated with socioeconomic status and region. The correlation between family income and distinctiveness of life-style for the sixteen denominations is −.66. The correlation between family income and denominational emphasis on evangelism is −.68. The correlation between family income and liberal theology is .60. Also the correlation between percent living in the West and distinctiveness of life-style is .71, and the correlation between percent in the West and emphasis on evangelism is .52. Whereas the patterns regarding socioeconomic status are consistent with past research, those regarding percent in the West are new and puzzling. Apparently, the culture in the American West is much more supportive of conservative, disciplined, evangelical churches than of more liberal, pluralistic churches.

Explanations for Recent Trends

We have discussed the general downturn in denominational growth rates from 1955-65 to 1965-75. Analysts have shown that the main changes from growth to decline came in the mid-1960s. What caused them? It could have been changes in contextual factors or changes in institutional factors. Whatever the explanation, it must point to factors that underwent short-term changes of a decade or so, not long-range trends, such as the rise of science, the increase in standard of living, or secularization. Short-term fluctuations must be explained by short-term factors.

In the present study we lack the information necessary to identify the contextual or institutional changes decisively. We have said that, in general, contextual conditions explain a little more than half the denominational differences; this, however, does not help much to explain recent trends, since a change in only one or two of the many determinants of denominational trends may be the whole explanation. Based on bits of evidence available, we believe that the major explanations for recent trends are contextual changes. Several indications suggest this.

First, the denominations have maintained a rather steady lineup of growth rates, relative to one another, since 1940. This leads us to look to factors common to many denominations, not just affecting particular ones, when trying to understand trends (see chapter 6 in this book on similarities in recent denominational trends). Second, the denominational trend graphs depict smooth lines and gradual curves, indicating that gradual, pervasive factors are at work, not immediate events, policy decisions, or shifts in denominational programs. Third, the arguments pointing to denominational changes as explanations for the recent downturn—arguments usually pointing to social action and ecumenism—lose their power when we see (in Table 8.4) that these are not necessary for explaining denominational trends. Other characteristics—such as theological liberalism vs. conservatism, distinctiveness of life-style vs. affirmation of mainstream culture, or uniformity vs.

pluralism in beliefs—are more crucial, and we doubt if these characteristics have changed greatly. Also, the denominational downturns started in the early 1960s, *before* the major social action thrusts of any Protestant denominations. (For related research de-emphasizing the impact of social action on trends, see Johnson and Cornell, 1972; Hoge, 1976b.)

What are the main contextual changes that are responsible? Again, we lack direct evidence and must rely on clues. Whatever they are, they have hit those denominations hardest that are highest in socioeconomic status and that are the most affirmative of American culture (the strongest contextual and institutional factors in our analysis). These two are related; across the sixteen denominations they correlate at .66. We believe Kelley is right when he says that denominations most embedded in the surrounding culture are most subject to favorable or unfavorable shifts in that culture. These denominations benefited from a favorable cultural context in the 1950s but suffered in the late 1960s.

Contextual changes are scrutinized in other chapters of this book. Here we note two changes that are most convincing as having an influence on denominational trends. First is the change in the birthrate. The birthrate is not only important in itself, in that fewer children have been born in recent years, but also the birthrate is an indication of deeper value shifts among young adults. Birthrates and church attendance rates have fluctuated together in America for as long as we have data. Second, a definite value shift has occurred among young people, and especially affluent and educated young people, since the 1950s. The shift has been toward individualism, cosmopolitanism, and greater freedom in the areas of marriage, sexuality, sex roles, and personal morality. The total value shift has created some barriers between certain young people and the churches. Such broad contextual changes as these seem most important for explaining recent trends.

CHAPTER 9

Factors Producing Growth or Decline in United Presbyterian Congregations[1]

Wade Clark Roof,
Dean R. Hoge,
John E. Dyble,
and
C. Kirk Hadaway

In 1974 the General Assembly of the United Presbyterian Church in the U.S.A. voted to establish a special committee to study the loss of membership and to determine its causes and implications. The committee began work in late 1974 and issued its final report in June 1976 (Presbyterian Committee, 1976). Dean Hoge was a member of the committee; John Dyble was on its staff. The committee collected and analyzed data on growth or decline of individual Presbyterian congregations. A large amount of data was gathered in autumn 1975, and initial tabulations were made for the committee report.

This chapter presents further multivariate analysis of the data set, carried out largely by Wade Clark Roof and Kirk Hadaway, as part of the Hartford working group. First, we review the conceptualization and procedures of the survey, then the hypotheses studied, and finally the empirical findings of the study.

CONCEPTUALIZATION AND PROCEDURES

The committee wanted information on the fastest growing and fastest declining congregations in the United Presbyterian Church. It decided to study a six-year period, from 1968 to 1974.[2] For each of the approximately 9,000 congregations in the denomination, the 1974 active membership figure was divided by the 1968 figure, producing a growth ratio. Since the entire denomination had lost 15.4 percent of its active members during these six years, the average ratio figure was .846.

On the basis of the ratio, we sampled from the 10 percent of the fastest growing, the 10 percent of the fastest declining, and the 30 percent in the middle. The sampling produced a list of approximately 350 with a growth of 5 percent or more (called "growing"), approximately 350 having some loss but not as much as 20 percent (called "typical"), and approximately 350 having losses of 30 percent or more (called "rapidly declining"). The sample of congregations was also stratified by size and geographic region.

Each of the 1,050 congregations was asked to take part, and 802 agreed to do so (293 growing congregations, 268 typical, and 241 rapidly declining). Two kinds of questionnaires were sent to them. First there was a "church questionnaire," which asked a number of factual questions about the community, the congregation, the church program, and so on, to be filled out by a knowledgeable person with access to church records. Second was a packet of six to fifteen "individual questionnaires," to be given to designated types of active parishioners.[3] A total of 617 of the church questionnaires were returned (233 or 76 percent from the growing, 204 or 76 percent from the typical, and 190 or 79 percent from the declining congregations). Of the 7,396 individual questionnaires sent out, 3,994 (51 percent in growing, 54 percent in typical, and 58 percent in declining congregations) were returned.

The data from the church questionnaires and individual questionnaires was combined by assigning mean or modal scores of the individuals from each congregation to that congregation's data. Also, additional data was added from questionnaires that arrived too late for the initial analysis. The result was a data set based on the congregation as a unit of analysis, with 681 congregations (for sampling details see Presbyterian Committee, 1976).

The data was extensive, with nearly 500 variables to be tested as possible determinants of congregational growth or decline. We made an initial scan of correlations between each of them and congregational growth, and on the basis of it eliminated over half (for details on these initial correlations and on criteria and procedures for variable reduction, see Appendix).

HYPOTHESES STUDIED

The questionnaires were constructed with a deductive logic, starting with a long list of hypotheses generated by the committee via interviews and research. The first hypothesis was based on a topic much debated today. Can church growth be gained only at some cost to other important goals of church life? Does a gain in numbers entail a loss in effectiveness, or mission, or community life? The church renewal movement of the late 1950s and early 1960s often said yes, and its writers tended to see the church's loyalty, mission, and effectiveness as more important than gains in numbers. They stressed mission, authenticity, discipleship, and a clear Christian identity apart from mainline American culture (for examples see Berger, 1961; Webber, 1964; for an overview see Reitz, 1969). Writers in the church renewal movement tended implicitly to give a low priority to numerical church growth, and sometimes they explicitly rejected growth as a primary goal of the church. They were not opposed to growth as such but believed that emphasis on growth would take a toll on more urgent objectives. Recently, Robert K. Hudnut, a Presbyterian minister of this theological persuasion, challenged present-day emphasis on church growth in a book entitled *Church Growth Is Not the Point!* (1975). Hudnut (1975:ix) argues:

> But church growth is not the point. The point is whether the church is being true to the Gospel. And, in city after city and town after town, it is. Indeed, *because* it is being faithful it is often *losing* members.
> Loss of growth in statistics has often meant increase in growth in the Gospel. The "dead wood" is gone. The "faithful remnant" remains. The church is lean and stripped for action in the '70s.

Later, he says that "most churches could be two-thirds smaller and lose nothing in power [1975:xi]." Hudnut fears that efforts to foster church growth will endanger personal growth, forgiveness, sensitivity, and discipleship.

The opposite argument is widely heard. It states that theology of the "faithful remnant" and stories of how Gideon conquered with a small band of soldiers are rationalizations. Nothing important would be sacrificed if churches made all-out efforts for growth. And anyway, growth is a foremost priority for Christians, as evidenced by the parable of the lost sheep and the Great Commission to preach the gospel to all nations (for examples of these arguments see McGavran, 1970; Wagner, 1976).

The crucial issue for us is not whether church growth is more or less important but whether the foremost church goals have a fixed-sum character, so that certain ones can be attained only at the cost of loss in others, and a gain in one necessitates a loss in another. The matter can be stated in hypothesis form even more precisely: *considering five church goals—numerical growth, level of individuals' religious commitment, level of members' satisfaction and enthusiasm, level of love and care within the membership, and effectiveness of social witness—they are not mutually exclusive, and they do not form a fixed-sum system.* Wagner would agree with this; Hudnut would not.

Beyond this, we were concerned to see if the main determinants of local congregational growth or decline were a congregation's own conscious efforts, programs, and leadership (local institutional factors) or external factors over which the congregation has no control (local contextual factors). We lacked information for a serious test of national contextual or institutional factors.

We viewed local contextual factors, over which the congregation has no control, as logically prior in a causal sense. We examined local institutional factors, while holding local contextual factors constant. A major research question then was: Do local institutional factors outweigh local contextual factors, assessing the former while holding the latter constant? Fifteen specific hypotheses were put forth describing the impact of specific local contextual or local institutional factors. We list them, beginning with local contextual factors:

(H1) *Congregations will tend to grow if the community in which they are located is affluent.* Past research on this question unanimously shows that Presbyterian congregations grow better in affluent than in poor communities. For example, Thorne (1964) studied census tracts in Pittsburgh and correlated various characteristics with the density of Presbyterian members per 1,000 population in each. The correlation was .57 with median family income, .65 with median years of schooling completed, and .65 with median gross rent of rental occupied dwellings. Somewhat earlier, Douglass (1942) studied Presbyterian congregations in Philadelphia; he divided all the census tracts into four levels, from best to poorest, based on twelve criteria (home ownership, adequacy of housing, degree of crowding, and so on), and found that Presbyterian congregations in each level had different patterns of growth or decline. From 1920 to 1941 those in the best areas had grown by 25.3 percent, while those in the poorest areas had declined 26 percent. The United Presbyterian Church is seen widely as a middle-class denomination, and it grows best where middle-class persons reside.

(H2) *Congregations will tend to grow if their communities are changing and have an influx of affluent, largely white families.* This is a corollary of H1.

(H3) *Congregations in suburban communities will tend to grow more than congregations in cities or rural areas.* This is a pattern recognized by church planners for decades. It is probably best explained by influxes, in many suburbs, of relatively affluent, largely white families.

(H4) *Congregations tend to grow if other churches, and especially other United Presbyterian congregations, are not nearby.*

Next, we turn to local institutional factors:

(H5) *If contextual factors are equal, congregations will tend to grow whose laypersons are satisfied with the church worship and program.*

(H6) *If contextual factors are equal, congregations will tend to grow when the pastor is perceived as warm, spiritually authentic, competent, and able to generate enthusiasm, and when the laypersons are satisfied with the pastor.* This is related to H5, but it specifically tests one aspect of church life—the role of the pastor.

(H7) *If contextual factors are equal, congregations will tend to grow when they are engaged in social action.* This hypothesis has been hotly argued. Some say that church social action is a positive witness to the community and often a way of engaging new prospective members in activities. Others argue that church social action turns off many laypersons and has contributed greatly to withdrawal of members from Protestant churches in recent years. On a related topic, Johnson and Cornell (1972) and Hoge (1976b) made empirical studies to see if objections to social action were a cause of some members' decreasing church contributions, and both found no support for the contention. Contributions are not the same as membership, but the factors underlying them are perhaps similar.

(H8) *If contextual factors are equal, congregations will tend to grow if they have internal harmony and cooperation.*

(H9) *If contextual factors are equal, congregations will tend to grow if the members participate actively in many activities in small groups.* This hypothesis states a theory of church growth espoused by Robert Raines in his book *New Life in the Church* (1961). The theory states that when members are engaged in supportive and intimate small groups, their commitment and their outreach will strengthen (for a similar theory see Schaller, 1975).

(H10) *If contextual factors are equal, congregations will tend to grow if they strive to keep a clear Christian identity over against their surrounding culture.* This hypothesis, as noted earlier, was important in the church renewal writings of the early 1960s. In a somewhat different form it was espoused by Dean Kelley in *Why Conservative Churches Are Growing* (1972). The basic point is that the church loses its attractiveness as a religious institution if it loses itself in the prevailing culture.

(H11) *If contextual factors are equal, congregations will tend to grow if they maintain a clear sense of doctrinal truth, a clear system of meaning and value, intolerance of inner pluralism or dissent, and a high level of demand on members.* This hypothesis states several of the variables central to Kelley's argument about strong religious commitment. Essentially, Kelley's point is that strength of commitment rests upon an unambiguous, forceful type of meaning system.

(H12) *If contextual factors are equal, congregations will tend to grow if they maintain a conservative theological stance.* This hypothesis is widely held by conservative theologians and is closely related to the variables of greatest interest to Kelley. In a 1971 study of twenty United Presbyterian fast-growing congregations, this hypothesis was explicitly studied but found no support (Board of National Missions, 1971).

(H13) *If contextual factors are equal, congregations will tend to grow if they stress recruitment of new members and have active programs to do so.*

(H14) *If contextual factors are constant, congregations will tend to grow if they are effective as organizations, including clear trust in leadership, good communication, sharing ideas, and a sense of an active community.*

(H15) *If contextual factors are constant, congregations will tend to grow whose members' involvement in secular or voluntary organizations, and whose participation in leisure or recreational activities, do not interfere with church life.*

Tests of these fifteen hypotheses should indicate the crucial local determinants of congregational growth or decline. These determinants may vary greatly, depending on variations in the context, such as whether the church is in a city, suburb, or rural area.[4] Many commentators on the American church, including early figures such as Douglass and Brunner (1935) and later Leiffer (1949) and Shippey (1960), have stressed how church trends differ by community type. They have pointed out not only how settings can affect churches, but also how the latter, as institutions, interact dynamically with their environment. With so many variables it is difficult to specify exactly how these should change, but our analysis must look inductively at the data to see what modifications, in fact, occur. Thus, another hypothesis is added for the sake of clarity:

(H16) *The strength of various determinants of congregational growth or decline will vary depending on whether the church is in a city, a suburb, or a rural area.*

CHURCH GROWTH AND OTHER INSTITUTIONAL GOALS: ARE THEY COMPATIBLE?

Our first hypothesis, perhaps the most basic of all, is concerned with whether or not church growth is attained at a cost to other important goals of churches, such as member commitment, love and mutual support within the membership, congregational satisfaction, and social witness. Is church growth incompatible or compatible with these other goals? Our data shed some light on this, since it included measures of four other congregational goals (see Table 9.1).

1. *Strong commitment.* A strong commitment of each member to the faith and to the church is a goal of every Presbyterian congregation. In the data set we have four aggregate measures of such commitment: (1) the percentage of membership attending worship services on a typical Sunday, and ratings on how important the congregation as a whole sees (2) sharing the faith personally, (3) ministering to the needs of others, and (4) bringing new members into the church. As shown by the correlation coefficients, church growth is positively associated with the percentage of members attending worship services and with the goal of bringing new members into the church. Correlations of growth with sharing the faith and ministering to the needs of others as goals, however, are too weak to be noteworthy.

2. *Love and mutual support.* To measure this we have three rating scales filled out by laypersons in each congregation. These ratings show that growing churches tend to be more united than

TABLE 9.1

CORRELATION OF OTHER CONGREGATIONAL GOALS WITH CHURCH GROWTH, 1968-1974*

	Growth, 1968-1974
Strong Commitment	
What percentage of your membership attends worship services on an average fall Sunday?	.18
In your congregation as a whole, which three of the following have you found to be the most important aspects of their faith? (ten responses given)	
Sharing their faith with others personally	.07
Ministering to the needs of others	-.03
Bringing new members into the church to share their faith	.13
Love and Mutual Support	
Rating of congregation on scales of 1 to 7:	
1=impersonal, 7=mutually supportive	.12
1=unfriendly, 7=friendly	.07
1=divided, 7=united	.18
Social Witness	
Does your congregation provide financial support to any non-denominational community agencies or organizations?	.06
Within its total program, to what extent does your congregation emphasize social involvement?	.03

	Growth, 1968-74
Is your congregation currently involved in the following?	
Providing aid to needy persons in your congregation	-.07
Providing aid to needy persons in your community	-.12
Helping to organize or support disadvantaged members of your congregation to petition for their cause (e.g., women, senior citizens, welfare mothers)	.08
Helping to organize or support disadvantaged groups to petition for their cause	.09
Satisfaction and Enthusiasm	
All in all, to what extent are you satisfied with your congregation compared with most others?	.27
All in all, to what extent are you satisfied with your membership?	.20
To what extent are you satisfied with each of these components of your congregation's life?	
Church administration	.03
Pastoral sensitivity to the needs of people	.12
Worship services (overall)	.11

*Correlations of .09 or stronger are significant at the .01 level. N = approximately 681.

others and somewhat more mutually supportive, although only slightly more friendly. While friendliness is often cited as a trait of a growing church, interestingly it shows up here as less important than unity and mutual support.

3. *Social witness.* It is often argued that emphasis on church growth precludes effective Christian social witness, not only because attention and energy are diverted from social witness but also because churches working for growth will shy away from any actions that might offend someone in the congregation. Table 9.1 includes six measures of congregational social witness. The first two are ratings of social involvement in general. The third and fourth are ratings of congregational activities in helping needy persons—involvement often labeled as charity rather than social action, since aid to individual needy persons usually has no impact on the social conditions generating distress. The fifth and sixth are ratings of congregational involvement in social action in this latter sense. These distinctions turned out to be unimportant, however, as the table shows. Only one of the six measures of congregational social witness—providing aid to needy persons—has a statistically significant inverse relationship to church growth, and it is too weak to be noteworthy; this is no doubt a result of the lack of needy persons in the affluent areas that, as shown below, are very conducive to membership growth. Several other correlations are positive rather than negative but all are very weak. Thus, there is little basis for concluding that church growth and social witness mutually exclude each other.

4. *Satisfaction and enthusiasm.* This goal is a bit ambiguous in that it is often instrumental to growth as well as a goal in itself. That is, many persons stress satisfaction and enthusiasm as generalized resources for achieving other goals, not as goals in themselves. In spite of this fuzziness, the data is enlightening. We have five measures: First and second are overall ratings of satisfaction with the congregation and with church membership generally. Third, fourth, and fifth are ratings of satisfaction with discrete elements of congregational life—church administration, pastoral ministry, and worship. The correlations with growth range in magnitude from .03 to .27, the strongest occurring with the generalized ratings. The two positive correlations of .20 and .27 indicate that growth and satisfaction are associated.

We can now answer the question, Is church growth attained at a cost to other foremost goals? The answer is no. Growing congregations appear to have slightly stronger commitment of members than other congregations, somewhat greater unity and support, and somewhat greater satisfaction and enthusiasm among their members. The relationship with social witness is weak and ambiguous. To summarize, growth has little impact, either positive or negative, on a congregation's achievement of other goals. If anything, growing churches appear to be achieving other goals a bit better than those that are stable or declining in membership.

LOCAL CONTEXTUAL FACTORS

We look next at the importance of local contextual factors for church growth. As pointed out earlier, these are factors over which the congregation has no control, and thus, they logically precede institutional considerations in our analysis. The data included many indicators of aspects of the local community. Five clusters of variables were identified in the preliminary analysis: affluence, demographic change, community facilities, community type, and church competition.[5]

First, we examine correlations for the five clusters, summarizing the degree of association with church growth (see Table 9.2). Shown are the simple correlations for the separate indicators plus the multiple correlation squares (R^2), or the total association for the combined set of indicators in each cluster.

All the affluence indicators relate to church growth and are among the strongest correlates uncovered. Age of church building and age of homes near the church are negatively associated with growth; economic level of the neighborhood is positively associated, percent renters negatively associated. Likewise, the demographic change indicators predict church growth in ways that would be expected. Economic expansion and growth of the school population of a community are the best predictors, with correlations of .28 and .25, respectively. Increasing numbers of young people, families, newcomers, and Protestants are all supportive of a growing church, whereas an influx of older persons and minorities is not. Both of these clusters—affluence and demographic change—reinforce the image of the healthy Presbyterian church as one catering to a white, upper-middle-class, family-centered clientele.

Facilities located near a church, except for farms, are all negatively related to church growth. Even the presence of public schools is not a correlate of growth. Rather, public schools, banks, and retail stores are slightly inhibitive, suggesting that the churches surviving best are those located in primarily residential

TABLE 9.2

CORRELATIONS OF LOCAL CONTEXTUAL MEASURES WITH CHURCH GROWTH

Local Contextual Clusters	Correlation*
Affluence (Total R^2 = .10)	
Age of homes near church	-.27
Age of church building	-.19
Economic level of people living near church	.22
Percent renters near church	-.19
Demographic Change (Total R^2 = .13)	
Increase in school population	.25
Increase in economic level	.28
Increase in older persons	-.10
Increase in younger persons	.13
Increase in minorities	-.15
Increase in families	.16
Increase in newcomers	.09
Increase in Protestants	.09
Community Facilities (Total R^2 = .05)	
Location near church of factories	-.05
Location near church of banks	-.13
Location near church of retail stores	-.14
Location near church of shopping centers	-.01
Location near church of railroad or bus station	-.04
Location near church of farms	.14
Location near church of public schools	-.15
Community Type (Total R^2 = .03)	
Suburb versus city, town and country (suburb=1, other=0)	.10
Suburb and town and country versus city (suburb, town and country=1, city=0)	.16
Church Competition (Total R^2 = .02)	
Other Protestant churches close by	-.15
Other Presbyterian churches close by	-.01

*Correlations of .09 or stronger are significant at the .01 level.
N = approximately 681.

areas. This interpretation is further supported by the community-type variations. Two differing combinations of community types were included in the analysis: suburb versus city, town, and rural areas; and city versus suburb, town, and rural. On the assumption that cities differ substantially in residential characteristics from either suburbs or town and country areas, it follows that the latter combination should better predict church growth. While the difference in size of correlations is not huge, this is indeed the case. Churches located in well-established residential areas are growing, compared with those in commercial and/or transitional areas, where people are moving out.

The presence of other churches is also a factor. It would appear that other Protestant churches nearby is more important than other Presbyterian churches. This may be because most communities have only one Presbyterian church. Also, many Protestant churches draw members from a similar social background as do the Presbyterians, and thus compete with one another for members. The greater the interdenominational competition, the greater the chances that Presbyterian growth will be affected.

Variations by Community Type

The patterns just described hold in a general sense, but do they apply across all types of communities? We repeated the foregoing analysis *within* each of six community types: growing areas of large cities, nongrowing areas of large cities, growing areas of suburbs, nongrowing areas of suburbs, small cities, and town and country settings (see Table 9.3).[6] One overall pattern in the table is that the correlations are almost always higher for the city and the suburban congregations than for those in small cities or in town and country settings. This is largely a result of low variation in the latter settings. Indeed, in the Presbyterian data set the typical congregations (neither growing nor declining much) were most often found in small cities, in small towns, and in rural areas; the fastest growing congregations were located disproportionately in suburban areas, while the fastest declining were most often in large cities. It seems that small cities and small towns have more stable churches because their populations are more stable. Hence, local contextual factors are relatively less influential than in cities and in suburbs.

Table 9.3 has several patterns regarding specific contextual factors. Community growth and affluence are important for church growth in all types of communities, but especially so in growing cities and suburbs. Level of affluence is important in all types of communities, but more so in growing areas than in nongrowing areas. In suburban communities, both growing and nongrowing, increases in school population, in younger persons, in families, and in higher status residents are all strong assists to church growth. These same demographic changes have less influence in large cities and in small cities and towns (where they occur much less). An increase in minorities is inversely associated with church

TABLE 9.3

CORRELATIONS OF LOCAL CONTEXTUAL MEASURES WITH CHURCH GROWTH
BY COMMUNITY TYPE

Local Contextual Clusters	Large City		Suburbs of Large City		Small City	Town and Country
	Growing Area (N=94)	Non-Growing Area (N=71)	Growing Area (N=86)	Non-Growing Area (N=85)	(N=111)	(N=161)
Affluence						
Age of homes near church	-.33*	-.28*	-.30*	-.36*	-.24*	-.11
Age of church building	-.17*	-.14	-.29*	-.23*	-.21*	-.15*
Economic level	.31*	.21*	.17	.00	.23*	.20*
Percent renters	-.11	-.16	-.21*	-.26*	-.03	.14*
Demographic Change						
Increase in school population	.13	.10	.34*	.33*	.30*	.09
Increase in economic level	.35*	.21*	.41*	.28*	.16*	.16*
Increase in older persons	-.04	-.18	-.05	-.17	-.06	-.13*
Increase in younger persons	.04	.02	.17	.18*	.15	.15*
Increase in minorities	-.25*	-.32*	-.19*	-.15	-.04	.00
Increase in families	.15	.08	.23*	.19*	.18*	.12
Increase in Protestants	.22*	.25*	.20*	.07	.08	.00
Community Facilities						
Church near Factories	-.06	-.06	.11	.10	-.12	-.12
Banks	.08	-.14	-.14	-.19*	-.08	-.19*
Retail stores	-.12	-.34*	-.17	-.18*	-.06	-.14*
Shopping centers	.04	-.04	-.03	.00	.06	-.03
Railroad or bus station	.02	-.12	-.05	-.22*	-.01	-.06
Farms	.24*	-.13	.12	.22*	.07	.12
Public schools	-.12	-.13	-.16	-.15	-.10	-.26*
Church Competition						
Other Protestant churches	-.20*	.10	-.37*	-.25*	.01	-.13*
Other Presbyterian churches	-.03	.22*	-.27*	-.12	.05	.01

*Significant at the .05 level.

growth in cities and suburbs, except in town and country areas where there are very few blacks and other minorities to begin with. An increase in Protestants, likewise, is a factor important to church growth in cities and in growing suburbs, but less so in nongrowing suburbs, in small cities, and in town and country settings.

Looking at community institutions and facilities, we see that their presence near the church is of greater significance in nongrowing city and suburban settings than elsewhere. Especially in cities, it is crucial whether the community is growing or not. If it is growing, the presence of banks, shopping centers, bus stations, and the like is of little relevance. Urban churches located in stable residential areas, and especially in areas benefiting from an influx of new people, are better able to hold onto and attract new members.

Competition from other churches has a greater effect in growing areas than elsewhere. In growing urban and suburban areas the presence of other churches nearby is associated with membership decline. The same holds for nongrowing suburbs, but not for nongrowing city areas, where the presence of other churches appears to encourage Presbyterian growth.

In sum, factors in church growth vary somewhat from one community type to another. Whether the congregation is located in a city, a suburb, a town, or a rural area is important. But even more important are two factors that may be present in any area—*affluence and favorable demographic shifts*. Affluence and favorable demographic shifts may occur in any ecological setting, and it is these rather than the type of neighborhood or city that most influence church growth or decline. Probably all the mainline religious institutions in America are strongly affected by factors such as these, since mainline denominations draw the majority of their members from a broad, middle-class constituency.

Relative Importance of Contextual Factors

If indeed affluence and favorable demographic change are the major contextual determinants of church growth, this should be even more evident when we control statistically for the several clusters of factors. In the analysis above we looked at the correlations without controls and hence did not assess fully the relative significance of each of the five contextual clusters. In a further analysis (shown in Appendix) we computed multiple-partial correlations with church growth for each cluster while holding constant all the other clusters.[7] This provides a more thorough basis for assessing the relative importance of the various factors. The outcome was that demographic change (with all else controlled) accounts for 8 percent of the variance, and affluence (with all else controlled) accounts for 4 percent. None of the other clusters accounts for over 1 percent. The conclusion is quite clear: *affluence* and *demographic change* are the best overall predictors of church growth among all these factors. Hypotheses concerning these factors receive greater support than do hypotheses about community type, institutions and facilities, or church competition.

LOCAL INSTITUTIONAL FACTORS

Next, we turn to our second set of factors—local institutional. They pertain to the internal dynamics and characteristics of churches and include a wide range of matters—such as congregational style, program, and activities—over which members have some degree of choice. Data on fifteen clusters of local institutional factors is depicted in Table 9.4. (See Appendix for the process of variable selection for institutional clusters.) The table shows the simple correlation of each variable with church growth and the variance explained in church growth by each cluster. Two of the clusters are clearly the most related to church growth—satisfaction with church worship and program, and congregational harmony and cooperation.

Satisfaction with church worship and program is clearly the strongest of the many institutional factors. All eight indicators within the cluster are related to church growth, as expected, and the total explained variance (.13) is greater than that for any other cluster. This is not very surprising, since membership growth in churches, as with many voluntary organizations, often creates internal strains and tensions, depending on the extent to which new members are assimilated into a group. Level of satisfaction is likely to reflect, among other things, social acceptance and a sense of belonging. Also, because churches are highly normative organizations seeking to influence people's values and beliefs, those unhappy with them tend to drop out or become inactive. In a religiously pluralistic society, dissatisfied persons can easily find another faith or organize a new congregation within the same denominational tradition more in keeping with their outlook. Thus, members' satisfaction with church worship and program is a critically important intervening factor. Churches that grow are those able to generate high levels of membership satisfaction,

TABLE 9.4

CORRELATIONS OF LOCAL INSTITUTIONAL FACTORS WITH CHURCH GROWTH

Local Institutional Factors	Correlation*
Satisfaction with Church	
Worship and Program (Total R^2 = .13)	
Need for Improvement in Recruitment	-.33
Need for Improvement in Lay Leadership	-.17
Need for Improvement in Congregation's Involvement in Community	-.16
Need for Improvement in Youth Programs	-.21
Need for Improvement in Financial Support	-.20
Need for Improvement in Worship Services	-.15
Need for Improvement in Sense of Purpose and Priorities	-.19
Satisfaction with Congregation	.27
Pastor (Total R^2 = .04)	
Rating on Ability to Generate Enthusiasm	.20
Rating on Warmth	.14
Rating on Competence	.16
Satisfaction with Pastor	.18
Social Action	
1. **Use of Facilities** (Total R^2 = .01)	
Use by Educational Groups	-.12
Use by Community Service Groups	-.05
Provide Meeting Room for Study of Social Issues	.07
2. **Organizing the Disadvantaged** (Total R^2 = .01)	
Help Organize Disadvantaged Members to Petition	.08
Help Organize Disadvantaged Goups to Petition	.09
3. **Financial Support** (Total R^2 = .03)	
Support for Rehabilitation Groups	.13
Support for Scouts	.11
Support for Adult Education	.05
Support for Educational Groups	.05
4. **Changing Society** (Total R^2 = .03)	
Importance for Pastor Trying to Change Society	-.17
Importance for Member Trying to Change Society	-.12
Congregational Harmony and Cooperation (Total R^2 = .10)	

	Correlation
Congregation United	.18
Congregation Friendly	.08
Congregation Mutually Supportive	.12
Congregation Inclusive	.08
Disunity as Result of Social Action Involvement	-.29

Small Groups and Activities (Total R^2 = .05)

Active Youth Program	.18
Men's Groups	.12
Prayer Groups	.09
Bible Study Groups	.07
House Church Clusters	.06

Apartness from Culture (Total R^2 = .03)

Congregation Stands Apart from Community	-.15
Congregation Is Dissimilar from Community	-.14
Congregation Is Uninvolved in Community	-.12
Congregation Is Opposed to Community	-.12

Demands on Members (Total R^2 = .03)

Regular Confirmation Class	.17
Procedures for Familiarizing People with Church Programs	.07
Procedures for Preparing New Members	.08

Sharing Beliefs (Total R^2 = .01)

Frequency That Members Share Beliefs and Insights	.10
Frequency That Respondent Shares Christian Beliefs	.07
Importance of Sharing Beliefs	.06

Intolerance (Total R^2 = .02)

Agree that no one has the right to impose beliefs on others	-.11
Congregation's Openness to People of Diverse Theologies	.07

Conservatism (Total R^2 = .04)

Agree that the Bible is the only infallible rule	.13
Importance Attached to Faith as Personal Guide in Daily Decisions	.08
Agree that it is not as important to worry about	

	Correlation
life after death as about what we do in this life	-.13
Agree that the different churches are saying the same thing but with different words	-.08
Importance of Personal Experience of Salvation	.09

Recruitment (Total R^2 = .03)

Members' Involvement in Recruitment	.17
Identification of Visitors at Worship	.05
Contact of New Residents in Community	.06
Follow-up Personal Contacts with Visitors	.05
Organized Program for Recruitment	.06

Integration of New Members (Total R^2 = .03)

Procedures for Integration of New Members	.11
Percent of Church Leaders New to the Congregation	.12

Coordination and Leadership Style (Total R^2 = .03)

Influence of Pastor on Church	.13
Congregation Style Encourages Hard Work by Members	.10
Influence of Church Groups on Church	.07
Session Is Sensitive to Congregation	.07
People Plan Together and Coordinate	.06
People Are Asked in Making Decisions	.06

Communication and Encouragement (Total R^2 = .03)

People Offer Each Other Ideas	.13
Information About Church in Local Newspapers	.06
Information on Church Programs Is Adequate	.06
Members Keep Each Other Informed	.10
Procedures for Dealing with Inactive Members	.06
Congregation Plan to Maintain Contact with Members	.04

Involvement in Secular Organizations (Total R^2 = .01)

Members Are Involved in Secular Organizations	.07
Outside Involvement Decreases Church Involvement	-.05
Involvement in Organizations Is a Barrier to Church Involvement	-.04

*Correlations of .09 or stronger are significant at the .01 level. N = approximately 681.

thereby averting, as much as possible, the loss of members to other religious groups, as well as congregational apathy and disinterest.

Much the same holds for the second strongest cluster, congregational harmony and cooperation. Congregations that are united, friendly, mutually supportive, and inclusive are inclined to grow. Disunity in a congregation (as a result of social action involvement or anything else) is associated with church decline. Almost as important to church growth as overall membership's satisfaction is the quality of relationships between members and the consensus about the church's purpose and mission.

Pastor ratings are important, especially whether or not the pastor generates enthusiasm in the congregation. About equally important are small group activities, particularly so in the case of active youth programs. Neither of these clusters, however, proves to be as strongly associated with church growth as some seem to think.

Social action involvement encompasses a diverse group of measures. Four subsets were identified: use of facilities, organizing the disadvantaged, financial support, and efforts at changing society. Both organizing the disadvantaged and financial support for activities customarily associated with churches—Scouts, rehabilitation for example—are positively related with membership growth; but the use of congregational facilities by groups concerned with social action and explicit efforts at changing society tend to be inversely related. Two conclusions appear to follow. One is that what is often labeled social action in churches means various things and may or may not affect congregational growth. Whether or not churches grow when engaged in social action depends on what aspects of social action are involved, the degree to which such programs touch upon the lives of the members themselves, and whether or not such activity is viewed as controversial in society. A second is that it is not social action involvement per se, but rather the *congregational tension and disunity* often associated with social action that is crucial. Social action that does not create disharmony is unlikely to have a negative effect on church growth.

All the remaining clusters are weakly related to church growth. Several of these—apartness from culture, demands on members, sharing belief, intolerance, and conservatism—bear upon Kelley's thesis about which churches in contemporary American society are growing. Our data offers only weak support for his argument. In its favor we see that demands on members and conservative theology relate positively to growth to a noteworthy degree. But apartness from culture, an important aspect of Kelley's concern for the church's distinctive meaning system, is negatively associated with growth. Among Presbyterian congregations, the ones growing are closely identified with the culture and community of which they are a part. Also, on another matter about which Kelley speaks—intolerance—our evidence is inconclusive. We have only two indicators of intolerance: one yielding a negative correlate of membership growth and the other a positive.

Other considerations—such as recruitment, integration of members, coordination and leadership style, communication and encouragement, and involvement in secular organizations—appear to have little impact on church growth. Relative to the other institutional factors previously examined, they exert less of an influence.

Controls for Contextual Factors

Knowing that contextual factors do indeed affect whether or not churches grow, we were interested in seeing if controls for these would influence, in any way, how the institutional variables operate. That is, does the importance of the institutional factors change when the contextual variables are statistically held constant? Are the institutional factors still as important "if all else is equal"? To check this we computed multiple-partial coefficients, simultaneously controlling for the two contextual sets that were of most significance (affluence and demographic change).[8] The results can be described concisely (for details see Appendix). Generally, the local institutional factors remain almost as strong after controls as before. The relative importance of the various institutional factors also remains nearly the same. The strongest institutional factor, "Satisfaction with Church Worship and Program," which accounted for 13 percent of the variance without controls, accounts for 11 percent with controls. The second strongest without controls, "Congregational Harmony and Cooperation," accounted for 10 percent without controls and 8 percent with controls. The third strongest, "Small Groups and Activities," dropped from explaining 5 percent without controls to 2 percent with controls. The fourth strongest, "Pastor," maintained its explanatory power at 4 percent of the variance both without and with controls.

Most of the institutional factors weakened moderately when controls were introduced. However, "Organizing the Disadvantaged," one portion of the social action factor, gained in explanatory power from only one percent without controls to 5 percent with controls (the more organization of disadvantaged, the more growth occurred). The reason for this is unclear. Possibly it is related to the presence or absence of disadvantaged persons in the community. Thus, where disadvantaged persons are present, organizational efforts in their behalf may contribute to church growth.

Analysis Within the Six Community Types

As we did earlier, again we computed the correlations within each of the six community types. Here we did so after controlling for the two main contextual clusters—affluence and demographic change (see Table 9.5). The main pattern in the table is that the institutional factors are most important in suburbs and least important in small cities and in town and country settings. It should be remembered that small cities and town and country areas had the largest number of stable churches and the fewest fast-growing or fast-declining churches. Since fast growth or decline is less likely in such settings, institutional influences will have less impact. By contrast, suburban churches seem to have greater power over their own growth or decline through institutional efforts than do city churches or small town churches.

A second pattern is that the institutional factors have greater impact in nongrowing areas (both city and suburban) than in growing areas (both city and suburban). This pattern is especially clear in the contrast of nongrowing suburban areas and growing suburban areas. For example, satisfaction with worship and program correlates .40 with church growth in nongrowing suburbs and .24 with church growth in growing suburbs. Also, congregational harmony and cooperation correlates .33 with church growth in nongrowing areas of large cities and .21 with church growth in growing areas of large cities. Apparently, in nongrowing areas church growth is largely dependent on holding onto members through congregational unity, communal life, and effective pastoral leadership.

EXPLANATORY SIGNIFICANCE OF THE VARIABLES

As a final part of the study, we sought to determine the explanatory significance of the entire set of variables examined. Table 9.6 summarizes the total variance accounted for by the various clusters, both contextual and institutional, looking at them in terms of their consecutive increments in explaining church

TABLE 9.5

CORRELATIONS OF LOCAL INSTITUTIONAL FACTORS WITH CHURCH GROWTH
BY COMMUNITY TYPE, CONTROLLING FOR AFFLUENCE AND DEMOGRAPHIC CHANGE:
MULTIPLE-PARTIAL CORRELATIONS*

Local Institutional Clusters	Large City		Suburbs of Large City		Small City	Town and Country
	Growing Area (N=94)	Non-Growing Area (N=71)	Growing Area (N=86)	Non-Growing Area (N=85)	(N=111)	(N=161)
Satisfaction with Worship Program	.24	.23	.24	.40	.15	.11
Pastor	.15	.21	.11	.13	.09	.09
Social Action Use of Facilities	.11	.13	.17	.44	.16	.06
Organizing the Disadvantaged	.09	.21	.19	.28	.15	.00
Financial Support	.06	.07	.07	.09	.00	.02
Changing Society	.06	.04	.00	.16	.02	.00
Congregational Harmony and Cooperation	.21	.33	.20	.30	.05	.04
Small Groups and Activities	.08	.10	.20	.17	.02	.02
Apartness from Culture	.01	.24	.09	.09	.08	.00
Demands on Members	.08	.00	.03	.20	.02	.07
Sharing Beliefs	.05	.01	.07	.17	.04	.00
Intolerance	.00	.07	.01	.06	.01	.01
Conservatism	.21	.14	.10	.18	.10	.00
Recruitment	.02	.04	.11	.10	.02	.09
Integration of New Members	.01	.00	.04	.05	.00	.04
Coordination and Leadership Style	.12	.04	.06	.14	.09	.02
Communication and Encouragement	.14	.27	.03	.22	.04	.00
Involvement in Secular Organizations	.05	.14	.07	.10	.01	.00

*Coefficients of .06 or stronger are significant at the .05 level.

TABLE 9.6

EXPLAINED VARIANCE FOR CONTEXTUAL AND INSTITUTIONAL CLUSTERS

	Total Adjusted R^2	Increments to Adjusted R^2
Contextual Clusters		
Affluence	.086	.086*
Demographic Change	.143	.057*
Community Type	.146	.003
Institutional Clusters		
Satisfaction with Church Worship and Program	.208	.062*
Pastor	.205	.000
Social Action (All 4 Sets)	.230	.022*
Congregational Harmony and Cooperation	.269	.039*
Small Groups and Activities	.263	.000
Demand, Sharing Beliefs, Intolerance, Conservatism	.266	.000
Recruitment	.260	.000
Integration of New Members, Coordination and Leadership, Style, Communication and Encouragement, and Involvement in Secular Organizations	.260	.000

*In the second column, statistically significant at .05 level.

growth. The multiple R^2 is shown after each cluster is added.[9] We were able to explain 26 percent of the total variance.

The size of the coefficients can be influenced by the order in which the clusters are introduced in the analysis. Therefore, we sought to enter them in an order consistent with our causal assumptions and in keeping with empirical findings up to this point. Affluence and demographic change clusters together account for over 14 percent of the adjusted variance. When we treat suburb and rural setting versus city setting as a community type variable, the variance explained is increased slightly, to 14.6 percent. The contextual factors combined account for 56 percent of the adjusted explained variance in church growth.

Among the institutional clusters, only three have much overall impact: satisfaction with worship and program, social action involvement, and congregational harmony and cooperation. Worship and program satisfaction is very important, accounting for about one half the variance explained by institutional factors. Congregational harmony and cooperation is the second most important cluster, followed by social involvement. These three explain 11.4 percent of the variance above and beyond that accounted for by the contextual factors, thus comprising about 44 percent of the total explained variance.

CONCLUSIONS

This research has inquired into the correlates of church growth to determine what types of factors operate and how strong they are. Most relationships were weak, with the majority of the correlations weaker than .10 and thus unable to explain very much variance in church growth.

Several conclusions follow from our analysis. First, among contextual factors, the hypotheses receiving the greatest support were H1 and H2, stressing the importance of affluence and of an influx of young, middle-class, largely white families into the communities in which the churches are located. The importance of these factors is not surprising, since most mainline Protestant churches rely upon these sources for their growth. Churches closely identified with an affluent, white middle-class clientele all benefit from an influx of such people. The impact of affluence and favorable demographic change on church growth is independent of, and more important than, the location of the church in a city, a suburb, or a small town. The basic currents of community change affecting churches are important in *all* types of communities.

Second, among institutional factors, the hypotheses receiving the greatest support were H5, H7, and H8, emphasizing members' satisfaction with worship and program, involvement in social action, and congregational harmony and cooperation. Both the satisfaction and harmony and cooperation factors are understandable, since in America, with its heritage of religious voluntarism, churches must attract and maintain their members, depending on how well they can meet the members' personal needs and preferences, both religious and social.

Social action involvement is more complicated because, as we have seen, it can have both positive and negative effects. Involvement in controversial actions can lead to congregational division and disharmony, and if so, it will likely lead to membership decline; yet, some types of social action attract newcomers and offer members a sense of religious and social responsibility. Quite clearly, generalizations about the effects of social action on church growth or decline are easily exaggerated, and analysts must scrutinize them carefully.

Equally significant as the hypotheses supported are those that are not. Two deserve comment. One is the role of the pastor as it relates to church growth. Contrary to Wagner and others who have recently stressed the responsibility of the clergy and of church leaders for growth, the findings here fail to offer strong support for this line of thinking. To be sure, pastors are important but mainly as they affect factors already mentioned, such as members' satisfaction, congregational harmony, and social action; apart from these, the ratings of pastors on various dimensions were quite unimportant. Given the complexities of the factors involved, clergy should not be singled out as primarily responsible for the trends in question. Rather, attention belongs to how they develop those institutional styles and qualities—especially satisfaction and harmony—most conducive to congregational growth. A second is that the conservatism of a congregation's theology turned out less important than many commentators seem to believe. Among Presbyterians, at least, theologically conservative congregations are not growing appreciably more than are liberal congregations.[10]

Finally, this study provides at least an initial answer to the general question faced by researchers of church trends for some decades—How much of the change is caused by local contextual factors and how much is caused by local institutional factors? Some, like H. Paul Douglass, have argued that "as the community goes, so goes the church," emphasizing the influence of local contextual forces over a congregation's destiny. Other analysts, such as McGavran, Wagner, and Kelley, emphasize the importance of pastoral leadership, evangelism, theology, and church discipline—all local institutional factors. In this study of Presbyterian congregations, we find that the two sets of factors are roughly equal in strength. Contextual factors are slightly stronger, accounting for 56 percent of the explained variance, while institutional factors account for 44 percent. Both sets operate, independently and probably in interaction with each other, in shaping church trends. The issue is not really one set of factors versus the other, but rather the conditions under which one or the other predominates in influence, or how the two together explain trends neither can account for alone. In the future more attention should be given to developing multi-causal and interactive approaches, which hopefully will provide a more thorough explanation for congregational trends.

Performance of United Church of Christ Congregations in Massachusetts and in Pennsylvania[1]

William J. McKinney Jr.

The United Church of Christ is one of the mainline Protestant denominations that has experienced declines in membership since the mid-1960s, after several decades of steady growth. From 1970 to 1975 reported membership declined 7.2 percent. Along with membership declines have come declines in church school enrollment and strains on financial support of local, regional, and national mission programming. Church school enrollment decreased 24.5 percent from 1970 to 1975. Support for local church programming increased at a rate less than that of inflation, and support for nonlocal denominational mission activity increased at a rate less than one third the inflation rate.

What happened? Sydney Ahlstrom (1972:1079), in the concluding chapter of *A Religious History of the American People*, points to the decade of the 1960s as the emergence of a new stage in the development of American religious life. This decade, he argues, brought to an end "a unified four hundred year period in the Anglo-American experience." The accuracy of Ahlstrom's assessment will be judged by future generations of historians. Yet, it does seem clear, from the perspective of the late 1970s, that the decade was one in which established patterns of religious participation in America began to change.

Our objective in this chapter is not to explain recent religious changes, whose causes are numerous and complex. Our effort is more limited, but it is set amid the context of wide-ranging discussions of secularization, religious trends, new religious movements, and church growth.[2] In such a context we must state precisely our purposes and point of view. First, in this chapter, we argue that numerical membership growth is one of a number of dimensions that need attention, as one examines the performance of local congregations of the United Church of Christ. Second, we examine relationships among five dimensions of local church performance using data from 263 United Church of Christ congregations in Massachusetts and in Pennsylvania. Third, we examine the relative impact of community factors external to the local church and factors internal to its life on those dimensions of congregational performance.

TOWARD AN UNDERSTANDING OF CONGREGA-TIONAL PERFORMANCE

The student of changes in religious commitment and participation in religious organizations must be sensitive to two questionable assumptions that occur frequently in discussions of church trends. The first is seen in a tendency to equate church growth with denominational growth. Denominational growth is a summation of local church growth and can be fully understood only through an analysis of local church conditions. While denominational growth patterns have received considerable attention, examinations of growing and declining congregations within denominations have been few in number (see chapter 9 for one such study). In the past most investigators have used a case study approach that is of limited value in understanding broad patterns of congregational growth.

The second questionable assumption is seen in a tendency to view numerical increases in church membership as a sole indicator of local church and denominational health. The question "Is church growth good?" presses one into the realm of theological values. It needs to be addressed from the perspectives of both theology and the sociology of organizations.

For some religious bodies in the United States, growth is *not* a value, and no new adherents are sought. The Shakers, for an extreme example, will cease to exist on the death of their few remaining members. The Amish seek no converts but expect to replenish their numbers from within. The various communities of Judaism stress preservation and retention of members as opposed to recruitment of non-Jews. By contrast, other religious bodies are aggressively evangelical, seeking the conversion of individuals and groups to their religious stance and to membership in their religious community.

The *anti*-growth stance is an uncommon one within American Protestantism, but it does have advocates. Robert Hudnut (1975) presents an articulate counter to concern about membership losses in his recent book, *Church Growth Is Not the Point!*, arguing that the task of the church is not to expand itself numerically, but to be faithful to its mission as servant in and for the world.

Carl S. Dudley (1977), from a different perspective, has addressed the question, "Why do small churches not grow?" Viewing small churches as primary groups or as single-cell organisms in which every member expects to know every other member, Dudley contends that the small church (200 members or less) is already the right size for its task.

> Small churches are already the right size for everyone to know everybody else. They are, in fact, much larger than many social scientists think they "ought to be." They cannot include more members without letting go of the contact they now have with the present body [1977:13].

Dudley's point is an important one: church growth can be organizationally undesirable, apart from theological considerations. On reaching a given size, the organization loses the capacity to do well what it is able to do and to provide for its members what they expect of it.

Expectations of Local Churches by Denominations

Membership growth is one of several aspects of congregational performance. For some churches and some denominations it is an extremely important goal; for others it is less important. Recent research on the performance of local churches, however, has tended to focus on this single dimension. Since data on membership is more readily accessible than other measures of performance, this focus is understandable. The focus on membership has also resulted from difficulty in arriving at criteria regarding other areas of performance. The very notion of performance implies a set of criteria or standards in relation to which a church is performing well or poorly, and such criteria are not easy to determine.

One way of addressing the question of congregational performance is to examine the goals the local church has set for itself and to assess its effectiveness in reaching these goals. Another is to give attention to the nature of relationships among the members of the congregation, on the assumption that the stated goals of an organization are frequently secondary to the maintenance of patterns of relationships among participants within a social group. A third is to formulate criteria of performance based on theological assumptions about the nature of a "good" or "faithful" local congregation.

Each approach has attractions. While recognizing these, we adopt still a fourth approach, attempting to identify the expectations a denominational body has of the local churches that comprise its membership. These expectations may or may not be held by all local churches of the denomination, but we shall ask, "What does the United Church of Christ expect of the local congregations that hold membership in the denomination?"

Within some denominations expectations or performance criteria for local churches are relatively clear. Adherence to specific doctrines, levels of clergy subsidies, and financial quotas for support of denominational mission programs are examples. Other expectations may be more informally articulated but just as clearly understood: emphasis on recruitment of new members, stances on sociopolitical issues such as abortion, alcohol consumption, or gambling, and so on.

The expectations a denomination has of its local churches can have considerable impact, since denominations have some sanctions to ensure conformity. The sanctions include the withholding of professional leadership from deviant congregations, influencing placement of clergy, and other forms of organizational pressure.

Denominations in the congregational tradition are less explicit in their expectations of local church performance than are those of a more connectional polity. The investigator cannot turn to a Book of Discipline to find them but must look to other sources to discern them.

The *Constitution and Bylaws* of the United Church of Christ, a document adopted in 1961, contains several references to the local church. It gives major attention to the protection of the autonomy of the local church, as exemplified in the following statement:

The autonomy of the local church is inherent and modifiable only by its own action. Nothing in this Constitution and Bylaws of the United Church of Christ shall destroy or limit the right of each local church to operate in the ways customary to it; nor shall it be construed as giving to the General Synod, or to any Conference or Association now, or at any future time, the power to abridge or impair the autonomy of any local church in the management of its own affairs [United Church of Christ, 1977:4].

Given the freedom and the responsibility each local UCC congregation has to set its own goals and order its own life, those who would presume to set forth expectations of local church performance do so with some hesitation. The Tenth (1975) and Eleventh (1977) General Synods of the United Church of Christ nevertheless adopted resolutions on the "vitality of the local church." These statements place an emphasis on the issue of viability as essential to the achievement of vitality and include recommendations to the agencies of the United Church of Christ for enhancing the work of local churches. The two statements stress five dimensions of local church life as especially important in the local churches' quest for viability.

1. Nurture of the present membership and the enlistment of new members;

2. Adequate finances to support the congregation's leadership, organizational, and facilities needs;

3. Pursuit of mission through which the congregation is actively engaged in outreach to its community, nation, and world;

4. Program that satisfies the needs of the membership, including worship life that celebrates the common life of the people, pastoral care and nurture to encourage growth in faith, and development of effective clergy and lay leadership;

5. Supportive relations with and financial support for the mission program of the United Church of Christ and its instrumentalities.[3]

AN EXAMINATION OF CONGREGATIONAL PERFORM-ANCE

Data and Methods

In the last several years the United Church Board for Homeland Ministries has collected data on three aspects of local church life: (1) membership, church school, and financial data for the years

1965-75; (2) tract-level data from the 1970 U.S. census on the communities in which churches are located; and (3) data on the background and attitudes of persons attending Sunday services of worship in United Church of Christ congregations. The last has been obtained through the use of a four-page Church Membership Inventory administered to all church attenders over the age of 15.[4]

From this bank of information, data on 263 United Church of Christ congregations in Massachusetts and in central Pennsylvania has been selected for the purpose of the present analysis.[5] The data was collected in the spring of 1976 with the cooperation of the staff and leadership of the Massachusetts and the Penn Central conferences. The choice of the Massachusetts and the Penn Central conferences was based on several considerations: administration of the Church Membership Inventory took place during the same period, both areas have a history of relatively complete and accurate statistical reporting, and both contain a mixture of urban, suburban, and rural communities and churches. In both cases the regional judicatory, the conference, is organized with a single executive and several staff generalists deployed regionally.

Two additional considerations weighed heavily in the choice of these areas. First, each is a major center of one of the traditions that united in 1957 to form the United Church of Christ. Massachusetts was a major center of Congregationalism and Pennsylvania of the German Reformed Church. This would make possible comparisons of trends and performance by denominational heritage. Second, the two conferences have had rather different membership patterns during the 1970s. From 1970 to 1975 the churches of the Massachusetts Conference experienced a net membership loss of nearly 25,000 persons, or 15 percent, while the churches of the Penn Central Conference experienced a slight membership gain—the only UCC conference in a northern industrial state to show a gain during the period.

Data was assembled on 135 Massachusetts and 128 Penn Central congregations. Included were rankings of each church on nine items by two or more conference staff, statistical data for 1975 and rates of change for 1970-1975 on various membership and financial items, data from the U.S. census, and aggregated results for the 24,052 persons completing Church Membership Inventories in these churches.[6]

For the most part, the participating churches are representative of the two conferences, ranging in membership from under 30 to over 1,500 members. Twenty-seven percent reported a 1975 membership of under 200, 38% between 200 and 399, 18% between

400 and 599, 9% between 600 and 799, and 9% over 800. Fourteen percent are located in major cities of Standard Metropolitan Statistical Areas, 14% in secondary cities of SMSAs, 19% in "older suburbs," 28% in "newer suburbs," and 25% in "town and country" settings.

The typical congregation averaged a membership loss of .9% per year from 1970 to 1975. Four percent averaged an annual gain of 5% or more, 11% a gain of 2.5 to 4.9%, 25% a gain of less than 2.5%, 28% a loss of less than 2.5%, 19% a loss of 2.5 to 4.9%, and 13% a loss of more than 5% per year.

Attendance at worship on the Sunday designated for administration of the Church Membership Inventory averaged 29.5% of reported membership. Church school enrollment averaged 42% of total membership. The median annual increase in current local expenses for the 1970-75 period was 6.6%, while the median annual increase in financial support for mission activity beyond the local community was 5.3%. The median annual contribution per family to church activity (calculated from Church Membership Inventory results) was $223, or 2% of annual family income.

Dimensions of Congregational Performance

We have discussed five areas of congregational performance given attention by the UCC's General Synods of 1975 and 1977. Our ability to develop measures for these five dimensions is limited somewhat by the data available or accessible for most local churches. Some measures are more precise than others, since some areas more readily lend themselves to quantification.[7]

1. *Membership change* is relatively straightforward. For each church we have calculated the average annual percentage change in reported membership for the years 1970-75 (inclusive).

2. *Current local expense change* is similarly straightforward. For each church we computed the average annual percentage change in reported current local expenses in actual dollars for the years 1970-75 (inclusive).

3. *Denominational support* is measured by an index comprised of two items: the percentage of the church's 1975 noncapital expenses given for support of UCC mission activity beyond the local level and 1975 per capita expenses for this activity.

4. *Congregational outreach* is also based on an index containing two items: rankings provided by conference staff on the extent to which the congregation is actively engaged in outreach or social action activity within its local community and per capita support

for the denomination's 17/76 Achievement Fund, a nationwide campaign to provide financial support for six predominantly black colleges historically related to the denomination.[8]

5. *Member satisfaction* is more complex. The Church Membership Inventory listed nine areas of church life. Persons were asked to what extent they seek help from their church in each area and to what extent they have received help in each area. They were given a choice of five responses, ranging from "very much" to "very little." Mean scores were calculated for each church on each item, and the measure of satisfaction is based on the mean discrepancy between expectation and receipt of help in the nine areas.

Relations Among Performance Dimensions

What are the relationships among these dimensions in real life? Is performance in some areas achieved at the expense of other areas of performance? Do our dimensions of performance complement one another? Are they independent?

Table 10.1 presents intercorrelations of the five measures of congregational performance for our total sample of Massachusetts and Pennsylvania churches. With the exception of a fairly strong positive correlation between membership change and change in current local expenses, the relationships are weak, for the most part. While there is little evidence to suggest that performance in a given area is in conflict with performance in others, neither is there evidence that performance in one area particularly enhances or complements performance in other areas.

To examine the possibility that relationships among aspects of local church performance might differ between different types of churches, we divided the sample into groups by denomination of origin (Congregational Christian and Evangelical and Reformed) and by community type (city, older suburb, newer suburb, town and country). Table 10.2 examines the intercorrelations between membership growth and the four other performance areas across these categories of churches.

The relationship between membership growth and increasing current local expenses seen in Table 10.1 is also evident when subgroupings are examined. UCC churches whose membership is growing tend to have growing budgets; those whose membership is declining tend to have budgets that are increasing less steadily or are declining.

As was true for the total sample, the intercorrelations in the subgroups between membership growth and member satisfaction,

TABLE 10.1

CORRELATIONS AMONG FIVE PERFORMANCE DIMENSIONS

	Member- ship Change	Local Expense Change	Denomi- national Support	Outreach	Member Satis- faction
Membership change	--	.31*	.12*	.00	-.12*
Local expense change		--	.06	.02	-.06
Denominational support			--	.13*	-.09
Outreach				--	.12*
Member satisfaction					--

*Correlations significant at the .05 level. N=236.

TABLE 10.2

CORRELATIONS OF MEMBERSHIP GROWTH WITH OTHER DIMENSIONS OF LOCAL CHURCH
PERFORMANCE BY DENOMINATION OF ORIGIN AND COMMUNITY TYPE

	Denomination of Origin		Community Type			
	E&R✝ (N=128)	CC✝ (N=135)	City (N=72)	Older Suburb (N=51)	Newer Suburb (N=50)	Town and Country (N=90)
Local expense change	.31*	.23*	.16	.19	.30*	.24*
Denominational support	-.17*	.08	.10	-.02	.18	-.10
Outreach	-.04	.15*	.04	.02	.23*	.01
Member satisfaction	-.15*	-.02	.03	.09	-.01	-.14

*Correlation significant at the .05 level.
✝E&R = Evangelical and Reformed; CC = Congregational Christian.

denominational support, and outreach are inclined to be weak, but there are exceptions. Growing churches located in newer suburban communities show a tendency to be more engaged in outreach than churches located in newer suburbs that are declining in membership; membership declines among Evangelical and Reformed background churches tend to be accompanied by lower scores on our index of denominational support. In both cases, however, the relationships are rather weak.

We also examined the intercorrelations among the other performance dimensions within these groupings (not shown here) and found that the patterns do vary. Member satisfaction and congregational outreach, for example, were weakly associated in the total sample, but among churches in newer suburbs they correlated at .40. This indicates that in these suburban communities, members of churches engaged in outreach tend to be more satisfied with the church's performance in meeting their needs. Similarly, denominational support and outreach are unrelated within city and newer suburban locations, but they are correlated at .30 for Evangelical and Reformed background churches, .22 for those of Congregational Christian background, and .23 for those in older suburban communities.

We began this section by asking whether or not performance in some areas of congregational life is achieved at a cost to other valued ends. We found that, with the exception of a fairly consistent positive relationship between membership growth and increase in local expenses, intercorrelations tend to be quite weak. Membership growth, change in local expenses, denominational support, outreach, and member satisfaction appear to be relatively independent dimensions, neither strongly complementary nor conflicting.

Correlates of Congregational Performance

Throughout this book one finds a number of theories proposed to account for changing patterns of church membership and participation. Some are in agreement. Others conflict. We turn now to an examination of the usefulness of a number of these theories in explaining membership growth and other dimensions of performance for United Church of Christ congregations in Massachusetts and in Pennsylvania.

From some seventy items available to us, we have selected for examination twenty-one independent variables.[9] For purposes of discussion and analysis we have grouped these variables into seven clusters plus an additional variable. The seven clusters can be divided into two sets—factors external to the congregation and factors internal to it.

The first set, composed of two clusters, measures factors external to the congregation over which it exercises little control or influence. The first, *community character*, contains four variables: community size, neighborhood socioeconomic status, percentage of the population black and Hispanic, and percentage of households owning their own homes. The second, *population change*, includes two items: the average annual rate of population change in the community from 1960 to 1970 and the average annual population change from 1970 to 1975. All these items are taken from the 1970 U.S. census and later published materials of the Bureau of the Census.[10] The early work of Douglass and Brunner (1935) and of contemporary social ecologists has shown the influence of the community context in which a church exists on its performance, especially on its membership growth or decline.

The second set of five clusters measures factors essentially internal to the life of the congregation. The first, *congregational socioeconomic status*, utilizes a composite index based on responses to the Church Membership Inventory and includes educational background, family income, and occupational status of those employed. It is included to measure the impact of social status on congregational performance, a factor emphasized by Niebuhr (1929) in his treatment of the evolution of denominations and by Lenski (1963) in his discussion of religious practices in the Detroit metropolitan area. Scholars are not in agreement concerning the direction of the influence of social and economic status on church participation, but nearly all have stressed its importance. We shall examine its impact on the various performance areas under investigation. The second internal cluster, *nuclear family orientation*, includes four items: church school enrollment as a percentage of 1975 reported membership, the average annual change in church school enrollment from 1970 to 1975, average household size, and average number of relatives living in separate households nearby. Numerous analysts, among them Warner (1959), Berger and Nash (1962), and Schroeder (1975), have stressed the relationship between the church and the maintenance of traditional family structures. We would expect that elements of family composition in the membership would be associated with performance in various areas.

The third internal cluster deals with *intensity of involvement* and includes four items: percentage of reported membership in attendance for worship on the Sunday designated for administration of the Church Membership Inventory, average frequency of church attendance, average number of memberships in church organizations reported by church attenders, and annual household contribution to the church as a percentage of annual household income (taken from Church Membership Inventory results). This is intended to reflect the level of commitment members have to their church, a factor identified by Kelley in his book on church growth. The fourth cluster, *leadership*, is comprised of two rankings provided by conference staff, one dealing with the aggressiveness of the church's pastor and one with the adequacy of the "fit" between the skills and interests of the pastor and the needs of the congregation. The role of the pastor has been given major emphasis by writers associated with the church growth movement. For C. Peter Wagner (1976:57), for example, "a pastor who is a possibility thinker . . . whose dynamic leadership has been used to catalyze the entire church into action for growth" is "Vital Sign Number One of a healthy, growing church."

The fifth internal cluster deals with the *theological orientation* of the congregation and is based on three items: an assessment of the theological stance of the congregation (ranging from very liberal to very conservative) provided by conference staff familiar with the congregation, and two items taken from the Church Membership Inventory completed by church attenders—the relative concern expressed by members for their church in helping them to "know of God's care and love for me" and the relative concern expressed for the church's helping them to "be aware of the needs of others in my community." Theological orientation has long been seen as associated with individual religious behavior and has more recently received attention with regard to the growth of denominations.

In addition to these seven clusters, we looked at an additional variable, *denomination of origin*, denoting the denomination of which the congregation was a member at the time of the formation of the United Church of Christ, in 1957. Campbell and Fukuyama (1970:94-97, 159-61), in a 1964 study of individual UCC members, found significant differences on indexes of organizational involvement, religious devotion, belief, and social acceptance of blacks between those reared in Congregational Christian and in Evangelical and Reformed households. We wanted to look at differences in patterns of performance between churches of the two traditions some twenty years after union.

Table 10.3 shows the correlations between the twenty-one variables (seven clusters plus one variable) and the five performance areas.[11]

We see that churches located in small communities are more likely to be growing, to be increasing their local budgets, and to be higher in denominational support than those in large communities. They also tend to have less satisfied memberships and to score lower on our index of outreach.

Location in a community of high socioeconomic status has little impact on membership growth, growth in local expenses, or member satisfaction. Churches in higher-status communities do tend to be higher in outreach performance, but lower in denominational support. Presence of minority persons and home

TABLE 10.3

CORRELATIONS OF CONTEXTUAL AND INSTITUTIONAL VARIABLES
WITH FIVE CONGREGATIONAL PERFORMANCE DIMENSIONS

	Member-ship Change	Local Expense Change	Denomi-national Support	Outreach	Member Satis-faction
Local Contextual Factors					
Community Character					
Community population: 1970	-.46*	-.24*	-.21*	.15*	.24*
Neighborhood socioeconomic status scale (5=high, 1=low)	-.14*	-.12*	-.21*	.25*	-.07
Neighborhood percent Black and Hispanic	-.24*	-.07	.03	.08	.15*
Neighborhood percent owning own home	.26*	.05	.11*	-.04*	-.17*
Community Population Change					
Community mean annual population change: 1960-1970	.14*	.08	-.04	.09	-.14*
Community mean annual population change: 1970-1975	.22*	.12*	-.03	.03	-.11*
Local Institutional Factors					
Socioeconomic Status					
Congregational socioeconomic status scale (5=high, 1=low)	-.14*	-.15*	-.04	.38*	-.04
Nuclear Family Orientation					
Church school enrollment as a percentage of total membership: 1975	.22*	.21*	.19*	-.22*	-.21*
Mean annual change in church school enrollment: 1970-1975	.28*	.12*	.03	-.12*	-.11*
Mean household size	.17*	.10	.06	.01	-.17*
Mean number of family members living in separate households nearby	.22*	.09	.23*	-.33*	-.02*
Intensity of Involvement					
Percent of members attending service of worship	.04	.21*	.04	-.22*	-.11*
Frequency of church attendance scale (5=high, 1=low)	-.07	-.04	.00	.11*	.03
Mean number of memberships in church related organizations	-.17*	-.12*	.09	.27*	.15*
Mean family contribution to church as percentage of annual income	.14*	.12*	.27*	-.01	-.22*
Leadership					
Clergy aggressiveness scale (5=high, 1=low)	-.00	.03	-.00	.31*	.23*
Clergy "fit" scale (5=high, 1=low)	-.06	.00	-.00	.36*	.22*
Theological Orientation					
Theological liberalism scale (5=high, 1=low)	-.28*	-.20*	-.13*	.40*	.14*
Relative member concern for God's care and love	.14*	.13*	.02	-.27*	-.01
Relative member concern for being aware of community needs	-.00	.04	-.01	.22*	-.02
Denominational Heritage					
Evangelical and Reformed background	.31*	.20*	.44*	-.22*	-.17*

*Correlation significant at the .05 level.

ownership levels in the community tend to be rather weak predictors of performance, with the exception of membership growth. Growing churches are inclined to be located in neighborhoods with low minority populations and with high levels of home ownership. Population change in the community, particularly in the 1970 to 1975 period, is associated with membership growth but has minimal impact on other areas of performance.

In summary, the items included in our community character and population change clusters have their greatest impact on membership growth and decline. They have limited impact on change in local expenditures, denominational support, member satisfaction, and (with the exception of neighborhood status) congregational outreach.

The next four variables reflect a nuclear family orientation. All four—church school enrollment as a percentage of membership, rate of church school enrollment change, household size, and presence of relatives living in separate households nearby—are associated with membership growth. For these churches, family-related factors seem very important in achieving membership growth. Low church school enrollments, church school declines, small families, and lack of extended family ties on the part of members are associated with membership losses. Changes in church school enrollment and in household size have little impact on other areas of performance.

When we look at the relationship between two of the items in this cluster—church school enrollment as a proportion of membership and presence of relatives nearby—and two of the performance dimensions—denominational support and outreach—we see a rather interesting interrelatedness. Churches with high church school enrollments and whose members have local extended family ties tend to be high on our index of denominational support and low on our index of outreach. This finding suggests that for local churches that have remained family-centered in their membership composition, the denomination represents a further extension of the family and is worthy of loyalty and support as an appropriate vehicle for expressing concern for mission. Local community outreach and support of distant colleges, neither of which is able to make clear claims to family loyalty, have less appeal. For churches whose family ties—nuclear and extended—have been broken, new communities of reference become, in effect, competition to those expressions that might have been important in another era, for example, the denomination. Concern for outreach in the local community and concern for the education of minority persons at some distance from that community emerge as alternative means of demonstrating concern for mission.

The third cluster of internal variables comes closest to what Dean Kelley (1972:56-57) has called "strictness." As is evident in the table, the items in the cluster are rather weak predictors of membership growth. Only membership in church organizations has a correlation of at least .15, and this is in the opposite direction from what we might have expected: churches with high levels of member participation in organizations within the church are less likely to be growing than those with low participation levels.

High levels of member attendance on the Sunday chosen for administration of the questionnaire are associated with increases in local expenses. Household contribution levels are related to denominational support and to the church's performance in satisfying member expectations. Churches whose members contribute high proportions of their income to church activities tend to be high in denominational support, while low giving levels are associated with low support. Interestingly, congregations whose contribution levels are high tend to be less satisfied than those whose members contribute less. Churches with high attendance levels score lower on the outreach index than do churches whose attendance levels are low, and those whose members are more involved in church organizations are higher in outreach.

Two items dealing with pastoral leadership comprise the sixth cluster. Aggressive pastoral leadership and the appropriateness of the "fit" between the minister and the church have no impact on membership growth, change in local expenses, or denominational support. Both items, however, have an important impact on member satisfaction and outreach performance. Since we have no data on the specific goals that the minister pursues aggressively, we should be cautious in assessing the validity of the hypothesis of Wagner and of others concerning the role of the pastor in membership growth. An aggressive pastor pursuing goals of outreach or congregational nurture, for example, may be very passive in the recruitment of new members or in raising an annual budget.

The three items in the theological orientation cluster are all related to congregational outreach. Churches that are seen by conference staff as theologically liberal, whose members place relatively low priority on "knowing of God's care and love for me" and whose members place high priority on "being aware of the needs of others in my community," score high on our outreach index. The two church priority items are unrelated to the other performance areas.

The theological liberalism/conservatism scale, however, is related to membership growth and to increase in local expenses. Growing churches do tend to be conservative churches in these two United Church of Christ conferences.

Finally, denomination of origin proves to be a strong predictor of local church performance. Churches of Evangelical and Reformed background tend to be higher in denominational support, membership growth, and change in local expenses. Those of Congregational Christian background, on the other hand, are higher on the outreach index and tend to have more satisfied memberships.

While we have argued that membership growth is but one of several dimensions of congregational performance valued by the United Church of Christ, the particular focus of this book warrants a more detailed look at the relationship of membership growth to the variables contained in our seven clusters. Table 10.4 presents the correlations within denominations of origin and community types. We see in Table 10.4 that the relationships vary within subgroupings of churches. Some items that showed no significant impact on church growth for the total sample—such as the two clergy leadership variables, frequency of church attendance, and relative concern for awareness of the needs of others in the local community—also have little impact on church growth within the subgroupings. Other items that were only weakly associated with membership growth within the total sample are more strongly associated within certain subgroupings.

City congregations whose membership is drawn from lower socioeconomic backgrounds, for example, are more likely to be growing than city churches whose membership is drawn from higher-status groups. Growing city churches also tend to be comprised of persons with large numbers of family members living nearby and to have low rates of member attendance at worship. Membership growth in city churches seems to be dependent on the maintenance of extended family ties within the congregation.

Perhaps most interesting are the cases in which an item is related to membership growth for the total sample but has no effect or a negative effect within certain subgroupings. The most striking example is with churches located in rural or country communities. While both community character and population change have consistently high impact on growth in other community settings,

TABLE 10.4

CORRELATIONS OF INDEPENDENT VARIABLES WITH MEMBERSHIP GROWTH
BY DENOMINATION OF ORIGIN AND COMMUNITY TYPE

	Denomination of Origin		Community Type			
	E&R	CC	City	Older Suburb	Newer Suburb	Town and Country
Local Contextual Factors						
Community Character						
Community population: 1970	-.36*	-.41*	-.24*	-.54*	-.27*	-.08
Neighborhood socio-economic status scale (5=high, 1=low)	-.02	.08	-.19	-.20	.08	-.09
Neighborhood percent Black and Hispanic	-.29*	-.23*	-.22*	-.12	.06	-.11
Neighborhood percent owning own home	.27*	.23*	.09	-.04	.23*	.06
Community Population Change						
Community mean annual population change: 1960-1970	.02	.33*	.23*	.22	.13	-.15
Community mean annual population change: 1970-1975	.06	.36*	-.01	.09	.11	.04
Local Institutional Factors						
Socioeconomic Status						
Congregational socio-economic status scale (5=high, 1=low)	-.10	.09	-.22*	.03	.07	-.07
Nuclear Family Orientation						
Church school enrollment as a percentage of total membership: 1975	.22*	.05	.10	-.13	.10	.15
Mean annual change in church school enrollment: 1970-1975	.35*	.19*	.18	.11	.33*	.24*
Mean household size	.26*	.13	.18	.09	.02	.01

	E&R	CC	City	Older Suburb	Newer Suburb	Town and Country
Mean number of family members living in separate households nearby	.05	.02	.26*	.19	.09	.03
Intensity of Involvement						
Percent of members attending service of worship	.05	-.11	-.33*	-.02	-.15	.06
Frequency of church attendance scale (5=high, 1=low)	.08	-.06	.02	-.05	.16	-.17
Mean number of memberships in church-related organizations	-.10	-.13	-.06	-.29*	-.04	-.05
Mean family contribution to church as percentage of annual income	.02	-.12	-.13	.28*	-.22	.20*
Leadership						
Clergy aggressiveness scale (5=high, 1=low)	.03	.13	-.01	.13	.12	.02
Clergy "fit" scale (5=high, 1=low)	-.07	.11	-.03	.01	.06	-.05
Theological Orientation						
Theological liberalism scale (5=high, 1=low)	-.26*	-.09	-.32*	.01	.03	-.20*
Relative member concern for God's care and love	.17*	-.05	.08	.12	-.13	.26*
Relative member concern for being aware of community needs	.12	.09	-.16	.18	.14	-.02

(N=128) (N=135) (N=72) (N=51) (N=50) (N=90)

*Correlation significant at the .05 level.

none of the local contextual items correlates significantly with membership growth and decline in rural areas. Only four of the twenty variables examined are related to membership growth among these churches.

Also revealing is the relationship between theological conservatism and church growth. Within the total sample, theological conservatism is associated with membership growth. When subgroupings are examined we see that the relationship holds for city churches, country churches, and those of Evangelical and Reformed background. Theological orientation is *unrelated* to church growth among Congregational Christian background churches or to growth within either category of suburban churches!

Evangelical and Reformed and Congregational Christian background churches differ in additional ways. Community population growth appears to be far more conducive to church growth for Congregational Christian background churches. Nuclear family orientation, especially as reflected in church school size as a proportion of membership, appears more important for those of Evangelical and Reformed origin.

Several conclusions can be drawn from the preceding discussion. First, to varying degrees, congregational performance is affected by conditions in the community that are largely beyond its control. This appears to be particularly true of membership growth. Second, the degree to which the community is urbanized appears to affect its performance in all six areas. Third, denomination of origin is significantly related to all five dimensions of congregational performance. Fourth, conditions internal to the life of the congregation are significantly related to performance in each area, but different aspects of the life of the congregation have differing effects on various dimensions.

We are left with a major unanswered question: Are the relationships we have seen between congregational performance and certain features of community and congregational life causal or merely an accidental function of community setting or denominational background? Such questions are addressed in the following section.

EXPLAINING CONGREGATIONAL PERFORMANCE

We have chosen to use multiple regression analysis as a means of examining the relative impact of the independent variables discussed in the previous section on our five dimensions of congregational performance. Multiple regression analysis is a statistical technique that allows us to look at the impact of an independent variable on an area of performance while controlling for several other variables.

Because the relationships between denomination of origin and the five performance dimensions were so striking, we examined the 135 Congregational Christian and 128 Evangelical and Reformed background churches separately.

The results from the analyses appear in Table 10.5 and in Table 10.6. In each table we have grouped the independent variables into seven clusters. The clusters were entered into the analysis one by one, beginning with those clusters of variables over which the congregation has relatively little control and then turning to those items reflecting characteristics of the congregation's internal life. The two tables indicate, first, the amount of variance in each performance area that is accounted for by all the clusters of variables that have been entered into the analysis, including the cluster being examined, and second, the amount of additional explanatory power that cluster has when we controlled for the clusters preceding it in the analysis. In Table 10.5, for example, we see that community character alone accounts for 22.6 percent of the variance in membership growth for churches of Congregational Christian background. When community growth is added, we are able to account for only slightly more of the difference in membership growth; population change adds only .3 percent more explanatory ability when we have controlled for the variables in the community character cluster.

At the bottom of each table we see the degree to which we are able to explain performance in the five areas using the data included in our study. For churches of Congregational Christian background the amount of variance explained ranges from 28.9 percent for outreach to just 5.2 percent for denominational support. For those of Evangelical and Reformed background we can account for 38.5 percent of the variance in outreach, but the variables in our study do little to explain changes in local expenses.

The tables suggest that conditions in the local community have substantially more impact on the performance of Congregational Christian background churches than for the Evangelical and Reformed background churches. This is evident when we look at various performance areas.

Fully 90 percent of the variance explained in membership growth for Congregational Christian background churches is accounted for by community factors external to the local church,

TABLE 10.5

EXPLAINED VARIANCE FOR CONTEXTUAL AND INSTITUTIONAL CLUSTERS: CONGREGATIONAL CHRISTIAN BACKGROUND CHURCHES

	Membership Change		Change in Local Expense		Denominational Support		Congregational Outreach		Membership Satisfaction	
	Total Adj. R^2	Incr. to R^2	Total Adj. R^2	Incr. to R^2	Total Adj. R^2	Incr. to R^2	Total Adj. R^2	Incr. to R^2	Total Adj. R^2	Incr. to R^2
Contextual Clusters										
Community Character	.226	.226*	.019	.019	.000	.000	.035	.035	.089	.089
Population Growth	.229	.003	.096	.077*	.000	.000	.037	.002	.092	.003
Institutional Clusters										
Socioeconomic Status	.235	.009	.090	.000	.041	.041*	.081	.044*	.097	.044
Nuclear Family Orienta-tion	.235	.001	.093	.003	.022	.000	.077	.000	.095	.000
Intensity of Involvement	.236	.000	.131	.038*	.029	.007	.071	.000	.072	.000
Leadership	.266	.031*	.128	.000	.057	.028*	.243	.172*	.135	.062*
Theological Orientation	.254	.000	.159	.031*	.052	.000	.289	.046*	.113	.000
Total Variance Explained	.254*		.159*		.052		.289*		.113	
Total Explained Variance Added by Institutional Clusters	.041		.072		.052		.262*		.066	

*Statistically significant at the .05 level.

TABLE 10.6

EXPLAINED VARIANCE FOR CONTEXTUAL AND INSTITUTIONAL CLUSTERS: EVANGELICAL AND REFORMED BACKGROUND CHURCHES

	Membership Change		Change in Local Expense		Denominational Support		Congregational Outreach		Membership Satisfaction	
	Total Adj. R^2	Incr. to R^2	Total Adj. R^2	Incr. to R^2	Total Adj. R^2	Incr. to R^2	Total Adj. R^2	Incr. to R^2	Total Adj. R^2	Incr. to R^2
Contextual Clusters										
Community Character	.117	.117	.014	.014	.000	.000	.040	.040	.080	.080
Population Growth	.115	.000	.011	.000	.000	.000	.052	.012	.090	.010
Institutional Clusters										
Socioeconomic Status	.108	.000	.012	.001	.002	.002	.126	.074*	.083	.000
Nuclear Family Orientation	.205	.097*	.033	.021	.022	.020	.140	.014	.077	.000
Intensity of Involvement	.188	.000	.004	.000	.088	.066*	.299	.159*	.197	.120*
Leadership	.191	.003	.000	.000	.104	.016	.381	.082*	.256	.059*
Theological Orientation	.222	.031*	.000	.000	.088	.000	.385	.009	.250	.000
Total Variance Explained	.222*		.000		.088		.385*		.250*	
Total Explained Variance Added by Institutional Clusters	.131*		.000		.088		.333*		.160*	

*Statistically significant at the .05 level.

while 52 percent of the explained variance in growth of Evangelical and Reformed origin churches is attributable to factors outside the congregation. For the former, only clergy leadership makes a significant additional contribution to an explanation of membership growth when prior factors are controlled. Nuclear family orientation and theological orientation remain important contributors to membership growth for the latter.

The twenty variables included in the analysis are relatively ineffective in accounting for changes in local expenses for Evangelical and Reformed background churches. They do account for 15.9 percent of the variance within the Congregational Christian sample, with population growth, intensity of member involvement, and theological orientation accounting for the largest proportions of the variance.

Even with controls, clergy leadership proves to be important for both groups in influencing congregational outreach and member satisfaction. In addition, congregational socioeconomic status has a considerable influence on outreach performance. Intensity of member involvement also affects outreach among Evangelical and Reformed background churches, but theological orientation, important for Congregational Christian origin churches, adds little to our ability to predict outreach performance within these churches. Intensity of involvement is an important predictor of member satisfaction for Evangelical and Reformed background churches, but not for those of Congregational Christian background.

CONCLUSIONS

We have looked at five areas of local church performance seen as important by a single denomination and have examined the relationships among these areas of performance, using data from 263 local United Church of Christ congregations in Massachusetts and in Pennsylvania. We have also studied the impact of a number of contextual and internal features of church life on these dimensions of performance. What was found?

First, we have seen that performance in one area of church life neither assures nor prevents achievement of other valued ends. Among membership growth, denominational support, outreach, and member satisfaction we found rather weak relationships. The one exception was a consistent positive relationship between membership growth and increasing local expenses. The data reviewed here suggests that a growing membership base is as important as any other single factor in insuring the financial health of the congregation. An increasing budget appears to be a by-product of a growing membership.

Second, we have seen that conditions in the community in which a church is located have more effect on some areas of congregational performance than on others. The character of the community and its growth patterns during the 1970s have a substantial impact on membership growth but relatively little effect on performance in other areas.

Third, the relative influence of the internal factors we have examined also varies. Clergy leadership proves to be a key factor in accounting for member satisfaction and congregational outreach. Congregational socioeconomic status was also related to outreach but had little effect on other areas of church life.

A correlation between theological orientation and the various performance areas weakened considerably when subjected to statistical controls. While growing churches tend to be conservative, there is little evidence of a strong causal relationship between conservative theology and membership growth.

Fourth, differences between churches of Congregational Christian and Evangelical and Reformed background remain striking. In no area is this more notable than with respect to membership growth. Churches of Congregational Christian background tend to reflect rather closely what is happening in their surrounding communities. In growing middle-class communities, these churches tend to be growing. In communities of lower status they tend to experience more rapid membership declines. Churches of Evangelical and Reformed background are not invulnerable to community changes, but these changes have had far less impact on their growth during the 1970s. This is due in large part to their ability to maintain strong familial ties. The differences are deeply rooted in the contrasting histories of the two denominations. From their early years in this country the Congregational churches of Massachusetts have tended to be community churches whose members were assimilated into the wider culture, while the Reformed churches of Pennsylvania provided an immigrant people with a link to a rich ethnic and theological past.

From an institutional perspective, the data presented in this chapter may be seen as containing both positive and troubling signs for the United Church of Christ. On the positive side, there is no evidence that membership declines have brought with them diminished strength in other areas of church life. Many churches that are declining in membership appear to be doing other things very well.

More ominous is the apparent dependence on location in growing middle-class communities for maintenance of a strong membership base among churches of Congregational Christian background and dependence on traditional nuclear family patterns among those of Evangelical and Reformed origin. Neither the concentration of the United Church of Christ in the nation's slowly growing industrialized Northeast and Middle West nor the considerable strains experienced by the American family in recent years are encouraging signs for future membership growth. That future will depend in large part on the ability of the denomination to transcend what are presently major strengths: an integral relationship between the church and its community and a capacity to conserve strong familial ties in the face of strains on these relationships.

CHAPTER 11

Social Change and Local Churches: 1951-75[1]

Douglas A. Walrath

Someone once remarked, "The greatest enemy of any institution is change." Certainly that statement applies to the church. Church organization, especially at the parish-local congregational level, is built on the assumption that society and its institutions will change very little, if at all. Tradition is given prominence in nearly every aspect of the church's life. Persons who are older and wiser tend to be seen as best equipped to hold leadership positions. The church's value system affirms social control over nearly every change.

This resistance to change has been a moderately difficult problem for the church throughout its history. In our era, however, this inability to adapt has thrown the church into a crisis situation.

Ours is a time of *rapid social* change. Both words that modify are important. Rapid social change pervades every dimension of life today. Economic expansion has tripled since World War II, drawing the majority of Americans from settled communities into a fast-changing, polymorphous urban sprawl to fuel the expansion. Hardly anyone lives out adulthood in the neighborhood where he or she grew up or works in the same neighborhood where she or he dwells. Metropolitan neighborhoods give way repeatedly as one social group displaces another. Rural areas send more and more of their youth to college, never to see them return. Basic attitudes and life-styles change so rapidly that not only do parents fail to understand their children (and vice versa), but college-age young people find their predominant attitudes and values very different from those of young people in high school; which, in turn, differ greatly from those of junior highs. At similar points in their life

248

careers, each group holds different views and is committed to goals much different from those that immediately preceded them. Thus, the generation gap is now a five-year matter.

Living life today is more complex and more difficult for nearly everyone. Instead of being able to follow well-established patterns to find their way into stable institutions of life, individuals are faced with the problem of having to make their way through life in the midst of institutions that are themselves attempting to cope with rapid social change. Many are forced to retrain for a new work career three or four times during their lifetimes. One out of every three marriages ends in divorce, wiping out the support provided by one intimate relationship and necessitating the development of another to continue the supports of human intimacy. Moreover, the steadily increasing pace of change exacerbates these problems.

SOCIAL CHANGE AND THE CHURCH

This deep social change brings huge problems to the stable-based, locally oriented church. We can begin to understand these problems by looking systematically at just two dimensions of the change.

The Movement from Community to Mass Society

In 1790, when the first U.S. census was taken, 95 percent of Americans lived in rural areas. In 1840 we were 90 percent rural and in 1890 two thirds rural. At the turn of the century we were still 61 percent rural. During the first half of the twentieth century, especially after World War II, we experienced massive urban growth. From 1900 to 1970, while our total population grew 2.6 times, our metropolitan population grew fourfold and our suburban population sixfold (Kahn, 1975). This crowding and massing of most people into metropolitan regions has raised significant obstacles for local congregations.

Often, when lecturing on recent social change, I show a slide of a dirt road followed by a slide of an interstate highway system interchange. I ask those viewing the slides near which road they would locate a church. Almost everyone chooses the dirt road. That inability to visualize a church near an interstate points to the difficulty most of us experience in locating the church where it is proximate to most of life. Our modern highway system illustrates the manner in which society has moved away from *communities* where people lived out all aspects of their lives (family, school, work, leisure activities, buying and selling, civic responsibilities) with the *same* people. Now most of us live in a *mass* society, where the various activities of life are conducted over a widely scattered region, usually each with different groups of persons.

One result of this change is the removal of many aspects of life from the effective orbit of the church's influence. In the minds of most people today, the church is expected to be present to only those activities that occur at or near one's residence. Individuals are still encouraged to carry their faith into other areas of life, but they receive little *institutional* aid from the church to do so. It is rarely present or even cognizant of what goes on in the worlds away from home where most people now live out most of their lives. Contemporary life patterns have effectively *distanced* the church as an institution from most of life.

Alienation

Persons massed together are forced to live segmented, fragmented lives and experience alienation. Even at the point of residence, most people are no longer neighbors or members of a community. Those in any given neighborhood have little more in common than proximity. Often they do not work with their immediate neighbors, nor do they socialize with them, pursue the same hobbies with them, shop in the same stores (at least not together). Neighbors do not need to get along with one another to make a living, to ski or bowl, to enjoy school or church or anything else. The private automobile has allowed most people to pursue a variety of interests and meet a variety of needs with various groups of people, mainly of their own choosing.

Even the poor who live deep within urban centers have much less overall interaction with their immediate neighbors than those who preceded them. Forced into overcrowded housing in the problem-ridden centers of our cities, they lock their doors against their neighbors and isolate themselves both for emotional survival and sheer safety. While some may still have more social interaction with their neighbors than their suburban counterparts, many no longer work near their immediate residence. The last U.S. census shows that large numbers of those who live in the center city now commute out of the city into the metropolitan area for employment.

Most people today live simultaneously within several social networks rather than within a simple neighborhood or community. They work with one network of persons, ski with another, seek to improve their children's schools with another, go to church with another, and so on. They have less invested in their residential community or neighborhood than previous generations because fewer of their basic needs are met there. Present trends in housing reflect these changing attitudes and life-styles. Multiunit dwellings aim to serve mobile persons who live much of their lives away from home and who expect to relocate frequently. Present marriage patterns among young adults, who delay marriage and who often choose to remain childless if they do marry, show a life-style that does not envision settling down and buying a home as an ideal.

Such highly mobile, regionally oriented persons find less meaning in and are less likely to support local institutions, including local churches. My own studies indicate that the two major sources of church dropouts are young adults and those who are socially, as well as geographically, mobile. Both groups tend to be oriented toward the larger society and to invest in regional, social networks as much or more than in their neighbors or local community.

In summary, the church finds itself among highly mobile persons who live fragmented lives. It is unable to be institutionally present to most segments of their existence, and most people do not expect it to be. Society itself has moved from communities of persons to regional conglomerates of functional areas (housing, work, shopping, for instance) linked together by a complex road system. Most persons live more of their lives with networks of persons unrelated to their residential locale than they live with their neighbors. In fact, many have little, if any, interaction with their neighbors.

In the past most churchgoers have related to the church through a primary local social context: their neighborhood. Present radical changes in life ways demand significant adaptation from the church, or it will become even more distant from people's lives. Fewer and fewer persons are primarily oriented to any single, local, social context. They live in several networks. Thus, even when the church is effectively present to their neighborhood, it is present to only a segment of their lives. The more distant the church becomes from the breadth of people's experience, the less likely they will be to relate to it. We shall note in the final section of this chapter that church participation drops away systematically, affecting, first, those in neighborhoods most deeply affected by social change and those persons most oriented toward the changing, larger, social context.

LOCAL CONTEXTUAL TYPES

In order to monitor the impact of this overall social change during the past twenty-five years and to trace its movement through various local social contexts, one needs, first, to describe these locales. Building upon previous work in the field of social or human ecology and social stratification, I have developed a series of metropolitan and nonmetropolitan social context types. A comprehensive, full description of these types is contained in two major reports published by the Synod of Albany, Reformed Church in America (Walrath, 1969; 1974; 1977). For present purposes, a clear enough picture of neighborhoods and congregations can be obtained by using brief descriptions of the types. Table 11.1 outlines the typology. Figure 11.1 provides a geographical distribution picture of the types.

The twelve types of locales are grouped into two major regional groupings—metropolitan and nonmetropolitan. Metropolitan regions are basically those included in the SMSA designation of the U.S. census.[2] Nonmetropolitan regions are those outside the SMSAs. Exceptions occur because SMSAs, by definition, include complete counties, and occasionally, locales within a county are too rural to be typed functionally metropolitan.

Within the metropolitan region are three subgroups—cities, suburbs, and fringe areas—which are further divided into a total of nine locales. Moving from the center of the city out:

Type 1 is the Midtown locale, the city's central business district, usually the location for banks, large department stores, state or city office buildings.

Type 2 is an Inner City locale, generally one of the most deteriorating parts of the city. There is usually high incidence of social problems, rundown housing, and so on.

Type 3 is an Inner Urban Neighborhood, basically a residential area, but with some mixture of neighborhood-type businesses. Housing is generally two-family, middle income or lower-middle income. This neighborhood tends to be an area of residence for ethnic groups. In the Park-Burgess designation, it would be the zone of independent working-class housing (Park and Burgess, 1925).

Type 4 locales, designated Outer Urban Neighborhood, tend to be toward the edges of the city. They have middle-class to upper-middle-class housing, almost entirely single family, and few or no business establishments.

Moving out of the city area to the suburbs, Type 5 locales are

TABLE 11.1

SOCIAL CONTEXT TYPOLOGY OUTLINE

Region	Area	Locale
I. METROPOLITAN		
	A. <u>City</u>	
		1. Midtown
		2. Inner City
		3. Inner Urban Neighborhood
		4. Outer Urban Neighborhood
	B. <u>Suburb</u>	
		5. City Suburb
		6. Metropolitan Suburb
		7. Fringe Suburb
	C. <u>Fringe</u>	
		8. Fringe Village
		9. Fringe Settlement
II. NONMETROPOLITAN		
	D. <u>Urban</u>	
		10. Independent City
	E. <u>Rural</u>	
		11. Rural Village
		12. Rural Settlement

designated City Suburb. These are classic suburban communities that usually grew up along steam or electric transportation lines. They are aptly termed sub-urb because they grew up over against the city as places of residence for commuters who were affluent and could afford to move out of the city. They still tend to be considered prestige residential locations and to have a community center and distinct community life.

FIGURE 11.1
SOCIAL CONTEXT TYPOLOGY: GEOGRAPHICAL PATTERN

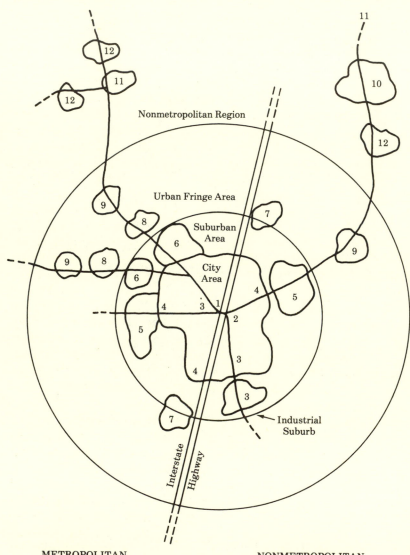

METROPOLITAN

1. Midtown
2. Inner City
3. Inner Urban Neighborhood
4. Outer Urban Neighborhood
5. City Suburb
6. Metropolitan Suburb
7. Fringe Suburb
8. Fringe Village
9. Fringe Settlement

NONMETROPOLITAN

10. Independent City
11. Rural Village
12. Rural Settlement

Type 6 suburbs are designated Metropolitan Suburb. They are suburbs that have grown up as residential neighborhoods in a ring around the city. They tend to be arranged in a patchwork pattern that intersperses residential locales, shopping centers, work locales, entertainment centers—all connected by roads that ring the city. Basic transportation movement is now around the ring rather than in and out of the city. Travel is via private automobile rather than by any kind of public conveyance. Major development of these suburbs generally occurred after World War II.

Type 7 suburbs, called Fringe Suburb, have grown up very recently, usually along interstate highway systems. They stand over against the entire metropolitan area much the same as, in earlier times, city suburbs grew up over against the city. Fringe suburbs tend to be middle- to upper-middle-class residential areas for those who are newly affluent. Most residents are younger middle-aged persons who are highly mobile. Zoning is strict and these locales have little or no business. Planned communities, sometimes called "new towns," are included in this grouping.

In larger metropolitan regions the pattern is often more complex than I have just described it. "Cities" containing locales of Types 1 through 4 are intertwined with residential suburbs (Types 5 to 7), as well as shopping centers, industrial centers, educational centers, and so forth, to form a quiltlike pattern much more complex than the simple, single central city with various locales arranged around it in rings. This clustering of areas is linked together by a network of highways. The distinctive characteristics of each type are still apparent, although the geographical patterns are less distinct.

On the edge of the metropolitan area, where the metropolitan area is expanding into the nonmetropolitan area, we find two fringe types. Type 8, the Fringe Village, was originally an independent rural village, but it has now been overrun by the metropolitan area. Increasingly, housing has been purchased by younger middle-aged couples with children, who are seeking a quiet village *residence*, but who in the rest of their lives are oriented toward the larger metropolitan area and world beyond the village. These communities tend to be a combination of long-term residents, many of whom are middle-aged or older, and these new arrivals.

At the edge of the metropolitan fringe area are Fringe Settlements, or Type 9. These are former rural settlements that have recently been overrun by metropolitan expansion. Zoning is often poor, and land use is unplanned and irregular. Various types of housing appear, including trailers, older houses, newer suburban-type homes, and a few estate-type residences. Some agricultural activity also remains in these areas. Most residents commute into the metropolitan area for employment.

Turning now to the nonmetropolitan region, we find, first of all, an urban area dominated by Type 10, a locale I designate Independent City. Independent cities have not given rise to a metropolitan area but stand alone, generally dependent on one major industry. Many of these industries produce one product for which raw materials are close at hand, for example, cement or bricks. Both the industries and the cities that depend on them have been hard hit in recent years. Automation, synthetic substitutes, and foreign competition have all taken their toll. With reduced employment, these cities often now suffer from urban blight. Only a fortunate few with an expanding industry (higher education, for example) have not declined.

The other area in the nonmetropolitan region is rural. It contains two local types, the first of which is Type 11, the Rural Village. This community is the traditional business, commercial, social hub of a surrounding agricultural area. However, with the decline of the number of people involved in agriculture over the last twenty years, many rural villages have either stayed the same size through out-migration of younger people or have actually declined in population.

The most remote nonmetropolitan type is Type 12, Rural Settlement. These settlements consist of a few houses, often a small church, sometimes one store or gas station, often now closed because of the competition of neighboring villages and the lack of travel through the settlements due to the bypassing interstate highway system.

THE PROCESS OF CHANGE

Early in this chapter I suggested that church participation would likely wane first among those in more urban locales and among those more oriented to the larger society. The series of figures to which we now turn seems to confirm these hypotheses. Data for the figures is drawn from United Methodist, United Presbyterian, and Reformed Church in America congregations in the Albany-Schenectady-Troy, New York SMSA and the nonmetropolitan counties immediately surrounding this SMSA. The patterns of change move in an orderly fashion through various local social contexts, beginning in the most urban locales and continuing outward.

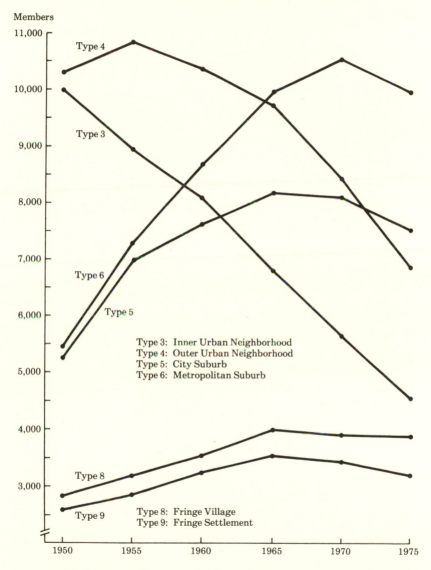

FIGURE 11.2
MEMBERSHIP CHANGE: PRESBYTERIAN, UNITED METHODIST,
AND REFORMED CITY, SUBURBAN, AND
FRINGE NEIGHBORHOOD CHURCHES

Type 3: Inner Urban Neighborhood
Type 4: Outer Urban Neighborhood
Type 5: City Suburb
Type 6: Metropolitan Suburb

Type 8: Fringe Village
Type 9: Fringe Settlement

In 1950 the churches in Type 3 neighborhoods from the three denominations have almost 10,000 members. By 1975 these churches have lost over half their members; only 4,500 remain. Churches in Type 4 have about 10,300 members in 1950. They go up to 10,800 members in 1955 and then drop away to less than 7,000 members by 1975.

Suburban Types 5 and 6 begin the period with a near identical rate of growth. City suburbs, however, taper off beginning in 1955 and then fall away steadily after 1965. Metropolitan suburbs,

FIGURE 11.3
MEMBERSHIP CHANGE: PRESBYTERIAN, UNITED METHODIST, AND REFORMED NONMETROPOLITAN CHURCHES

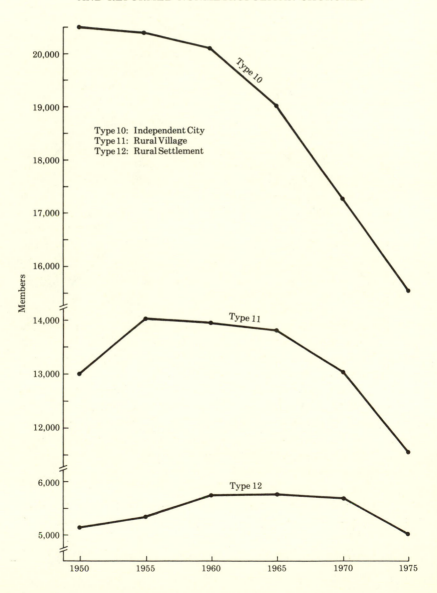

which are farther away from the core of the city, continue their rapid growth through the middle 1960s. After 1965 they also taper off and then decline after 1970. The orderliness with which change moves through the types, beginning in city neighborhoods and reaching out to the suburbs, is impressive.

My case studies of churches in each type of neighborhood help to explain the change pattern. Membership peaked in most inner urban neighborhood churches immediately before or after World War II. While males in these neighborhoods left to go into the service, population held up in the neighborhoods because of their proximity to industry. However, the social change facilitated by the war seriously disrupted the life patterns of these neighborhoods. The war gave those who went into the service a cosmopolitan experience. Many did not return to the old neighborhood to take their place in the factory, as they would have had they not been uprooted. Furthermore, the GI bill gave many an opportunity to go to college. More education enabled them to be socially and economically mobile, which encouraged them to be geographically mobile. They left the old neighborhoods behind as they moved up the social ladder. This opened the neighborhoods to other ethnic and social groups farther down the social ladder, many of whom are Roman Catholic and lower middle class. The existing mainline Protestant churches were unable to adapt. Although some of their former neighborhood members continued to drive back from their new suburban homes to support the city churches, as their children grew into adolescence, or as they relocated farther out or to another region, more and more of these people were lost.

Outer urban neighborhoods have been traditionally residential areas for middle- to upper-middle-class Protestant nuclear families. While these neighborhoods held their own against the suburban migration longer than the inner urban locales, they too fell victim to the Protestant quest for more space. As Protestants have left these neighborhoods, their houses have increasingly been sold to Jews and to middle-class Roman Catholics. Those Protestants who remain tend to be older middle-aged. Churches in these neighborhoods, built and programmed for middle- or younger middle-aged adults with children, find their traditional positions increasingly difficult to maintain.

What the cities have lost the suburbs have gained—at least in the way of church members. My interviews and sampling reveal large numbers of persons currently members of City, Metropolitan, and Fringe suburban churches who were formerly residents of and members of city neighborhood churches. In the older suburbs these members tend to be older in age and in length of membership in the suburban church. In summary, what Figure 11.2 represents is, to a large degree, a redistribution of members among types of churches, reflecting the migration patterns of white Protestants over the last twenty-five years.

A close study of membership change and types of membership accession among Reformed churches during decline tends to support the associations we have been describing. Decline becomes more extreme as the rate of transfers of adults into the congregation also declines. During the years of loss, the correlation coefficients of adult transfers in and loss of members for Types 3, 4, and 5 are .89, .78, .82 respectively. Thus, congregations' inability to attract new adults, either from within or to their neighborhoods, is significantly associated with their decline.

Before moving on to describe change in the fringe area, I should mention why I have omitted Types 1 and 2 from the present series of figures. In the case of Type 2, inner city, neither Reformed nor Presbyterian denominations have any congregations in those neighborhoods during the period 1950-75. The Methodists have only two, both struggling for survival. Mainline, predominantly white, Protestant denominations rarely have any congregations in Type 2 neighborhoods anymore. Most churches representing these groups in the inner city closed their doors, merged, or relocated prior to World War II.

Type 1, midtown, congregations are omitted for a different reason. They draw their members from *throughout* the city and suburbs. Therefore, their change patterns are related to changes in a variety of contexts beyond their immediate locale. They draw only a few of their members from their immediate locale. The key local context issue for these congregations is whether or not their participants continue to see their locales as safe and accessible. If the neighborhood around a midtown church deteriorates significantly, it tends to decline not so much because people move out of the neighborhood as because nonresidents refuse to come into the neighborhood to participate in the church. So long as their immediate neighborhood does not significantly decline, the change pattern of midtown churches is more closely associated with life-style changes in the social groups from which they draw their members. These social groups are most like those resident in Type 4 neighborhoods. For this reason, the change patterns of midtown churches closely resemble those of outer urban neighborhoods, which is apparent in Figure 11.4, on which both types are plotted.

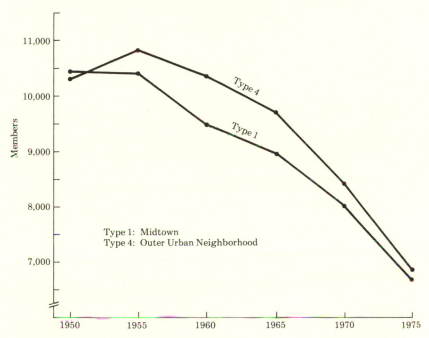

FIGURE 11.4
MEMBERSHIP CHANGE: PRESBYTERIAN,
UNITED METHODIST, AND REFORMED TYPES 1 AND
4 CHURCHES

Also, there is a remarkable similarity among the patterns of the individual denominations. Figures 11.5 and 11.6 illustrate this similarity. Figure 11.5 shows the change patterns for each denomination within outer urban neighborhoods; Figure 11.6, similar data within city suburbs. While there is some variation, the patterns have the same basic shape. Thus, the basic pattern of change for congregations of the same type can more likely be attributed to contextual factors, while denominational variations of the basic pattern are more likely attributable to internal factors in the congregations and/or their selective appeal to differing social groups.

Figure 11.2 shows the combined church membership of the three denominations in congregations located in fringe villages and fringe settlements. Churches show a moderate rate of growth in these locales on the edge of the metropolitan region through the middle sixties and then a stable pattern after that. Case studies reveal the pattern is largely the result of values and life-style conflict between old residents and newcomers. Newcomers make

FIGURE 11.5
MEMBERSHIP CHANGE: PRESBYTERIAN, UNITED METHODIST, AND
REFORMED OUTER URBAN NEIGHBORHOOD (TYPE 4) CHURCHES

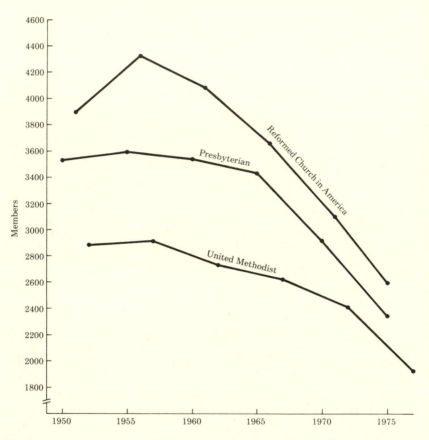

their way into the churches early in the period, usually welcomed at first by the old-timers. However, as newcomers press for changes in the church's program and life-style, old-timers resist. With the general loss of interest in church participation among younger adults and the upwardly mobile middle class, the fringe churches are back in control of the area natives and the few new arrivals who identify with natives or have intermarried with natives.

Figure 11.3 shows the change patterns in nonmetropolitan congregations. Again, we see a pattern of change beginning in the city and moving outward. The urban problems of independent cities already noted have an effect on mainline Protestant congregations similar to that which we have seen in metropolitan city neighborhoods.

FIGURE 11.6
MEMBERSHIP CHANGE: PRESBYTERIAN, UNITED METHODIST,
AND REFORMED CITY SUBURB (TYPE 5) CHURCHES

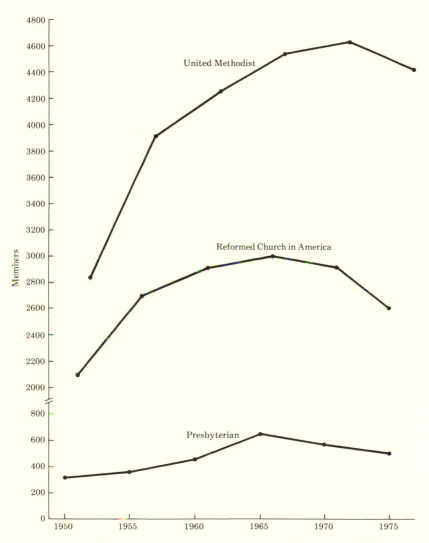

Rural village churches show the effect of heavy out-migration from the middle fifties on. Rural settlements that experienced heavy out-migration much earlier than village churches now have a relatively stable pattern. Also, on the average, settlement congregations are much smaller, tend to be composed of several extended families, and thus show very little meaningful statistical variation.

In summary, even change in nonmetropolitan churches is associated with quantitative and qualitative population shifts. The pattern of church membership change in all locales is systematically associated with changes in the local social context.

LOCAL SOCIAL FACTORS AFFECTING THE CHURCHES

Table 11.2 shows some significant social data from various types of neighborhoods and congregations located within the respective neighborhoods.[3] I have included only Reformed congregations because they are the only congregations from which I have participant sample data. The similarity of change patterns for the three denominations mentioned in The Process of Change section tends to support my belief that sample data from Methodist and from Presbyterian congregations of the same types would show similar social groups participating. Presbyterians would tend to be slightly farther up the social ladder in a given locale, while Methodists would probably be slightly down the social ladder. Presbyterians would thus experience social change a bit earlier than Reformed Church members, while Methodists would tend to experience it somewhat later, all other things being equal.

The table is very revealing. It illustrates the interaction of many of the factors we have been examining. Reviewing the data, we see first the striking association between neighborhood population changes and changes in church membership and church school enrollment. Column 5 shows the tendency of churches to lag behind neighborhood changes; most church participants represent long-established residents. Column 6 further develops this association. Within major type groups (city, suburb), the greater the social distance between the church participants and the neighborhood residents, the greater the percentage of membership loss the churches have experienced and the earlier the losses began. Evidently, churches are not able to keep up with social change in their immediate neighborhoods. Therefore, their memberships become increasingly socially distant from their neighborhoods. This distance between churches and their neighborhoods compounds the problem by decreasing the churches' ability to attract persons from the immediate area.

Especially in the city, congregations become increasingly dependent upon nonresident members for leadership and support. However, insofar as these members encourage the congregations' leadership and program to meet their needs and interests, they

TABLE 11.2

CHURCHES IN SYNOD OF ALBANY, REFORMED CHURCH IN AMERICA

	1	2	3	4	5	6
	Year Decline Begins	1960–70 Neighborhood Population Change (in %)	1960–70 Church Membership Change (in %)	1960–70 Church School Enrollment Change (in %)	Church Participants in Community More Than 10 Years (in %) 1974	Median Age Difference Church (1974) vs. Neighb. (1970) (in %)
CITY AND SUBURBAN NEIGHBORHOOD CHURCHES						
City:						
Type 3: Inner Urban Neighborhood	1946	-12.3%	-33.2%	-50.3%	89.7%	10.7 years
Type 4: Outer Urban Neighborhood	1957	2.1	-23.5	-53.8	83.3	4.2
Suburb:						
Type 5: City Suburb	1963	23.7	-0.5	-39.0	77.8	5.2
Type 6: Metropolitan Suburb	1969	29.9	32.9	12.0	74.6	3.5
FRINGE CHURCHES						
Fringe:						
Type 8: Fringe Village	1966	18.3	0.0	-33.3	75.3	7.8
Type 9: Fringe Settlement	1966	42.2	-5.3	-47.4	73.5	1.2
NONMETROPOLITAN CHURCHES						
City:						
Type 10: Independent City	1957	-8.6	-9.7	-26.4	83.3	4.9
Rural:						
Type 11: Rural Village	1959	-1.6	-15.7	-28.7	76.7	8.0
Type 12: Rural Settlement	1963	15.6	-4.3	-15.8	76.6	5.8

draw it even farther away from the neighborhood. When these nonresident members drop out or move away, the congregations are returned to those few participants still residents of the immediate area. Tragically, the churches are now seriously weakened and have little experience in programming for those different ethnic and social groups now close by.

Suburban churches are also experiencing a similarly widening gap, although for somewhat different reasons. Their participants overrepresent those oriented primarily to the local context, while new residents often are younger adults primarily oriented to the larger social context, as described earlier. Thus, distance tends to be more a matter of differences in life-styles, goals, directions, and values than differences in socioeconomic status or ethnic group.

Rural locales, as listed at the bottom of Table 11.2, show the progressive impact of social change within their area. The villages have been hardest hit recently by population loss, while rural settlement areas show some growth. Social distance between churches and their immediate neighborhoods is greatest for villages that, in turn, show the most decline in church membership and church school enrollment.

Independent cities have a pattern of change and especially social distance that resembles urban neighborhoods (especially Type 4) within metropolitan regions. The decline within independent city churches is moderated somewhat by the churches' ability to draw more easily from a wider area and the comparative lack of magnitude of the urban blight in an independent city as compared with a larger metropolitan city. The independent city church thus combines some of the characteristics of an urban neighborhood church with the more favorable characteristics of a midtown church.

The fringe types are probably not so systematic as the other types, because their area is in such a state of social confusion. Housing is mixed; types of persons are mixed. Churches are generally small, especially settlement churches. Usually, they are unable to attract and even less likely able to hold newer residents. Thus, they benefit little from population growth. The confusing social and church patterns lead to a lack of clear church trends.

Robert Merton's concept of manifest and latent functions helps us to understand more clearly the powerful impact on churches of growing distance between their participants and residents of the immediate area around the church (Merton, 1949). Briefly stated, the manifest functions of an organization are apparent in its stated purposes. In the case of a local church, worship and Christian education are manifest functions, carried out in the Sunday morning service and in the Sunday school.

Latent functions are just as important to participants, although not as apparent. Latent functions of congregations that encourage people to participate might include being seen with the right people, aid in the search of a mate, being able to play on the church's baseball team, holding a position of power and/or influence, and so forth. Because latent functions are not so apparent, their importance and, especially, their disruption in a time of change are also not so apparent.

When congregations experience neighborhood change and distancing, they also often lose their ability to meet latent functions of those to whom they have traditionally related and, at the same time, lack ability or willingness to develop latent functions that would appeal to new groups of persons becoming available to them. A formerly large city neighborhood church that met prestige needs for its members can no longer meet them when its neighborhood and its size have both seriously declined. A small fringe congregation that provided opportunity for area residents to hold positions of power and influence may well lose its appeal to those persons if an influx of better educated, more articulate, upwardly mobile suburbanites greatly increases its size and then attempts to alter its style and program in response to their needs. In fact, in the ensuing struggle, both groups may not be satisfied and may withdraw. Thus, while congregations appear unchanged (they continue their manifest functions by holding worship services, Sunday school, and so forth), they can lose their ability to meet important needs of their traditional supporters. The changes are not apparent because the functions are latent, not manifest.

What influence do factors other than social factors—for example, quality of leadership and church program—have in the overall health of congregations? Obviously, they do have power to influence the quality of a church's life and its overall performance. Perhaps the best way to understand the relative influence of internal institutional factors like leadership and program quality is to look again at a membership change trend line and recognize that the trend line for a given type group of congregations represents the average performance of that group through time. The limits of the group are defined by those congregations that perform at the top of the group (have the best record of membership change) and those that perform at the bottom (have the worst record of membership change). Such a typical band appears as Figure 11.7. The solid lines trace actual change in five-year intervals for six urban neighbor-

FIGURE 11.7
VARIATIONS IN MEMBERSHIP TRENDS IN SIX URBAN NEIGHBORHOOD CONGREGATIONS: CHANGE FROM 1960 BASE

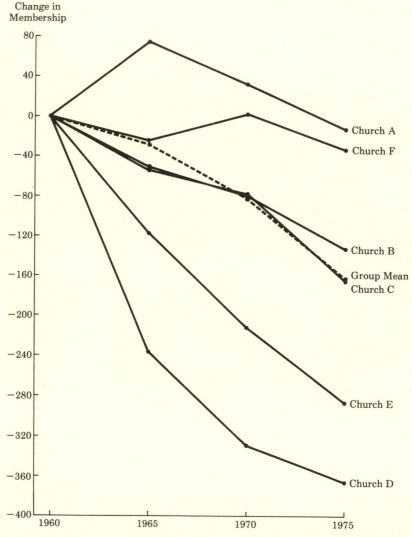

hood congregations in the Albany area; the dotted line, the average for the group.

Internal factors largely determine whether a congregation performs at the top or the bottom of its context group. The local context factors determine what overall changes limit congregations of a given type. Generally speaking, what leadership and program cannot do is enable a congregation to "escape" from its group entirely, that is, to perform through time in a manner consistently different from the basic pattern for congregations of its type. For this reason, church leaders in an urban neighborhood congregation who compare themselves with a metropolitan suburban congregation, even one of the same size with an equally able pastor and program quality, are making an unrealistic comparison. The local contexts are miles apart. The given opportunities of the two churches are so different that any comparison is very unfair.

In summary, the social contextual factors are very powerful. Churches rarely escape their overwhelming influence, especially in a time of rapid social change. Congregations that thrive amid change generally are those that are able to relate effectively to their contexts, maximizing the positive factors, minimizing the negative factors, programming toward the context's future rather than hanging on to a past that sooner or later is bound to vanish.

CHAPTER 12

Church Growth Research:
The Paradigm and Its Applications

C. Peter Wagner

The so-called church growth movement, with which I personally identify, has developed a fairly distinctive research paradigm for studying the dynamics of church health and growth. The movement itself emerged from the missiological research done by Donald McGavran in India from 1936 to 1955 and is reported in his three foundational works (McGavran, 1955; 1959; 1970). Since 1965 the institutional center of this continuing research has been the Fuller Theological Seminary School of World Mission and Institute of Church Growth in Pasadena, California.

Although interdenominational in scope, this approach operates within a set of theological presuppositions that decisively influence its goals and methodologies. In broad brush strokes this can be described as an evangelical theology. It takes seriously the sovereignty of God, the lordship of Jesus Christ, the absolute authority of the scriptures, the reality of sin and eternal judgment, the divine will that all men and women be reconciled to God through Jesus Christ, the need for a born-again experience, and the requirement placed on all believers to share their faith. These theological themes will not be expanded upon here, but they need to be displayed so that some of the later suggestions may be understood in context.

Church health and church growth are presumed to be closely associated. If a church is fully healthy, it will grow. Conversely, if a church is not growing in membership, there is probably something wrong with its health.

THE RESEARCH PARADIGM

The research paradigm within which the church growth movement operates is frankly task-oriented. It is deeply rooted in theological traditions, but it does not study theology for theology's sake. Theology is seen as a tool, and a necessary one at that, for the development of good church health. Most church growth researchers, theoreticians, and practitioners hold graduate degrees in theology.

Likewise the findings of social scientific research are used by the church growth movement when such findings are perceived to contribute to the task. To date, the discipline that has made the most direct contribution to the movement has been cultural anthropology. However, important input has also been received from sociology, psychology, social psychology, communications, and marketing research.

The conclusions of the church growth movement are not entirely new or unique. The movement's particular contribution to the practical knowledge of ecclesiastical growth dynamics has been its systematization of bits and pieces of data from theology and the social sciences into a coherent whole that provides useful handles for church practitioners. It is a common experience to hear a person who has just taken a training seminar in church growth say, "Everything I heard I have known before. But this is the first time it has all come together for me in a useful way."

Much of the data used in church growth research is gathered from case studies of individual churches. A large amount comes from pastors who learn the research paradigm and then apply it to their own parishes. Other case studies are made on selected churches that have shown some unusual characteristic in their growth pattern. They might be growing very rapidly, they might have reversed a negative growth trend in unlikely circumstances, they might have declined when other churches around them are growing, they might have recovered from an apparently serious disease. In one way or another they have distinguished themselves from the ordinary church. Because research models do exist, the church is checked against reference points representing principles that have been developed as hypotheses. Correspondence to or divergence from these principles is identified, described, and added to the body of knowledge.

The field of missiology, a science of the cross-cultural communication of the Christian faith, provided the original academic context for the church growth research paradigm. The paradigm began to develop in the mind of Donald McGavran while he was yet a Disciples of Christ missionary in India. The missiological research of Methodist Bishop J. Waskom Pickett (1933) on Christian mass movements (as they were then called) furnished key input to McGavran's thinking. In 1955 McGavran published his influential *The Bridges of God* and with it sparked the church growth movement. Since then the literature in the field has become quite extensive. The fundamental principles and the basic outlines of the research paradigm are to be found in embryonic form in *The Bridges of God* but principally in *Understanding Church Growth* (1970).

The church growth paradigm began to be applied in America in the early seventies. Although McGavran's *How Churches Grow* (1959) included American churches in its purview, the impact was minimal compared to the literature that has appeared more recently (McGavran and Arn, 1973; Wagner, 1976; McGavran and Arn, 1977; Orjala, 1978; Chaney and Lewis, 1977, for example). The church growth research paradigm is now being introduced in graduate programs of American theological seminaries, making it more accessible to American pastors and denominational executives.

It has been mentioned that the church growth research paradigm is task-oriented. Now the task needs to be defined. It is basically that of world evangelization. The theological presuppositions of the church growth movement bear strongly on its commitment to obey the so-called Great Commission of Jesus: "Go and make disciples of all nations [Matt. 28:19]." Every person who does not acknowledge Christ as Savior and Lord is a proper subject for evangelization according to this point of view. While some truth may be present in many human religious expressions, no theological or religious system is considered complete without the central motif of reconciliation to God through Jesus Christ. Furthermore, it is felt that the most satisfactory way to give tangible expression to commitment to Jesus Christ is through responsible membership in Christian churches. The theologically determined task thus becomes to persuade men and women (1) to establish a vertical relationship with Christ and (2) to establish a horizontal relationship with Christians in a community of believers. As this happens, churches grow, and thus the rationale for the expression "church growth."

I repeat: not all missiologists feel comfortable with the church growth paradigm, nor do all church leaders in America. Some believe that the burden for the evangelization of all peoples is

Christian arrogance and that many non-Christians can and do find God other than through Jesus Christ. Some would emphasize the social dimensions of the Christian gospel rather than the need to persuade people to become followers of Jesus and responsible church members. Others reject the emphasis on the growth of churches and argue that church growth is not necessarily related to faithfulness to God. Those in the church growth movement, therefore, recognize that their research paradigm will not be suitable for helping all churches, but their expectation, based on accumulating field experience, is that it will prove to be helpful to a significant number.

STEPS IN THE RESEARCH PARADIGM

The first step of church growth research in any given geographical area is to identify the peoples living in the area. A "people" is defined as a significantly large sociological grouping of individuals who perceive themselves to have a common affinity for one another. Although there is no way to predetermine the lines along which perceptions of group affinity or peoplehood will develop in a given situation, some of the factors that seem to be most influential in America include ethnic group (race, religion, national origin, language, rate and degree of assimilation), social class (vocation, economic status, formal schooling), regional identity, and rural-urban orientation. These groupings are referred to as "ethclasses" (Gordon, 1964:51-54) and "homogeneous units" (McGavran, 1970:85), as well as "peoples."

Peoples are identified first because empirical data indicates that Christian churches tend to grow along people lines. They almost invariably develop and bring together those of one homogeneous unit at a time. This is the way the earliest Christian churches grew in the Roman Empire, it is the way they grew through the twenty centuries of Christian history, and it is the way they grow in the 221 nations of the world today. As McGavran (1970:198) says, "People like to become Christians without crossing racial, linguistic or class barriers."

Because this research paradigm seems to provide both biblical and empirical reasons why Christian congregations can and should be encouraged to grow separately along homogeneous unit lines, it raises serious ethical problems for some who advocate that the church should take the lead in the battle against racism, segregation, and social injustice. Opponents of the homogeneous unit principle of church growth do not contest the "is" of the empirical data, but they warn against the "ought" of its ethical implications. Martin Marty (1978b:3) expresses it well when he says,

> Wagner, McGavran, and Company win hands down on the pragmatic issue and present some convincing and some tantalizing arguments to rationalize cultural separatism as the Christian model. You can tell from my comments that I do not dismiss them out of hand. But it is hard not to be troubled when we see such principles and ideologies grow out of the insights.

Many Christian theologians and ethicists feel that Christianity should break down peoplehood and group loyalty. The church growth paradigm, however, operates from a high view of culture. To use the typology of H. Richard Niebuhr (1951), the church growth paradigm would fit somewhere between "Christ of culture" and "Christ the transformer of culture," leaning toward the former. The church growth movement argues that Christianity spreads best when people are converted with a minimum of social dislocation.[1]

Any examination of factors contributing to church growth and decline in America should, according to this paradigm, proceed people by people. A study of the growth and decline of churches in New England, for example, needs to report on church growth among two million French Canadians there, or the hundreds of thousands of Portuguese-speaking Cape Verdeans in Rhode Island and in Massachusetts. Data gathered on the growth of churches in the Los Angeles five-county metroplex as a whole would be relatively meaningless by itself. Separate data needs to be gathered for the 3.7 million Hispanics, the 870,000 blacks, the 600,000 Jews, the 100,000 Koreans, the 40,000 Armenians, and the other non-Anglo groupings that comprise over 75 percent of the total population. Furthermore, churches do not grow uniformly among Hispanic Americans or Native Americans or any other general ethnic category, but these, in turn, must be broken down into significant homogeneous units within the larger groups. On a broader scale, church growth among Anglo-Americans in America also needs to be studied regionally. While there are many commonalities among subcultural groupings of Anglo-Americans, the differences are also significant as one moves, for example, from the Rio Grande area of Texas and New Mexico to the Northern Appalachian coalfields, to the corn belt of the Midwest, to the Pacific Northwest, and so forth. Churches grow differently in each region.

Once the peoples or homogeneous units are identified, the second step is to determine which churches, if any, are growing well within that particular people. The following scale has been proposed as a guideline for locating churches most likely to reveal growth dynamics:

> 25 percent per decade—poor growth
> 50 percent per decade—fair growth
> 100 percent per decade—good growth
> 200 percent per decade—excellent growth
> 300 percent per decade—outstanding growth
> 500 percent per decade—incredible growth

Usually, no church that shows a growth rate of under 100 percent per decade is selected for a case study. In most areas of the country, churches can be found in every category, although the 500 percent decadal rate is relatively rare.

When several churches that are growing at significant rates within a homogeneous unit are studied, common growth factors become evident. Even churches that have adopted differing philosophies of ministry will usually be functioning alike in crucial areas. In order to locate the growing churches in context, a survey is ordinarily made of the growth of all churches in the homogeneous unit, and comparisons are made with plateaued and declining churches.

The church growth research paradigm does not operate in a vacuum. A decade of investigation has accumulated enough data to formulate principles that seem not to be culturally specific, but which have cross-cultural validity. It would be well now to take a look at a sample of such principles.

NONTHEOLOGICAL GROWTH PRINCIPLES

It is recognized by students of church growth operating within varying research paradigms that the dynamics of growth and decline are always complex. There is no one simple reason why a given church or denomination grows or declines. Roozen and Carroll (chapter 1) have described the very helpful fourfold scheme of factors influencing growth used by the Hartford working group: (1) national contextual factors, (2) national institutional factors, (3) local contextual factors, and (4) local institutional factors.

The above order appears to move from the least to the most significant growth factors. There are undoubtedly some conditions in the world where national contextual factors are decisive. I could see how Afghanistan, North Korea, or South Africa could serve as contemporary examples. But it seems to me that in the United States, while long-range church membership trends suggest that national contextual factors have exerted significant influence from time to time, they probably are not as crucial as the other three sets. Of course, national contextual factors do influence national institutional factors to a degree.

The influence of national institutional factors depends largely on the connectional nature of the denomination concerned and on the degree of self-determination of each local parish. For example, the Church of the Nazarene is strongly connectional. Therefore, decisions made in its Kansas City offices regarding denomination-wide programs of leadership training, publications, and motivation for growth at the grass roots will, in all probability, affect most of its local churches. Also, priority decisions made by some mainline denominational bureaucracies during the sixties have affected growth of their churches negatively. However, in every one of the declining denominations there are cases of vigorous growth in some parishes that did not allow themselves to be affected by the negative national institutional factors.

In the final analysis, denominations grow or decline as local parishes grow or decline. Church growth research therefore must ultimately focus on the local church.

There is some debate among researchers as to the relative importance of institutional and contextual factors on the local level. I would rank local institutional factors higher, but only slightly higher, than local contextual factors as an influence in congregational growth or decline. Some growth problems are certainly beyond the control of the congregation and can be clearly ascribed to contextual factors. But many, probably the majority, of growth problems can be corrected by appropriate decisions and action on the part of the congregation. Examples of both will be given when church pathology is discussed below.

A fifth factor has not been discussed by the Hartford working group, which is intentionally dealing with the sociological phenomena of church growth. This factor is the sovereign and nonsociological work of the Holy Spirit. The Holy Spirit uses sociological factors but is not restricted by them, at least according to the theological assumptions of the church growth movement. This, in itself, increases the complexity of understanding ecclesiastical growth trends.

As mentioned earlier, research within the framework of the church growth paradigm has uncovered a number of apparently cross-cultural principles of growth. These have not yet been systematized and categorized, but four of the most important appear to be:

1. *Motivation.* Churches, in order to grow, must want to grow. The pastor is usually the starting point for this motivation, with the laypeople of the church close behind. A lack of motivation for growth may well turn out to be the most crucial factor causing church decline. Whereas almost every church will verbalize a vague desire to add new members, in many cases the congregation and its leaders are not at all willing to pay the price for growth. It requires hard work for a church to grow, and many churches prefer to coast along with a minimum of effort. Growth disturbs the status quo cherished by many. New church members tend to complicate patterns of interpersonal relationships, so their number is kept under control by existing members. To use Lyle Schaller's analogy (1975:93-96), pioneers tend to resent the intrusion of homesteaders and construct, sometimes subconsciously, invisible barriers to keep them out. A combination of spiritual and psychological motivation is necessary to overcome these attitudes in local parishes as a prerequisite to vigorous church growth.

2. *The homogeneous unit.* Some aspects of the homogeneous unit principle were discussed previously in relationship to the need for identifying the peoples among which churches grow. Churches that realistically evaluate themselves culturally and that gear their ministry toward meeting the needs of people most like themselves are in a position to grow. On the other hand, churches which decide to try to meet the needs of a variety of people usually find that they have growth problems. It is not possible for one church to meet the needs of everyone in the community for an extended period of time. Conglomerate congregations that grow well are a rarity.

This does not mean that the Christian ethical code permits deliberate discrimination or racism. It only means that the most natural way for a church to grow is among one people at a time. Churches in mixed communities may well find that some individuals from other homogeneous units will join their church and feel comfortable. In an open society there are always some who desire to leave the culture of their roots and assimilate into another culture. Hispanic Americans, for example, may choose to adopt an Anglo-American life-style. And there are areas where significant numbers of individuals from two or more homogeneous units are in the process of mixing through intermarriage and will seek out the fellowship of others who will accept their status. In any of these cases a church membership might appear to be heterogeneous. The larger the church, the more built-in tolerance there is for a wider spectrum of peoples, since smaller fellowship groups will usually form within them among people of differing homogeneous units.

Thus, while there are churches that include people from more than one homogeneous unit, they (1) are few in number across the board and (2) have a more difficult time growing than do homogeneous unit churches.

3. *Resistance-receptivity*. Other things being equal, it has been discovered that among some peoples there is an openness to the reception of the Christian message, while others seem closed to it. At the present time, animistic peoples are among the most receptive worldwide. Where the gospel is preached among animists, churches usually multiply. However, where the gospel is preached among Muslims, sparse results for church growth have been forthcoming. To cite another example, Jews in the State of Israel appear presently to be more resistant to the Christian gospel than Jews in the United States.

Two research tools have been developed to quantify the status of a given group of people in terms of their readiness for receiving the gospel: the Engel scale and the resistance-receptivity axis. The Engel scale, developed by James Engel (Engel and Norton, 1975:45), of Wheaton College, is a model that describes eight stages along the process of conversion to Christ and three afterward.[2] By studying a given people and determining what percentage of them are located at the various stages of the Engel scale, appropriate strategy for evangelization can be developed (see Figure 12.1).

The resistance-receptivity axis is a horizontal axis that starts at − 5 on the left and runs to + 5 on the right. People toward − 5 are known to be strongly opposed to Christianity (see Figure 12.2); those toward + 5 are known to strongly favor Christianity. In America, for example, Black Muslims and many Native American tribes would be located toward the left, while upper-middle-class-Anglo suburbanites and Korean immigrants would be located toward the right. The resistance-receptivity axis is thus used to plan the most effective deployment of Christian evangelists and missionaries.

Specific applications of the resistance-receptivity principle are used in local situations. When a local church is able to identify its own homogeneous unit, as well as the mosaic of homogeneous units in its community, it can then construct a resistance-receptivity axis by locating those homogeneous units most likely to respond to their style of Christianity toward the right side and the least

FIGURE 12.1
THE SPIRITUAL-DECISION PROCESS (ENGEL SCALE)

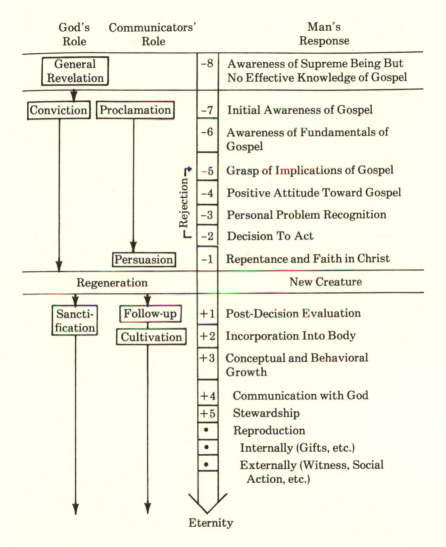

God's Role	Communicators' Role		Man's Response
General Revelation		−8	Awareness of Supreme Being But No Effective Knowledge of Gospel
Conviction	Proclamation	−7	Initial Awareness of Gospel
		−6	Awareness of Fundamentals of Gospel
		−5	Grasp of Implications of Gospel
		−4	Positive Attitude Toward Gospel
		−3	Personal Problem Recognition
		−2	Decision To Act
	Persuasion	−1	Repentance and Faith in Christ
Regeneration			New Creature
Sanctification	Follow-up	+1	Post-Decision Evaluation
	Cultivation	+2	Incorporation Into Body
		+3	Conceptual and Behavioral Growth
		+4	Communication with God
		+5	Stewardship
		•	Reproduction
		•	Internally (Gifts, etc.)
		•	Externally (Witness, Social Action, etc.)

Rejection

Eternity

Source: *What's Gone Wrong with the Harvest?* by James Engel and W. Wilbert Norton. Reprinted by permission. Copyright © 1975 by the Zondervan Corporation.

FIGURE 12.2
THE RESISTANCE-RECEPTIVITY AXIS

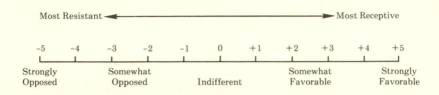

likely toward the left. For example, among the many indicators used to predict receptivity, change of life situation is prominent (Pentecost, 1974:91-111). Thus, when culture is held constant, new arrivals in the community would be more likely to respond than long-term residents. Some churches have discovered that they are having growth problems because they have been concentrating on a predictably resistant target audience. When they change the focus, growth is more likely.

4. *Redemption and lift.* Redemption and lift is a religious phenomenon that has been described by many students of religion (see, for example Niebuhr, 1929:26-76). However, McGavran (1970:260-77) provided the label and has sensitized church growth researchers to be aware of its relationship to church growth. Growth in churches can stop when and if those who have become Christians allow themselves to become so separated socioeconomically from their own people that they effectively become a separate homogeneous unit, cut off from meaningful contact with the non-Christians from which the church was originally formed.

THE MEDICAL MODEL AND THE ECCLESIOLOGIST

The Bible frequently uses the metaphor "body of Christ" to describe the church (Ephesians 1:22-23; Colossians 1:8). It has been useful to extend this analogy somewhat and to look at church health and sickness in much the same way that we look at physical health and sickness. Human bodies, for example, have vital signs that provide indicators of physical vitality. Pulse, respiration, blood pressure, and temperature alone can tell the physician a good deal about the health of the patient. Likewise, vital signs of healthy churches are being identified. On the negative side, human pathology is a highly sophisticated science. Church pathology is less sophisticated, but church growth leaders have found a helpful set of concepts for diagnosing the health of a church and making suggestions for either preventative or therapeutic measures.

In making a case study of a church or cluster of churches, church growth researchers approach the situation with a preconceived hypothesis as to why the church is or is not growing. This hypothesis is based on preliminary observations and measurements of the growth history of the church, demographic studies, and a degree of intuition gained from training and field experience. The case study reinforces or invalidates the hypothesis. When a particular hypothesis has seemed to fit a satisfactory number of cases, predictions as to how it will fit others become more reasonable. No final conclusions can be drawn because church growth is so complex. There needs to be room for modification in the light of feedback. Each principle will have many exceptions, and when the exceptions themselves form a pattern, they become another principle.

To illustrate, the seven vital signs and the eight diseases I have thus far identified are listed below. It is recognized that this is only a beginning, and a tentative one at that, toward an increase in our knowledge of what makes American churches grow or decline and of what can be done to promote vigor and health in these churches. My suggestions are made for Anglo-American churches, since they have been tested only on them. Whether or not they apply to other kinds of churches in America and in other parts of the world further research and testing will determine.

First, the vital signs (Wagner, 1976):

1. *The pastor.* Leadership is a key to church growth in any given parish. The pastor must want the church to grow and must be willing to pay the price if the church is to grow. He or she must have the faith and the vision to project where God wants the church to be in the future. The pastor must take the lead in goal-setting and must be willing to work hard for growth. The people will not believe in growth if the pastor does not. A pastor who is an active visionary leader is a vital sign of church health.

There are some pastoral qualities that limit growth. If the pastor is a "shepherd" type rather than a "rancher" (Schaller, 1977:52-54), the church will probably not pass 200 members. If the pastor is incapable of sharing leadership, both with staff peers and with lay leaders, the same ceiling will usually apply. Generally, pastors with short tenures of one to five years will not be able to establish and implement growth goals.

2. *The laity.* Mobilized laypeople are a sign of good church health. The biblical teaching of the church as a body and every

Christian functioning as one member or another of that body needs to be implemented for growth. Few churches, even growing churches, have 100 percent of their members mobilized. A more realistic goal in most churches is two thirds of the members working regularly. Of the total membership about 40 percent should be directing their energies toward tasks within the congregation itself, while another 20 percent direct their energies outside the church in efforts of evangelism and social concern.

3. *A big enough church.* Almost any church is big enough to do something, but for many significant church functions a critical mass is required for the ministry to seem appropriate to the market it serves. A ministry to single adults, particularly the formerly married, is an example. Large churches that can gather groups of 300 or more formerly married on a regular basis are "big enough" for a strong ministry in that area. Again, a certain size is necessary to provide resources geared to meet certain needs, such as those requiring the services of professional counselors. In some geographical areas, such as suburban Los Angeles, large churches seem especially attractive, but in others, such as rural communities, they do not seem to fit. As Carl Dudley (1978) has shown, a small church of, say, 100 is large enough to meet the needs of intimacy, mutual sharing, and Christian commitment for many Christian people. It should be observed, however, that the potential for growth in such a church is limited, since significant growth would inevitably turn it into a large church that would then not be able to preserve the qualities of a small church. Many such congregations intuitively resist growth while continuing to verbalize their need to evangelize and bring new members in.

4. *Structural balance.* The three significant components of the infrastructure of a church are celebration (the membership group), the congregation (the fellowship group), and the cell (the spiritual kinship group). Although there are types of churches which provide exceptions, the rule is that the three structures need to be balanced for optimum church health. Churches that have 50 to 60 percent of the adults who attend celebration (worship) also participating in congregations of about 40 to 120 each are in very good shape. If 30 to 40 percent are active in cell groups where more intimate relationships are built, the infrastructure will usually be strong.

5. *One homogeneous unit.* As mentioned previously, churches that have developed around the homogeneous unit principle are, in the main, healthier than those that have mixed significant percentages of people from more than one group. If a church

discovers that it has more than a token representation of members from different homogeneous units, it may be experiencing growth problems.

6. *Efficient evangelistic methods.* No one evangelistic methodology is adaptable to all local situations. Each situation needs a tailor-made approach fitted specifically to its needs. Research is needed to explore this further and also to test and determine appropriate market segments for popular evangelistic methodologies. Nevertheless, the healthy, growing church has obviously discovered some method that is effective in adding new members.

7. *Properly arranged priorities.* The most crucial area for arranging priorities in church growth seems to be the relationship between evangelism and social service in the outreach ministry of the church. It was previously mentioned that certain decisions of mainline denominational bureaucracies in the sixties produced national institutional factors that had a negative effect on church growth. In my opinion, the crux of those decisions involved the issue of priority. Due to the social upheavals of the decade, church leaders who were deeply involved caused their denominations to put a ministry of social concern in a higher priority position than evangelism. This produced a wave of dissatisfied customers, so to speak, who deserted their churches in droves. It now appears that the problem was not so much that the churches undertook ministries of social concern, particularly those of a noncontroversial nature; church members expect this. The problem was, rather, that the priority of evangelistic outreach slipped from the number one position (Kelley, 1977:ix-xi). As Johnson and Cornell (1972:108) say:

> Summing up, America's churches are chiefly dedicated to that old-time endeavor that never grows old, spreading the Gospel. . . . Whether they see it in terms of prayer or evangelism, however, it is considered the local church's central imperative by Christians across the continent, black and white, city folks and back countrymen.

These seven vital signs are intended to be initial concepts toward which further research can be geared. This has been done on many occasions since *Your Church Can Grow* (Wagner, 1976) appeared on the scene, but one significant test of their validity has been published and circulated. It is found in the December 1977 issue of *Home Missions*, a publication put out by the Southern Baptist Home Mission Board in Atlanta. A computerized research design studied 475 of the fastest growing Southern Baptist churches and raised the issue of the vital signs. The two that did not seem to be totally valid for Southern Baptists were the mobilized laity concept (chiefly because many Southern Baptist leaders have an aversion to spiritual gifts) and the balanced infrastructure (because cell groups do not seem to be a factor in Southern Baptist growth). Overall, however, they scored fairly well.

If the vital signs approach looks at church health in a positive way, pathology looks at it negatively. Here is a brief description of the eight church growth diseases that have been identified thus far (Wagner, 1979b):

1. *Ethnikitis.* Ethnikitis is a disease produced by local contextual factors, in this case a changing community. It is terminal. The people who started the church were people from the neighborhood. Then a new kind of people moves in, and church members move out to new neighborhoods but commute back to the church for services. It becomes an island of one kind of people in the midst of a community of another kind of people. Given time (as little as four years and as long as a generation) it will pass away. By making a transition from a congregation of the old kind of people to the new kind of people, the old congregation can die with dignity. Ethnikitis has been described by many authors under a variety of names, and several options for solving the problem (not curing the illness) have been suggested (Jones and Wilson, 1974:17-19; Driggers, 1977; Noyce, 1975).

2. *Old age.* Of the eight diseases, only ethnikitis and old age are terminal, and both are produced by local contextual factors. Old age is caused by a disintegrating community. While ethnikitis is normally an urban disease, old age is normally a rural disease. It should not be confused with a high age profile, although a disproportionate number of senior citizens is commonly one of its later symptoms. When population declines at a steady rate, schools close, businesses move out, and churches die. A church with old age can die with dignity if it gracefully accepts its situation and if adequate provision is made for the pastoral care of its members during its last years.

3. *People-blindness.* People-blindness is the malady which prevents the people in a church from recognizing the significant cultural differences that separate people into groups, differences that tend to obstruct the communication of the gospel message. It is the assumption that "our" church is capable of winning anyone at all to faith in Christ and of folding them into the fellowship of our church. Here is where the ubiquitous homogeneous unit principle touches pathology. In extreme cases, people-blindness can lead to

"sociological tissue rejection," analogous to the phenomenon that the human body prefers death to the reception of incompatible tissue. Groups of people, including Christians, often prefer disintegration of the group rather than receiving large doses of people perceived by the group to be incompatible.

4. *Hypercooperativism.* Christian cooperation is a virtue, but if carried too far it can become an obstacle to church growth. A common, but false, assumption in American ecclesiastical circles is that the more churches cooperate, the more evangelism will get done. In fact, research on such movements as Evangelism in Depth (Wagner, 1971:139-60; Peters, 1970:72-77) and Here's Life, America (Arn, 1977:4-7; Wagner, 1977:12-19) indicates that usually it is just the opposite; the more a church cooperates interdenominationally, the less evangelism occurs. Until more successful models are developed, it can be assumed that area-wide ecumenical evangelistic efforts will tend not to enhance rates of church growth.

5. *Koinonitis.* The biblical concept of *koinonia* (fellowship), like cooperation, is a good thing, but if overdone it will stop church growth. This can happen in two ways. First, what I call "fellowship inflammation" occurs when the people in a church become so concerned for the welfare of one another that they lose their vision for outsiders yet to believe. Outreach programs wither, the church is afflicted with "evangelistic myopia," and growth is halted. Second, a kind of "fellowship saturation" can set in when a fellowship group gets too large. Fellowship groups that reach 100 to 150 members tend to plateau, and unless they divide, growth can be stunted.

6. *Sociological strangulation.* Sociological strangulation is the only disease on the list specific to growing churches. It occurs when the volume of people flow exceeds the ability of the facilities to handle it. The two most prominent danger areas are parking and sanctuary. Parking facilities that do not have empty spaces during peak traffic hours are probably already choking off potential growth. When the church is growing and the sanctuary is 80 percent full, sociological strangulation is usually setting in. The strong growth mix of some churches can overcome these potential growth obstacles, but as a general rule, they will inhibit growth if steps are not taken to correct the problems.

7. *Arrested spiritual development.* When church members fail to mature in their spiritual life, church growth will ordinarily suffer. Religious vitality cannot be maintained among groups of people who operate at low levels of faith, prayer, doctrinal

conviction, biblical knowledge, and morality. While some churches may grow for a time as social clubs, in the long run the general public is attracted mostly to churches that display strictness (Kelley, 1977). In the area of arrested spiritual development the nonsociological factor, the activity of the Holy Spirit, becomes more prominent than in the other diseases. It is a theological assumption of the church growth movement that people become Christians and responsible church members as a result of a supernatural working of the Holy Spirit, mediated through the witness of Christian men and women. When the Christian men and women are not mature, they are, to that degree, ineffective channels for the work of the Holy Spirit, and the health and growth of the church thereby suffers. The cure for arrested spiritual development is church renewal, which can take a variety of forms.

8. *Saint John's syndrome.* Like several human diseases, Saint John's syndrome is named after the person who discovered it. The apostle described it in chapters 2 and 3 of the book of Revelation, in the letters to the seven churches in Asia Minor. The churches were about forty years old when John perceived them as having left their first love (2:4). They were second-generation churches that had become nominal or "lukewarm" (3:15-16). This kind of life cycle of rise, plateau, and decline has frequently been observed (Moberg, 1962:118-24). It can be avoided if new first-generation Christians are continually brought into membership.

The Emerging Ecclesiologist

The ecclesiologist is a professional who has the aptitude, training, and experience to help a specific church or cluster of churches with their health problems. The term is a new one, derived from the Greek *ecclesia* and parallel to ecclesiology, which is used by systematic theologians for the study of the church. The ecclesiologist, as I am using the term, is not a theorist nor a theologian as much as a practitioner. He or she can detect both vital signs and diseases and, in many cases, prescribe what is needed for a church to regain health, vitality, and growth.

The supply of ecclesiologists is still rather small. The church market in America is not yet accustomed to their presence or availability, since concepts of church sickness and health have not constituted significant parts of the curricula of ministerial training programs. Most ministers have been trained to theologize or spiritualize growth problems rather than to diagnose them as they would expect human diseases to be diagnosed. Church budgets typically do not contain line items for consultants or ecclesiologists on the assumption that the pastor has been trained to handle health problems. This fallacy is becoming more widely recognized, and the demand for ecclesiologists is increasing. Some denominations and judicatories are retooling in-house personnel as resident ecclesiologists. Others are using outside professionals, who work on an interdenominational basis.

A great deal of research is yet needed for the development of the therapeutic phase of ecclesiastical medicine. Given the complexity of church growth, there will be no patent medicines. However, at least one attempt to standardize diagnostic procedures has been made (Fuller Evangelistic Association, 1978), and others will undoubtedly follow. Much of the help that churches need is in the areas of planning and of management. Perhaps the curricula in seminaries will eventually be changed to equip ministers to at least be para-ecclesiologists. Even in that case the demand for professionals will, in all probability, continue to rise. The whole field is challenging and promising. As increasing numbers of ecclesiologists emerge to meet the demand, hopefully many present trends of church stagnation and decline will be reversed.

CHAPTER 13

Recovering the Church's Transforming Middle:
Theological Reflections on the Balance Between Faithfulness and Effectiveness

Robert A. Evans

While attending a symposium on church growth, both a pastor and a lay leader confronted me: "I am convinced that our church's ministry to the community is valuable, and a solid core of our members are dedicated to the kind of ministry in which we are involved," the pastor declared. "But few new people in our urban- and youth-oriented culture seem inclined to join or even regularly attend services in a church they perceive as mainline tradition-al. . . . There is enormous pressure to grow, or at least not to decline, so that our church and its mission will survive. Yet everything around us is changing. Can and should *we* change?"

The lay leader joined the pastor by adding, "*What* shall we change? The program, the worship, our recruitment style? I am not sure we are doing everything wrong, yet we and hundreds of other mainline churches are losing members. In the face of all the conflicting data offered at this conference," the elder inquired, "how, for God's sake, can we as Christ's body be both faithful and effective?"

A concrete response to the questions of these two Christians, pastor and layperson, is the focus of this essay. In my judgment, these two people have placed the issue of church growth in an appropriate theological perspective. The problem of church membership and participation has been concisely put, in terms of the nature of the church. The question is not "to grow or not to grow," but rather, "growth at what cost and for what purpose."[1] What priority should numerical growth be given within the total ministry and mission of the church? As this lay leader so aptly phrased it, how can the church respond to its calling to be both faithful and effective? Ultimately, this question calls us to face the problems inherent in the relationship between Christ and culture; problems that demand theological responses that have more to do with the "whither" of church growth than with the "what" and the "why." The what and why of recent changes in church membership and participation have been assessed in previous chapters. This chapter addresses the whither.[2] Whither, according to Webster, means to what point, end, conclusion, or design.

A Vision with Presuppositions

For mainline American Protestant churches in the final quarter of the twentieth century I would like to explore a vision of a theologically credible and sociologically viable model of Christian commitment. The vision focuses on God's joyful expectation that Christians be both faithful and effective as they point to Christ as the transformer of culture.

This vision is founded on four basic presuppositions:

1. The church is called by Christ to be a transformer of culture. The vision would mean a change for some mainline Protestant Christians toward the direction of the conversionist motif of H. Richard Niebuhr (1951), in his *Christ and Culture*. We may not need a thrust toward the personal conversion of new church members, many of whom may already be inoculated against the gospel. Rather, we need commitment to a Christ who is a transformer of culture. The call is for participation in the conversion of the values of a culture.

2. The influence of the church in contemporary American culture is marginal but not inconsequential. As institutions, mainline Protestant church bodies have assumed a minority status that frequently reflects a cultural captivity. However, there is a potential for the church again to significantly influence a culture it helped to shape.

This kind of witness requires a modeling, facilitating role rather than a dominating, forming, guiding role. It demands final acknowledgment of Thomas Luckmann's (1967) thesis that the church is socially located on the periphery of modern society. Yet, this very position on the boundary of culture may be essential for its transforming function. For the church to witness to Christ as the transformer of culture would demand a new self-perception and reorientation of commitment.

3. There has been a collapse of the theological middle. We have experienced, theologically, in the 1970s a collapse of the middle ground between liberalism, that is basically culture affirming (a Christ-of-culture model), and fundamentalism, that is basically culture denying (a Christ-against-culture model). The church presently lacks a theological foundation for engaging the culture creatively. There is a need to rediscover and repopulate the middle ground, which is basically culture challenging (a Christ-trans-forming culture model).

This new middle ground must be rebuilt on the basis of a view of Christian commitment that is both theologically and sociologically authentic. It must, in my judgment, be rebuilt on the foundation of a doctrine of the church which expresses the essential dialectic between faithfulness and effectiveness. The church must live into a model of ministry which emphasizes the quality of relatedness among its members and to those unchurched whom it touches. This quality must be both caring and prophetic, comforting and liberating, challenging and transforming.

4. Numerical church growth is important but not primary to the transformation of the church and the culture. If quantitative growth is perceived by either liberal or conservative as the primary mark of commitment and health in the church and thus a demand of faithfulness, then Christ of culture is the normative model. The church will tend to affirm present cultural values and will seek to attract as many members as possible by meeting their expectations through programs and proclamation. A by-product of this approach is often the postponement of ethical awareness. Avoidance of conflict with the culture is pursued with the hope of gradually bringing a new member to see the wholeness of what the gospel demands of a committed disciple.

If growth is seen as an unimportant or even a negative mark of commitment and survival of the present life of the church, then a Christ-transcending culture is the normative model. Among mainline Protestant churches this takes at least two forms. A church will tend to reject cultural values outside itself through high demands of conformity in program participation, the level of Christian education, spiritual discipline, or positions on social issues. New members are viewed as distractions from the mission or accommodation to the culture unless they are willing to submit to the demands and perhaps a probationary period. The other form of this model is perhaps as much a disengagement from culture as a transcending of it. The church will tend to be so self-satisfied with its present patterns and styles that new members are seen as nuisances or threats. An encounter with the culture is simply avoided by seldom seeking to engage it.

If numerical growth is understood as neither the primary nor an unimportant mark of commitment in the life of the church and as neither a demand of faith nor a distraction from mission, then Christ the transformer of culture may become a normative model. Following this model the church may recover a commitment to understand, challenge, and influence the values of culture. Growth may be understood as a possible consequence of ministry and mission but not as the central or sole methodology of mission. Evangelism becomes important because sharing the faith becomes an expectation, and new members or allies of the church are received as a gift of the Holy Spirit (see Costas, 1976). Church membership and participation, both in quality and quantity, are then evaluated in light of how faithful and effective a facilitator the church has become in the dialogue between Christ and culture. Transformation consistent with the love of God and neighbor becomes the criterion to be examined in a particular time and place with a specific type of congregation.

For the church to be on the periphery of society does not negate periodic penetration into its core. Marginality could be like the liminality of being on a sacred threshold. This position provides the perspective to model and urge transformation. My vision for the church is the recovery of the transforming middle by the balance of faithfulness and effectiveness with the model of Christ as the transformer of culture. The application of my hypothesis is explored in three areas: (1) a biblical and theological thesis, (2) implications for the church, and (3) applications for the church.

A BIBLICAL AND THEOLOGICAL THESIS

What God requires of the church is not growth but faithfulness. This thesis points to the biblical norm that is at the core of the Old and the New Testaments and is summarized by Jesus: "Love the

Lord your God with all your heart, and with all your soul, and with all your mind. . . . Love your neighbor as yourself [Matt. 22:37, 39]."

In theological terms, H. Richard Niebuhr (1951:27) translates this biblical core to define the purpose of Christ's body the church as "the increase of the love of God and neighbor." God has made a covenant with those who believe. This covenant requires *faithfulness* to God as the central commitment. It also calls for a gospel of love, justice, and liberation for all God's creatures. The gospel message, the εὐαγγέλιον which Christians are expected to share, promises that we shall be "new creatures" in Jesus Christ and shall have a fullness of life in the midst of joy or suffering, praise or persecution. God's demand of faithfulness carries no guarantee for growth, health, prosperity, or even temporal survival.

There is a constant temptation in the history of the community of faith, Niebuhr reminds us, to allow the scriptures, the church, or even Christ to become the focus of the church's commitment. Neither the authority of scripture and the dissemination of biblical truth, nor loyalty to the church and participation in its saving fellowship, nor even a Christ-centered devotion and striving to gain disciples to his lordship can be the ultimate goal of the church. Jesus himself has rejected these alternatives by refusing to bear primary witness to the scriptures, the community, or even to himself. He directs us to the God who sent him, who loves him, and who is loved by him. "Nothing less than God—albeit God in the mystery of his being as Father, Son, and Holy Spirit—is the object toward which Scriptures, Church, and Jesus Christ himself direct those who begin by loving them [Niebuhr, 1956:31]."

Faithfulness to God is the central mark of Christian commitment. It is lived out in love of God and neighbor. "God requires" or "God demands" is the covenant language, but this ought not to weigh down the church or individual Christians as heavy duty or constraint. Love of God and neighbor is both law and gospel. It is a love demanded by God as creator, but it is also a gift supplied by God as redeemer and a power nurtured by God as sustainer. The commitment to love of God and neighbor, as seen in the biblical context, brings joy and fulfillment even in the midst of struggle, pain, conflict over what God and the neighbor expect. Faithfulness to this loving provides meaning, belonging, and empowering for the quality of human relatedness, but it does not insure numerical growth.

What is the relationship between faithfulness and growth? Compare what I have been suggesting with this quote from the

Office of Evangelism of the Episcopal Church (*The Episcopalian*, 1977): "God wants this parish to grow. . . . It is biblical and what God wills. . . . Growth is holy, healthy, normal and to be expected. . . . Church growth is not an option. It is central to our gospel task. If we are not growing, we are not doing what God wants." The theme that God wants your church to grow is characteristic of the church growth movement, as articulated by Peter Wagner in chapter 12. It is also representative of the approach being taken by many mainline churches as they strive to address the decline in membership and participation. But can this suggestion that God demands growth be justified from a biblical and theological perspective?

I can find no emphasis in the New Testament on a self-conscious strategy for church growth. It simply "happens" sometimes in the course of being faithful and should be understood as the mysterious work of the Holy Spirit. A small or mixed response to sharing the gospel at Athens and at Ephesus is as important an event for celebration as large numbers of converts in Jerusalem. The criterion of commitment modeled in the New Testament is faithfulness to a quality of life in Jesus Christ that provides for shared love, devotion to justice, and hope of liberation. John Yoder's (1973:45) view of the church's purpose spells this out.

> The other New Testament element that is also difficult to relate to the "church growth" system is the kind of vision of the church in the world we have especially in the books of *James*, *Peter*, and *Revelation*. This is the vision of an innocently suffering, patient, scattered, little group of people. Their faithfulness is not that they talk a lot or that they win a lot of people. Their only call is to be sure that when they suffer it is innocent. Only that they can explain when the world asks them what their hope is. There is no attention to self-critical, self-analytical, or self-conscious strategy, but rather being the little flock in the midst of the world and facing the hostility of the world without losing hope.

The central issue is how the church lives and defines itself in relationship to the world. It is to the culture that the church addresses its gospel in word and deed. The biblical stress is on transformation—the renewal of one's mind and heart when committed to the love of God, not to any particular institutional affiliation. As Paul writes in Romans 12:1-2 (NEB):

> I implore you by God's mercy to offer your very selves to him:
> a living sacrifice, dedicated and fit for his acceptance, the

worship offered by mind and heart. Adapt yourselves no longer to the pattern of this present world, but let your minds be remade and your whole nature thus transformed. Then you will be able to discern the will of God, and to know what is good, acceptable, and perfect.

Faithfulness is the requirement and the model of commitment.

One of my concerns is to ask how church growth came to be perceived as the priority of the ministry and mission of the church. I think there are some important theological reasons why some dedicated church leaders have equated growth with God's will and church health. Much of this understanding stems from an interpretation of the Great Commission, which appears to make evangelism the central if not the sole priority of the new community of disciples. Jesus commands, "Go forth therefore and make all nations my disciples; baptize men everywhere in the name of the Father and the Son and the Holy Spirit [Matt. 28:19, NEB]." There are comparable passages in Mark 13 and in Luke 24 that make the expectation and the assignment to testify, proclaim, and witness to the gospel before all nations.

Setting aside some unresolved exegetical difficulties with the authorship of the commissions, there are two additional components present in one or another of these three accounts. The most important component, for me, is the second section of the Great Commission. The requirement Jesus places on the disciples is not simply to witness and to baptize, but *also* to "teach them to observe all that I have commanded you [Matt. 28:20, NEB]." This full sharing of the gospel, when we teach *all* that Christ commanded us (including his demands of humility, loving our enemies, forgiving seven times seventy, and selling what we have to give to the poor), is not a minimal request. Nor can there be a realistic expectation that those who really understand the application of this gospel will flood into the church. There is a temptation among many of us, certainly myself, to selectively interpret the Great Commission by putting the stress on "making disciples" rather than on "sharing the fullness of the gospel."

The majority of the Synoptic Gospel accounts of commissioning put the stress on proclaiming to nations rather than to individuals. This seems to imply not only extensiveness but inclusiveness. Christ offers us hope that before the end, nations will be united in God across their dividing boundaries. Another component in Mark 13 seems clear: those who testify to the completeness of the gospel should not expect an enthusiastic reception. What Christians should prepare for is resistance in the form of floggings, arrests, and betrayal. It is even declared that the one sharing the gospel may be hated. Yet, he or she is asked to hold out to the end. Here the call to faithfulness sounds similar to Yoder's previous description of the early church.

The second persistent element in commissioning for commitment is the promise that Christ will be with us "always, to the end of time." In Luke 24 the proclamation of the gospel means "repentance and the forgiveness of sins." One can only assume this is true for both those who hear and those who proclaim that complete gospel. There is an assurance that commitment to faithfulness will not put an unmanageable burden of responsibility or guilt on the believer because of the result or consequence of one's sharing. The expectation of faithfulness is to share, not necessarily to succeed. In fact, the principal tone of the biblical witness is to be on guard, lest we inappropriately expect some product, benefit, or result of our faithfulness and thus stand in defiance of God's grace, assuming a stance of pride or guilt about the result. Mark 13 dramatizes God's responsibility for the conclusion of the transaction. Even if one who testifies is persecuted, "do not worry beforehand about what you will say, but when the time comes say whatever is given you to say; for it is not you who will be speaking, but the Holy Spirit [Mark 13:11, NEB]." It is our natural predisposition to segment and isolate the full context of the commissioning event, yet this has led to an isolated and theologically unwarranted priority being given to evangelism. The implication of this priority is that God *requires* church growth.

God requires faithfulness. However, faithfulness must always be applied to a specific situation. Love of God and neighbor must be effectively embodied if faithfulness is to have any meaning or power. Effectiveness can be defined in theological terms as the appropriate embodiment or expression of faithfulness in a given human context. Thus, God requires not only faithfulness, but also effectiveness.

Another way of understanding effectiveness is in terms of goals and the means applied to achieve those goals to which a Christian or a church is committed. The appropriateness of the goals must be decided on the grounds of faithfulness. However, effectiveness is the measure of how those goals are fulfilled. Effectiveness involves the appropriate coordination of means and ends for the sake of the overall purpose. One is unfaithful if the aims are misdirected. One is ineffective if the goals are disembodied.

The New Testament is filled with accounts of God's expectations of effectively embodied faithfulness. Jesus' account of the parable of the talents, as recorded in Matthew 25, is a striking example. To receive the praise "Well done, my good and trusty servant" entails not only appropriate intentions, but effective application of one's resources. This depends on the conditions and talents available. Whether the measure is one, two, or five seems less critical than effective application of the treasures given to God's servants. The connection of the parable in verses 1-30 with the final sixteen verses of chapter 25 concerning the effective embodiment of love of God and neighbor is critical. In the kingdom the Son of man will measure the effectiveness of our love, of our faithfulness, in the feeding, clothing, visiting, and caring for one of our "brothers here, however humble." The weight of effective application is so great that it will be counted as being done for the Lord himself.

What is the relationship between faithfulness, effectiveness, and growth? First, it must become clear that to respond to God's faithfulness and its effective application ought not to be understood as an antigrowth position or as setting church growth over against faithfulness.

I do not suggest that God never desires the church to grow. Nongrowth or decline is not necessarily a sign of faithfulness any more than it is an indelible mark of unfaithfulness. The point is the Holy Spirit alone knows if, when, and how the increase will be given. Evangelism alone can never be an isolated priority of the church. Faithfulness to love of God and neighbor is the priority. However, the expectation that members of the church, by God's grace, will seek to discover effective ways to share the complete gospel in word and deed follows in proper theological perspective. This leads me to confirm, on biblical and theological grounds, the thesis that God requires not growth but faithfulness.

IMPLICATIONS FOR THE CHURCH

The research in this book contains important learnings for me, and I would like to examine these in the context of the biblical and theological thesis just explored.

It is important to recognize, particularly in certain denominations, the anxiety or exhilaration that was involved in the descending or ascending membership attendance and financial curves from 1965 to 1975. Many whose rolls were dropping were in real pain. Large numbers of persons became unemployed—missionaries, pastors, Christian educators, church executives—due to the cutback in ecclesiastical budgets on national and local levels.

Perhaps more significant were the demoralization and sense of failure among some persons in the declining churches who could not understand what was happening to them and to their congregations. Some pastors left the active ministry. Many creative and responsible mission projects died on the vine. Guilt, anxiety, and defensiveness were rampant.

Meanwhile, dramatic growth was taking place in churches like Garden Grove Community Church of Southern California, with Pastor Robert Schuller, and Coral Ridge Presbyterian Church, in Fort Lauderdale, Florida. Both churches grew by the thousands and built multimillion-dollar buildings to celebrate and sustain their own growth. Coral Ridge sponsored workshops on growth and produced a movie about itself entitled *Like a Mighty Army*. Robert Schuller accepted national speaking engagements for churches as well as commercial sales groups. He proposed "possibility thinking," in which the secret to success was finding a need and filling it. Pastors and lay leaders in several burgeoning suburban congregations among the mainline denominations shared hints with their urban colleagues about how to turn the trend around. One suburban pastor expressed to me what he called "justifiable pride" for the booming expansion of his membership, worship, and mission budget.

The prevailing question was "Why?" As a result of the research summarized in this volume, there are some persuasive clues to the answers. Carroll and Roozen remind us, in chapter 1, that simple causes or simple patterns of causes to account for church growth and decline are rejected by virtually all the findings of competent research. We must look to multiple and interacting factors that will be distinctive to particular congregations at particular periods in the life of that church and the culture.

After examining the four categories of causal factors that might account for church growth and decline at the congregational level, I am convinced that there is strong evidence that they can be ranked in order of actual impact for mainline churches at this point in history, beginning with the factor having the greatest impact, down to the one having virtually no significant influence, in this sequence: (1) local contextual, (2) national contextual, (3) local institutional, and (4) national institutional. There is a complex interaction between the factors, and they can be distinguished from one another only for purposes of critical analysis. The factors described as local institutional and as national institutional are critical issues of faithful and effective ministry. These are very important issues, but there is little evidence that they can be considered significant determining factors in church growth and decline.

It is noteworthy that the significant line of demarcation is between contextual factors over which the church has virtually no control and institutional factors over which the church has primary control. The inclination to stress institutional factors as foremost, even in the face of strong data to the contrary, exists among many persons. Two positions that have major stakes in the importance of institutional issues at either a national or a local level are represented in this volume by Kelley (chapter 15) and by Wagner (chapter 12).

The views of Dean Kelley, which have been very provocative for the whole study, need attention. Kelley generally ignores contextual factors; institutional factors dominate his argument. For Kelley, most of the growing churches are conservative in theology, but strictness is the key issue that correlates with strength and thus growth. Informative as this theory is for a certain type of church orientation, research by Hoge, McKinney, Roof, and others does not indicate that the criteria are causal or predictive for mainline denominations in accounting for growth or decline. Concurring with Hoge (chapter 8), I suspect that Kelley's churches grew in special social contexts and were characterized by what I would describe, following Niebuhr, as a Christ-against-culture model. This is fundamentally an authoritarian, intolerant, and exclusivist model that will appeal to only certain types of people on the fundamentalist side of the middle.

Peter Wagner (chapter 12) has also presented a program of principles for church growth that emphasizes institutional factors as the keys to growth. A self-conscious strategy with emphasis on the homogeneous unit is pivotal. While influenced by conservative-evangelical theological presuppositions, the research paradigm of the church growth movement is pragmatic. It uses the findings of social research—especially those of anthropology, psychology, and market research—to strategize for the sake of church growth. Motivation is the foundation; theology is one tool. Given the creative energy to apply the principles, certain churches willing to pay the price and to make growth the unqualified priority as a demand of God may experience growth. The question I raise is whether or not the price is too high, when one analyzes principles such as the homogeneous unit on the grounds of faithfulness. Wagner (chapter 12) acknowledges that the church growth paradigm is most identified with the Christ-of-culture model.

Free from Guilt or Pride

The first implication for the church is based on my biblical and theological thesis and on my evaluation of the sociological findings. For me, it is the most important learning from my engagement of the empirical research. It can be summarized as follows: We are free from inappropriate guilt or pride about whether our congregations have declined or increased. The most persuasive reasons in the midst of multiple factors for church growth and decline are contextual factors, on both local and national levels. These are fundamentally beyond the control of the church at either the national or local level. This liberation from guilt and pride, accompanied by a renewed trust in God's grace, is the important theological message we are called to share with those who are so anxious about church growth.

We are now *free* to concentrate on what I believe the biblical tradition values most: the level of faithfulness whereby the church accounts for the hope that characterizes us as the body of Christ in the world. Perhaps we can now become liberated to pursue anew the criterion of faithfulness: love of God and neighbor. We can be released to give our time and energy to deciding how our congregations, at a given moment in time and history and placed in a specific geographical setting and value climate, are required to be faithful. For some congregations, faithfulness will expect growth; for others it will mean stability. For yet others, faithfulness may actually mean numerical decline without being described as having a pathological illness. There is no universal set of principles for faithfulness. Faithfulness focuses on extending the love of God and humanity but can only be explored and evaluated in a specific situation to which the church finds itself called.

Balance Between Faithfulness and Effectiveness

The second implication for the church must be stated immediately, lest an imperative dialectic be distorted. The church must find a balance between faithfulness and effectiveness. There is a need to nurture a creative dialectic between:

Biblical Faithfulness to Love of God and Neighbor
and
Pragmatic Effectiveness in Ministry and Mission

The church has often tended to skew this delicate balance. This is especially true in relation to evangelism. In some periods and places there has been radicalized theological commitment to proclaiming the offense of the gospel as faithfulness in such a way that many people inside and outside the church were blocked from effectively hearing the complete gospel in its comforting, liberating, and even prophetic concern. Smylie (chapter 3) recalls the commitment of some members of the mainline churches to their Reformation heritage in the application of the prophetic Protestant principle to the transformation of culture. This is reflected in those same church leaders' own involvement in the civil rights movement and in protests against poverty and the Vietnam War. These stands were honest and prophetic yet appear in retrospect to have sometimes involved one's own ethical justification as much as theological nurture. I believe that the message was faithful. The method was clearly not effective. As one senior pastor humorously remarked, "I regret that I have but one assistant to give for my country." In the dialogue between Christ and culture, some proclamations and sermons represented more of an "against culture" than a "transformation of culture" view.

On other occasions we, as church interpreters, have so accommodated the message of the gospel to the needs and presuppositions assumed in our listeners that we also block the full gospel by selectively filtering our message to one particular group of people. This filtering is done on grounds such as race, sex, or economic strata or in terms of particularly acceptable themes, such as the justification of the individual work ethic or the central need for family stability and spiritual peace. The church's lack of carry-through on programs to combat racism and sexism is an example of a selectively interpreted gospel message.

The dynamics of life in the church require what I have called a creative dialectic between faithfulness and effectiveness that is not dissimilar to the dialectic in the great commandment between love of God and neighbor. The elements of the commandment are inseparably interrelated. Niebuhr reminds us that "God's love of self and neighbor, neighbor's love of God and self, self's love of God and neighbor are so interrelated that none of the relations exists without the other [Niebuhr, 1956:34]." So also the church cannot ultimately be faithful without informed and compassionate effectiveness. Neither can the church be finally effective as Christ's reconciling body without taking into account the faithfulness God requires of the church as God did of Christ himself in matters of love and justice.

Many of us are struggling with the balance between faithfulness and effectiveness. The biblical tradition calls us not only to covenantal faithfulness, but also to pragmatic effectiveness in all phases of our ministry and mission. Acts records the events of an early church whose members sought creative means of effectively embodying faithfulness whether that reaped honor or persecution. Effectiveness applied to church growth may be understood as an appropriate expectation of an anticipated gift from the Holy Spirit. On other occasions, expectation of membership growth may inhibit effective ministry. Whether faithfulness expects or inhibits growth depends on the focus of ministry and mission of a particular church. The question, as we noted originally, is "church growth at what cost and for what purpose."

Guard Against the Seductiveness of Effectiveness

Before I explore a faith hunch for the future, let me note one more basic implication for the church: The seductiveness of effectiveness in balancing the demand to be faithful.

John Yoder, in his critique of the church growth movement, notes its tendency to reject theological scrutiny in the scramble for efficiency (1973:27). He then reports on conversations with Latin American theologians who have directly experienced church growth programs in their own countries. They were worried by the seeming concurrence between this approach to membership and an American cultural style, which is success-, management-, and computer-oriented. Rene Padilla suggested that "Church Growth people assume that you make Christians the way you make cars and sausages. Mass production, achieved by having the machinery properly regulated, is the way to do anything [Yoder, 1973:29]." This critique is dismissed by Yoder as a matter of "style not substance." I am not so sure. The style in which we carry out the ministry and mission of the church may witness to critical issues of faithfulness and effectiveness. Danger lies in the seductiveness of supporting effectiveness or efficiency at the cost of faithfulness. New Testament scripture is filled with accounts of Jesus and the disciples giving compassionate concern for the means by which they accomplish their goals, particularly if action involves human relationships. Jesus' response to the blind beggar Bartimaeus may be illustrative (Mark 10:46-52). Rather than assuming the blind man wanted most to be given sight and thus immediately and efficiently performing the healing, Jesus says to him, "What do you want me to do for you?" The participation of Bartimaeus in the healing and transforming event is part of its redemptive power. It is on the grounds of faith as well as effective embodiment that renewal occurs. "Jesus said to him, 'Go; your faith has cured you.'

And at once he recovered his sight and followed him on the road [Mark 10:52, NEB]."

Three principles seem to have influenced the evangelism approaches of some mainline denominations. I wish briefly to explore their theological implications. I believe these to be examples of the seductiveness of effectiveness when separated from or not balanced with faithfulness.

1. Donald McGavran (1970) distinguishes between "discipling," which moves a person over the threshold of minimal commitment to the Christian movement, and "perfecting," which follows later and involves continuing education to unfold the meaning and implications of one's new loyalty. Theologians like John Yoder (1973:31ff) have challenged this distinction on theological grounds. I wish, as well, to underline what I believe is a compromise in sharing the gospel in its full integrity for the sake of effectiveness and growth.

The functional distinction between discipling and perfecting can take many forms. The term was developed by the church growth movement, but the idea affects most churches at some point in their ministries. The minimal requirements of discipling may take the form of confessing the name of Jesus and water baptism, as McGavran suggests, or may take a more subtle form, such as requiring church membership as an implicit prerequisite for being married, having one's children baptized, or acquiring access to recreational or educational opportunities, as church programs sometimes do. The issue, from my perspective, is that the distinction and prioritizing of discipling over perfecting violates the biblical understanding of conversion and straitjackets the perception of religious experience. In addition, it carries the danger of introducing a process akin to Bonhoeffer's "cheap grace." When the perfecting is finally pursued, it may cause a negative reaction and a falling away by the person originally discipled—as is indeed predicted in the New Testament. Perhaps most damaging from the perspective of love of God and neighbor, this superficial discipling may produce a kind of vaccination against the full meaning of the gospel.

It is not always clear what discipling involves, and therefore, it is difficult to discern what constitutes minimal commitment. We are all aware of denominations and congregations that have such low expectations and/or requirements for membership that minimal commitment is a functional reality. However, it becomes a serious matter from the perspective of faithfulness when this process becomes a self-conscious strategy. The church growth movement and those in leadership positions in evangelism who have adopted this paradigm speak of the "postponement of ethical awareness" in presenting the gospel to potential converts. This attempt to make the gospel attractive and as palatable as possible seems, to me, a direct contradiction of the meaning of conversion in the New Testament. Conversion appears to mean a substantial change in one's being and perspective, a turning around that is never completed in this life but is on the way. Any self-conscious editing of the gospel requirements, resulting in ethical postponement in order to make the message initially more acceptable, seems especially contradictory to what Jesus asks of new disciples. Jesus' demand for a radical new obedience to the love of God and neighbor is accompanied by demands to remove the obstacles to this full obedience—whether that means selling your goods and giving to the poor or not stopping to plow your fields or bury your kin.

A simple analogy that perhaps overstates the point but can be applied in our context comes from a recent conversation. In the midst of the turmoil over busing in South Boston, a pastor advocated and pursued a new evangelism program that explicitly avoided discussing racism as a sin. His rationale was that this issue could only be perceived properly within the context of the faith and the loving nature of the church. He argued, "A temporary delay is more justifiable than no access." I believe that to disciple or evangelize in this way—even if ethical awareness concerning fuller comprehension of the gospel is not long postponed—violates biblical and theological faithfulness. The very process lacks not only integrity but credibility. Faithfulness and perhaps effectiveness are both sacrificed.

Lest any of us feel too self-righteous, we must inquire which components in the gospel we tend to modify for the sake of initial or sustained acceptance. The one with which I am most in touch revolves around the level of my life-style and consumption in relation to my neighbors in the developing countries of the world. As an American, I live off their labors and resources, as I participate in the consumption of almost 70 percent of the world's resources. I suspect each of us has his or her own form of postponed ethical awareness.

2. The second principle that exemplifies the seductiveness of effectiveness is the much publicized homogeneous unit. Wagner (1976:110) states: "A 'homogeneous unit' is simply a group of people who consider each other to be 'our kind of people.' " It is the ecclesiological parallel to "birds of a feather flock together." As

McGavran (1970:198) notes, "People like to become Christians without crossing racial, linguistic, or class barriers." No one doubts the sociological accuracy or the pragmatic efficiency of the principle. Many mainline churches may discover the principle when they reflect on the pattern that has been actually pursued when a program of outreach, either formal or informal, is conducted. The question I raise with Wagner and with denominations or congregations that are reassessing the priority of church growth in their ministry and mission is that of faithfulness.

Jesus frequently related the image of the kingdom to a great feast or banquet. Those at table would be Samaritans and Jerusalemites, Pharisees and slaves, harlots and the holy. It is, if I understood the image correctly, the greatest breaking down of homogeneous units we will ever know. Eating at table with Jesus was a critical symbol of fellowship. It is precisely here that Jesus rejected all lines of social distinction. Lest one believe his demands were based only on a temporary preference that requires a minimum of discomfort, Jesus' ultimate analogy of the kingdom is calling people in from the highways and byways to join the banquet (Matthew 22; Luke 14). At the table of fellowship in his presence, Christ makes possible a radical sense of community that transcends the walls and barriers of race, class, sex, and age.

In Ephesians 2 and 3 Paul affirms God's intent to break down the dividing wall between Jew and Gentile and make of them a new humanity through the cross. Within the New Testament context, Jews and Gentiles were the most striking example of different kinds of people. Paul's great fight with Peter, recorded in Galatians 2, is about Paul's insistence that there cannot be two separate churches of Jews and Gentiles. As John Yoder (1973:44) helps us understand in theological terms, the oneness of the unity in Jesus Christ, the bridging of ethnic barriers, "is not a fruit of the gospel; it is not an *object lesson* in the gospel; it is not a *vehicle* of the gospel, it *is* the Gospel." The account in Acts 10—12 demonstrates that the church can and must grow across cultural barriers. It is in this very act that the transformation of culture in Christ's name occurs. In the final analysis the homogeneous unit principle may not only be unfaithful on theological grounds, but pragmatically ineffective in a ministry and mission particularly to the young and better educated.

3. The third theme is what I describe as the strictness principle. It is represented by Dean Kelley's theories on church growth (see chapters 8 and 15). Kelley notes, in chapter 15, the desire to have entitled his controversial book "Why Strict Churches Are Strong."

He pleads for doctrinal and life-style control and for such a high level of commitment as to almost necessitate intolerance of other views, even to the extent of avoiding other Christians who fail to conform. This is a call for the radical purity of the church at all cost.

It is actually a sectarian argument that is not really indifferent to culture because of the depth of its own seriousness and commitment. Rather, the strictness principle demands a stance over against culture in order to maintain a sect mentality that stresses purity and the avoidance of contamination. As Kelley illustrates, this mindset is effective for producing allegiance, because it is very clear about what it means to be saved and what qualifies one to be counted among the elect.

Most mainline Christians have a touch of guilt when they are accused of not being serious or disciplined enough about their faith, and there is certainly some justification for the critique. However, to make strictness a principle and to link this to absolute clarity on what constitutes Christian obligations in belief and practice must be questioned from a faithfulness perspective. It is difficult to justify such a stance from many New Testament scenes. Jesus' own ministry and that of disciples like Paul do not seem to be characterized as sectarian with a strictness of belief, practice, or association. Jesus not only lives out a contrast with the puritanical and hypocritical Pharisees, but calls attention to their superficial stance on eating, working on the sabbath, and narrow interpretations of the Mosaic law and their intolerant, unloving pattern of avoiding contact with the ethically or religiously unpure. Paul's position on taking care not to cause a neighbor to stumble by one's own freedom or finding it imperative to be all things to all people for Christ's sake seriously challenges the faithfulness of the strictness principle.

At its core, the strictness principle seeks to create community by simplistic clarity and by avoidance of the ambiguity that is at the heart of the human experience. The parabolic nature of the New Testament teachings defies a simplistic return to the self-justification of the law. It is the discipline of the heart that the gospel seems to require: acceptance and forgiveness of all God's creatures; openness to the ambiguity involved in being made new creatures in Christ; and a commitment in love to one's neighbor as defined by presence, not his or her beliefs or actions. The strictness principle is finally suspect on the standards of faithfulness and effectiveness, despite its seductive appeal to create a strong and growing church.

These three effectiveness principles are so seductive, because they have led us almost unconsciously into allowing American church membership and participation to become the definitive criteria of commitment. Many of the working group would reject these criteria as would church leaders among the clergy and the laity. Yet, these criteria subtly undergird our sociological surveys and our ecclesiological strategizing.

APPLICATIONS FOR THE CHURCH

A humbling conclusion of the research contained in this book, one that should highlight our constant dependence on God's grace, is that reliable predictions about future religious trends are not in order. However, I do want to risk a "faith hunch." It is a "hunch" rather than a prediction, because it is based on a strong intuitive feeling, not on a direct extrapolation from the data. It emerges from my own attempt to analyze the research conclusions. Yet, it goes beyond any of the established results. It is a "faith" hunch, because it is based on the firm conviction that God will use the church of Jesus Christ for God's purposes, even if we misunderstand or mistakenly respond.

The critical question is, *Can* and *should* the church change the thrust of its ministry and mission in the next half decade? If the answer is "yes" or even "hopefully," then *what* should it change? My vision of the church's task in the immediate future centers on the recovery of the transforming middle. Specific themes constructed on the foundation of a balance between faithfulness and effectiveness may provide some form to this vision for the "whither" of Christian commitment.

In contrast to the three seductive dangers identified earlier, these themes are (1) church typology, (2) ministry to young adults and the unchurched, and (3) quest for community.

Identify Church Typologies

The first theme is in direct contrast to the strictness principle. I doubt if any set and final list of characteristics will disclose what it is to be a "strong" or, in my language, "faithful" church. Dean Kelley has suggested that mainline churches could grow if they would pay the price in strictness of style and doctrine; he doubts that they will. I doubt they *should*, if it implies a universal model of the church and measures its strength by growth.

A Christian congregation must discover and own its distinctive identity as a church of Jesus Christ in a particular time and place—its own church type. Awareness of this identity may or may not demand change. If change is necessary, then the ability and willingness to make adjustments may be assessed over against their purpose and cost. To unearth or restore a church's identity and mission is often very difficult. This is particularly so in the American church, which tends to prescribe plans for evangelism, social action, stewardship, or spiritual discipline as if most congregations, particularly within the same denomination, were essentially similar. One learning attained from the research is that there are different types of churches and there are different forms of ministry and mission that can be evaluated as equally faithful and effective. In reference to membership and participation, these applied criteria could mean growth, stability, or decline, depending on the identity and context of the church.

The notion that there are different "types" of churches is prevalent in the literature, and it is not possible to spell out the emerging comparative typologies here. It is important, however, to underscore the theological significance of knowing and owning the type of church in which one ministers. The expectations and demands of one type of congregation will be quite different from those of another. The vision concerning themes and methodology appropriate for the penetration of culture by a church on the periphery will vary, depending on church type and constituency. To understand the type of one's congregation and thus discover its identity may be theologically faithful and pragmatically effective.

My hunch is that the continued exploration of church types is a crucial element in the development of several persuasive models of Christian religious commitment. This individual assessment is also crucial to the authentic repopulation of a theological middle ground concerning the nature and purpose of the church.

Ministry to Young Adults and the Unchurched

There is one fascinating piece of data about which virtually all the researchers agree. There has been a disproportionately sharp decline in the level of church membership and participation for persons between the ages of 18 and 30. This is especially intriguing when there is some indication that this trend reflects a disaffection of youth from the established church but not necessarily a disinterest in religious experience or religious themes. Much recent work (Wuthnow and Glock, 1974; Roozen, 1976; Hale, 1977; Gallup Opinion Index, 1978b) has made it clear that rejection of churchgoing practice does not necessarily mean the rejection of religion in terms of belief in God, prayer, and significance of life after death. But this should not be taken to excuse the fact that there has been a major loss of young people from church life at a formative stage in the development of their world view. There is some evidence that this defection is an early indication of the decrease in significance of the institutional church among the population as a whole. This warning is particularly evident in the views of the unchurched who are young, affluent, and college educated.

Basic trends in Christian beliefs, even with acknowledgment of the limitations of some assessment instruments, have remained relatively unchanged over the last three to four decades. However, the saliency or importance of religion in people's lives shows an appreciable decline (see chapter 1). Belief is steady; church participation and saliency of religious practice is down.

What is the image of the church carried by the unchurched? A recent Gallup Survey (Gallup Opinion Index, 1978b) adds new fuel to old stereotypes. It finds the unchurched saying that the institutional church is not effective in helping people find meaning in life; is not warm or accepting of outsiders; is not concerned enough with social justice; is too concerned about organizational issues; has lost the real spiritual part of religion. Surprisingly, on all the issues cited except too little concern with social justice and not welcoming outsiders, the churched agree with the unchurched. Even given my skepticism about national surveys, this information suggests a considerable indictment of the institutional church.

The situation calls the church to a faithful and effective response to the image that many young adults and unchurched have of the role of the church in society. The relationship between Christ and culture emerges particularly in the more detailed studies of Hoge and Wuthnow. Hoge (chapter 4) makes the case that a specific interrelated set of values is essential in understanding the attitude of college-educated young adults. Wuthnow argues specifically that prior contact with the counterculture was a primary causal factor in the disaffection of youth from the church. Although a minority of youth actually belonged to the counterculture, there was a significant effect on shaping the values and attitudes of large portions of American youth.

These young adults perceived, perhaps not incorrectly, that there was a contrast between the life-style and quality of commitment of many in the institutional church and the Christian values that they proclaimed (Wuthnow, 1976b). One may acknowledge that many manifestations of that experimental counterculture were superficial and at times bizarre. Yet, it is now difficult to ignore or dismiss the impact of some central commitments of that generation on those who are in or are about to emerge from the category of young adults. A few have suggested, including this author (Evans, 1971:97), that some of the fundamental values of this counterculture were embodiments of the Christian gospel: liberating love, revitalized community, transforming peace, and sacrificial concern. The young appeared really to believe what the church, in its more authentic moments, proclaims about love of God and neighbor.

Countercultures virtually never replace the dominant culture. Their purpose is to encounter, penetrate, challenge, and eventually transform or at least modify the mainline stream of culture. According to the research of Wuthnow, this penetration from the periphery for the sake of transformation has actually occurred. One consequence for many young people was an anti-institutional or at least skeptical attitude about the institutional church, combined with positive attraction and need for some of the religious and spiritual values associated with the Christian gospel.

Part of my faith hunch is that in the future many types of congregations will come to see their ministry and mission in terms of the human need for an accepting community and support of social justice for those outside as well as inside the official church boundaries. Cultural dominance by the church, if it ever existed in this century for America, is not a viable model for the next two decades. Dominance in numbers has often meant capitulation to the norms of the culture rather than sacrificial service of those struggling to implement Christian-informed motifs of liberation, acceptance, compassion, justice, and forgiveness. This seems to be true whether the implementation is inside or outside the religious camp. This latter distinction of being inside or outside the religious structure did not seem to be very critical to Jesus if there was evidence of love of God and neighbor.

A commitment to service rather than size may call a church to be as much concerned with allies as with members. Research reveals that in the eyes of many the church has suffered a credibility decline concerning the model of commitment it urges for others on biblical and theological grounds. This model includes a promise of meaning for life, belonging with acceptance, and empowerment for spirituality and social justice. Yet, the disappointment with the church, combined with a more anti-institutional and anti-authoritarian attitude in the culture, may not make this a period when high participation of membership should be expected or would even be faithful. The church's desire to dominate by membership and participation, without a change in its commitment model, may result in an inoculation against the gospel in some areas. The faith hunch suggests that the church must try to restore its credibility by relating to allies, especially among the young and the unchurched, who sometimes share similar values and goals but are dubious about the value of official membership and participation. They are seeking evidence that the church is a reliable ally and is committed to a transformation of culture, not simply an accommodation to culture. Alliance-building will come about by living into a model of commitment that is more faithful and may, in the long haul, be more effective.

The church may not be amiss in taking a hint from the counterculture in its attempt to influence rather than control the culture. One of the most refreshing elements of the alternative life-style associated with the counterculture was that there was little attempt to recruit new members or to demand conformity of those who affiliated themselves with the movement. Rather, certain values such as love, peace, and community were emphasized, and the persons who were the most authentic representatives of this counterculture approach embodied these commitments. Credibility and this influence were exerted by modeling for, not by controlling of, those persons encountered. In fact, the collapse of the counterculture came when the lived paradigms deserted or distorted the commitments of the movement. We are learning that some influence among those never part of the counterculture remained, even when the more obvious experiments faded. This may have resulted from the concentration on a strategy of influence rather than control.

If the church is on the boundary of society, engaging the culture for the sake of transformation, then it may need more of a prophetic cutting edge than a culture-affirming core concerned with institutional maintenance. If this is true, then what is not needed is a distinction between "discipling" and "perfecting," with the stress on minimal commitment and the postponement of ethical awareness for the sake of the attraction of large numbers of new believers. What is needed is more commitment and credibility from the very beginning, not less. The accessible, if not easy, religion supplied by the market research approach of the church growth movement lacks not only faithfulness, but in the long run may also be ineffective. The search for many of the unchurched seems to be for evidence of effectively embodied faithfulness on the part of the church that contains a challenge and some confrontation with the values of culture—even of a culture with which one may have reached an uneasy and accommodating alliance.

The task for the church in the immediate future may involve more creative conflict than satisfied solidarity. The demand for love of God and neighbor causes conflict in priorities and commitments. A decision, a conversion, is demanded by God, in which a continuing struggle for the fullness of life is the goal. This goal does not guarantee satisfied solidarity. Many young adults and the unchurched could be seen as borderline allies of a church aiming at Christ's transformative effect on culture. We are called in this time, I believe, to be faithful and effective as we ask, listen, and heal. This is perhaps the beginning of a serving, influencing, and transforming model of Christian commitment.

The Quest for Community

The final dimension of this vision for the future—to rediscover the transforming middle—focuses on another undisputed element in our research: the church is perceived as unaccepting. The most poignant evidence came from interviews with those who have dropped out of the church (see chapter 2). Warren Hartman describes this point well in summarizing his research on the reasons for church dropout: "The most frequently mentioned reason on their list was their failure to feel that they were accepted, loved, or wanted." One half of those interviewed in another study cried during the session, revealing the depth of feeling about involvement in the community of faith.

The data reveals that churches are perceived as too rigid and narrow, while members are viewed as less tolerant and accepting of a diversity of viewpoints than the nonchurch member. While there are obviously many ways of explaining and interpreting this data, there is an inescapable and overwhelming impression that the church is characterized in the eyes of members and nonmembers as lacking warmth, personal concern, openness, and acceptance.

This reality of the current religious climate is particularly disturbing when one contrasts this with a theological theme of Paul Tillich, who declares that the crucial factor in the Christian gospel is "to accept that you are accepted." The church has a profound problem with the quest for community at the very moment when it seems so desperately needed by the culture. Walrath (chapter 11) makes a compelling case for the consequence of rapid social change: "Persons massed together are forced to live segmented, fragmented lives and experience alienation." For the church to be faithful and effective at this moment in American history—a time characterized by rapid social change and the constant threat of alienating forces that would sever us from the fragile roots we have—requires a new concern for community. Yet, this may demand a transformation of our understanding of community. It is clear that persons are not long deceived by superficial friendliness or incorporation into the group by assigning them a task immediately upon entry. A sense of community based on role, status, and structure dissolves when a change in the structure is demanded by external or internal forces. Fellowship built primarily on support but which lacks loving and transforming critique will not weather the storm of conflict. The church has often attempted to create community by organizing itself around task or turf. Perhaps this superficial desire for constantly harmonious cooperation and complete satisfaction in the church is what makes the homogeneous principle appear so attractive and workable. The problem is that the structural community one can create lacks depth.

The biblical image of community, which I wish to refer to by the Latin term *communitas* (to distinguish it from "community," which may be understood as an "area of common living" [see Turner, 1969]), is represented in the book of Acts. The reality of such phrases as "there was never a needy person among them" and "the whole body of believers were united in heart and soul" points to a quality of relatedness I describe as *communitas*. This sense of *communitas* cannot be created or organized, and it is not based on task or turf. Rather, the biblical image of *communitas* is a quality of relatedness combining intimate support and loving critique. It is based on "spirit" and "spontaneity" and is always a gift of God that breaks open our established patterns in order to allow us to be transformed anew by Christ.

This third theme of the vision, *communitas*, stands in revealing contrast to the seductiveness of the homogeneous unit. *Communitas* is a quality of relatedness that the Holy Spirit allows to emerge, over against a human strategy of inclusion through which persons feel at home with their "own kind." Genuine community brings critique and support, conflict and comfortableness. The Spirit will regularly confront us on the boundaries—both the boundaries of our culture and of our lives. There is a breaking open at the point of liminality for persons and groups that continually transforms them into creatures and new communities. This is a radical and regular remaking of the mind and heart that creates a new homogeneity in

Christ to transcend the superficially ordinary cultural bonding. This is the terrifying and tremendous promise of the meaning, belonging, and empowering function of the love of God and neighbor. It is beyond anything we can create and guarantee.

Community in the sense of *communitas* is by its very nature boundary-breaking. This is true whether the boundaries are race, class, or time. Genuine community is the art of loving and caring that cannot avoid challenge and transformation. The very form of being made new creatures in Christ is traumatic. To believe the church can minister effectively and faithfully apart from emersion in this transformative process is an illusion. The church should be most vulnerable to the transforming power of Christ within its own churchly culture.

This *communitas* will not have effectiveness apart from the recognition of the pluralistic nature of the world in which both the church and the culture stand. The power of *communitas* is in antistructure or metastructure (for a detailed discussion, see Evans, 1975). Note that this sense of community, informed by the vision of the early church as seen in Acts, goes beyond and penetrates any particular structure in order to transform it. Acceptance is not on stance or condition, but on Christ's power to make us members one of another. This quality of *communitas* will not be easily achieved. However, it is desperately sought by those inside and outside the church and is experienced by many in both these locations. To experience this mutual at-oneness does not require that one be an official member of the religious community. No such prerequisite appears in scripture. Rather, *communitas* is a gift of the spirit that binds together those who thirst for the love of God and neighbor.

Personal Conclusions

There is, I believe, hope for reconstructing and repopulating the middle ground between a culture-affirming liberalism and a culture-denying fundamentalism. Neither of these theological positions holds promise for a ministry that seeks to balance the creative dialectic between faithfulness and effectiveness. Hope for the future is based on a model of Christian religious commitment that points to Christ as the transformer of culture *and* the church. Each congregation must discover its identity and evaluate its ministry and mission in terms of the criteria of faithfulness and effectiveness appropriate to its own context.

Personally, I do not think the next decade necessarily will or should be a period of great numerical church growth. To mature into the "fulness of Christ" as communities of faithfulness is the call I perceive. This call may mean a transformation in many churches' understanding of this ministry and mission in relation to the culture. Many of these congregations will be stable or slightly declining if the neighborhood or constituency is stable. Others may grow. It is misleading, however, to declare that churches must grow or even that they must change. What a specific congregation is called by God to do in a specific context must be discovered on the grounds of individual commitment to faithfulness and effectiveness—not on the basis of externally devised criteria. It is the quality of community among the members and their creative commitment to the transformation of themselves and their culture that is an essential mark of the body of Christ. This sense of *communitas* will occur through the power and gift of the Holy Spirit and through a commitment to the love of God and neighbor.

The call to faithfulness and effectiveness carries with it promises of joy and hope. Smylie (chapter 3) reminds us that the heritage of the mainline Protestant churches is a witness to Christ as the transformer of culture in the public as well as the private realm. While I am less convinced than Smylie about the present extent of commitment to renewal, I believe he correctly recalls that God never allows this transforming spirit to be underground for long. The repopulation of the theological middle ground will come through emigration from left and right of the middle and eventually perhaps from some allies of the love of God and neighbor who are currently not even on the church map.

Martin Marty (1978a) declares, "The bustling 'conservative' churches have not successfully reshaped American culture, or arrested cultural trends to which they objected, or prevented their own internal adaptation to worldliness." My question is, Can nonbustling but committed mainline churches respond more faithfully and effectively to this call to facilitate the transformation of culture by the Christ in whose grace they ultimately trust? The research in this volume suggests some directions and provides some hope. The sustaining promise, however, comes at the conclusion of that Great Commission we have been struggling to interpret, when Jesus said, "I am with you always, to the end of time."

CHAPTER 14

Some Sociological Conclusions About Church Trends

Dean R. Hoge
and
David A. Roozen

What is happening, how should we best conceptualize it, and why is it happening? With these three questions we approached recent church trends in America. The studies of the Hartford working group have produced some conclusions that are convincing, at least to us. They can be categorized into sociological conclusions and conclusions for church policy. This chapter reviews some sociological conclusions of possible interest to future researchers.

ASSUMPTIONS INFLUENCING THE RESEARCH

For sake of clarity, we should restate some of the assumptions and parameters of the project. We have looked at the church as an institution and at individuals' involvement in it, not at religiousness more generally. We have tried to avoid premature assumptions or judgments about sources or motivations for church involvement. Most of our attention has been devoted to the major Christian denominations, and we have said virtually nothing about sectarian groups or new religious movements. We have tried to be guided by reliable empirical data rather than by personal observation or speculation, and this has led us to stress topics on which empirical data was available. We have accepted some of these limitations to make the project manageable.

315

Much attention has been given to the years since World War II. All the sociological studies have been limited to this period of time, partly because the available data is richer for these years. Our historical studies have spanned more years, in an effort to avoid a foreshortening of vision. We scrutinized longer-term trend data (see Presbyterian Committee, 1976; Gaustad, 1976) but were unable to draw firm conclusions without more information. Limiting ourselves to the post-World War II years could be misleading, because the 1940s and early 1950s might be somehow abnormal. Then the denominational declines after the late 1950s could be seen as a "return to normalcy" and as an event to be explained in its own right. We considered this possibility at some length. Without doubt the 1950s were a time of relatively great growth in the mainline denominations, and in a long-range view the growth rate after the 1950s would be expected more likely to curve downward than to curve even more steeply upward. But beyond this initial statement we were unable to apply the notion of "return to normalcy" with any explanatory rigor. In a period of rapid social change the notion of normalcy may be unclear, and it seems so for the years under study here.

DESCRIPTION OF THE TRENDS

For basic data on trends in church membership and attendance we were dependent on (1) denominational data published in yearbooks and compiled in the annual *Yearbook of American and Canadian Churches* and on (2) replications in nationwide polls. The question arises whether this data reports actual church trends reliably, and we tried to be cautious. Two problems should be noted in this regard.

First, a possible source of unreliability in denominational data is changes in definition of membership or changes in data collection methods. We looked into the issues and concluded that membership definitions changed little in the years covered by our study (see chapter 6).

Second, a problem in the accuracy of denominational membership reports is the variation in roll-cleaning practices. This problem gives rise to one widely cited theory of the reported downturn in membership of several denominations—that those denominations have not really declined in membership but have merely cleaned their rolls more carefully in recent years. The theory is difficult to test, since the information needed to do so is

DEE KUENNING

not available. The Presbyterian Committee tried to assess the theory within that denomination. It asked a sample of congregations if they had reviewed their membership lists more rigorously in recent years than a decade earlier, and the majority said yes (1976:226). Presbyterian congregations had acquired an economic reason for doing so, since the congregational apportionments for denominational programs had increased greatly during the early 1970s, and the apportionments were based directly on congregational membership size. These facts supported the "cleaner rolls theory." However, other facts conflicted with the theory. Other denominations, such as the United Church of Christ, the Episcopal Church, and the United Methodist Church, have had trend lines similar to the United Presbyterian trends in membership, yet these denominations had no visible economic reason for more rigorous cleaning of rolls in recent years. The Presbyterian Committee decided that the cleaner rolls theory was probably true but weak. It accounts for only a small amount of the membership trends depicted in annual yearbook reports.

We recognize that membership reports and survey data do not capture the total picture of church trends. Some examples of important but unmeasured changes demonstrate this. In 1935 H. Paul Douglass reflected on some changes in mainline churches in the 1920s and 1930s. He said that the use of revivals was waning and that the practice of family devotions was also appearing to weaken. Also during the 1920s and 1930s, midweek services were gradually abandoned. (In subsequent decades Sunday evening services were also eventually given up.) Also Douglass saw a tendency away from dogma and toward discussion in both Sunday school and preaching (1935:151). Another interesting finding occurred in a 1960 restudy of a 1948 study of Pittsburgh area churches (Thorne, 1967). The percentage of members living a mile or less from their churches declined about 6 points over that time; the churches were decreasingly based on neighborhood areas. Isolated bits of information such as these are intriguing but often difficult to interpret theoretically.

EXPLANATION OF THE TRENDS

To help conceptualize the factors possibly influencing church trends we divided them into four categories, created by cross-cutting contextual factors versus institutional factors and national factors versus local factors. This is a rudimentary conceptualization needing refinement later. The contextual versus institutional distinction is based partly on the concern about church action; any factor judged to be not reasonably changeable by intentional church effort was classified as contextual. Thus, for example, socioeconomic status of parishioners in any congregation or denomination is seen as contextual, even though church action in the areas of evangelism and new church development could conceivably have an impact over the span of some years. Family size is also classified as contextual. The national versus local distinction is rooted in decades of Protestant church planning research (for summaries see Douglass and Brunner, 1935; Leiffer, 1961), in which neighborhood characteristics were thoroughly researched and distinguished from overall social changes in the nation. National institutional factors include denominational policy, practices, mission programs, theology, and image. Local institutional factors are characteristics of the local congregation, such as type of leadership and program and management of tensions.

In a study of why some congregations grow while others decline, all four sets of factors must be investigated. In a study of why some denominations grow while others decline, the national factors are foremost in importance, and the local factors are included in the analysis only when it can be demonstrated that they differ systematically from denomination to denomination. For example, geographic shifts in the U.S. population affect all denominations, but if it can be proven that one denomination more successfully develops new congregations in newly built suburbs than other denominations, then these neighborhood-level factors are important. In a study of why overall church participation in the United States is growing or declining, the national factors would again be foremost.

Regional factors are not clearly conceptualized in this fourfold rubric. Regional location of any denomination would be included, along with other denominational characteristics, as a national institutional factor. Changing regional contextual factors, such as the growth of a regional subculture, are tentatively included with national contextual factors but only preliminarily. They require an additional level of analysis, which we were not able to do (see chapter 8).

The four sets of factors are tentatively seen as additive and recursive, producing a four-factor model:

$$\text{Growth} = b_1 \text{ NCF} + b_2 \text{ NIF} + b_3 \text{ LCF} + b_4 \text{ LIF}$$

NCF, NIF, LCF, and LIF are indexes of national contextual factors, national institutional factors, local contextual factors, and local institutional factors, respectively, and b_1, b_2, b_3, and b_4 are weights indicating the importance of each. This is an appropriate conceptual model for local congregations; for denominations the last two factors and their weights would be deleted.

Thus, if empirical research found that national and local factors were equally weighty and that contextual factors in both settings were 1.5 times as powerful as institutional factors, the weights might be $b_1 = .3$; $b_2 = .2$; $b_3 = .3$; and $b_4 = .2$. Insofar as the four sets of factors have overlapping explanatory power, we would see the contextual factors as causally prior and assign the overlapping explanatory power to them, not to the institutional factors. Thus, in the studies in this book we have seen the contextual factors as exogenous.[1]

This model implies that the tasks of analysis are (1) to identify the principal factors causally important in each of the four overall sets and (2) to determine the weighting to be given to each set. The questions of possible interaction effects or feedback loops are postponed until more precision is possible. Available evidence related to both tasks is reviewed below. But first, we must clarify the question of short-term versus long-term trends.

SHORT-TERM VERSUS LONG-TERM TRENDS

A researcher attempting to explain trends must determine how short-term or long-term the trends really are, and therefore, what kinds of explanations are convincing. Decade-long fluctuations, for example, cannot be explained by century-long trends in contextual factors. How long, in years, are the trends in the data? Are there several patterns visible? Are the trends recurrent or cyclical?

Our studies have repeatedly concluded that trends in American church membership and attendance are rather short-term in nature. The downturn in membership in many denominations has occurred only since the middle 1960s, and in 1978 there were signs that the abruptness of the decline is lessening. Looking farther back in history, the trends during the 1930s changed in about 1938-42, when church growth began showing an increase. It continued through the 1950s and began showing signs of a turning point at the end of the 1950s and in the early 1960s. One could conclude that the most suitable historical unit for explaining such trends would be the decade or half-decade. This is also the view of other investigators (McGavran, 1970; Wuthnow, 1976b).

Are there long-term trends distinguishable from the decade-long fluctuations, which demand another order of explanation? This is a distinct possibility. Hoge (1974:ch. 6) argued that in college-student trend data, long-term trends of a half century or more could be distinguished from decade-long fluctuations. Is this true of church membership and attendance trends too? This vexing problem occupied much of our thought but without any clear solution.

Are there cycles visible in the trends? If so, how long are they? Some investigators of American church history have spoken of waves or pulses in church growth. William McLoughlin (1974) identified five pulses of revivalism in American history, the first being in 1600-40 and the last two being in 1875-1915 and 1950-80. He sees each as a sort of collective conversion experience in the midst of fundamental political-social issues in the American national identity. The issue underlying the revivalism period today is, Is the Protestant ethic and our capitalistic system capable of meeting our domestic and international responsibilities? McLoughlin's is a theory of awakenings more than of denominational histories. It alerts us to the repeated outbreaks of new religious fervor in church history. How it helps to explain the church membership trends in the last two decades is not clear.

Lyle Schaller identified three main waves of new church development in recent American history. "The first was the period between 1890 and the beginning of World War I, the second was in the 1920's, and the third was the 1948-63 period [1975:51]." Phillip Jones's data (in chapter 7) partly confirms this statement for the Southern Baptist Convention except that the first and third waves were much stronger than the second described by Schaller, in the 1920s. The explanation for these waves is unclear, but generally, Schaller stresses national contextual factors.

In the British Isles, church trends over several centuries were analyzed by Currie, Gilbert, and Horsley (1977). They found two kinds of regularities in the trends, of which one is somewhat relevant to us.[2] They found that several denominations seemed to have similar patterns of growth and then decline during their history. After an early vigorous period of growth—the progressive phase—came later phases of routinization and then gradual losses. In recent decades the newer sectarian groups (the Mormons, the Seventh-Day Adventists, and the Jehovah's Witnesses, for instance) have grown steadily, while older, established middle-class denominations have been declining. This pattern has been noted in modern church history by numerous observers (for example, Weber, 1963; H.R. Niebuhr, 1929; McGavran, 1970). There is, for some reason, an association between the age of a denomination and lack of vigorous growth. Currie and his associates concluded that contextual factors were more important than institutional factors in explaining this (1977:37).

We are left with diverse analyses and explanations. Our tentative conclusion is that no obvious regular cycles are visible in denominational trends in recent U.S. history, nor are there obvious long-term trends distinct from the decade-long fluctuations described above. Economic conditions and urbanization trends do not seem to coincide with church growth trends. There seems to be greater growth among the younger denominations than among the older ones, but this does not produce any regular cycles in church trends.

It follows that future projections and predictions are credible for only a short period of time, perhaps a decade at most. Trend lines do not hold steady for longer than that. To the urgent question of whether recent mainline denominational downturns are here to stay or whether they are short-term aberrations of history, we can say little. But we are inclined to doubt statements alleging or predicting precipitate changes. One occasionally hears statements of the "we are at the end of an era" variety, predicting great changes in a few years. They are not convincing. Church trends are inherently more stable and less dramatic than that.

IDENTIFICATION OF NATIONAL CONTEXTUAL FACTORS

We turn to a discussion of each of the four sets of factors influencing church trends, beginning with national contextual factors. It is important to remember that the downturn in mainline Protestantism is a relatively recent phenomenon. Early signs of a slowdown began to appear in the early 1960s, then downturns came in the middle 1960s, followed by a decade of constant losses. By 1978 one saw some indications that the losses were beginning to diminish. Whatever contextual factors contributed to this trend must have arisen in the period 1955-65. Before that time all the denominations were growing.

This conclusion is important, since it renders incredible many arguments heard today that point to centuries-long social or intellectual trends allegedly explaining recent Protestant losses. Such arguments invoke the rise of science, increasing living standards in America, increasing educational levels in America, increased leisure, the rise of mass media, increased geographic mobility of the population, increased urbanization, or other long-term elements of modernization. Also, secularization is not a credible explanation, both because the term is difficult to understand operationally and because it refers to a gradual cultural trend. Possibly certain combinations or interactions among such long-term trends produce dramatic short-term developments, but we have never seen demonstrations of such occurrences.

One finding has strong implications for understanding national contextual factors. It is that *age differences* in church attendance and religious attitudes occurred progressively after about 1960. Most of the decline in church attendance and membership since 1960 has been among persons 39 years old or less. This important pattern is visible only in nationwide survey data, not in denominational data, since the latter rarely contains age distinctions. The fact that young adults are the main group staying away from the church in recent years helps solve a riddle arising from denominational trend data—that although membership in several denominations is down since 1965, total contributions and per capita contributions are up. The solution is that membership losses have occurred in a category of persons who never have given much money—young adults.

Another important finding is that the birthrate in the United States has closely paralleled church participation rates and (among college students) traditional religious beliefs for about five decades. They increased or decreased in parallel. What is the linkage? One obvious linkage is that fewer births produce fewer children for Sunday schools and fewer new church members about fourteen years later. Two other linkages have also been empirically demonstrated. One is that adults with school-age children participate more in churches than other adults their age; thus, if more adults have school-age children, the overall church participation rate would be higher and vice versa. The other is that the determinants of birthrates are partly in value commitments of young adults, and these value commitments are related to attitudes about churches. In this sense the birthrate is a symptom of underlying value patterns, not directly causal in itself. Whatever causes births to rise or fall somehow causes church participation to rise or fall. For whatever reason, the birthrate was high during the 1950s but plummeted beginning about 1959 and remained low through the middle 1970s.

Age differences and birthrates are intriguing, but they don't provide us a clear explanation of church trends. We lack adequate information and must rely on indirect proof. We do know that attitudes have changed on a number of topics from the late 1950s until today, and the topics are proven to be associated with church commitment and attendance. They include the areas of sex behavior, abortion, ideal family size, civil liberties, marijuana legalization, and political party identification. In every instance the attitude trends are in the direction of individualism, personal freedom, and tolerance of diversity. The associated change in the realm of religion has been toward individualism and away from church commitment. The change has been much greater among young adults, and especially college-educated young adults, than elsewhere. Whatever is causing the attitude shift in the area of religion seems to be broader in scope, causing multiple attitude shifts.

Whether the attitude changes should be seen mainly as a generational phenomenon resulting from disruptions in childhood socialization during the 1950s and 1960s, or whether they are an indication of broader value change in the total society (which is first evidenced in the volatile youth population), is unclear. Whether the changes originated in certain attitude areas and spread to others, or whether they occurred in all, due to outside pressures, is also unclear.

IDENTIFICATION OF NATIONAL INSTITUTIONAL FACTORS

National institutional factors include denominationwide characteristics such as polity, theological orientation, moral teachings and standards, new church development, and mission emphases. Many observers have pointed to such factors as explanations for recent denominational trends.

In chapter 8 we tested some of these factors in the sixteen-denomination study. We found that in recent decades denominations which strongly emphasized local evangelism, maintained a distinctive life-style and morality apart from mainstream culture, maintained a unitary set of beliefs, and de-emphasized social action and ecumenism were the ones that grew. We also tested two other characteristics but found them weak—strength of ethnic identity and congregational versus centralized polity.

Denominations could be seen as arrayed on a single overall axis, with "conservative-disciplined-distinctive from culture" at one pole and "liberal-pluralistic-culture-affirming" at the other. Those near the first pole have grown, while those near the second have declined.

The questions still remain about which of these factors are most causal, which are merely correlates and not causes, and how strong these institutional factors are apart from contextual factors. These questions cannot be answered decisively with existing research. However, we tend to agree with Dean Kelley that ecumenism is best seen as a correlate, not a cause, of growth or decline. Also, social action is only indirectly related to growth or decline; several studies have failed to find a strong direct relationship. The impact of social action seems to be mostly in the church conflicts that social action sometimes arouses and in reallocation of mission energies and monies. We believe that the impact of evangelism, theological conservatism, distinctiveness of life-style and morality, and maintenance of unitary beliefs on growth or decline is more direct and stronger.[3]

IDENTIFICATION OF LOCAL CONTEXTUAL FACTORS

Our studies agree with many past investigations of local contextual factors enhancing congregational growth. In chapters 9, 10, and 11 we found that the most powerful local contextual factors helping mainline Protestant church growth are affluence of the community, presence of middle-class residential neighborhoods near the church, percent homeowners near the church, absence of minorities in the neighborhood, and absence of other Protestant churches nearby. Any neighborhood changes are important if they change these factors; for example, an increase in economic level is favorable for church growth and a decrease is unfavorable. While our research is mainly on middle-class mainline denominations, certain principles apply to all denominations—that increases in their constituency populations nearby are favorable and increases in nearby residential neighborhoods are favorable.

IDENTIFICATION OF LOCAL INSTITUTIONAL FACTORS

The working group helped produce several studies of local institutional factors. The most thorough, based on United Presbyterian congregations and reported in chapter 9, found that the most important factors are overall satisfaction of laity with church worship and program, and congregational harmony and cooperation. Member dissatisfaction or conflict within the congregation are clearly sources of decline. Also, members' ratings of pastors, the presence of small groups in the congregation, and certain traditional forms of social involvement are slightly associated with growth. Theological conservatism is a slight asset for growth. Distinctness from the surrounding culture was tested but found to be more a liability than an asset for growth of Presbyterian congregations; this was in contrast to our findings about distinctness from culture as a denominational characteristic.

Chapter 10, based on United Church of Christ congregations, found that theological conservatism is strongly correlated with congregational growth and that the relative size of the church school, compared with the total church, is a correlate of growth. Measures of clergy aggressiveness and of the "fit" between clergy and congregation turned out to be weak factors for growth.

Peter Wagner, in chapter 12, set forth his conclusions about foremost institutional factors based on his case studies of growing churches. He stressed pastors who were motivated to grow and were willing to pay the price, laity who were actively involved in outreach as well as congregational activities, a large enough congregation to provide the functions desired by church members, cultural and social homogeneity within the church membership, and a high priority on evangelistic efforts among culturally similar people.

The Southern Baptist study (noted in chapter 7) of fastest-growing congregations concluded that the pastors are crucially important. The pastors of the fastest-growing congregations were "Bible-believing, evangelistic, strong leaders, and accessible and warmly human." Also, the growing congregations were theologically conservative, with minimal energies going toward social ministries and social issues.

These investigations vary in method and in conclusions. They disagree on the importance of the pastor and his or her leadership methods. Also they disagree on how much theological conservatism is associated with congregational growth.

ESTIMATED WEIGHTING OF FACTORS

The research reported in this book permits a more reliable estimate of the weights of the four sets of factors than was possible in the past. In chapter 9 the relative weights of local contextual and local institutional factors in the Presbyterian study were most reliably estimated: 56 percent of the explained variance was attributed to local contextual factors, and 44 percent was attributed to local institutional factors. No estimate of national contextual or institutional factors was possible; hence, they were ignored.

In the study of United Church of Christ congregations in chapter 10, the findings for the formerly Evangelical and Reformed congregations differed substantially from the findings for the formerly Congregational Christian congregations. This was due, in part, to the different regions and community settings in which the sample churches were located. In former Evangelical and Reformed congregations, local contextual factors were seen as explaining 52 percent of the explained variance, with 48 percent attributed to local institutional factors. In former Congregational Christian congregations, local contextual factors were seen as explaining 90 percent of the explained variance, with 10 percent attributed to local institutional factors. This sizable divergence can be traced partly to the strong explanatory power of family size in the community and to the number of children in church school in former Evangelical and Reformed churches but not in the others. McKinney saw these as institutional factors, but we doubt if they should be so categorized (in this respect we disagree with McKinney), and we believe that the variance seen as explained by "institutional factors" for former Evangelical and Reformed churches is too high. The 52 percent explained by contextual factors is correspondingly too low and should be more like 60 or 70 percent.

As noted in chapter 9, we found that the relative importance of local contextual versus local institutional factors varied from community setting to community setting. The institutional factors were most influential in suburbs and least so in small cities and rural areas. Also, they were more influential in nongrowing suburban areas than in growing suburban areas. Probably a variation of this sort is behind the differences in the relative importance of local contextual and local institutional factors in the United Church of Christ study. As a summary statement, in any event, we believe that in mainline Protestant congregations, local contextual factors are relatively more powerful than local institutional factors. The contextual factors explain about 50 to 70 percent, as an estimate, while the institutional factors explain about 30 to 50 percent.

The relative weights of national contextual and national institutional factors were studied only in chapter 8. That study concluded that the national contextual factors were more powerful than the national institutional factors, accounting for a bit more than half the explained variance in 1965-75. They were a bit weaker in 1955-65. The weights are not constant from decade to decade, making research more difficult. Due to paucity of data, we could not be precise about changes in weights over time.

What is the relative power of national as compared with local factors? This important question is unanswered by available research. No estimate can be made.

We should note that people hold different views about the relative importance of the four sets of factors. For example, Wagner stated in chapter 12 that local institutional factors are more important than local contextual factors, basing his view on his experience. Also, Kelley's influential theories of church growth and decline are based almost entirely on the scrutiny of institutional factors (both national and local), with the implication that contextual factors are much less important. It seems to us that action-oriented church analysts and consultants tend to estimate the weight of local institutional factors more highly than the best research would warrant.

EXPLANATION OF DENOMINATIONAL TRENDS SINCE THE EARLY 1960s

One of our basic aims has been to evaluate current purported explanations of denominational trends since the early 1960s. We have begun to zero in on the most plausible explanations and to eliminate others proven by available data to be impossible.

Since throughout American church history the "normal" pattern has been growth, we have tended to emphasize the dramatic declines in several denominations since the early 1960s as the phenomenon needing explanation. Hence, we have scrutinized these recent patterns of decline more carefully than the rather continuous growth patterns in certain denominations over the years.

Second, we maintain that short-term religious trends can be explained only by short-term factors.

Third, we believe that national factors, not local factors, explain the denominational trends. It is logically possible that local factors could explain denominational trends if those factors are specific to denominations or families of denominations, but we have not found any such argument to be convincing. The analysis of local neighborhoods or community types is crucial for understanding dynamics of individual congregations, but it is not very helpful in explaining decade-long denominational trends common to groups of denominations.

Our attention is therefore directed to national factors changing in a decade or two; they could be either contextual or institutional. We believe that the major explanation for recent trends is to be found in national contextual factors, for two reasons. First, our research has indicated that, in general, national contextual factors are more powerful than national institutional factors in explaining trends in major Protestant denominations. Second, the arguments made pointing to changes in denominations during the 1960s and stating that those changes account for the membership trend lines have not been convincing. The arguments about social action, although often made, are not powerful because research linking social action with membership trends has consistently been inconclusive and also because the smooth trend lines showed declines before the main social action occurred. The arguments about evangelism and new church development are a bit more convincing, but in the case of new church development the trends across the denominations are not different enough to provide a major explanation for denominational differences in trends (see Hadaway, 1978).

The main explanations for the recent denominational trends are to be found in the social context more than in the institutional churches. They are more cultural than demographic in nature, as shown by our research (especially chapter 5) indicating the weakness of demographic explanations (looking at numbers of persons in various age, education, and regional categories) in explaining trends. It seems that a broad cultural shift has occurred that has hit the churches from the outside, and it has hit the affluent, educated, individualistic, culture-affirming denominations hardest. The shift occurred much more among the youth than the older adults. It was most visible among the affluent young people, especially those on college campuses. It began in the early 1960s and achieved momentum during the middle and late 1960s. Many observers indicate that it has been strongest in the West, although we lack clear data on the question. The value shift was in the direction of greater individualism, personal freedom, tolerance of diversity, and distance from many traditional institutions. We agree with Wuthnow's (1978:143) conclusion:

> These losses [in the mainline churches] can be explained to a significant degree as the result of young people being thrust together by a variety of historical events into a countercultural generation unit whose values and life styles did not include,

and were often in active opposition to, participation in organized religion. The new religions formed a part of the counterculture, of course. But the losses experienced by the churches cannot be attributed solely to the gains of the new religions. They must be traced to the counterculture in its broadest sense and ultimately to the strains giving rise to the counterculture.

This conclusion that outside pressures are the most important explanation for declines in many denominations is consistent with our research finding that denominational membership trends are more the result of failure of recruitment of new members than of the dropping out of existing members. It is also consistent with the widespread feeling of bewilderment among church leaders in declining denominations as to what is happening. The dismay is understandable when we realize that external forces not visible from the midst of church life and not even very visible to the naked eye apart from sociological trend research are responsible for the declines.

We have stated that the value shifts have been strongest among educated, cosmopolitan, middle-class youth, and that consequently, the denominations composed mostly of such persons have been hardest hit by a loss of youth. Indeed, the membership losses have been greatest in those denominations (1) filled with cosmopolitan, middle-class persons and (2) maintaining minimal distance, if any, from the life-style and morality of mainstream American culture (see chapter 8).

This point has a noteworthy implication. Research indicates that value changes in America have been greatest among youth, but they have been diffusing from college youth to non-college youth and also from youth to larger sectors of adults (see Yankelovich, 1974 and chapter 4 of this book). Investigation suggests that changes in college students' values anticipate the direction of changes in many other adults' values within a few years. It would follow that the experiences of cosmopolitan, middle-class denominations would occur also in other Protestant denominations within a few years—notably, a loss of youth commitment. Indeed, in 1978 there were indications that this is happening. The most important sign is that some Protestant denominations of moderate and conservative theology have experienced membership decline in the last few years. Kelley (1977:vii) reports in the preface to the second edition of his book that in 1973 three conservative denominations—the Presbyterian Church in the U.S., the Lutheran Church-Missouri Synod, and the Christian Reformed Church—peaked in membership and began to decline. In 1978 the Southern Baptist Convention showed signs that its growth is coming to an end.

In short, the data shows a historical sequence of impacts on denominations from the changing values of young adults, first impacting the middle-class, cosmopolitan, theologically liberal denominations; next the less cosmopolitan, theologically moderate denominations; but not at all those denominations keeping a definite distance from the prevailing American culture, such as the Seventh-Day Adventists and the Latter-Day Saints. Probably a diffusion of values is taking place in American society that affects these denominations in more or less predictable sequence. Hargrove (1976) described just this historical sequence in her analysis of changes in campus ministries of different denominations; what happened first to the theologically liberal groups next happened to the Catholics and to the theologically conservative groups but not yet to the Latter-Day Saints.

CULTURAL POLARIZATION

To point out the shift in values among youth toward greater individualism, personal freedom, and tolerance of diversity does not explain some of the patterns in church trends. If such a shift has occurred, why don't the Protestant denominations most characterized by individuality, freedom of belief, and tolerance of new life-styles gain adherents? If there is a liberal shift, why don't the liberal churches benefit? The evidence is that they do not. Also, it must be asked, If there is a shift in values away from traditional religion, why is there evidence at present of increased fervor in conservative Christian religious groups, especially those involving youth?

The current situation can, we believe, best be understood if we look at the broader outlines of American culture today. Hoge (1976b) has argued that American culture is grounded in two main worldviews, the traditional Christian and the secular humanistic. The first is institutionally based in the traditional churches; the second is based in the American scientific and intellectual establishment, especially higher education. The meaning systems of most individuals or institutions are based in either an evangelical Christian worldview or a scientific humanistic worldview. The credo of almost any individual and institution, if examined and pressed back to its foundation, will be seen to rest on one or the other or some combination of the two. Some institutions such as church-related universities assert the unity of the two as their basic identity, but in fact, they find it difficult to embody in present-day American culture. More often the two are felt as existing in tension, and among college students especially, an observer can collect examples of conversion from one to the other, in both directions.

This shorthand depiction of American culture is an oversimplification, but it is consistent with other analysts' views (for example, Bellah, 1976) and contains some important implications. It is important that the main changes in American culture since the Cold War years have been a rising dominance of the secular humanistic culture and its attendant values of individualism and rationalism. In Bellah's words, "utilitarian individualism" has become the dominant ethos. Even though dominant, it is not a sustaining culture for individual persons. As Hoge (1976b:122-23) notes:

> The secular culture says little about personal meaning of individuals, especially individuals not intimately involved in the scientific, technological, or political systems. It also lacks meaning for those instances in which technological, organizational, or political efforts fail and their adherents despair. Secondly, the secular culture assumes justification by works. . . . Thirdly, the secular culture says little about authentic human community, with its own movement of the spirit and its own sacramental life.

Ever since the late nineteenth century, as this culture was gaining power in America, mainline Protestantism has been a major bridge and synthesis between it and traditional Christianity. In certain periods the bridge has been vital and strong. The 1950s was such a period, but in the 1960s the bridge was greatly weakened. Hoge speaks of the "collapse of the middle," borrowing a phrase from James I. McCord. The reason for the collapse of the mainline synthesis is not clear. Bellah suggests that the events of the 1960s brought strains it could not bear. The intense alienation felt by youth in the 1960s arose because of "the inability of utilitarian individualism to provide a meaningful pattern of personal and social existence, especially when its alliance with biblical religion began to sag because biblical religion had been gutted in the process [1976b:339]."

In a decade of increased dominance of the secular individualistic culture in educated circles, one should not be surprised by widespread experimentation with new religious movements based in the secular culture but answering inner needs of individuals.

Indeed, the 1960s saw a flurry of quasi-religious spiritual efforts, including the human potential movement, the sensitivity-encounter groups, *est*, Transcendental Meditation, Scientology, and some Eastern movements transformed to be consistent with the prevailing culture. These were seen as philosophically and ethically consistent with the secular worldview and with science. They were individualistic, and they demanded only low levels of personal commitment. Their recruits came from young educated adults immersed in the secular ethos but experiencing personal malaise.

Recent research on new religious movements in America since the early 1960s is instructive at this point. In a review of the research, Robbins, Anthony, and Richardson (1978) categorized the new religious movements as (1) mystical-therapeutic and (2) neofundamentalist. The first type, as described above, synthesized scientific and religious themes in a quest for personal meaning in the midst of the secular worldview. The second represented a protest against this worldview, especially its relativism and "permissiveness." Adherents of the second made strident reaffirmations of theocentric ethical dualism and traditional morality, especially visible in the Jesus movement and neopentecostal groups. Several observers of the second type have described a "returning fundamentalist" syndrome, in which a person from a conservative Christian background went through a period of countercultural rebellion against parental values, later became disenchanted with the counterculture, and then became involved in an unconventional Christian sect that synthesized countercultural and conservative Christian elements (Robbins et al., 1978:102). Prototypically, they came to the Jesus movement after tragic experiments with drugs, sex, and hippyism. Of the two kinds of movements, the first is numerically larger and represents the "normal" development of spiritual experimentation in the new cultural setting. The second is a reaction to it and a quest for authority in traditional Christianity. Although the Jesus people, the Moonies, and others have received much publicity, they represent a minority of youth today, not the dominant type.

The new spiritual energies have polarized and have not turned in the direction of the mainline Protestant bridge. Somehow the Protestant synthesis is not experienced as being personally orienting or sustaining, and greater identity and authority are experienced at one or the other basis of authority. The wellsprings of Christian church commitment do not seem to exist in or near the secular humanistic ethos, where intense individualism, relativism, and transient commitments seem to channel spiritual energies in other directions. Church commitment is found mainly in a gradually shrinking sector of the culture anchored at the traditional evangelical pole.

The exact interpretation of recent religious trends is open to debate, and we cannot be certain that our interpretation is correct. More research and even the mere passage of time will help future researchers sort out the correct from the misdirected interpretations and will clarify both the spiritual outlines of our time and its lessons for understanding human religiousness.

CHAPTER 15

Commentary:
Is Religion a Dependent Variable?

Dean M. Kelley

This volume is an earnest effort to grapple with one of the most intriguing sociological conundrums of the century: Why the so-called mainline denominations of the United States, which had been growing in membership rather steadily for more than a century, suddenly began to *lose* members in the 1960s, while some nonmainline denominations continued to grow. I appreciate the opportunity to share in this stimulating study and to have, in a way, a Last Word.

The authors have generally been very conscientious in focusing attention on time-specific factors—those that would have effect within the time span under study. They have also sought explanations which would embrace all the denominations that began to lose members; single-denomination factors were rightly considered insufficient to explain why the same thing was happening in other denominations at about the same time. What they did not always do was to account for the continued growth of still other denominations: why did decline hit only certain denominations and not all?

The last factor is the most intriguing and often the most neglected, partly because the denominations that have continued to grow are not well known to our researchers and are not viewed by them with the same degree of understanding, identification, empathy that they feel for the denominations they know better.

Such religious groups are, to some degree, not just *terra incognita* to the well-trained, perceptive researchers of this company, but *terra aliena*. They just don't "dig" the Assemblies of God, the Jehovah's Witnesses, the Seventh-Day Adventists, the Mormons, the neocharismatics, and all those "lesser breeds without the law." I'm not sure I do either, but I am proposing that "mainline" readers entertain the notion that such groups may be doing something right.

Our authors, for better or worse, eschew the effort to obtain data on the most intense forms of religious behavior—"new religious movements, sects and cults"—and confine themselves to the culture-affirming mainline churches. This is probably a necessary self-limitation, since data on the former is scarce and doubtless difficult to obtain, but it should not be lost sight of that *a whole wing of the spectrum of religious behavior in this country*—by far the most interesting and informative—*has been left out*, or nearly so. Only in the attenuated form visible in some of the more stable evangelical or pentecostal denominations is it even referred to, and these are groups already nearing the middle of the spectrum! Those left out are not so much culture-rejecting as they are culture-indifferent, being so preoccupied with religious concerns as to have little interest in anything else.

This book, probably necessarily, occupies itself with the commoner, more generally recognizable forms of religious behavior in American society and does a very adept job of interpreting them. The forms omitted, although intense, are relatively infrequent; that is, few people, proportionately, are caught up in them, and so they remain somewhat exotic, alien patterns to most people. (Some of the "strange" traits of the Jesus people, the Children of God, the Unification Church of Sun Myung Moon, or Hare Krishna, which have seemed so alarming to some, might have been less so if recognized as, in many respects, similar to earlier religious movements at a corresponding stage in their development.)

But because of their relative infrequency, we seldom encounter these intense forms of religious life and therefore tend to assume that the relatively attenuated forms that involve 1,000 or 10,000 times more people are normative, that the mainline church on the corner is an example of what religion *is*, and therefore, we can confine our study of religion to it and its (very similar) counterparts down the street and across the country. For many purposes, that may be a justifiable conclusion, but only if we remember continuously that the most significant—or most virulent—forms, from which we might learn even more, have been omitted. Much of what this chapter can offer as a commentary and corrective to the book is predicated upon the contrasts between what is here and what *isn't*.

This book is organized around the sorting of causal factors for trends in (mainline) church membership and participation into four categories: national contextual, national institutional, local contextual, and local institutional. One can find little fault with that principle of organization, but a great deal with the causal priority accorded to each. It is the assumption of the authors—to which a great amount of discussion has been devoted—that the *contextual* factors are prior to the *institutional* ones.

> Insofar as the four sets of factors are intercorrelated, and hence have overlapping explanatory power, we would see the contextual factors as causally prior and assign the overlapping explanatory power to them, not to the institutional factors [chapter 4; see also chapter 8, chapter 10, chapter 14].

That is a theoretical assumption, in the sense that statistical analysis could just as well have operated in the opposite direction, and is based on the authors' understanding of the causal priority of the two kinds of variables. Peter Wagner disagrees with that assessment (chapter 12), and so do I. Wagner would see local institutional factors as crucial for achieving church growth, since it must occur in *local* churches or it will not occur. I would see *national* institutional factors as potentially prior to contextual factors for explaining why some *denominations* are growing and others are not.

The actual national contextual factors that were found to have some statistical relationship to growth in church membership and participation were not the expected demographic ones. Age distribution, birthrate, income, mobility, education, regionalization, and so forth showed weak or irregular correlations at best (see summary of chapter 5). Instead, the stronger factors were qualities characterized as cultural rather than demographic: value patterns underlying changes in the birthrate and the shift of *attitudes* in favor of individualism, personal freedom, tolerance of diversity and away from institutional commitments. These rather generalized traits are said to show a correlation with trends in church participation, at least in mainline denominations, and are characterized as the cultural climate in which the churches must operate.

The cultural climate may indeed be a dominating causal factor in the growth or decline of mainline churches, which are apparently very susceptible to transient shifts in public opinion about what's "in" and what's "out" this decade, year, or month. But other churches are not as clearly affected by the cultural climate. Not knowing perhaps or more likely not caring what that climate is supposed to be, they go on attracting and retaining members, even young adults, in spite of the supposedly adverse cultural climate.

In fact, rather than being victims of changes in cultural climate, religious movements or emphases have often determined or modified the cultural climate themselves. Among many people, it is religion that shapes the value-system which determines whether they have more or fewer or any children, not the other way around. It is religion that shapes their outlook on individualism, freedom, diversity, and institutions, not the other way around. For such persons, causality works in the direction *opposite* to that assumed by our authors.

In discussing whether or not their assumption of the direction of causality in multivariate analysis was justified, some of the authors asked one another what a congregation or denomination could do to "break out of the box" of contextual factors. Only a surge of evangelism or new church development seemed to offer a solution, and these were seen to be both unlikely and as susceptible to the environing contextual factors as the churches are (said to be) in their present condition. But the ability of churches to "break out of the box" of cultural captivity is not the question with which this study started. That question was how to account for the startling change in trends in church membership and participation in the mid-1960s, and (I would emphasize) why it hit certain churches and not others. The question was how they got "*into* the box."

It is quite possible that there are institutional factors that could account for more of the answer than contextual factors, but whether churches can *change* those institutional factors at will does not make them less institutional. Suppose that a church with a premillennial theology finds itself losing members and is advised that it will grow if it changes its theology. That may be true, but the church may feel that to change its theology would transform it into another church, so it refuses to change, even at the price of decline. So the test of an institutional factor is not whether the church can change it, but whether it is part of the institution rather than of its environment.

Chapters 8 and 14 indicated that if churches are arrayed in a continuum from conservative-disciplined-distinctive from culture at one end to liberal-pluralistic-culture-affirming at the other, those

near the former end have grown, while those near the latter end
have declined (chapter 14:323). The former group were characterized by "strongly emphasized local evangelism, maintained a
distinctive life-style and morality apart from mainstream culture,
. . . a unitary set of beliefs, and de-emphasized social action and
ecumenism [ibid.]." Whether a denomination at the other end of
the continuum could acquire these characteristics and consequently begin to grow is not the question; it is sufficient for the
purposes this study set for itself to note that these institutional
factors seem to make a significant difference. Is it a greater
difference than contextual factors? That depends on which the
researcher takes first.

The three contextual factors the researchers found strongly
related to denominational growth (chapter 8) were (1) family
income, (2) percent living in the West, and (3) number of children
in family. These together are said to "explain over half the total
variance in denominational growth rates in 1965-75 and a bit less
in 1955-65 [8:190]"—*if they are taken first.* If the institutional
factors—(1) theological conservatism, (2) emphasis on evangelism,
(3) distinctive life-style and morality, and (4) unitary set of
beliefs—are taken first, they explain virtually *all* the total variance,
and little is left for contextual factors to explain!

Is the assumption that contextual factors are causally prior a
valid one? In the sense that all churches must operate within the
context of an external environment, yes. But they respond
differentially to that environment. Some grow in it and some
decline, depending upon their institutional stance. It may well be,
then, that contextual factors *are* determining over institutional
factors for the mainline churches: that's one way to state the reason
they are declining. In those churches, *religion has become a
dependent variable.* When set in a propitiously affluent neighborhood, with the right age, sex, and race mix (or nonmix), it will
prosper, but change one or two of the environmental factors a little
and it will wane and wither.

Does that mean they can and should change the institutional
factors that seem to correlate with decline? Perhaps they should,
but that doesn't mean they can or will. Elsewhere I have explained
that I don't think they can or will change in the ways that would
make them vigorously growing denominations (Kelley, 1972,
1977). (If they had the vigor to change, they'd have the vigor to
grow.) And the crowning irony is that those denominations that
most closely resonate to the supposed newly dominant cultural

values—individuality, freedom of belief and action, and tolerance of differing life-styles—are not attracting the very young people supposedly embodying those new values; to the contrary. They are diminishing, while the denominations, as Hoge and Roozen note, that do not resonate to or sympathize with the trendy new "values" continue to grow! [See chapter 14:330.]

Is it because the latter types of churches are appealing with increasing success to a dwindling "market," while the former are appealing with diminishing success to a growing "market" (chapter 1:38)? This suggestion, first put forth by George R. LaNoue, is cited in Why Conservative Churches Are Growing (1977:93), where I found it not entirely persuasive. In this query, much turns on the meaning of market. In the population at large, are there two latent subpopulations, one susceptible to religious appeals that are supposedly consonant with mod cultural values (whatever they may be; in this instance, individuality, freedom of belief and action, tolerance of differing life-styles) and another susceptible to appeals that are—in essence—antimod? Is there a third subpopulation in between, the indifferents, who are not at the time susceptible to either kind of religious appeal? Or is there some kind of continuum present, ranging from those hyperresponsive to change through the indifferents to those resistant to change? Or are there other dimensions present, such as religious needs, viewed independently of receptivity to cultural change?

It may be that it is the meeting of people's religious needs that makes the market, and when people experience such needs, they go to the religious groups that seem likely to meet them best or keep hunting until they find such groups. That might account for the observation that mod churches do not seem to attract (even) mod people; they may not be effective at meeting anyone's religious needs.

Hoge and Roozen have suspected something similar in their reflections on Robbins' theory that the new and growing religious movements take one of two directions—either reaffirming traditional Christian theology and ethics or resonating to the scientific, secular, humanistic themes in modern culture—but they do not follow the liberal, semi-individualistic path of mainline Protestantism. Hoge and Roozen note that Protestantism has historically been a bridge between these two, but it does not seem to be functioning in that capacity today, at least not for the young seekers who are turning to the two more dynamic alternatives. Hoge and Roozen conjecture, "Somehow the Protestant synthesis is not experienced as being personally orienting or sustaining, and greater identity and authority are experienced at one or the other basis of authority [chapter 14-332]."

This excursus by Hoge and Roozen and by Robbins into theology and the history of ideas is remarkable for three sociologists, who may have overlooked something closer to their own expertise. It may not be the theological content of the reaffirming sects or the scientific cults—or even of the Protestant synthesis—that makes the difference. Rather, it may be the way they go about gathering in religiously perplexed persons, nurturing them, fitting them into a supportive regime, inculcating authoritative answers to their perplexities (whether those answers be scientific or traditional is of secondary importance). In that sense, Hare Krishna, the Unification Church, Scientology, and various evangelical movements may all be *religiously effective* in a way that mainline Protestantism is not. Thus, Hoge's and Roozen's conjecture might be revised to read: "Somehow the Protestant synthesis is not seen as being *serious,* while the other two alternatives are."

In my book (Kelley, 1972; 1977) I tried to make clear what I think "seriousness" means in religion, and I am disappointed to discover that so little of it has registered in an otherwise very perceptive volume. (I had hoped to complete this chapter without harking back to my own work, but it offers a still-needed corrective to much thinking in contemporary religion, and research into religion.) In chapter 1, Roozen and Carroll state: "Since the publication of Dean Kelley's *Why Conservative Churches Are Growing* . . . , it has been common to distinguish growing denominations from dwindling denominations in terms of their *theological orientation* [1:24, emphasis added]." Such a characterization would be appropriate if derived solely from the title. But Roozen and Carroll have correctly stated a misconception committed by Common Parlance, with the assistance of Harper & Row, the publisher, who insisted on that title rather than one I thought more accurate, "Why Strict Churches Are Strong" (whether theologically conservative or not, whether growing at a particular time or not).

A fairly accurate summary of my thesis is presented by Hoge at the beginning of chapter 8 and does not need repeating here. Suffice it to say that it does not give much attention to the *theology* of the churches whose growth rates were being compared, and what attention it did give was not to the *content* of those beliefs but to the way they were held, the role they played in the religious organization. The main factors in my comparison of the denominations were those showing organizational strictness, which were seen as an evidence of seriousness and thus of social strength, irrespective of content.

A person with religious needs, I contended, would tend to be attracted to a religious group that seemed to take itself seriously by insisting that it knew what it was doing and that its members practice what they preach. That is hardly an unreasonable supposition and does not require sophisticated ventures into comparisons of trends in theology or plausibility, which are regions of interest only to the relatively few adherents (or nonadherents) of religion who concern themselves with intellectual distinctions. For most of humankind, I insist, what matters in religion is not so much its doctrines and tenets as how it gathers the lambs unto its bosom and protects and supports and strengthens them and thus keeps them there.

My concern for strictness/seriousness/strength was reflected in some aspects of the comparisons made of United Presbyterian and United Church of Christ congregations (chapters 9 and 10). Those studies compared growing with static or declining local churches on various variables, among which were conservative theology (chapter 9:203), rigorousness of membership standards, and measures of intensity of involvement (chapter 10:238). They found that "the factors stressed by Kelley were not very important" (UCC) or that "all the tests of the Kelley hypotheses . . . came out very weak . . . for Presbyterian congregations [chapter 8:182]." Of course they are "weak" or "not very important" for Presbyterian and United Church congregations (even growing ones). That is part of the condition that, in my view, has caused the deterioration of membership and participation in those denominations.

When studies of nonmainline churches—the ones that are growing—are added, a different result is found. Chapter 8 includes correlations between membership trends in sixteen denominations and certain ratings of those denominations on eight criteria by twenty-one experts. (Their ratings of those denominations on ecumenism matched mine with a Spearman rank-order correlation of $+.96$ out of a possible 1.00!) Hoge summarizes these findings:

> We conclude that the denominational characteristics attributed by Kelley to growing denominations are strongly upheld by independent ratings of experts. The factors Kelley stressed most—emphasis on evangelism, emphasis on distinctive life-style and morality, and disallowing individualism in belief—came out of the strongest [chapter 8:192].

This observation is quoted, not as a vindication (since it relies not solely on direct empirical data but includes ratings by experts who may not have had direct experience of all traits of all denominations rated), but as a clue to the excluded range of data that might be found in the nonecumenical, nonmainline churches "farther out" than the somewhat "domesticated" ones included in the ratings (Assemblies of God, Mormons, Nazarenes, Seventh-Day Adventists, Southern Baptist Convention). A very different picture might be presented by such a study of the groups in which religious behavior is most intense, most pure, most virulent. Instead, to a large extent, this volume approaches the study of the epidemiology of religion by rather tenuous extrapolations from intense analysis of the condition of a large number of "patients" who have long since "recovered" from it! (Or at least it is dormant in them; they are not even very good "carriers.")

How much more we might learn from a study of the "active" cases! Unfortunately, they are difficult, if not impossible, to study. They don't keep statistics, and if they do, they won't share them with anyone outside their own group. They don't answer questionnaires or consent to interviews (unless for the purpose of converting the interviewer). They often do not belong to a national hierarchy or connectional system, so they are very difficult to locate, to categorize, to analyze. By the time they have settled down sufficiently to be studied, they are already becoming part-time or partially inactive disciples.

An example may be the Southern Baptist Convention, which reports that 27 to 28 percent of its members since 1950 have been nonresident (chapter 7:164), meaning not attending the local church in which they hold membership because of residence elsewhere, and have not yet transferred to a church near their new home. When I was a parish pastor (Methodist), we called such members inactives and tried to get them to become active in a church near where they lived. In 1952 the Methodist Church discontinued use of the inactive category, contending that members who were not active should not be carried on the rolls (although some of them still were). But a 27- to 28-percent level of inactive members is incredible! That means that when the Southern Baptist Convention passed the Methodist Church in size in 1966, its claimed membership of 10,949,493 was actually under 8,000,000—if it counted members the way the Methodist and most other churches do. And it may not have caught up with the United Methodist Church yet—in active members! Is the not-quite-so-rapidly-growing Southern Baptist Convention slowing down? Are its nonresident members more active than active United Methodists? A little research here would be instructive.

It is probably too much to imagine, let alone expect, that the mainline churches are going to become centers of full-time religious activity. (One might contend that the study of real religious behavior should begin with those laypersons who put in more than fifty hours per week in religious activity, or clergy more than 100; below that they are not even *visible* as religious activity and can only be considered religious *inactivity*.) But one could at least hope and expect that they would be serious about what they do undertake in the name of religion.

Unfortunately, most people have the notion that a religious organization can be serious only if it is authoritarian, and that the only content it can be serious about is fundamentalism. That may indeed be the case, but it is hard to see why it need be. There is no reason the members of a nonfundamentalist congregation could not sit down and ask themselves (as the Anabaptists did) what, if anything, they are prepared to be serious about, and then *do* it. (If they are anxious to avoid authoritarianism, they can make the preacher stay outside while they decide.) They could center on just a few things for a start, but those few would be *binding* on *all members*. Perhaps choosing one or two of the ten commandments would be a bit severe as a beginning, so they might decide to join together in Bible study one evening a week; not every night, as some monastic communities or Jehovah's Witnesses do; maybe a trial period of three months would be as strenuous as could be expected for beginners. This *reductio ad absurdum* may suggest how far most mainline churches are from serious discipleship.

If the mainline churches could muster sufficient seriousness about what they profess to believe, they might cease to be blown from pillar to post by every breeze of cultural climate, every shift in demography or other "contextual" factors. They might even begin to affect some of the circumstances around them, to influence the cultural climate themselves, as their forebears did. They might, in fact, cease to be a dependent and become an independent variable.

CHAPTER 16

Commentary:
What Are the Alternatives?

Lyle E. Schaller

What alternatives are open to the pastor or the lay leader who advocates church growth but is discouraged by some of the research findings presented in this volume? This book provides a wealth of material to feed the discussions on alternative courses of action.

If the leaders are members of a long established, white, middle-class congregation, meeting in a building located in a changing neighborhood in the central city or in an older suburban community, someone may declare, "I told you there is no chance for us to grow unless we relocate! The United Presbyterian study proved that very clearly. We either relocate to where our kind of people live or we stay here and see this church die."

Another alternative is to shift the debate to a search for a scapegoat. "There's no chance for our church unless we get a dynamic pastor who can attract new members. The research on church growth shows the pastor is the key!" A defender of the minister may reply, "But that's not true! The research shows it is the local context, not the pastor, that is the key variable in whether a congregation grows or doesn't grow!"

Someone else may add, "I've always said that the Sunday church school is the feeder for the church, and that's been proved now by what Warren Hartman has discovered. I think we need to find the money to hire a full-time professional director of Christian education to rebuild our Sunday school. If we don't, we might as well get ready to watch our church die." The person opposing this can point out, "But another United Methodist study showed the

344

churches with a full-time, professional director of Christian education were more likely to have a declining Sunday church school than similar churches with a Sunday school run by lay volunteers!"

From a denominational perspective, the debate may be over whether or not the regional and national agencies of the denominations have any significant control over those very important local contextual factors. Or it may shift to a choosing up of sides over whether God is calling the churches to be faithful and obedient—and therefore probably to decline—or to grow. Some of the chapters in this volume suggest that is the basic issue, while others suggest the issue cannot be defined in that either-or frame of reference.

INSTITUTIONAL EXCLUSIVISM

Another alternative, which may be more productive, would be to shift the focus of the debate. Instead of using the research data to reinforce previously held opinions or to identify a scapegoat or to provide excuses for the lack of growth, it may be more creative to focus first on the characteristics of the congregation and to use sociological research findings to understand the dynamics of congregational life. Many of these institutional factors produce strong anti-church growth tendencies within the worshiping congregation and cause it to become an exclusionary group.

Perhaps the best beginning point for this approach is to recognize that a normal institutional characteristic of the typical congregation is that, like other organizations, it tends to be benign toward insiders (members) and hostile toward outsiders (nonmembers). Institutions and organizations do not naturally find numerical growth to be automatic or comfortable or satisfying. The normal stance of any organization is to perpetuate the status quo. A numerical increase in size is disruptive. Rapid numerical growth tends to be very disruptive. This becomes a major point of tension between the imperative of the Great Commission and the normal institutional pressures on congregational values and behavior.

Frequently, the institutional pressures to perpetuate the status quo prevail over the biblical imperative to evangelize. This pattern can be seen in thousands of small congregations that have included approximately the same number of active members for several decades. These congregations can receive and assimilate replacement members because that is a means of perpetuating the status quo. They have not been able to grow because numerical growth would be disruptive. A parallel pattern can be seen in the strongly evangelistic congregation which grows at a rapid pace for several years until it has reached a size that a major expansion of the meeting place is required. Frequently, but not always, that produces a change in congregational priorities from church growth to institutional maintenance. Leaders are chosen, not on the basis of evangelistic gifts, but because of their skills in finance, real estate, and construction. These new leaders revise the action priorities of that congregation. Once that change in the agenda has been made, the natural institutional pressures cause that congregation's growth curve to turn into a plateau. After that has happened, it becomes very difficult to change back to an agenda dominated by church growth priorities.

A second institutional fact that must be recognized in evaluating the potential for growth of any church is that every congregation, by its actions and programs, causes some people to feel excluded. The congregation that conducts all its worship services, classes, and meetings in English will cause Korean or Spanish-speaking people to feel left out. The congregation that builds its program to meet the needs of husband-wife couples with children under 18 at home and that places the decision-making power in the hands of adults from these families will cause many people in the other two thirds of the adult population to feel they are neither wanted nor needed. The congregation that, in the 1960s, emphasized the value system of the traditional culture caused members of the counterculture of the 1960s to feel unwelcome.

If the leaders of a church are insensitive to the fact that their congregational life-style causes some people to feel excluded, it will be extremely difficult for that congregation to identify the people it is trying to reach. A large part of the medical research for a cure for cancer is devoted to discovering the causes of cancer. Likewise, the congregation that wants to grow must discover what it is doing or not doing that keeps people away. Identifying the people a congregation excludes is a useful step in sharpening the focus of that church's evangelistic outreach. To cite an example of this, the congregation that seeks to reach and minister to deaf persons must first recognize that its heavy reliance on the spoken word is an exclusionary procedure. After this has been acknowledged, it is relatively easy for the members to understand the need to have someone available at every worship service, meeting, social event, study group, and class to translate the spoken word into sign language.

The congregation that claims it is trying to reach everyone in its efforts to grow is engaged in a venture guaranteed to produce frustration, disappointment, and unfulfilled goals.

In theological or doctrinal terms, this issue can be described as the difference between the universal Church—the capital C Church—and the individual congregation—the lower case c church—which is one of the millions of institutional expressions of the universal Church. The universal Church has a clear-cut biblical imperative to reach every living person with the good news that Jesus Christ is Lord and Savior. Each individual congregation has a piece of that total responsibility, but I cannot believe God is expecting any one congregation to do it all. There are, however, congregational leaders and ministers who apparently are convinced that if their congregation does not do it all, it will not get done!

A third institutional factor that influences the capability of a congregation to grow numerically can be described simply as "the cutback syndrome." This is a natural institutional tendency to reduce the size and complexity of a church's total ministry and program to a size that can be comprehended and managed more easily.

The cutback syndrome takes many forms. It is reflected in the decision to merge the youth choir into the adult choir, or to combine two Sunday school classes of older adults, or to shift from two worship experiences on Sunday morning to one service, or to reduce the size of the program staff, or to merge two circles within the women's organization, or to eliminate the traditional Wednesday evening Thanksgiving service in order to support the interdenominational service on Thursday morning, or to combine the junior high and senior high youth into one group, or to scrap the Sunday evening service because of low attendance.

There are natural institutional pressures operating in every congregation to cut back on the size, variety, complexity, and scope of the total program in order to reduce it to a point that the members can more easily keep track in their heads of everything that is happening. This is a widespread anti-church growth tendency that can be found in nearly every congregation.

A fourth factor which encourages an institutional exclusivism in churches is that the vast majority of Protestant congregations on this continent already have more members than they are able to accept, love, and care for. (See the section on church dropouts in chapter 2.) These congregations have not been able to assimilate and accommodate all their members. They resemble a glass of water filled to the brim. It is possible to pour more water into the glass, but that will result in some overflowing. Some will be new water and some will be old water. Unless a congregation increases its institutional capability to accommodate and care for more people, it may be able to receive a large number of new members, but it will not show much net growth.

Expanding the congregational capability to accommodate a larger number of people usually means enlarging the number and variety of face-to-face small groups, creating new groups to accommodate new members, changing the nominating procedures to make it easier for new members to become policy-makers, increasing the number of offices and committees, possibly enlarging the program staff, adding new ministries and programs, increasing the number of available worship experiences each week, and providing new opportunities for the personal and spiritual growth of people. That is a long list, and many congregations would like to grow without paying that institutional price for change.

A fifth, and one of the more subtle institutional factors that tend to limit a congregation's capacity for growth, is the nature of the self-image and the basic criterion for defining size. The typical, almost universal, pattern for defining the size and nature of a congregation is to identify the number of members: that is a 160-member church, or that is a 500-member congregation, or that is a 700-member parish. This automatically causes growth to be defined in terms of an increase in the number of members. It then follows that a strategy for church growth will be developed primarily around a set of goals to increase the numerical size of that congregation.

A more realistic, creative, and productive way of defining the institutional nature of the growing church is to see it as a congregation of congregations or groups, organizations, classes, circles, cliques, fellowships, and task forces. Some of these subcongregations appeal to certain individuals, while others appeal to a different group of people. In many growing congregations the numerical increase in size has resulted from (1) an increase in membership of these existing subcongregations and (2) an increase in the number and variety of subcongregations.

One example of this concept that has some provocative implications for potential church growth is offered by Warren Hartman (see chapter 2). Hartman has defined four different audiences of church members—the fellowship audience, the evangelistic concerns audience, the study audience, and the social concerns audience. A fifth audience consists of the members who are interested in two or three of these concerns. This type of conceptual framework is far more helpful in defining a congregation's potential for growth than simply referring to this church as a congregation of 345 members, which hopes to double in a decade.

While this is not offered as an exhaustive list, the five factors identified here do illustrate how research on the nature of institutions can be useful in explaining why some congregations have difficulty in growing. A fail-safe assumption in looking at these and other similar factors is that religious institutions tend to behave more like secular institutions than one might expect, on the basis of their proclaimed religious values and goals.

One alternative open to persons interested in promoting church growth is to identify the institutional factors and pressures that tend to restrain congregational growth. The five identified here can be used as a beginning point in building that list.

ASSUMPTIONS BEHIND A DENOMINATIONAL STRATEGY FOR CHURCH GROWTH

Another alternative for the person interested in church growth is to use the insights and knowledge accumulated by research in the behavioral sciences in developing a denominational strategy for church growth. Much of the research reported on in this volume lends itself to this approach, since it comes from denominational studies.

The five-point approach to a denominational strategy outlined here is based on several assumptions that require identification before going on to suggest an action strategy.

The first, and by far the most important, is a theological question. James H. Smylie raises this in his historical essay (chapter 3). Has God decided that Christians will be a minority in the world of today and tomorrow? Is it God's divine will that the membership of the mainline denominations in America should continue to decline? Or has God given the leaders of the churches in the last quarter century the freedom to create trends in church membership? Are the churches reactors to what God already has decided? Or has God given the leaders the freedom to influence the future?

In this essay it is assumed that God has given church leaders a large degree of freedom, which will enable them to influence the shape of the future.

The second assumption is that the order of priorities on a denominational agenda influences what will happen within that denominational family in the years ahead and that the denominational leaders do have considerable freedom in determining those priorities.

The third assumption separates my definition of reality from the thinking represented by a number of the other contributors to this volume. A dominant theme of many observers of the religious scene has been to suggest that a reason for the lack of continued growth in several mainline denominations has been the increasing preoccupation of the leaders, and especially the clergy, with social action and a variety of issue-centered ministries. A variation of this basic theme is offered by Robert A. Evans, when he suggests the choice may be between faithfulness and growth (see chapter 13). My perception of contemporary reality indicates the basic division is not a social action versus evangelism division, but rather a choice between placing the highest priority on evangelism and church growth or placing institutional maintenance concerns at the top of the priority list. One reason for suggesting this is that both the United Church of Christ (chapter 10) and the United Presbyterian (chapter 9) studies suggest that the evangelical church members and the growing churches place as much or more emphasis on social welfare efforts and on ministries to people beyond the membership as do the liberal church members and the stable or declining congregations. Another reason is that in the declining denominational families, I frequently see a high priority being assigned to institutional maintenance, while in the growing denominations the highest priorities often are given to items related to evangelism and church growth. The Baptist General Conference, for example, has set a denominational goal to "double in a decade," with a major emphasis on starting new congregations. Between 1968 and 1983 most of the annual conferences in the United Methodist Church are placing a high priority on funding pensions for pastors and will raise between $150 million and $200 million in special, second-mile designated giving for that purpose. In the State of Illinois the Southern Baptists started approximately forty new racial, nationality, language, and ethnic congregations in 1978 (plus nearly sixty new missions to Anglos). The United Presbyterian Church, the Presbyterian Church in the U.S., and the United Church of Christ have been giving considerable attention to the surplus of clergy and to the increasingly limited mobility of pastors because of the shortages of vacant pulpits in congregations with at least 300 members and able to offer an adequate salary for the pastor. In 1978 the combined efforts of these three denominations did not produce as many new congregations in the entire nation as the Southern Baptists started in northern Illinois. In other words, the third assumption behind this suggested outline for a denominational approach to church growth is that an effective strategy requires a change in the agenda, but it may be a change from institutional maintenance concerns to church growth rather than placing a low priority on social action in order to encourage numerical growth.

The fourth assumption is a simple and obvious one but must be stated, lest it be overlooked. A denominational strategy will not be the same as a congregational strategy for church growth, because the nature of the denomination and its responsibilities, resources, authority, perspective, and role are not the same as that of a congregation. The fifth assumption is that the higher priority items in a denominational strategy for growth should be those over which it has the greatest degree of control, and the lower priority items should be those over which it has more limited control. Sixth, it is assumed that any generalized proposal, such as this one, must be revised before it can be implemented, in order to match the distinctive characteristics of a specific denomination. Seventh, it also is assumed the denominational strategy should be developed with the expectation that it will encourage and facilitate congregational growth. Finally, it is assumed the denominational strategy will take advantage of the insights and findings that have come out of research into church growth.

A SUGGESTED ACTION STRATEGY

While denominational statistics are not fully comparable on a year-to-year basis nor across denominational lines, there are four statements that can be derived from statistical reports which deserve the careful attention of anyone interested in developing a denominational strategy for church growth. Every denomination reporting an increase in membership reports an increase in the number of congregations. Every denomination reporting an increase in the total number of congregations reports an increase in members. Every denomination reporting a decrease in membership reports a decrease in congregations. Every denomination reporting a decrease in congregations reports a decrease in members. While this does not prove a cause and effect relationship, it does introduce the first component of a denominational strategy for church growth.

The first step in developing a denominational strategy for church growth should be to organize new congregations. This is an effort that can be undertaken unilaterally by regional and/or national judicatories or it can be a cooperative effort of one or more congregations and the appropriate denominational agency. It is the one component of an overall strategy that can be initiated unilaterally by denominational leaders. It is one program that is within the control of denominational leaders.

The Division for Mission in North America of the Lutheran Church in America is one of several denominational agencies which has demonstrated that a program for new church development can be designed to reach people who are not active in any worshiping congregation (as contrasted to the strategy of starting new churches to serve "our people" who have moved here). A reasonable goal is that 60 to 80 percent of the members of the typical new mission will be persons who, immediately before joining that mission, were not actively involved in the life of any worshiping congregation.

There is an increasing body of research which suggests that the financial cost to the denomination need not be as high as it has been in several mainline denominational families. In fact, there is considerable evidence to suggest that the healthiest new congregations are the ones which received only a comparatively modest financial subsidy from the parent denomination. It appears that large financial subsidies may not be compatible with church growth for new missions nor for existing congregations.

The second component of a denominational strategy requires a far larger degree of participation from existing congregations. This is a denominationally initiated effort to provide training experiences in church growth for both the laity and the clergy. This component of an action plan is based on the belief that researchers in the behavioral sciences have learned some things about church growth that can be transmitted and that people can take advantage of these learnings to help their congregation to grow. The contributions to this volume by Hoge, Roozen, Doyle, Kelly, Jones, Walrath, Roof, Dyble, Hadaway, McKinney, and Wagner represent examples of what has been learned that can be transmitted to congregational leaders to help them develop a congregational strategy for growth. In most cases, however, the initiative for creating these training events rests with the denominational leaders.

The third component of a denominational strategy rests on the belief that there is a relationship between the staffing of a congregation and the potential for growth. Approximately one

Protestant congregation out of six averages more than 200 at worship on Sunday morning. This means they are approaching and perhaps have passed the point at which they can function effectively with only one minister and no other professional program staff *and also expect to grow.* Some of these large congregations are staffed for growth. Many are staffed to remain on a plateau. Others are staffed for decline.

This can be illustrated by looking at three examples. The first is a 900-member congregation established in 1850 in what is now an exurban community that doubled in population between 1950 and 1965, doubled again between 1965 and 1975, and is expected to double again by 1985. This congregation averages 485 at worship and is staffed with an exceptionally gifted pastor and a part-time college student. It is unlikely that it will grow, and when the present pastor leaves it will probably begin to decline. If it were staffed to grow, it would have the equivalent of four full-time professional program staff members and would be expecting to add a fifth within two or three years.

A second example is the 1,100-member, 19-year-old congregation in what is now a large, mature suburban city. It averages 650 at worship, down from 785 at its peak four years ago. The staff includes (in order of seniority) a full-time minister of music, a full-time director of Christian education, a full-time 26-year-old associate minister, and the newly arrived full-time 49-year-old senior pastor. It appears to be staffed for continued decline and an eventual leveling off with an average attendance at worship of between 400 and 500. It has a large staff, to be sure, but not large enough to grow, given its peculiar situation.

The third example is the 445-member congregation now averaging 215 at worship. This congregation is located in an exrural community sixty miles from the heart of a large city. During the past five years the population of the community doubled, and this congregation also doubled in size. Expenses are climbing more rapidly than income, however, because this congregation has had to relocate to a new parcel of land and build a new, larger meeting place. The leaders believe it will be at least seven or eight years before this congregation will be financially able to expand the program staff.

A denominational strategy for church growth might include (1) encouraging the first congregation to add a second ordained minister and a lay program assistant to the staff immediately and to plan to create and fill two additional staff positions within the next two years; (2) encouraging the second congregation to add a staff person on lay leadership development and a person-centered staff person to specialize in reaching and assimilating new persons immediately, plus perhaps a part-time minister of visitation; (3) offering financial assistance to the third congregation, perhaps on a dollar-matching basis to enable it to expand its staff immediately.

All three congregations already have more members than they are able to care for. It is unrealistic to expect them to be able to reach, assimilate, and minister to more people without either adding staff or neglecting some of the present members. As part of an overall denominational strategy for church growth, denominational leaders could take the initiative in encouraging large congregations to staff for growth rather than for maintenance of the status quo.

The fourth element in this suggested strategy also assumes a willingness by denominational leaders to take the initiative and is based on the personal observation that a very substantial portion of today's growing congregations are nongeographical parishes. Their growth is a result of developing specialized ministries to reach and serve those segments of the population largely ignored by most worshiping congregations. These specialized ministries are directed at such groups as the deaf, the parents of developmentally disabled children and those children, the recently widowed, young single and never married adults in the 20 to 26 age bracket, the upwardly mobile lower-middle-class and middle-class parents (and especially black parents) who desire an excellent Christian education for their children and are reached through the Christian day school for children in the 3 to 10 age bracket, single parents, the "empty nest" generation in their late forties and fifties, the recently divorced, persons in wheelchairs, parents who recently experienced the death of a child, alcoholics and spouses of alcoholics, young single adults in their middle and late twenties who are engaged in a personal religious search and who also are seeking an outlet for expressing their creativity and commitment through serving as volunteers, the intentionally childless couples who feel ostracized in the conventional family-centered parish, and newcomers to the United States from South America, Asia, and Africa. These are examples of some of the people being reached and served by growing churches through a variety of specialized ministries.

This proposed plan of action suggests that denominational leaders vigorously encourage congregations to develop specialized ministries to reach and serve the people who are largely ignored by most congregations today.

This fourth component of an overall denominational strategy also runs counter to a large stream of conventional thinking in denominational circles. For many years the stereotyped approach has been to urge congregations to specialize as geographical parishes and to seek to reach and serve the people who happen to reside in close proximity to that congregation's meeting place. This is a bankrupt approach to church planning and has only limited relevance to sparsely populated rural communities and to the first residents of new housing. Instead of identifying the people to be reached by their place of residence, a far better approach is to identify the people to be reached by their distinctive needs and to develop ministries in response to those needs.

While it is a far more productive approach than the conventional procedure of securing a map and drawing a circle with a one-mile radius from the meeting place, it also is a more difficult strategy to implement. First, it runs counter to the wishes of many congregational leaders who would prefer a strategy of reaching young families with children at home. (A reasonable estimate is that today the first priority on the outreach agenda of at least 85 percent of all urban and suburban congregations is to attempt to reach and win those husband-wife couples with children at home—and who constitute 34 percent of the adult population of the United States.) In other words, denominational leaders must persuade congregational leaders to shift their priorities from focusing on one third of the adult population to identifying the needs of the other two thirds of the adult population who are largely ignored by the typical family-centered congregation. That is not an easy assignment!

A second reason denominational leaders will find difficulty in implementing this suggestion is that few congregations, and also few denominational agencies, possess an adequate level of experience and skill to help congregations develop and implement a specialized ministry. A third difficulty is that in many denominational families the approach to congregational consultations has been to facilitate the process by which a congregation formulates and implements its own outreach goals. That emphasis on a nondirective process usually results in the formulation of goals concerned with (1) institutional maintenance, (2) reaching more "people who are just like us, only younger," and (3) perpetuating the past rather than breaking new ground and developing new ministries. In other words, this fourth component of a suggested denominational strategy for church growth often will require a more prophetic, a more highly skilled, a more aggressive, and a more directive role for the staff of the regional judicatory than has been the style in many denominational families. That may be asking more than is reasonable.

One alternative is for the denomination to model this concept by developing new specialized congregations to reach people who are largely ignored by existing churches. Examples of this include the new congregation for the deaf, the new congregation composed entirely of French-speaking newcomers from Haiti, the new congregation built around a ministry to families with mentally retarded and mentally handicapped children, or the new congregation composed almost entirely of persons who have been turned off or burned out or rejected or frustrated by a traditional church. Here again, a "both-and" approach by the denomination may be superior to an "either-or" decision.

The last component of this suggested five-point denominational strategy for church growth is directed at the tens of thousands of small congregations that have been on a plateau in size for decades. Thanks to the work of Carl Dudley, of the Small Church Project of the United Church of Christ, and others who have become concerned about the future of the small church, it now appears that it is possible to help some of these congregations with less than 200 members become effective evangelistic forces in their communities. An effort to help static small churches to grow may be the most difficult suggestion to implement of any of the five points in this proposal, but it should be included in a denominational strategy for growth.

A reasonable approach would be that because of (1) the very large number of small congregations in most denominational families, (2) the reluctance of many small congregations to adopt and implement a plan of action that may disrupt traditional patterns, (3) the limitations of what can be undertaken because of scarce denominational resources including staff time, and (4) the critical importance of a strong initiatory role by the leaders of the small congregation in any such venture, the regional (or national) judicatory concentrates its efforts on those congregations that take the initiative in responding to the announcement of available help and that also are willing to invest financial resources in a program for church growth. In many small congregations the only truly meaningful formal decisions that represent how people feel about a subject are those which involve the expenditure of scarce financial resources. Therefore, a logical component of a denominational strategy would be to require each participating congregation to pay at least part of the total financial cost of a program designed to help small churches grow.

This is not intended to be an exhaustive listing of the components of a denominational strategy for church growth. It is offered only as a suggestion of how denominational leaders can move from a discussion of the research presented in this volume to developing an action plan designed to take advantage of the insights that have been accumulated by the church growth movement and to incorporate these findings into a denominational strategy. Research, debate, discussion, and analysis can be very interesting in isolation, but they should lead to action if we are to be responsible stewards of the freedom and resources God has given us.

Notes

CHAPTER 1: RECENT TRENDS IN CHURCH MEMBERSHIP AND PARTICIPATION: AN INTRODUCTION

1. For a reconstruction of the membership trends of major U.S. denominations from colonial times to the present, see Gaustad (1976) or Kelley (1977).

2. The Gallup poll percentages shown in Figure 1.5 are based on an annual average of responses to questions asking whether or not a person attended a religious service in the week prior to the survey. An annual average is used to compensate for seasonal fluctuations in religious attendance. For example, church attendance is typically higher during Lent and Advent than during the summer. Unfortunately, the Gallup organization has only conducted its annual audit of church attendance since 1955. The yearly percentages presented in Figure 1.5 for the Survey Research Center are from single surveys conducted at the time of the Presidential election in each respective year. They represent the percentage of respondents indicating that they attended religious services "regularly." The Survey Research Center has continued to conduct a national survey in every Presidential election year, but regrettably, it radically altered the wording of its church attendance question after 1968.

The Gallup Annual Audit of church attendance has been conducted in every year since 1955. Figure 1.5 only presents the Gallup Annual Audit percentages in four-year intervals, because that is the time span between the Survey Research Center's Presidential election surveys. A complete rendering of the Gallup Annual Audit figures can be found in the Gallup Opinion Index (1978a).

3. At the time of this writing, another major study is in progress. It is an analysis of the 1978 Unchurched Americans Survey, conducted by the Gallup poll for a coalition of twenty-nine denominations convened by the National Council of Churches. A preliminary report of findings for the Unchurched Americans Survey can be found in the Gallup Opinion Index (1978b).

4. The term mainline has become a rather common, although ambiguous, adjective in recent commentaries about American religion. The best explanation of the term in the sense it is used in this book is contained in Martin Marty's A Nation of Behavers (1976:52-79). In general, we use the term to refer to the members and/or churches of the United Church of Christ, Episcopal Church, United Presbyterian Church, Lutheran Church in America, United Methodist Church, American Baptist

Convention, Reformed Church in America, and Southern Presbyterian Church; and, with a bit of hesitancy, to the Southern Baptist Convention, Lutheran Church-Missouri Synod, and American Lutheran Church.

5. The one situation in which denominational differences in definition of membership affect a comparison of denominational membership trends is a radical change in the number of children in the population. Such a change has more immediate effect on the membership of denominations that count persons as members from infancy on than on denominations that only count confirmed or adult baptized persons. But the effect should balance out over time.

6. A related problem is encountered when using the grand totals reported in such interdenominational reports as the *Yearbook of American and Canadian Churches*. It is the way that denominations new to these reports are added to the membership totals. For example, Winthrop Hudson (1955) points out that in 1952 the Christ Unity Church, with 682,172 members, was included for the first time in the *Yearbook of American and Canadian Churches*. Its addition alone accounted for more than one third of the overall church membership gain reported for that year.

7. In interpreting these percentages for the churched, it should be kept in mind that approximately 4 percent of the persons classified as churched are non-Christian.

8. The 1952 and 1965 *Catholic Digest* surveys (Marty, Rosenberg, and Greeley, 1968) contain a similar, although not identical, question about one's belief concerning the Bible. The surveys show a slight falloff from 1952 to 1965 in the percentage of the total sample believing the Bible to "really be the revealed word of God." For persons 18 to 24 years old, however, the decline is three and one half times as great as that for the total sample.

9. The first interpretation has considerable affinity with arguments set forth in Kelley's *Why Conservative Churches Are Growing*. The second has some affinity with the "collapse of the middle" thesis suggested in Hoge's *Division in the Protestant House* (1976).

CHAPTER 2: RESEARCH ON FACTORS INFLUENCING CHURCH COMMITMENT

1. This chapter reports on a major review of existing research, carried out before most of the other chapters in the book were finished. Hence, it does not include the new research reported in the book.

2. This question has been researched with regard to values of college alumni, and the main conclusion is that the cohort and the period effects are stronger than the aging effect (see Freedman, 1962; Feldman and Newcomb, 1969; Hoge and Bender, 1974). The main period effect was a time of relatively traditional and conservative values in the mid-1950s. Similar research on political alienation among adults found the period effect to be strong, the cohort effect to be weak, and the aging effect to be zero (Cutler and Bengtson, 1974). Two studies of political attitudes found the period effect to be greater than the aging effect (Glenn and Hefner, 1972; Glenn, 1974).

3. In this part we have grouped existing theories into six types without, we believe, very much distortion. Two theories have been espoused in addition, but we hesitate to see them as separate. Yinger (1970:130-31) proposes a social learning theory to account for most existing variation in church commitment. The theory states simply that persons most interested in religion and the church are members of those groups most concerned to train their members to be religious. In short, the main predictor of any person's church commitment will be the religious group from which she or he comes. Bibby and Brinkerhoff (1974:74) make the same argument in setting forth a "socialization factor" for explaining levels of church involvement. These theories are intended to explain group differences rather than individual differences in church involvement. We have discussed them in Part I under the heading of denominational differences. They are related to theories of individual differences in that they describe exogenous background factors prior to several more immediate intervening variables. For example, childhood socialization into religion is logically prior, and in that sense exogenous, in relation to doctrinal beliefs, value orientation, or local-versus-cosmopolitan orientation at present.

4. Max Weber had a more complex analysis emphasizing personal meaning and adjustment (Gerth and Mills, 1958). He suggested that lower-class persons associate themselves with religious groups for relief from dissatisfying aspects of their lives. Upper-class members involve themselves in churches because religion serves to justify their good fortune; their religious need is not redemption so much as legitimation.

5. Another study supports the theory, but the sample is so unusual that we hesitate to accept the results as theoretically valid. It was done in a single Catholic parish having both college students and resident adults (see Christopher et al., 1971).

6. The theoretical discussion of political belief systems by Converse (1964) has been influential. It is consistent with Hoge's depiction of meaning-commitment systems but goes beyond it in specifying the amount of interrelatedness of belief elements for different kinds of persons and the circumstances that cause change.

7. Length of residence in the community correlated strongly with Roof's localism measure, but it correlated weakly with church attendance (r = .17). Although several past studies have found an association between length of residence and church activity (Davis, 1962; Metz, 1965; Main, 1967; Alston, 1971), other studies have found either no relationship or a weak relationship (for example, Hoge and Polk, 1976; Hoge and Carroll, 1978). The reason for the discrepant findings is unclear; perhaps it is important that the studies finding no relationships are those based on church members only, while some of the studies finding a relationship are based on surveys of total adult populations.

8. Research on congregation size is relevant here. Church planning research has generally shown that smaller churches have higher attendance/membership ratios (Thorne, 1964; Maloney and Schaller, 1965), with the greatest differences occurring in churches that have under 300 members. Above that size, attendance/membership ratios change little. Wicker (1969) studied two churches and found higher membership commitment in the smaller one, but in a later study (Wicker et al., 1972)

involving many churches, the pattern was not found. Also Hoge and Polk (1976) failed to find the pattern. The reason for the discrepant findings is unclear.

CHAPTER 4: NATIONAL CONTEXTUAL FACTORS INFLUENCING CHURCH TRENDS

1. H. Paul Douglass, the most prominent sociologist of the American church in 1920-50, agrees in stressing short-range variations in the social climate: "Ideally perhaps religion ought always to be a vital energy, dominating every age. Actually it ebbs and flows. Subjective factors, like fervor, sincerity, sense of reality and relevance, depth of motivation, now rise and now fall. . . . Obviously the religious climate reflects the still more general intellectual and moral currents of the age [Douglass and Brunner, 1935:287]."

2. Much of Wuthnow's theory and data come from the Religious Consciousness Project at Berkeley in 1971-74, of which he was a member. The summary report of the project (Glock and Bellah, 1976) was written by fourteen authors, based on a variety of separate investigations. All agree that the religious turmoil in the 1960s was the result of a broad disaffection of middle-class youth from established American institutions—business, government, education, the churches, and the family; the religious events were one component of a broader phenomenon. Also, the investigation by Barbara Hargrove into campus ministries indicated that the main social turmoil took place among middle-class, urban, cosmopolitan youth; it occurred much less among ethnic, sectarian, less cosmopolitan youth, or those belonging to religious groups keeping a distance from mainstream culture (such as the Mormons or fundamentalist sects). Hence, such churches were less affected.

3. In preparing this part we made a major search for replications of attitude items. We included only the most typical and instructive in Table 4.4; others are shown in the Appendix. Several came to our attention after the chapter was written and are merely noted in the text. I wish to thank Desiree Holubowicz for assistance in compiling the data.

4. We may note that trends in political alienation in recent years have the same kinds of patterns as other attitude areas we analyzed. Foner (1974) studied political alienation in survey data from 1952 to 1968 and found greater change among young adults than older adults; most of the age differences occurred after 1960. Foner argued that political climate, not demographic change, is the main explanatory factor in the shifting attitudes. House and Mason (1975) did a similar analysis and agreed that changes in traditional demographic aggregates had little explanatory power; the changes in alienation came from events and changes in value structures.

5. Researchers attempting to explain the baby boom in the 1950s and the subsequent rapid drop in the birthrate have used economic arguments exclusively. The most discussed attempt is that by Easterlin (1961, 1966), who used theories of economic well-being of young couples compared with their expectations about their own futures. Easterlin cited availability of jobs and promotions at different points in time, changes in earning

362

power of young couples, and availability of veterans' benefits. It seems fair to conclude that his explanations are mostly after-the-fact and that no one has been able to foresee the drastic fertility changes in recent decades. Attempts to explain the changing birthrate by monitoring changes in broader value structures of young adults would seem helpful.

CHAPTER 5: THE EFFICACY OF DEMOGRAPHIC THEORIES OF RELIGIOUS CHANGE: PROTESTANT CHURCH ATTENDANCE, 1952-68

1. The research reported in this chapter was supported by funds provided by the Lilly Endowment, Inc. and The Hartford Seminary Foundation. The data used has been made available to the author by the Social Science Data Center of the University of Connecticut. Computer services have been provided by the University of Connecticut Computer Center.

2. The term demographic is often used in survey research to refer to those background or facesheet items that have become taken-for-granted inclusions on all surveys, for instance, age, sex, race, education, occupation, marital status, location and size of community. I do not so limit my usage of the term. According to the term's broader meaning, any variable that can meaningfully describe the population, can differentiate between "kinds of people," is a demographic variable, and this is the sense in which I use the term.

3. A more detailed discussion of massification and polarization effects can be found in Glenn (1967) and in Davis (1975b).

4. The five surveys in my study are the 1952, 1956, 1960, 1964, and 1968 American Election Surveys. This series of surveys has continued on a regular basis since 1968, but the data on religious participation collected since then is incompatible with the data used in our study because of changes in question wording. Futher information concerning the surveys used in our study, including sampling details, can be found in Campbell et al. (1968, 1970, 1971) and in Political Behavioral Program (1971, 1973). In all cases the weighting and selection procedures suggested by the principal researchers in the codebooks for obtaining the least biased national sample is followed.

5. If past research on religious participation agrees on anything, it is that Catholics attend church more frequently than do Protestants, who, in turn, attend more frequently than Jews, who, in turn, attend more frequently than those expressing no religious preference. The five SRC surveys present nothing to contradict this. The data does suggest, however, that the trends in religious participation for these religious groups are somewhat dissimilar. Figure 5.2 plots the trend for white Protestants. It shows a very gradual increase in religious participation from 1952 to 1964 (a total increase over the twelve years of 5.5 percentage points), followed by a rather sharp decrease from 1964 to 1968 (losing almost the total amount gained over the previous twelve years). In comparison, the Catholic trend, as measured in our surveys, shows a relatively steep increase from 1952 to 1956 and from 1956 to 1960 (twelve percentage points over the eight-year

period), followed by an extreme decrease from 1960 to 1964 (ten percentage points over the four-year period), which continues but at a slower rate through 1968 (losing another three percentage points). The number of Jews and others appearing in the samples is too small to provide a reliable measure of their respective trends in religious participation.

6. I focus on these variables because past research has indicated that they are related to religious participation and because data presently exists that would allow for at least a partial test of the impact demographic changes associated with them have had on religious participation. Accordingly, some variables are not included because appropriate data is not available—religious belief and mobility, for example; and some variables are not included because despite popular belief, past research has shown them to be unrelated to religious participation, at least at the level they are typically measured on national surveys—community size, for instance.

7. I would hope that future national surveys containing religious variables would take more seriously the potential importance of value commitments for understanding religious change. In this regard it is important to note the recent National Opinion Research Center series of General Social Surveys (NORC, 1977) and a recent national survey dealing with churched and unchurched Americans, conducted by the Gallup poll for an ad hoc coalition of denominational agencies (see Gallup Opinion Index, 1978b). Both contain value and religious indicators. These surveys should prove to be valuable baselines for future studies of the relationship between value change and religious change.

8. In the 1960 survey this question was asked only of those expressing a religious preference. In all other years it was asked of all respondents. Because I have limited my analysis to those persons expressing a Protestant preference, the 1960 departure from otherwise standard procedure should have no bearing.

9. In the 1956 and 1960 surveys, respondents were coded as having no school-age children present in the household if (1) they indicated having only one child under 18 years of age and also indicated that their youngest child was less than 5 years old; (2) they indicated having no children under 18 years of age; or (3) they indicated having two children under 18 years of age, the youngest child being less than 2 years old. All other respondents were coded as having children of school age present in the household. Such a constructed measure of the presence or absence of school-age children does not, of course, provide a perfect match to the direct "any children in school" measure. However, in the 1968 survey we were able to test the goodness of the fit between the two measures. Less than 3 percent error was found.

10. "Married" refers to persons married and currently living with their spouses. "Not married" refers to anyone else. All persons over 55 years of age were placed in the same family life cycle stage regardless of marital status or the presence of school-age children because past research (Carroll and Roozen, 1975) has found that finer differentiations in this age category do not affect religious participation.

11. The demographic effect on religious participation change associated with a particular explanatory variable is removed by setting the T_2 distribution of the explanatory variable equal to the T_1 distribution of the

explanatory variable. The joint-period effect on religious participation change associated with any given explanatory variable is removed by setting the T_2 percentages of religious participation within categories of the explanatory variable equal to their respective T_1 percentage.

Although the tables in the text present only the demographic, joint-period, and interaction effects, the actual percentage distributions over time for the explanatory variable and religious participation by the explanatory variable used in the calculation of these effects can be found in the Appendix.

12. A number of other massification and differentiation effects present themselves in Figures 5.3 through 5.7. They are, however, with one exception, either relatively insignificant and/or seem related to the age and education effects discussed above. The one exception is the unusually low level of religious participation found in the West in 1956. Its presence in the data is puzzling, especially since it does not appear to be present in the Gallup Poll National Church Attendance time series (Gallup, 1972). Probably it is due to sampling peculiarities.

CHAPTER 6: COMPARISON OF TRENDS IN TEN DENOMINATIONS 1950-75

1. The authors gratefully acknowledge the assistance of Warren J. Hartman, of the Board of Discipleship, the United Methodist Church.

2. They include Doyle and Kelly (1976); Doyle and Murnion, (1978); Evangelical United Brethren Yearbook, 1951-68; General Minutes of the Annual Conferences of the Methodist Church, 1951-67; General Minutes of the Annual Conferences of the United Methodist Church, 1968-76; Hartman (1976); Hoge (1977); Jones (1977); Journal of the General Convention, 1952-76; Minutes of the General Assembly of the United Presbyterian Church in the United States of America, 1976; Lutheran Council in the U.S.A., 1978; Official Catholic Directory, 1951-76; The Episcopal Church Annual, 1951-76; United Church of Canada Yearbook, 1976; United Church of Christ Yearbook, 1962-76; United Presbyterian Committee (1976); Whipple (1976); Yearbook of the Evangelical and Reformed Church, 1952-61; Yearbook of the Congregational Christian Churches, 1950-61.

3. The Church of Jesus Christ of Latter-Day Saints is one of the ten largest U.S. denominations. It was not included in this paper because its membership is concentrated in a few states.

4. When the Constitution of the United Church of Christ was declared in force in 1961, the 2,726 congregations and 814,124 members of the Evangelical and Reformed Church became members of the United Church of Christ. This was true only for those of the 5,458 Congregational Christian congregations (1960 membership: 1,432,486) that voted to become part of the United Church of Christ. By the end of 1965 a total of 994 Congregational Christian churches, with a 1960 membership of 181,682, had abstained from voting, had voted not to become part of the United Church of Christ, or had affiliated with the National Association of

Congregational Christian Churches. All the membership losses during the 1960-65 period and 81 percent of the decline in the number of churches can be accounted for by nonaffiliation of Congregational Christian churches.

5. The nine U.S. census regions are the following: *New England*—Maine, New Hampshire, Vermont, Massachusetts, Rhode Island, Connecticut; *Middle Atlantic*—New York, New Jersey, Pennsylvania; *East North Central*—Ohio, Indiana, Illinois, Michigan, Wisconsin; *West North Central*—Minnesota, Iowa, Missouri, North Dakota, South Dakota, Nebraska, Kansas; *South Atlantic*—Delaware, Maryland, District of Columbia, Virginia, West Virginia, North Carolina, South Carolina, Georgia, Florida; *East South Central*—Kentucky, Tennessee, Alabama, Mississippi; *West South Central*—Arkansas, Louisiana, Oklahoma, Texas; *Mountain*—Montana, Idaho, Wyoming, Colorado, New Mexico, Arizona, Utah, Nevada; *Pacific*—Washington, Oregon, California, Alaska, Hawaii.

6. Roman Catholic figures are for children in elementary parochial schools and public school pupils attending elementary religious education programs; Episcopal enrollment includes pupils in Sunday and in released-time classes and excludes full-time parochial schools. Southern Baptist and United Methodist figures are for all students, nursery through adult, enrolled in Sunday schools; Lutheran figures are for students through high school; United Presbyterian and United Church of Canada figures include all age groups of pupils, as well as officers and teachers. The congregations of the United Church of Christ do not follow uniform reporting practices (some include officers and teachers, while others do not), and it could not be determined what percent of the total UCC figures represent the various categories of church school students.

CHAPTER 7: AN EXAMINATION OF THE STATISTICAL GROWTH OF THE SOUTHERN BAPTIST CONVENTION

1. Of the 35,073 currently existing churches, the year organized could not be obtained for 272 (0.8 percent) due to insufficient data on the Uniform Church Letters. In addition, not all the churches organized in 1976 had been reported at the time of preparation for this graph; thus, 1976 is not included. Of the existing churches, 12,783 were organized before 1900 and were not included in the graph. Over 3,000 of these churches were organized before the formation of the Southern Baptist Convention in 1845 due to a split between Baptists of the North and the South.

2. Churches sponsoring missions were eliminated from the breakdown because data for their missions is included with their data, and it is impossible to separate them. In 1976 approximately 2,400 missions were sponsored by about 1,500 churches, which together accounted for about 10 percent of the total number of baptisms. Other churches were eliminated because they either did not make a yearly report or they did not report their date of organization.

CHAPTER 8: A TEST OF THEORIES OF DENOMINA-TIONAL GROWTH AND DECLINE

1. Several persons helped greatly on this project. Constant Jacquet, Dean Kelley, Everett Perry, John Dyble, David Roozen, and Raymond Potvin gave helpful advice and read early drafts of the chapter. Wade Clark Roof computed the NORC data. William McKinney Jr. was especially helpful, suggesting a number of improvements and compiling the geographical distribution data.

2. The distinction between institutional and contextual factors is found throughout this book. It is made partly for policy reasons; institutional factors are those amenable to manipulation through deliberate church action, while contextual factors are beyond church control. As an example of the latter, migration of people from one region to another or changes in sex-role definition are such strong social forces that they are beyond reasonable impact by church action and hence are classed as contextual factors. Similarly, the social class, race, and family size of members is classified as contextual in this chapter. It could be argued that they are institutional, since evangelism efforts and new church development efforts can be deliberately directed at one social class or another. But they are not easily changed by church effort and hence are classified as contextual.

3. Interviews with seven denominational officials responsible for new church development provided evidence that denominations vary in their investment of funds and energy in new churches. Also historical trends have occurred—in the mid-1960s several denominations shifted from developing traditional types of congregations to developing new styles of congregations, sometimes centering on social involvement or specific life-styles (see Hadden and Longino, 1974). These efforts were terminated in the early 1970s, with a return to development of traditional congregations (for trend data see Schaller, 1967).

4. In order to test if institutional changes produced membership changes, we needed ratings for each of two decades, 1956-65 and 1966-75. Although our pretest questionnaire asked for this, the pretest experts convinced us that such a task was too long and ponderous. Hence, we limited the rating form to one decade only. This limitation prevented some of the direct tests of effects that we desired and forced us to rely on inferences. The twenty-one experts who filled in the rating form were (1) church historians: Edwin Gaustad, Winthrop Hudson, Martin Marty, Richard Pierard, John Woodbridge; (2) sociologists of religion: Earl Brewer, Ronald Enroth, Douglas Johnson, David Moberg, Everett Perry; (3) denominational and ecumenical leaders: Constant Jacquet, Arleon Kelley, Harold Lindsell, Harold Ockenga, Floyd Robertson, David Schuller, William P. Thompson; (4) seminary educators: Glenn Barker, Donald Shriver, C. Peter Wagner, Robert Wilson.

5. Five denominations lacked current membership statistics in the *Yearbook*. Since our pretest experts did not know the Canadian denominations, we had to delete them. We deleted three American denominations for the same reason. This left seventeen that were included in the rating form. Later, we found inexact membership statistics for the

Churches of Christ and deleted that denomination, leaving sixteen. We would have much preferred keeping more denominations in the analysis. Ratings for the Churches of Christ are shown in Table 8.1 for informational purposes.

6. The rating form included a don't know option but asked that the raters not use it more than one fourth of the time. Actually, they used it 6 percent of the time. For analysis we used the mean of the experts' ratings, not including the don't know responses.

7. The mean standard deviation across the seventeen denominations for the eight dimensions were (1) 1.38; (2) .89; (3) 1.03; (4) 1.24; (5) 1.06; (6) 1.04; (7) 1.13; and (8) 1.13. The denominations whose standard deviations were largest across the twenty-one raters were the Churches of Christ and the Christian Church (Disciples of Christ).

8. The expert ratings on ecumenism strongly support Kelley's (1972:89) "Exclusivist-Ecumenical Gradient." Fourteen denominations appear in both lists, and the rankings are almost identical, never varying by more than two ranks. Spearman's rank-order correlation for the two is .96.

CHAPTER 9: FACTORS PRODUCING GROWTH OR DECLINE IN UNITED PRESBYTERIAN CONGREGATIONS

1. The analysis in this chapter was made possible by funds from the Lilly Endowment, Inc., granted to The Hartford Seminary Foundation, and from the University Computing Center at the University of Massachusetts, Amherst.

2. The decision to look at a six-year period was made because six years seemed to be a long enough time that short-range fluctuations, errors, and chance occurrences would have little impact, yet short enough that the influence of particular pastoral leadership styles and program emphases could be isolated. It was feared that trends of eight years or more would have unclear determinants due to multiple pastors, changes in personnel, and shifts in program.

3. Individual questionnaires were to be given to two to four session members (elected governing board of laypersons), one trustee, one church school teacher or administrator, one women's group leader, one youth, one choir member or music leader, and several members only moderately active in church life. The questionnaires were therefore not filled out by random samples of members, but rather by relatively active members. We asked that the persons selected be a diversified group in terms of background, age, and viewpoints. Large congregations were sent more questionnaires than small ones. The average returned per congregation was 6.5.

4. It was thought that there would also be variations by size of congregation. However, in preliminary analysis we found small, statistically nonsignificant differences across three size groups. Consequently, we decided not to distinguish congregation size, but to focus instead on community type.

5. Several items used in testing these clusters were recoded or reconstructed from the questionnaire:

a. The item dealing with change in the school population was recoded so that the response indicating a decrease is given a 1, no change a 2, and an increase a 3.

b. Other items dealing with demographic change in the area were also recoded. A nonresponse was taken to mean no change, and the item was then coded similarly to the question on change in the school population.

c. The item on increase in the percent of Protestants was derived by subtracting the percentage of Protestants living near the church ten years ago from the percentage now living there.

d. The city/suburb/town and country classification was derived in the following manner: Cities over 250,000 and cities 50,000 to 250,000 were combined into the city category; suburbs of these cities made up the suburb category; and small cities (10,000 to 50,000), small towns under 10,000, farm and open country were combined into the town and country category. The general guidelines determining choice of variables included are discussed in the Appendix.

6. In this typology, communities of 50,000 or more population are large cities, 10,000 to 50,000 are small cities, and small towns under 10,000 and farm and open country are combined into the town and country category. A city or suburb was defined as growing if the area was increasing in newcomers, nongrowing if either stable or declining in newcomers.

7. A multiple-partial correlation is analogous to a partial correlation and is useful for summarizing relations among variables utilizing multiple indicators. It is a multiple coefficient in the sense that the measure allows one to look at a relationship between a dependent variable and a *cluster* of independent variables, while controlling for another *cluster* of variables. For a discussion see Blalock (1972:458-59).

8. Because there were so many variables in these two clusters, we used only eight measures as controls. They were age of homes, age of church building, economic level, percent renters (measures of affluence), increase in economic level, increase in proportion of young, increase in proportion of minorities, and increase in proportion of school population (measures of demographic change).

9. In Table 9.6 the R^2s are adjusted to minimize chance increases in variance explained due to the large number of independent variables. The adjusted coefficients are more reliable for drawing conclusions about relative importance of factors when a large number of variables are in the analysis. In the previous analyses this was less of a problem because fewer variables were involved or because our focus was on single clusters of variables only. Unfortunately, the adjusted coefficients are intuitively more difficult to understand because the amount of explained variance does not necessarily increase as variables are added. The more independent variables are in the analysis, the more drastic the reduction in R^2 is when adjusted. The adjustment procedure reduced the total variance explained in Table 9.6 from 38 percent to 26 percent.

10. After our analysis was finished, the Southern Baptist Convention published the results of a somewhat similar study of its fastest growing congregations (Home Missions, 1977). The SBC scanned its 35,000 congregations to find the fastest growing between 1972 and 1976 based on a threefold criterion—total membership, Sunday school enrollment, and baptisms. The top 1.5 percent (N = 425) were selected for study, and

reporters were sent to do stories on the fifteen fastest growing. No control group of stable or declining congregations was included.

Of the 425 churches contacted, 277 cooperated by returning completed a pastor's questionnaire and a layperson's questionnaire. The growing churches were mostly in growing suburban areas. Seventy-four percent said their church's neighborhood was growing; 59 percent said the neighborhood was rising in economic status; 70 percent were located in a suburb or urban fringe. Most congregations were rated by their pastors as middle class or lower middle class—70 percent of the pastors said the predominant groups were "clerical, mid-level management" or "blue collar." The churches were larger than the average SBC churches at the start of the growth period (1972). The median age of the congregations (as of 1977) was twenty-one years, and the median years the pastors were in the ministry was seventeen. Laypersons described the pastors as "Bible-believing, evangelistic," "strong leader," "strong counselor-pastor type," and "accessible and warmly human." They did not check other responses, such as "non-directive style of leadership" and "depends on laity for church direction."

Due to the methodology of the SBC study, no weights can be attached to the various factors influencing growth. Doubtless both local contextual factors and local institutional factors were important, as they were in the Presbyterian study. Reporters who visited the fastest growing churches and interviewed experts (including Phillip Jones and C. Peter Wagner, both authors represented in this book) made estimates. They said that the growing churches are deeply Bible-believing, based on absolute Bible authority; churches give little attention to social ministries and social issues; their pastors are experienced, dynamic, enthusiastic, and hard-working; the preaching is expository, using verse-by-verse exposition; and they are very active in evangelistic efforts.

The reporters, at least, believed that theologically conservative churches grow faster than others, and that the dedication and personality of the pastor is a foremost factor in growth. These two hypotheses were tested in the Presbyterian data but found little support. Whether or not this difference in conclusions results from different research approaches or from denominational differences is unclear.

CHAPTER 10: PERFORMANCE OF UNITED CHURCH OF CHRIST CONGREGATIONS IN MASSACHUSETTS AND IN PENNSYLVANIA

1. Support for this study has been provided by the United Church Board for Homeland Ministries and The Hartford Seminary Foundation. The author is indebted to both organizations for their support.

2. A current intense interest in such themes is evident in the debate over theories of secularization (Berger et al., 1973; Caporale and Grumelli, 1971), in renewed interest in the nature of religious experience (Glock and Bellah, 1976; Wuthnow, 1976a), and in a variety of studies of individual and group church participation patterns (Roof, 1976; Greeley et al., 1976). It is also seen in the emergence of a significant body of literature dealing

370

with church growth (Roozen, 1978a; Wagner, 1976; Shannon, 1977; Kelley, 1977).

3. The Tenth General Synod (United Church of Christ, 1975) reaffirmed an earlier statement urging each local church to provide for the "Basic Support" of Our Christian World Mission (the denomination's chief source of financial support) an amount equal to at least 25 percent of its current local expenses.

4. A copy of the Church Membership Inventory appears in the Appendix.

5. The Massachusetts Conference is comprised of 453 churches and 139,699 members (1975) and includes the entire state of Massachusetts. The Penn Central Conference includes 256 churches and 77,484 members located in fifteen central Pennsylvania counties, extending from the Lancaster area in the east to Mercersburg in the west and north to the New York border.

6. A small number of Pennsylvania churches of Congregational Christian background were eliminated from the sample, as were two Massachusetts churches that retain membership in the Conference but are not affiliated with the United Church of Christ. The churches participated in the study at their own expense with the encouragement of the conference and the Board for Homeland Ministries staff. Due to program emphases in the conferences, there is a slight overrepresentation of churches in the Metropolitan Boston area of Massachusetts and in nonmetropolitan communities of Pennsylvania.

7. Further information on the construction of measures is contained in the Appendix.

8. Our use of these two items in constructing our index of outreach was based on two considerations. The General Synod statements to which we have referred emphasize the local church's role in both community and worldwide outreach. The 17/76 Achievement Fund was presented to churches during the early 1970s as a concrete means of expressing concern for racial justice in the United States through support of black colleges historically related to the Congregational Christian denomination and for overseas educational programs for racial minority persons. Second, we found strong correlations between conference staff ratings of congregational outreach and support of the 17/76 Achievement Fund among churches of both traditions.

9. Examination of the intercorrelations between some seventy items for which data was available and the five performance resources eliminated a large number due to very weak relationships. A complete correlation matrix is contained in the Appendix.

10. We chose to rely on census material rather than on clergy or lay perception of community trends. The larger project from which data presented here is taken has indicated that perceptions of clergy and laity about local population characteristics frequently differ from actual census findings.

11. In an earlier draft of this paper we included a sixth performance dimension, which we labeled congregational inclusiveness. This dimension was intended to reflect the degree to which the congregation reflects in its membership the diversity of the community in which it is located. Implicit in various statements of the denomination's General Synod and of

other agencies of the United Church of Christ is a value on heterogeneity at both the congregational and denominational levels. The 1977 statement on the vitality of the local church cited earlier, for example, calls on the agencies of the denomination to assist local churches in integrating persons of a variety of life-styles within the life of a single congregation. We did develop a measure of inclusiveness based on socioeconomic status, age, and mobility of church attenders and community residents. (Too few churches or communities included in the study had sufficiently large minority populations to include race in our index of inclusiveness, and adequate data on other types of inclusiveness was unavailable to us.) We found that churches located in higher-status communities were far more likely to be inclusive in their membership than those located in lower-status neighborhoods, and that nonmetropolitan communities were more likely to include a full range of community residents than those in more urban areas. The question of congregational inclusiveness needs further attention and awaits the development of more adequate measures than we had available to us.

CHAPTER 11: SOCIAL CHANGE AND LOCAL CHURCHES: 1951-75

1. Research on which some of the material in this chapter is based was supported by a grant from the Lilly Endowment, Inc. Some material in this chapter also appeared in Jackson W. Carroll, *Small Churches Are Beautiful* (New York: Harper & Row, 1977).

2. The U.S. census defines an SMSA: "Except in the New England States, a standard metropolitan statistical area is a county or group of contiguous counties which contains at least one city of 50,000 inhabitants or more, or 'twin cities' with a combined population of at least 50,000. In addition to the county or counties containing such a city or cities, contiguous counties are included in an SMSA if, according to certain criteria, they are socially and economically integrated with the central city. In the New England States, SMSAs consist of towns and cities instead of counties."

3. Data sources of Table 11.2 are as follows: Columns 1, 3, and 4 are based on church yearbook data. Column 2 is based on 1960 and 1970 data for census tracts from the neighborhoods around the church buildings and from which the congregations in a given type group have traditionally drawn their members. Columns 5 and 6 are based on either data gathered from the congregations at Sunday morning worship services during 1974, or 1970 census tract data for neighborhood tracts, or both. The data gathered at Sunday morning worship services comes from a sample of forty-eight churches (N=3800), representing at least 25 percent of the churches in each type. For complete data see Walrath (1974).

CHAPTER 12: CHURCH GROWTH RESEARCH: THE PARADIGM AND ITS APPLICATIONS

1. Space prohibits a full discussion of the ethical implications of the homogeneous unit principle. For those interested, see Wagner (1978; 1979a).

2. The model of spiritual decision presented in Figure 12.1 has undergone an interesting history. In rudimentary forms it was first suggested by Viggo Sogaard while he was a student in the Wheaton Graduate School. It was revised by James F. Engel and published in such sources as the Church Growth Bulletin and elsewhere during 1973. Since that time, modifications have been introduced as others have made suggestions. Particularly helpful comments have been advanced by Richard Senzig, of the communications faculty at the Wheaton Graduate School, and professors C. Peter Wagner and Charles Kraft, of the Fuller School of World Mission.

CHAPTER 13: RECOVERING THE CHURCH'S TRANS-FORMING MIDDLE: THEOLOGICAL REFLECTIONS ON THE BALANCE BETWEEN FAITHFULNESS AND EFFEC-TIVENESS

1. It is important to define church growth for the purposes of this chapter. Latin American theologian Orlando Costas (1976:6), in an analysis of the incredible membership gains of the Chilean Protestant Church, declares, "Numerical and organic growth does not necessarily mean that a church is growing. A church which grows numerically and organically may just be getting fat." Costas goes on to describe holistic growth, which includes conceptual and incarnational growth as well as numerical and organic. While it is theologically appropriate to define growth, as Costas suggests, more holistically, I prefer to reserve the term maturity for an increase in knowledge, discipline, spirituality, or mission and to confine the term growth to an increase in numbers of members, levels of attendance, and financial contributions.

2. Given my concern with the "whither," this chapter cannot be primarily about church growth. In the present cultural climate, to focus on numerical membership is deceptively seductive, because such concentration may be based on the uncritical assumption that church growth is unqualifiably good and indisputably central. In this sense, the whole book carries the danger of being unintentionally seductive. From my theological perspective, even my participation in the project is unfaithful unless I direct my reflections toward the nature and purpose of the church and not simply the issue of growth. The concern with growth and decline in mainline churches can be appropriately evaluated only in relationship to the priorities established for and by the body of Christ. Faithfulness and effectiveness are the criteria I propose. Christ as the transformer of culture is the standard by which the church is judged.

CHAPTER 14: SOME SOCIOLOGICAL CONCLUSIONS ABOUT CHURCH TRENDS

1. The model is useful for helping conceptualize the problem, but it has some limitations of which two should be noted. First, as set forth, it has no

interaction terms, even though interactions occur in reality. For example, we found evidence that denominations are influenced by national contextual factors to the extent that they are embedded in the mainstream culture (see chapter 8). This argues for including interactions in the model in future use. Second, the distinction between local contextual and local institutional factors is ambiguous. Our definition is that a contextual factor is one "not reasonably changeable by intentional church effort." Such a variable as neighborhood socioeconomic status seems clearly contextual, since church effort can do little about it. Family size is less clear, but we have classed it as contextual, since research has identified some strong determinants of family size not easily influenced by churches. How about a congregation's ethical stance toward the surrounding culture, either withdrawal and separation from it or affirmation of it? We have classified this factor as institutional, since it seems changeable by intentional church effort, yet in real life, to change it would be difficult and costly. An effort to make a change in a factor of this kind, which is central to the congregation's identity, would cause a sense of anomie among many members, loss of commitment among others, and withdrawal from membership among others. Such a factor is theoretically changeable by church effort, but it is not politically feasible (to borrow a political term) due to the great cost it would incur. At best, it would have to be attempted slowly. In short, the distinction between local contextual and local institutional problems is more akin to a gradation of factors, from those least changeable to those most changeable, by intentional church effort (assuming that the church leadership clearly desires to attempt the change).

2. The other regularity found by Currie, Gilbert, and Horsley is a five- or six-year sawtooth-like pattern of conversions, especially in the nineteenth and the early twentieth century. It seemed most explainable by the dynamics of revivals and conversions themselves, which disappeared in all denominations that ceased to grow. For a similar pattern in the United States, see Weber (1927).

3. A specification is necessary at this point. We found that denominations which most strongly embrace the mainstream culture are most affected by shifts in that culture—either for the better or for the worse (see chapter 8). We found that since 1965 the tendency of any denomination to identify with the surrounding American culture has been a strong correlate of decline. Apparently, the reason was that cultural forces in this period were unfavorable to the church. We doubt if this was true in the period 1948-55, for which we lack data; probably the cultural forces then were favorable for churches, and culture-embracing denominations benefited.

Bibliography

Ahlstrom, Sydney E.
  1970 "The radical turn in theology and ethics: why it occurred in the 1960's." *The Annals of the American Academy of Political and Social Sciences* 387:1-13.
  1972 *A Religious History of the American People.* New Haven, CT: Yale University Press.
  1978 "National trauma and changing religious values." *Daedalus* 107:13-29.
Allport, Gordon W.
  1966 "The religious context of prejudice." *Journal for the Scientific Study of Religion* 5:447-57.
Alston, Jon P.
  1971 "Social variables associated with church attendance, 1965 and 1969: evidence from national polls." *Journal for the Scientific Study of Religion* 10:233-36.
  1972 "Review of the polls." *Journal for the Scientific Study of Religion* 11:180-86.
Alston, Jon P., and William A. McIntosh
  1977 "An assessment of the determinants of religious participation." Paper presented to the American Sociological Association, Chicago.
Alston, Jon P., and Francis Tucker
  1973 "The myth of sexual permissiveness." *Journal of Sex Research* 9:34-40.
American Association of Theological Schools
  1972 "Voyage: Vision: Venture. Report of the Task Force on Spiritual Development." *Theological Education* 8:152-205.
Anders, Sarah F.
  1955 "Religious behavior of church families." *Journal of Marriage and Family Living* 17:54-57.
Argyle, Michael, and Benjamin Beit-Hallahmi
  1975 *The Social Psychology of Religion.* London: Routledge & Kegan Paul.
Arn, Winfield C.
  1977 "A church growth look at Here's Life, America." *Church Growth: America,* January-February: 4-7.
Babchuk, Nicholas, Harry J. Crockett Jr., and Jon A. Ballweg
  1967 "Change in religious affiliation and family stability." *Social Forces* 49:59-71.

Bahr, Howard M.
  1970 "Aging and religious disaffiliation." *Social Forces* 49:59-71.
Baltzell, E. Digby
  1964 *The Protestant Establishment, Aristocracy and Caste in America.*
       Westminster, MD: Random House.
Barth, Karl
  1948 "No Christian Marshall Plan." *The Christian Century* LXV:
       1330-33.
Bayer, Alan E., and Jeffrey E. Dutton
  1976 "Trends in attitudes on political, social, and collegiate issues
       among college students." *Journal of Higher Education* 47:159-71.
Bell, Bill D.
  1971 "Church participation and the family life cycle." *Review of*
       Religious Research 13:57-64.
Bell, Robert R., and Jay B. Chaskes
  1970 "Premarital sexual experience among coeds, 1958 and 1968."
       Journal of Marriage and the Family 32:81-84.
Bellah, Robert N.
  1976 "New religious consciousness and the crisis in modernity." Pp.
       33-52 in Glock and Bellah (eds.), *The New Religious Conscious-*
       ness. Berkeley: University of California Press.
Bender, Irving E.
  1968 "A longitudinal study of church attenders and non-attenders."
       Journal for the Scientific Study of Religion 7:230-37.
Berger, Peter L.
  1961 *The Noise of Solemn Assemblies.* Garden City, NY: Doubleday.
Berger, Peter L., Brigitte Berger, and Hansfried Kellner
  1973 *The Homeless Mind: Modernization and Consciousness.* New
       York: Random House.
Bibby, Reginald W.
  1978 "Why conservative churches really are growing: Kelley revisited."
       Journal for the Scientific Study of Religion 17:129-37.
Bibby, Reginald W., and Merlin B. Brinkerhoff
  1974 "Sources of religious involvement: issues for future empirical
       investigation." *Review of Religious Research* 15:71-79.
Biersdorf, John E.
  1975 *Hunger for Experience: Vital Religious Communities in America.*
       New York: Seabury Press.
Blaikie, Norman W.H.
  1972 "What motivates church participation? review, replication, and
       theoretical reorientation in New Zealand." *Sociological Review*
       20:39-58.
Blake, Judith
  1971 "Abortion and public opinion: the 1960-1970 decade." *Science*
       171:540-49.
  1974 "Can we believe recent data on birth expectations in the United
       States?" *Demography* 11:25-44.
Blalock, Hubert M.
  1972 *Social Statistics.* New York: McGraw-Hill.
Board of National Missions
  1971 "A study of some growing churches in the United Presbyterian

Church, U.S.A." Multilithed. New York: United Presbyterian Church.

Bouvier, Leon F., and Robert H. Weller
1974 "Residence and religious participation in a Catholic setting." *Sociological Analysis* 35:273-81.

Brackenridge, R. Douglas
1978 *Eugene Carson Blake: Prophet with Portfolio.* New York: Seabury Press.

Brown, Robert McAfee
1961 *The Spirit of Protestantism.* New York: Oxford University Press.

Campbell, Angus, Philip Converse, Warren Miller, and Donald Stokes
1968 *The 1956 Election Study* (Revised ICPR Edition). Ann Arbor, MI: Inter-University Consortium for Political Research.
1970 *The 1960 Election Study* (Revised ICPR Edition). Ann Arbor, MI: Inter-University Consortium for Political Research.

Campbell, Angus, Gerald Gurin, and Warren Miller
1971 *The 1952 American Election Study* (Revised ICPR Edition). Ann Arbor, MI: Inter-University Consortium for Political Research.

Campbell, Thomas C., and Yoshio Fukuyama
1970 *The Fragmented Layman.* Philadelphia: Pilgrim Press.

Caporale, Rocco, and Antonio Grumelli (eds.)
1971 *The Culture of Unbelief.* Berkeley: University of California Press.

Carlos, Serge
1970 "Religious participation and the urban-suburban continuum." *American Journal of Sociology* 75:742-59.

Carr, Leslie G., and William J. Hauser
1976 "Anomie and religiosity: an empirical re-examination." *Journal for the Scientific Study of Religion* 15:69-74.

Carroll, Henry K.
1893 *The Religious Forces of the United States Enumerated, Classified, and Described on the Basis of the Government Census of 1890.* New York: Christian Literature Co.

Carroll, Jackson W.
1978a "Continuity and change: the shape of American religion." Pp. 1-45 in Carroll, Johnson, and Marty (eds.), *Religion in America: 1950-Present.* New York: Harper & Row.
1978b "Understanding church growth and decline." *Theology Today* 35:70-80.

Carroll, Jackson W. (ed.)
1977 *Small Churches Are Beautiful.* San Francisco: Harper & Row.

Carroll, Jackson W., and David A. Roozen
1975 *Religious Participation in American Society: An Analysis of Social and Religious Trends and Their Interaction.* Hartford, CT: Hartford Seminary Foundation.

Chaney, Charles L., and Ron S. Lewis
1977 *Design for Church Growth.* Nashville: Broadman Press.

Christensen, Harold T., and Christina F. Gregg
1970 "Changing sex norms in America and Scandinavia." *Journal of Marriage and the Family* 32:616-27.

Christopher, Stefan, John Fearon, John McCoy, and Charles Nobbe
1971 "Social deprivation and religiosity." *Journal for the Scientific*

Study of Religion 10:385-92.
Cobb, John B. Jr.
1975 *Christ in a Pluralistic Age.* Philadelphia: Westminster Press.
Congregational Christian Churches
1951- *The Yearbook of the Congregational Christian Churches.* New
1961 York: General Council of the Congregational Christian Churches.
Converse, Philip E.
1964 "The nature of belief systems in mass publics." Pp. 206-61 in D.
Apter (ed.), *Ideology and Discontent.* Glencoe, IL: Free Press.
1976 *The Dynamics of Party Support: Cohort-Analyzing Party
Identification.* Beverly Hills, CA: Sage Publications.
Costas, Orlando
1976 "Church growth, in-depth evangelism and human liberation."
Multilithed. New York: United Church Board for Homeland
Ministries.
Cox, Harvey
1965 *The Secular City.* New York: Macmillan.
Current Opinion
1973 Report on survey data on ideal family size. Vol. 1:39.
Currie, Robert, Alan Gilbert, and Lee Horsley
1977 *Churches and Church-goers: Patterns of Church Growth in the
British Isles Since 1770.* Oxford: Clarendon Press.
Cutler, Neal E., and Vern L. Bengtson
1974 "Age and political alienation: maturation, generation and period
effects." *Annals of the American Academy of Political and Social
Science* 415:160-75.
Davis, James A.
1975a "Communism, conformity, cohorts, and categories: American
tolerance in 1954 and 1972-73." *American Journal of Sociology*
81:491-513.
1975b "The log linear analysis of survey replications." Pp. 75-104 in
Land and Spilerman (eds.), *Social Indicator Models.* New York:
Russell Sage Foundation.
Davis, James H.
1962 *The Outsider and the Urban Church.* Urban Pamphlet No. 19.
Philadelphia: Board of Missions of the Methodist Church.
DeJong, Gordon F., and Joseph E. Faulkner
1972 "Religion and intellectuals: findings from a sample of university
faculty." *Review of Religious Research* 14:15-24.
Demerath, Nicholas J. III
1965 *Social Class in American Protestantism.* Chicago: Rand McNally.
1968 "Trends and anti-trends in religious change." Pp. 349-445 in
Sheldon and Moore (eds.), *Indicators of Social Change.* New York:
Russell Sage Foundation.
Dittes, James E.
1971 "Conceptualization and statistical rigor: comment on 'Social
deprivation and religiosity.'" *Journal for the Scientific Study of
Religion* 10:393-95.
Dorchester, Daniel
1888 *Christianity in the United States from the First Settlement Down to
the Present Time.* New York: Phillips and Hunt.

Douglass, H. Paul
1942 *The Presbyterian Church in Metropolitan Philadelphia.* Mimeographed. New York: United Presbyterian Church. Also available as report #2768 in the H. Paul Douglass collection (New York: National Council of Churches).

Douglass, H. Paul, and Edmund de S. Brunner
1935 *The Protestant Church as a Social Institution.* New York: Harper & Row.

Doyle, Ruth T., and Sheila M. Kelly
1976 *Church Membership and Participation Trends in the Episcopal Church, 1950-1975.* Multilithed. New York: The Executive Council of the Episcopal Church, Evangelization and Renewal Office.

Doyle, Ruth T., and Philip J. Murnion
1978 *Catholic Membership and Church Participation.* Multilithed. Washington, D.C.: United States Catholic Conference, Bishops' Committee for Pastoral Research and Practice.

Driggers, B. Carlisle
1977 *The Church in the Changing Community.* Atlanta: Home Mission Board, Southern Baptist Convention.

Dudley, Carl S.
1977 *The Unique Dynamics of the Small Church.* Washington: The Alban Institute.
1978 *Making the Small Church Effective.* Nashville: Abingdon Press.
1979 *Where Have All Our People Gone? New Choices for Old Churches.* New York: Pilgrim Press.

Duncan, Otis Dudley, Howard Schuman, and Beverly Duncan
1973 *Social Change in a Metropolitan Community.* New York: Russell Sage Foundation.

Easterlin, Richard A.
1961 "The American baby boom in historical perspective." *American Economic Review* 51:869-911.
1969 "On the relation of economic factors to recent and projected fertility changes." *Demography* 3:131-53.

Edwards, Jonathan
1855 *History of the Work of Redemption.* First of 4 volumes of *The Works of President Edwards.* New York: Leavitt and Allen.

Engel, James F., and H. Wilbert Norton
1975 *What's Gone Wrong with the Harvest? A Communication Strategy for the Church and World Evangelism.* Grand Rapids, MI: Zondervan.

The Episcopal Church
1951- *The Episcopal Church Annual.* Wilton, CT: Morehouse-Barlow
1976 Co.
1952- *Journal of the General Convention of the Protestant Episcopal
1976 Church in the United States of America.* Printed for the Convention.

The Episcopalian
1977 Bi-monthly Newsletter, #9. New York: Episcopal Church Center.

Erskine, Hazel Gaudet
1966 "The polls: the population explosion, birth control, and sex education." *Public Opinion Quarterly* 30:491-501.

Estus, Charles W., and Michael A. Overington
 1970 "The meaning and end of religiosity." *American Journal of
  Sociology* 75:760-78.
Evangelical and Reformed Church
 1952- *Yearbook of the Evangelical and Reformed Church*. Philadelphia:
 1961 Eden-Heidelberg Bookstores.
Evangelical United Brethren
 1951- *Yearbook (Church Annual) of the Evangelical Brethren*. Dayton,
 1968 OH: Board of Publications.
Evans, Robert A.
 1971 *Belief and the Counter Culture*. Philadelphia: Westminster Press.
 1975 "The quest for community." *Union Seminary Quarterly Review*
  30:188-202.
The Evanston Report
 1955 Second Assembly of the World Council of Churches, 1954. New
  York: Harper & Row.
Fairchild, Roy W., and John C. Wynn
 1961 *Families in the Church: A Protestant Survey*. New York:
  Association Press.
Faulkner, Joseph E., and Gordon F. DeJong
 1966 "Religiosity in 5-D: an empirical analysis." *Social Forces*
  45:246-54.
Feldman, Kenneth A., and Theodore M. Newcomb
 1969 *The Impact of College on Students*. 2 vols. San Francisco:
  Jossey-Bass.
Finger, Frank W.
 1975 "Changes in sex practices and beliefs of male college students."
  Journal of Sex Research 11:304-17.
Finney, John M., and Gary R. Lee
 1977 "Age differences on five dimensions of religious involvement."
  Review of Religious Research 18:173-79.
Fischer, Claude S.
 1975 "The effect of urban life on traditional values." *Social Forces*
  53:420-32.
Foner, Anne
 1974 "Age stratification and age conflict in political life." *American
  Sociological Review* 39:187-96.
Forell, George W.
 1960 *The Protestant Faith*. Philadelphia: Fortress Press.
Foster, Shannon H.
 1977 *The Growth Crisis in the American Church: A Presbyterian Case
  Study*. South Pasadena, CA: William Carey Library.
Freedman, Mervin B.
 1956 "The passage through college." *Journal of Social Issues* 12:13-28.
 1962 "Studies of college alumni." Pp. 847-86 in Nevitt Sanford (ed.),
  The American College. New York: Wiley.
Freedman, Ronald, Pascal K. Whelpton, and Arthur A. Campbell
 1959 *Family Planning, Sterility, and Population Growth*. New York:
  McGraw-Hill.
Fuller Evangelistic Association
 1978 *Diagnostic Clinic*. Pasadena, CA: Fuller Evangelistic Association.

380

Gaede, Stan
  1975 "An empirical specification of some correlates of religious participation." Paper presented to the American Sociological Association, San Francisco.
  1977 "Religious participation, socioeconomic status, and belief-orthodoxy." *Journal for the Scientific Study of Religion* 16:245-53.
Gallup, George H.
  1972 *The Gallup Poll: Public Opinion 1935-1971.* 3 vols. New York: Random House.
Gallup Opinion Index
  1975 *Religion in America.* Report #114. Princeton, NJ: The American Institute of Public Opinion.
  1978a *Religion in America: 1977-78.* Princeton, NJ: The American Institute of Public Opinion.
  1978b *Unchurched Americans.* Princeton, NJ: The American Institute of Public Opinion.
Gaustad, Edwin Scott
  1962 *Historical Atlas of Religion in America.* New York: Harper & Row.
  1976 *Historical Atlas of Religion in America.* Rev. ed. New York: Harper & Row.
Gerth, Hans H., and C. Wright Mills (eds.)
  1958 *From Max Weber: Essays in Sociology.* New York: Oxford University Press.
Glenn, Norval D.
  1967 "Massification versus differentiation: some trend data from national surveys." *Social Forces* 46:172-80.
  1974 "Aging and conservatism." *Annals of the American Academy of Political and Social Science* 415:176-86.
Glenn, Norval D., and Ted Hefner
  1972 "Further evidence on aging and party identification." *Public Opinion Quarterly* 31:31-47.
Glock, Charles Y., and Robert N. Bellah (eds.)
  1976 *The New Religious Consciousness.* Berkeley: University of California Press.
Glock, Charles Y., Benjamin B. Ringer, and Earl E. Babbie
  1967 *To Comfort and to Challenge.* Los Angeles: University of California Press.
Glock, Charles Y., and Rodney Stark
  1965 *Religion and Society in Tension.* Chicago: Rand McNally.
Goode, Erich
  1966 "Social class and church participation." *American Journal of Sociology* 72:102-11.
Gordon, Milton M.
  1964 *Assimilation in American Life: The Role of Race, Religion and National Origin.* New York: Oxford University Press.
Gorlow, Leon, and Harold E. Schroeder
  1968 "Motives for participating in the religious experience." *Journal for the Scientific Study of Religion* 7:241-51.
Greeley, Andrew M.
  1972 *The Denominational Society.* Glenview, IL: Scott, Foresman.
Greeley, Andrew M., William C. McCready, and Kathleen McCourt

1976 *Catholic Schools in a Declining Church.* Kansas City: Sheed and Ward, Inc.

Greer, Scott, and E. Kube
1959 "Urbanism and social structure: a Los Angeles study." Pp. 154-271 in N. Sussman (ed.), *Community Structure and Analysis.* New York: Crowell.

Hadaway, Christopher Kirk
1978 *Sources of Denominational Growth in American Protestantism.* Unpublished Ph.D. Dissertation, University of Massachusetts.

Hadden, Jeffrey K., and Charles F. Longino Jr.
1974 *Gideon's Gang: A Case Study of the Church in Social Action.* Philadelphia: Pilgrim Press.

Hale, J. Russell
1977 *Who Are the Unchurched?* Washington, D.C.: Glenmary Research Center.

Hargrove, Barbara
1976 "Church student ministries and the new consciousness." Pp. 205-26 in Glock and Bellah (eds.), *The New Religious Conscious-ness.* Berkeley: University of California Press.

Harrison, Paul M.
1969 "Religious leadership in America." Pp. 957-79 in Donald R. Cutler (ed.), *The Religious Situation: 1969.* Boston: Beacon Press.

Hartman, Warren J.
1976 *Membership Trends: A Study of Decline and Growth in the United Methodist Church 1949-1975.* Nashville: Discipleship Resources.

Hastings, Philip K., and Dean R. Hoge
1976 "Changes in religion among college students, 1948 to 1974." *Journal for the Scientific Study of Religion* 15:237-49.

Hayes, Kenneth E.
1969 *Migrant Baptists.* Atlanta: Sunday School Board of the Southern Baptist Convention.

Herberg, Will
1955 *Protestant, Catholic, Jew.* Garden City, NY: Doubleday.

Hobart, Charles W.
1974 "Church involvement and the comfort thesis in Alberta." *Journal for the Scientific Study of Religion* 13:463-70.

Hoge, Dean R.
1969 *College Students' Religion: A Study in Trends in Attitudes and Behavior.* Unpublished Ph.D. Dissertation, Harvard University.
1974 *Commitment on Campus: Changes in Religion and Values Over Five Decades.* Philadelphia: Westminster Press.
1976a "Changes in college students' value patterns in the 1950's, 1960's and 1970's." *Sociology of Education* 49:155-63.
1976b *Division in the Protestant House: The Basic Reasons Behind Intra-Church Conflicts.* Philadelphia: Westminster Press.
1977 "Analysis of membership trends in the United Presbyterian Church." Unpublished.

Hoge, Dean R., and Irving E. Bender
1974 "Factors influencing value change among college graduates in adult life." *Journal of Personality and Social Psychology* 29:572-85.

382

Hoge, Dean R., and Jackson W. Carroll
   1978 "Determinants of commitment and participation in suburban Protestant churches." *Journal for the Scientific Study of Religion* 17:107-28.
Hoge, Dean R., and David T. Polk
   1976 "Determinants of Protestant church participation and commitment." Paper presented to the Society for the Scientific Study of Religion, Philadelphia.
Hollingshead, August B.
   1949 *Elmtown's Youth.* New York: Wiley.
Home Missions
   1977 "Off the top of the charts: the 425 fastest growing churches in the SBS—and why they've grown." *Home Missions* 48:11.
House, James S., and William M. Mason
   1975 "Political alienation in America." *American Sociological Review* 40:123-47.
Hudnut, Robert K.
   1975 *Church Growth Is Not the Point!* New York: Harper & Row.
Hudson, Winthrop
   1955 "Are the churches really booming?" *The Christian Century* 72:1494-96.
Inglehart, Ronald
   1977 *The Silent Revolution: Changing Values and Political Styles Among Western Publics.* Princeton, NJ: Princeton University Press.
Jacquet, Constant H. Jr. (ed.)
   1977 *Yearbook of American and Canadian Churches, 1977.* Nashville: Abingdon Press.
Johnson, Arthur L., Milo L. Brekke, Merton P. Strommen, and Ralph C. Underwager
   1974 "Age differences and dimensions of religious behavior." *Journal of Social Issues* 30:43-67.
Johnson, Douglas W., and George W. Cornell
   1972 *Punctured Preconceptions: What North American Christians Think About the Church.* New York: Friendship Press.
Johnson, Douglas W., Paul R. Picard, and Bernard Quinn
   1974 *Churches and Church Membership in the United States.* Washington, DC: Glenmary Research Center.
Jones, Ezra Earl, and Robert L. Wilson
   1974 *What's Ahead for Old First Church?* New York: Harper & Row.
Jones, Phillip B.
   1977 "An examination of the statistical reports of the Southern Baptist Convention through 1976." Multilithed. Atlanta: Home Mission Board, The Southern Baptist Convention.
Kahn, E.J. Jr.
   1975 *The American People.* Baltimore: Penguin Books.
Kando, Thomas M.
   1975 *Leisure and Popular Culture in Transition.* St. Louis: C.V. Mosby.
Kegley, Charles W.
   1965 *Protestantism in Transition.* New York: Harper & Row.
Kelley, Dean M.
   1972 *Why Conservative Churches Are Growing.* New York: Harper &

Row.

1977 *Why Conservative Churches Are Growing.* Updated edition. New York: Harper & Row.

Kelsey, George D.

1965 *Racism and the Christian Understanding of Man.* New York: Charles Scribner's Sons.

Kerr, Hugh T.

1950 *Positive Protestantism, A Return to First Principles.* Englewood Cliffs, NJ: Prentice-Hall.

Kersten, Lawrence L.

1970 *The Lutheran Ethic: The Impact of Religion on Laymen and Clergy.* Detroit: Wayne State University Press.

Killian, Lewis M.

1964 "Social movements." Pp. 426-55 in Robert E.L. Faris (ed.), *Handbook of Modern Sociology.* Chicago: Rand McNally.

King, Morton B., and Richard A. Hunt

1975 "Measuring the religious variable: national replication." *Journal for the Scientific Study of Religion* 14:13-22.

Landis, Benson Y.

1959 "A guide to the literature on statistics of religious affiliation with references to related social studies." *Journal of the American Statistical Association* 54:225-57.

1960 "Trends in church membership in the United States." *The Annals of The American Academy of Political and Social Science* 332:1-8.

Laumann, Edward O.

1969 "The social structure of religious and ethnoreligious groups in a metropolitan community." *American Sociological Review* 34:182-96.

Lazerwitz, Bernard

1961 "Some factors associated with variations in church attendance." *Social Forces* 39:301-9.

1964 "Religion and social structure in the United States." Pp. 426-39 in Louis Schneider (ed.), *Religion, Culture, and Society.* New York: Wiley.

1970 "Contrasting the effects of generation, class, sex and age on group identification in the Jewish and Protestant communities." *Social Forces* 49:50-59.

Lee, Gary R., and Robert W. Clyde

1974 "Religion, socioeconomic status, and anomie." *Journal for the Scientific Study of Religion* 13:35-47.

Lee, Robert

1962 "The organizational dilemma in American Protestantism." Pp. 187-211 in Cleveland and Lasswell (eds.), *Ethics and Bigness.* New York: Harper & Row.

Leiffer, Murray H.

1949 "Interfaith marriages and their effect on the religious training of children." *Lumen Vitae* 4:442-52.

1961 *The Effective City Church.* 2d. ed. Nashville: Abingdon Press.

Lenski, Gerhard E.

1953 "Social correlates of religious interest." *American Sociological Review* 18:533-44.

384

1963 *The Religious Factor*. Rev. ed. Garden City, NY: Doubleday.
Life
1955 "Christianity." December 26.
Lifton, Robert Jay
1969 "Notes on a new history." *New Journal* 3:5-9.
Lindsey, Hal
1970 *The Late Great Planet Earth*. Grand Rapids, MI: Zondervan Press.
Littell, Franklin H.
1962 *From State Church to Pluralism*. New York: Macmillan.
Lofland, John, and Rodney Stark
1965 "Becoming a world-saver: a theory of conversion to a deviant perspective." *American Sociological Review* 30:862-75.
Luckmann, Thomas
1967 *The Invisible Religion*. New York: Macmillan.
Lutheran Church Council
1950- "Lutheran Church Bodies in the United States and Canada."
1975 Unpublished material. New York: Lutheran Council in the U.S.A., Research and Information Center.
McGavran, Donald A.
1955 *The Bridges of God*. New York: Friendship Press.
1959 *How Churches Grow*. New York: Friendship Press.
1970 *Understanding Church Growth*. Grand Rapids, MI: Eerdmans Publishing Co.
McGavran, Donald A. (ed.)
1972 *Eye of the Storm: The Great Debate in Mission*. Waco, TX: Word Books.
McGavran, Donald A., and Winfield C. Arn
1973 *How to Grow a Church*. Glendale, CA: Regal Books.
1977 *Ten Steps for Church Growth*. New York: Harper & Row.
McIntosh, William A., and Jon P. Alston
1977 "Acceptance of abortion among white Catholics and Protestants, 1962 and 1975." *Journal for the Scientific Study of Religion* 16:278-94.
McLoughlin, William G.
1974 "Revivalism." Pp. 119-53 in E.S. Gaustad (ed.), *The Rise of Adventism*. New York: Harper & Row.
Main, Earl D.
1967 "Participation in Protestant churches." *Review of Religious Research* 8:176-83.
Maloney, William E., and Lyle E. Schaller
1965 *The Lutheran Churches of Northeastern Ohio*. Cleveland: Regional Church Planning Office. Also available as report #1514 in the H. Paul Douglass Collection (New York: National Council of Churches).
Marty, Martin E.
1968 "The Spirit's holy errand: the search for a spiritual style in secular America." Pp. 167-83 in McLoughlin and Bellah (eds.), *Religion in America*. Boston: Houghton Mifflin Company.
1970 *The Righteous Empire: The Protestant Experience in America*. New York: Dial Press.
1976 *A Nation of Behavers*. Chicago: University of Chicago Press.

1977 "Denominations: surviving the '70s." *The Christian Century* 94:1186-87.

1978a "Congregations Alive." *A.D. Magazine* 7:28-31.

1978b "Is the homogeneous unit principle of church growth Christian?" *Context* (March 15).

Marty, Martin E., Stuart E. Rosenberg, and Andrew M. Greeley
1968 *What Do We Believe?* New York: Meredith.

Merton, Robert K.
1949 *Social Theory and Social Structure.* New York: The Free Press.

The Methodist Church
1951- *General Minutes of the Annual Conferences of the Methodist*
1967 *Church.* Evanston, IL: Section of Research Records and Statistics Under the Supervision of the Council on World Service and Finance.

Metz, Donald L.
1965 "The invisible member: a report on inactive Methodists." Multilithed. Berkeley: California Bureau of Community Research.

Moberg, David O.
1962 *The Church as a Social Institution.* Englewood Cliffs, NJ: Prentice-Hall.

Monoghan, Robert R.
1967 "Three faces of the true believer: motivations for attending a fundamentalist church." *Journal for the Scientific Study of Religion* 6:236-45.

Moss, Milton
1968 "Consumption: a report on contemporary issues." Pp. 449-524 in Sheldon and Moore (eds.), *Indicators of Social Change.* New York: Russell Sage Foundation.

Moynihan, Daniel P., and Nathan Glazer
1963 *Beyond the Melting Pot.* Cambridge, MA: MIT Press.

Mueller, Charles W., and Weldon T. Johnson
1975 "Socioeconomic status and religious participation." *American Sociological Review* 40:785-800.

Nash, Dennison
1968 "A little child shall lead them: a statistical test of an hypothesis that children were the source of the American 'religious revival.' " *Journal for the Scientific Study of Religion* 7:238-40.

Nash, Dennison, and Peter Berger
1962 "The child, the family, and the 'religious revival' in suburbia." *Journal for the Scientific Study of Religion* 2:85-93.

National Opinion Research Center
1972- General Social Survey: Codebook. Annual editions.
1977 Chicago: National Opinion Research Center.

Newman, William M.
1975 "Religion in suburban America." Pp. 265-78 in Barry Schwartz (ed.), *The Changing Face of the Suburbs.* Chicago: University of Chicago Press.

Newman, William M., Peter L. Halvorson, and Jennifer Brown
1977 "Problems and potential uses of the 1952 and 1971 National Council of Churches' 'churches and church membership in the United States' studies." *Review of Religious Research* 18:167-72.

Nie, Norman H., Sidney Verba, and John R. Petrocik
1976 *The Changing American Voter.* Cambridge, MA: Harvard University Press.
Niebuhr, H. Richard
1929 *The Social Sources of Denominationalism.* New York: Henry Holt.
1951 *Christ and Culture.* New York: Harper and Brothers.
Niebuhr, H. Richard, Daniel Day Williams, and James Gustafson
1956 *The Ministry in Historical Perspective.* New York: Harper & Row.
1956 *The Purpose of the Church and Its Ministry.* New York: Harper & Row.
1957 *The Advancement of Theological Education.* New York: Harper & Row.
Niebuhr, Reinhold
1941 *The Nature and Destiny of Man: A Christian Interpretation.* Vol. 1, *Human Nature.* New York: Charles Scribner's Sons.
1943 *The Nature and Destiny of Man: A Christian Interpretation.* Vol. 2, *Human Destiny.* New York: Charles Scribner's Sons.
1959 "From progress to perplexity." Pp. 135-46 in Huston Smith (ed.), *The Search for America.* Englewood Cliffs, NJ: Prentice-Hall.
Novak, Michael
1972 *The Rise of the Unmeltable Ethnics.* New York: Macmillan.
Noyce, Gaylord B.
1975 *Survival and Mission for the City Church.* Philadelphia: Westminster Press.
Nunn, Clyde Z., Harry J. Crockett Jr., and J. Allen Williams Jr.
1978 *Tolerance for Nonconformity.* San Francisco: Jossey-Bass.
Ong, Walter J.
1970 *The Presence of the Word: Some Prolegomena for Cultural and Religious History.* New York: Simon and Schuster.
Orjala, Paul R.
1978 *Get Ready to Grow.* Kansas City: Beacon Hill Press.
Packard, Vance
1959 *The Status Seekers.* New York: David McKay Company.
Park, Robert E., Ernest W. Burgess, and Roderick D. McKenzie
1925 *The City.* Chicago: University of Chicago Press.
Pentecost, Edward C.
1974 *Reaching the Unreached.* Pasadena, CA: William Carey Library.
Perlman, Daniel
1974 "Self-esteem and sexual permissiveness." *Journal of Marriage and the Family* 36:470-73.
Perry, Everett L.
1973 Review of "Why Conservative Churches Are Growing," by Dean Kelley. *Review of Religious Research* 14:198-200.
Peters, George W.
1970 *Saturation Evangelism.* Grand Rapids, MI: Zondervan.
Petersen, William
1975 *Population.* 3d edition. New York: Macmillan.
Photiadis, John D., and Jeanne Biggar
1962 "Religiosity, education, and ethnic distance." *American Journal of Sociology* 67:666-72.
Pickett, J. Waskom
1933 *Christian Mass Movements in India.* Nashville: Abingdon Press.

Political Behavior Program
1971 *The 1964 Election Study* (Revised ICPR Edition). Ann Arbor, MI: Inter-University Consortium for Political Research.
1973 *The 1968 American National Election Study* (Revised ICPR Edition). Ann Arbor, MI: Inter-University Consortium for Political Research.

Pope, Liston
1942 *Millhands and Preachers*. New Haven, CT: Yale University Press.
1948 "Religion and the class structure." *Annals of The American Academy of Political and Social Science* 256:84-91.

Pratt, Henry J.
1972 *The Liberalization of American Protestantism*. Detroit: Wayne State University Press.

Presbyterian Committee
1976 *Membership Trends*. New York: United Presbyterian Church in the U.S.A.

Price, Clay
1977 "A study of denominational change to and from the SBC." Multilithed. Atlanta: Home Mission Board, The Southern Baptist Convention.

Prince, A.J.
1962 "A study of 194 cross-religious marriages." *Family Life Coordinator* 11:3-7.

Raines, Robert A.
1961 *New Life in the Church*. New York: Harper & Row.

Reed, John S.
1972 *The Enduring South: Subcultural Persistence in Mass Society*. Lexington, MA: Heath Press.

Reitz, Ruediger
1969 *The Church in Experiment*. Nashville: Abingdon Press.

Rindfuss, Ronald R., and James A. Sweet
1977 *Postwar Fertility Trends and Differentials in the United States*. New York: Academic Press.

Robbins, Thomas, Dick Anthony, and James Richardson
1978 "Theory and research on today's 'new religions.' " *Sociological Analysis* 39:95-122.

The Roman Catholic Church
1951-*The Official Catholic Directory*. New York: P.J. Kennedy & Sons.
1976

Roof, W. Clark
1972 "The local-cosmopolitan orientation and traditional religious commitment." *Sociological Analysis* 33:1-15.
1976 "Traditional religion in contemporary society: a theory of local-cosmopolitan plausibility." *American Sociological Review* 41:195-208.
1978 *Community and Commitment: Religious Plausibility in a Liberal Protestant Church*. New York: Elsevier.

Roozen, David A.
1976 "Belief without the church." *Praxis* (Fall):9-10.
1977 "Family life cycle, regionalism, value orientation and religious participation: a cross-sectional model." Unpublished.
1978a *Protestant Church Membership and Participation: Trends,*

388

Determinants, and Implications for Policy and Planning. Hartford, CT: The Hartford Seminary Foundation.

1978b The Churched and the Unchurched in America: A Comparative Profile. Washington, D.C: Glenmary Research Center.

Rosenberg, Morris
1961 "Test factor standardization as a method of interpretation." Social Forces 41:53-61.

Saldahna, Shirley, William McCready, Kathleen McCourt, and Andrew Greeley
1975 "American Catholics—ten years later." The Critic 33:14-21.

Savage, John S.
1976 The Apathetic and Bored Church Member. Pittsford, NY: Lead Consultants.

Scalf, John H., Michael M. Miller, and Charles T. Thomas
1973 "Goal specificity, organization structure, and participant commitment in churches." Sociological Analysis 34:169-84.

Schaller, Lyle E.
1967 "The coming crisis in new church development." Report #40, Regional Church Planning Office, Cleveland. Also available as report #1518 in the H. Paul Douglass Collection (New York: National Council of Churches).

1975 Hey, That's Our Church! Nashville: Abingdon Press.

1977 Survival Tactics for the Parish. Nashville: Abingdon Press.

Schrag, Peter
1973 The Decline of the Wasp. New York: Simon & Schuster.

Schroeder, Widick
1975 "Age cohorts, the family life cycle, and participation in the voluntary church in America: implications for membership patterns, 1950-2000." Chicago Theological Seminary Register 65:13-28.

Shannon, H. Foster
1977 The Growth Crisis in the American Church: A Presbyterian Case Study. South Pasadena, CA: William Carey Library.

Shippey, Frederick A.
1960 "The variety of city churches." Review of Religious Research 2:8-19.

Smith, M. Brewster, Jerome S. Bruner, and Robert W. White
1956 Opinions and Personality. New York: Wiley.

Stark, Rodney, and Charles Y. Glock
1968 American Piety: The Nature of the Religious Commitment. Los Angeles: University of California Press.

Stouffer, Samuel A.
1955 Communism, Conformity, and Civil Liberties. New York: John Wiley and Sons.

Stringfellow, William
1973 An Ethic for Christians and Other Aliens in a Strange Land. Waco, TX: Word Books.

Strommen, Merton P., Milo L. Brekke, Ralph C. Underwager, and Arthur L. Johnson
1972 A Study of Generations. Minneapolis: Augsburg Publishing House.

Stub, Holger R.
1972 Status Communities in Modern Society. Hinsdale, IL: Dryden.

Sweazey, George
1958 *Evangelism in the United States.* London: Lutterworth Press.
Sweet, William W.
1948 "The Protestant Churches." *Annals of The American Academy of Political and Social Science* 256:43-52.
Thorne, Charles
1964 "An overview of Presbyterianism in Allegheny County, Pennsylvania, including Pittsburgh." New York: United Presbyterian Church, Board of National Missions. Also available as report #2732 in the H. Paul Douglass collection (New York: National Council of Churches).
1967 "Membership distribution in relation to distance from the church." Mimeographed report. Also available as report #3689 in the H. Paul Douglass Collection (New York: National Council of Churches).
Tillich, Paul
1948 *The Protestant Era.* Chicago: University of Chicago Press.
Troeltsch, Ernst
1931 *The Social Teaching of the Christian Churches.* 2 vols. Translated by Olive Wyon. New York: Harper & Row.
Turner, Victor
1969 *The Ritual Process.* Chicago: Aldine.
Udry, J. Richard, Karl E. Bauman, and Naomi M. Morris
1975 "Changes in premarital coital experience of recent decade-of-birth cohorts of urban American women." *Journal of Marriage and the Family* 37:783-87.
United Church of Canada
1976 *Yearbook.* Toronto: United Church of Canada, General Council Research Office.
United Church of Christ
1962- *United Church of Christ Yearbook.* New York: United Church of
1976 Christ.
1975 *Minutes, Tenth General Synod, United Church of Christ.* New York: United Church of Christ.
1977 *The Constitution and By-Laws.* New York: United Church of Christ.
United Methodist Church
1968- *General Minutes of the Annual Conferences of the United*
1976 *Methodist Church.* Evanston, IL: Division of Administrative Services.
United Presbyterian Church in the U.S.A.
1976 *Minutes of the General Assembly of the United Presbyterian Church in the United States of America, Part II, The Statistical and Presbyterian Rolls, January 1-December 31, 1975.* New York: Office of the General Assembly.
U.S. Bureau of the Census
1957 *Statistical Abstract of the United States: 1957.* (78th edition.) Washington, DC.
1975 *Historical Statistics of the United States, Colonial Times to 1970, Bicentennial Edition, Part 2.* Washington, DC.
1977 *Statistical Abstract of the United States: 1977.* (98th edition.) Washington, DC.

390

Wagner, C. Peter
  1971 *Frontiers in Missionary Strategy.* Chicago: Moody Press.
  1976 *Your Church Can Grow: Seven Signs of a Healthy Church.* Glendale, CA: Regal Books.
  1977 "Who found it?" *Eternity* (September):12-19.
  1978 "How ethical is the homogeneous unit principle?" *Occasional Bulletin of Missionary Research* (January):12-19.
  1979a *Our Kind of People: The Ethical Dimension of Church Growth in America.* Atlanta: John Knox Press.
  1979b *Your Church Can Be Healthy.* Nashville: Abingdon Press.
Walrath, Douglas A.
  1969 "The congregations of the Synod of Albany." Parts I and II. Multilithed. Schenectady, NY: Synod of Albany, Reformed Church in America.
  1974 "The congregations of the Synod of Albany." Part V. Multilithed. Schenectady, NY: Synod of Albany, Reformed Church in America.
  1977 "Types of small congregations and their implications for planning." Pp. 33-61 in Jackson W. Carroll (ed.), *Small Churches Are Beautiful.* New York: Harper & Row.
Warner, W. Lloyd
  1959 *The Family of God.* New Haven, CT: Yale University Press.
Warner, W. Lloyd, and Paul S. Lunt
  1941 *The Social Life of a Modern Community.* New Haven, CT: Yale University Press.
Webber, George W.
  1964 *The Congregation in Mission.* Nashville: Abingdon Press.
Weber, Herman C.
  1927 *Presbyterian Statistics Through One Hundred Years—1826-1926.* Philadelphia: General Council of Presbyterian Church in the U.S.A.
Weber, Max
  1963 *The Sociology of Religion.* Boston: Beacon Press.
Westoff, Charles F., Robert G. Potter Jr., Philip C. Sagi, and Elliott G. Mishler
  1961 *Family Growth in Metropolitan America.* Princeton, NJ: Princeton University Press.
Whelpton, Pascal K., Arthur A. Campbell, and John E. Patterson
  1966 *Fertility and Family Planning in the United States.* Princeton, NJ: Princeton University Press.
Whipple, Kathie
  1976 "A first look, LCA trends during the period 1963 to 1974." Multilithed. New York: The Lutheran Church in America, Office for Research and Planning.
Wicker, Allan W.
  1969 "Size of church membership and members' support of church behavior settings." *Journal of Personal and Social Psychology* 13:278-88.
Wicker, Allan W., Joseph E. McGrath, and George E. Armstrong
  1972 "Organization size and behavior setting capacity as determinants of member participation." *Behavioral Science* 17:499-513.
Wingrove, C. Ray, and Jon P. Alston
  1974 "Cohort analysis of church attendance, 1939-69." *Social Forces* 53:324-31.

Winter, Gibson
1962 *The Suburban Captivity of the Churches*. New York: Macmillan.
Wirth, Louis
1938 "Urbanism as a way of life." *American Journal of Sociology* 44:1-24.
Wuthnow, Robert
1976a *The Consciousness Reformation*. Berkeley: University of California Press.
1976b "Recent pattern of secularization: A problem of generations?" *American Sociological Review* 41:850-67.
1978 *Experimentation in American Religion*. Berkeley: University of California Press.
Wuthnow, Robert, and Charles Y. Glock
1974 "The shifting focus of faith: a survey report." *Psychology Today* (November):131-36.
Yankelovich, Daniel
1974 *The New Morality: A Profile of American Youth in the 70's*. New York: McGraw-Hill.
Yinger, J. Milton
1970 *The Scientific Study of Religion*. New York: Macmillan.
Yoder, John
1973 "Church growth issues in a theological perspective." Pp. 25-48 in Wilbert R. Shenk (ed.), *The Challenge of Church Growth*. Scottdale, PA: Herald Press.
Zald, Mayer N., and Roberta Ash
1967 "Social movement organizations: growth, decay and change." Pp. 461-85 in Barry McLaughlin (ed.), *Studies in Social Movements: A Social Psychological Perspective*. New York: The Free Press.
Zaretsky, Irving I., and Mark P. Leone (eds.)
1974 *Religious Movements in Contemporary America*. Princeton, NJ: Princeton University Press.
Zimmer, Basil G., and Amos H. Hawley
1959 "Suburbanization and church participation." *Social Forces* 37:348-54.

Index